D0406077

The Practical Nomad Guide

TO THE

Online Travel Marketplace

Edward Hasbrouck

AVALON
TRAVEL
publishing

The Practical Nomad Guide to the Online Travel Marketplace
First Edition
By Edward Hasbrouck

Published by
Avalon Travel Publishing
5855 Beaudry St.
Emeryville, CA 94608, USA

Please send all comments, corrections, additions, amendments, and critiques to:
THE PRACTICAL NOMAD GUIDE TO THE ONLINE TRAVEL MARKETPLACE
AVALON TRAVEL PUBLISHING
5855 BEAUDRY ST.
EMERYVILLE, CA 94608, USA
email: info@travelmatters.com
www.practicalnomad.com

Printing History
1st edition—February, 2001
5 4 3 2 1

ISBN: 1-56691-250-4
ISSN: 1531-0582

Editors: Angelique S. Clarke, Jeannie Trizzino, Erin Van Rheenen
Copy Editor: Gina Wilson Birtchil
Series Manager: Angelique S. Clarke
Index: Monica Smersh
Graphics Coordinator: Erika Howsare
Design and Production: Kathleen Sparkes, White Hart Design

Front cover photo: Courtesy of NASA/JPL/Caltech

Distributed in the United States and Canada by Publishers Group West

Printed in United States by R. R. Donnelley

Although every effort was made to ensure that the information was correct at the time of going to press, the author and publisher do not assume and hereby disclaim any liability to any party for any loss or damage caused by errors, omissions, or any potential travel disruption due to labor or financial difficulty, whether such errors or omissions result from negligence, accident, or any other cause.

CONTENTS

Song of the Open Road

Afoot and light-hearted I take to the open road,
Healthy, free, the world before me,
The long brown path before me leading wherever I choose.

I think whatever I shall meet on the road I shall like,
    and whoever beholds me shall like me.
I think whoever I see must be happy.

From this hour I ordain myself loos'd of limits and imaginary lines,
Going where I list, my own master total and absolute,
Listening to others, considering well what they say,
Pausing, searching, receiving, contemplating,
Gently, but with undeniable will, divesting myself of the
    holds that would hold me.

Allons! The road is before us!
It is safe—I have tried it—my own feet have tried it well—
    be not detain'd!
Let the paper remain on the desk unwritten, and the book
    on the shelf unopened!
Let the tools remain in the workshop! Let the money remain
    unearned!
Let the school stand! mind not the cry of the teacher!
Let the preacher preach in his pulpit! let the lawyer plead
    in the court, and the judge expound the law.

Camerado, I give you my hand!
I give you my love more precious than money,
I give you myself before preaching and law;
Will you give me yourself? Will you come travel with me?
Shall we stick by each other as long as we live?

          —Walt Whitman, *Leaves of Grass*

The Practical Nomad Web site

This book is published in conjunction with the Practical Nomad Web site at **www.practicalnomad.com**. Some information is repeated in both places, but not everything in this book is on the Web site, and not everything on the Web site is in this book. I've tried to put each type of information in the place where it will be most useful.

It's easier to read explanations and descriptions in a book. It's easier to use lists of Internet resources on a Web site, where they can be linked directly and you don't have to type in Internet addresses. So this book concentrates on the advice, tips, techniques, and general information you need to know before you start using the Internet for travel planning and purchasing, or while traveling. There's a short list of key Internet resources at the back of the book, including all those mentioned in the text. But there are many more, and more detailed, reviews of specific Web sites, along with links to them, on the Practical Nomad site. That's also the place to look if something mentioned in the book has moved, or if you want to find out about new Web sites or other changes since this book went to press.

Research and final revisions to this book were completed in July 2000. Undoubtedly many things will have changed by the time you are reading this. If you find something that should be updated, and it isn't already on the Practical Nomad Web site, please let me know so I can pass it along to other people.

You can e-mail your comments to me at edward@hasbrouck.org. I don't promise to answer every message individually, although I try my best, but I do welcome your feedback, read it all personally, and use it to guide future editions.

In an effort to be helpful, I give opinions on many matters on which others would disagree; realize that these are only my opinions. Don't take anything you read here as gospel. Be as skeptical of what you read here as you would be of any other advice. If you think I'm wrong, please write and tell me so. If something is unclear, I've left something out, or there's something you found especially useful, please let me know.

Introduction

Travel and the Internet

Travel and the Internet go hand-in-hand. That should be no surprise: the movement of information has always paralleled the movement of people, power, and money. Historically, global electronic networking actually was pioneered by the travel industry long before the Internet existed. Today, travel reservations, especially airline ticket sales, are the leading edge of e-commerce.

The Internet might seem to provide an alternative to travel, or to render it unnecessary. But the reverse has been the case. Those who predicted that the Internet would be the death of travel, like those who predicted that the Internet would be the death of ink-on-paper books, have been proven dead wrong. Travel (followed by books) is the largest seller on the Internet. The present Internet age is distinguished not just by ease of communication, but by personal mobility and opportunities for travel unprecedented in human history. And for more and more people, long distance communication and travel are part and parcel of the same style of life, business, and leisure.

E-mail, instant messaging, electronic chat rooms. Internet discussion groups and mailing lists. Internet phone calls and video conferences. Internet personals and virtual matchmaking services. While none can replace the face-to-face meetings and personal experience of distant places, the Internet-fueled globalization of human and business relationships is driving people to travel farther and more often, for business and pleasure alike.

What the Internet Can and Can't Do for Travelers

- A tool for researching and planning your trip
- A tool for making travel reservations and purchases
- A tool for staying in touch and taking care of business while on the road
- Not all-knowing, infallible, or always superior
- A supplement, not a substitute, for other travel planning and buying resources
- A tool to enable you to be your own travel agent; not a substitute for the knowledge you need to be a successful do-it-yourself travel agent
- Not a substitute for travel itself! No matter how much time you spend online, never forget that real travel takes place in the real world, face-to-face with real people, perceiving and experiencing places directly with all your senses.

Highway engineers and planners know wider, faster roads lead to more traffic, not less. "A good road creates its own traffic." The same is true for the Internet. Business travel has increased because the Internet fosters and facilitates long-distance relationships. Similarly, travel for leisure and learning has increased—people are driven by a greater awareness of distant places and cultures, especially the person-to-person connections made possible by the Internet. And as a tool of globalization that transcends national borders, the Internet has given a special boost to international travel of all types.

On the Internet, you can read what's happening and what the weather is today in the place you want go to tomorrow. You can see what it looks like, and what people who were just there thought about it: which places, sights, and activities they liked and disliked. You can find descriptions and pictures of travel facilities (hotels, cruise ships, etc.), sights, and attractions. You can find logistical information, maps, timetables, and directions. You can get prices and make reservations for everything—airline and Amtrak tickets, package tours, cruises, hotels, hostels. You can rent a car or buy a Eurailpass.

Even better, you can use the Internet to find and communicate directly with people everywhere. People who live in the place you want to visit. People who share your interests. People who can tell you what it's like there and give you advice and recommendations. If you're lucky, you might find people who you can meet when you actually get there. They may show you around, invite you to their home, or simply tell you about the places and things only locals know to look for. Best of all, perhaps, you can use the Internet to find people with whom you can become long-distance friends. Who

knows? Maybe some of these people will eventually come to visit *you*.

And, of course, you can do all of this at any time, wherever you are (as long as there's an Internet connection), at your convenience.

Who is This Book For?

This book is for every traveler who uses or wants to use the Internet for travel planning or purchasing or while traveling. It's written primarily for people in the USA, but I hope much of it will be useful to readers in other countries as well. Whether you're a laptop-toting frequent business traveler, or you're contemplating using your new computer to make your vacation plans online for the first time, I hope you'll find this book useful.

This book is for the 11 million Americans who, in 1999, went online and spent $7 billion on travel products. It's also for those who are predicted to join them in spending more than $20 billion a year by 2001. And it's especially for those who are arranging their own travel for the first time, those who aren't sure whether they are really getting the best deals, or those who want to know how to tell when they're being misled or ripped off (and what to do about it if they are).

This book is for the 20 million Americans (about a third of all regular Internet users) who visit travel websites every month to help plan their travels. It's for everyone who'd like tips from industry experts and professional researchers on what's available for travelers, via the Internet. And it's for those who want information with fewer wild-goose chases. *Practical Nomad Guide to the Online Travel Marketplace* will help you separate useful information and great advice from online scams and hype.

Finally, this book is for every road warrior and cybercafe user, every sunbird with a laptop in an RV, and everyone who might become one. It's for anyone who wants to use the Internet to make life on the road easier and more fun.

WHAT THIS BOOK IS

This book is part consumer adviser, part research assistant, part road map, and part technical manual. It includes:

- a user's guide to the virtual travel library of websites, newsgroups, and other Internet travel planning tools;
- a buyer's guide to the virtual travel bazaar of online reservations and ticket purchasing;
- a consumer's guide to consumer protection, privacy protection, and online security;
- a road warrior's guide to using the Internet while traveling;
- an elementary textbook and reference manual for would-be, do-it-yourself, online travel agents.

The last item may require some special explanation. Why would you need a manual to teach you how to be your own travel agent on the Internet? What if you don't want to be a travel agent? Doesn't the Internet give you all the tools to be your own travel agent—without needing any training?

In a word, *no*. Contrary to anything you may have heard or read, the Internet does not give you access to most of the information or tools used by travel agents. It gives you access to only a small part of that information, and to only a very limited subset of the tools available to travel agents in querying electronic sources of travel information.

No doubt about it, the Internet does give you powerful tools with which you can accomplish almost every travel-related task. But that doesn't mean it automatically gives you the skill to use them well or to understand their risks.

Travel planning and decisions involve hundreds or thousands of

— DO-IT-YOURSELFING TAKES SOME EFFORT

You wouldn't try to build your own house just because someone gave you a set of all the tools you'd need for the job. It makes no more sense to try to be a do-it-yourself travel agent without spending at least a little time learning what travel agents do, and some of the skills they use to do it.

dollars, as well as valuable and irreplaceable vacation time. Good travel agents aren't nearly as stupid or unskilled as you may think if you've only dealt with bad ones. If you're going to be a travel do-it-yourselfer, do yourself a favor and spend at least a little time learning some of the tricks of the trade.

WHAT THIS BOOK ISN'T

This isn't a guide to how to get on the Internet. I assume that you are already on the Internet. If you aren't, and this book makes you want to be, you can learn how to get on the Internet from many other excellent books and resources. There's no need to repeat that information here. It can be confusing at first, but it's not that hard. The Internet is more complicated than it ought to be, but it's getting easier to use all the time.

This isn't primarily a list of websites, or of directions for how to use them. Most of what I could say about any specific website or its interface would be out of date by the time this book got to bookstores and libraries, or into your hands. New travel websites appear and disappear every day. So I've put most of the lists of links and site reviews on the companion website to this book at **www.practicalnomad.com**, where they can be updated more often. Instead, this book focuses on general principles, techniques, tips, and consumer advice that will remain true wherever you go on the Internet.

Most important, this isn't an infomercial or puff piece for the Internet travel industry. There are already plenty of, "Gee whiz, you can do everything on the Internet!" books. Too many press releases get printed as travel "news." Too often Internet information is little more than infomercials. Flush with billions of dollars in venture capital, Internet travel companies are still flooding us with their advertisements. What Internet users and travelers alike need most—and get least—is skepticism and critical advice.

A CONSUMERIST BIAS

I don't claim to be unbiased. I am emphatically and unequivocally biased toward the interests of people and consumers against the interests of corporations and the travel "industry".

That's why I wrote this book. Too many people are either led to spend more than they need to, misled by online propaganda, or give up more of their personal privacy than they normally would. Too often, they don't even know it.

I work for an online travel company, AirTreks.com, in my "day job." But I'd much rather risk alienating my travel industry associates than risk being accused of selling out the ordinary traveler. The recommendations in this book are my opinions, not advertisements. No one has paid me to be mentioned, or to be mentioned favorably, and I would refuse any such offers.

I don't need to tell you why, as a traveler, you would want to use the Internet. If you didn't think there was any reason to use the Internet as a traveler, you probably wouldn't be reading this book. The potential value of the Internet to travelers is obvious; the drawbacks and potential pitfalls are less so. I won't insult your intelligence by telling you how to push the "Buy" button. It's figuring out *whether* to push it and *when* that's more important. The most tempting and dangerous fallacy of Internet travel is to assume that because you can do everything on the Internet, you should. Some of my most valuable advice may be what *not* to do online, what might be more expensive online, and why.

A User's Guide to the Virtual Travel Library

Introduction: What's on the Internet for Travelers?

THE GOOD

More people use the Internet for travel research and planning than for reservations or travel purchasing, and with good reason: the Internet makes unprecedented amounts of information available from any connected computer. On the Internet, you can get information from the other side of the world as quickly and easily as from next door. It's cheaper than a phone call or fax, available whenever you are, and quicker than having printed literature sent to you by "snail mail."

In a few minutes today on the Internet, a skilled amateur can find information that a decade ago either took a professional (e.g., a librarian) weeks or months to find, or cost hundreds of dollars to access in proprietary databases.

While most airfare ticketing rules are still available only to travel agents, more travel planning and reference information is now available to consumers, thanks to the Internet. We travel agents increasingly rely on the Internet for reference, background, and destination information other than fares and prices.

For window-shoppers and armchair travelers, there are online

>> KEY ADVICE
About Internet Travel Planning and Research

■ Don't believe anything just because you read it on the Internet. Anyone can say anything on the Internet—and they do. The Internet is the most effective medium in history for the rapid global propagation of rumor, myth, and false information.

■ Watch out for advertisements disguised as impartial reviews or ratings. Many "recommendations" on Web sites, newsgroups, and bulletin boards are really paid ads, or written by people with a hidden financial interest in whatever they are recommending. If you can't tell, assume it's an ad.

■ Think about who is giving you advice and what their knowledge is based upon. Don't confuse form with substance as a guide to reliability. The best looking sites aren't necessarily the most accurate or the most useful.

■ Evaluate advice by its relevance to your tastes. People are different. That's one of the joys of the Internet: there's something for everyone, and you don't have to rely on "one size fits all" advice.

■ Look to the Internet especially for finding specialized and special interest, detailed, time sensitive, personalized, and international travel information.

■ Don't limit your Internet travel research to travel sites or to the World Wide Web. Some of the most useful online travel resources aren't on the Web, or are on Web sites that aren't specifically for travelers. You can get lots of useful travel information through Usenet newsgroups and e-mail, or by using the Internet to locate offline resources.

For much more advice and more resources for travel planning and research, see the Practical Nomad Web site at **www .practicalnomad.com** and, for international travel, the companion volume in this series, *The Practical Nomad: How to Travel Around the World* (2nd edition, 2000), available from Avalon Travel Publishing.

brochures galore, complete with everything from photographs of hotel rooms to virtual-reality tours. A live Web cam will show you—as it's happening—when the sun is shining and when the surf's up.

The Internet is interactive, connecting (surprise!) real people. You can ask questions and get answers and advice from around the world. If some detail is crucial to your trip, there is probably someone sitting at a computer somewhere who was there last month—or who lives there—and has just the information you need. You can find people to share travel stories with. People you can learn from. People you might hook up with as traveling companions in the "real world," or people who will come visit *you*. Some of the high points of my travels have been face-to-face meetings with people I'd never have found without the Internet.

FROM ANTARCTICA TO ALICE SPRINGS

On the Net, you can find amazing amounts of detail on the most obscure places and interests. You can read the latest newspaper from Antarctica or Alice Springs, the bus routes in Bangkok or Boston, a map of Manhattan or Madagascar, the current weather in Tobago or Timbuktu, how to get from the airport to downtown in San Francisco, California, or Santiago de Chile, or travelers' accounts of their recent visits to North Carolina or North Korea.

THE BAD

Gathering travel information on the Internet is not without its pitfalls. The Internet is rife with obsolete, misleading, self-serving, and simply wrong information. And the glut of information available on the Internet makes it essential to find efficient tools and strategies for selecting what's relevant, credible, and accurate—and avoiding scams, shills, and stupidity.

So, before we start looking at specific travel resources and research tools on the Internet,

"NOISE" TO "SIGNAL" RATIO

Imagine television if there were an hour of advertisements for every minute of entertainment or news, and you'll have a pretty good picture of the state of the Internet in 2001.

let's step back briefly to look at the big picture of online travel information. What's really out there, and how can you best find and make use it?

What the Internet Is and Isn't

MORE THAN THE WORLD WIDE WEB

The Web is only one aspect of the Internet. The Internet also includes e-mail, instant messaging, list servers, Usenet newsgroups, auto-responders, chat rooms, and other forums and tools, all of which have their uses for travel planning.

Why is this important? E-mail is invaluable as the most universal means of Internet communication. E-mail reaches far more people than the Web, especially in poorly connected parts of the world. Unlike browsing the Web, e-mail doesn't require as powerful a computer or as fast a connection. How many people do you know who send and receive e-mail yet don't have their own Web page? The people who have the answer to your travel question are much more likely to have an e-mail address than a Web page.

Similarly, Usenet newsgroups involve people from everywhere on the Internet, and beyond—not just members of a proprietary service like AOL, or visitors to one Website. Usenet newsgroups were the first interactive aspect of the Internet, 15 years before the Web. Today, they have the largest and most diverse participation of any Internet communication tool. If you want to draw on the widest possible pool of advice—for example, to obtain guest feedback on a hotel—nothing comes close to the reach of the Usenet.

That said, don't ignore the Web. In the rest of this chapter, I'll talk first about the Web. It's the easiest, and usually the first place to look on the Internet. And it's easier to search the Web than to search for e-mail addresses or newsgroup postings. But don't think that if you can't find what you want on the Web, it's not on the Internet. Send an e-mail message to the right address, or post a query in the appropriate newsgroup, and you still might find what you're looking for.

A COMMUNICATION MEDIUM, NOT A SOURCE

The Internet is not, strictly speaking, a *source* of information. The Internet is a medium of communication through which you can gather information from millions of sources.

That may sound like semantic nitpicking. It's not. The single most important thing to keep in mind when you're doing research about anything on the Internet is that, "I found it on the Internet" says *nothing* about where it came from, who provided it, why, or—most important of all—whether or not there is any truth to it.

So what? you may ask. The same could be said about books or television. But books, TV, and other media are *not* the same. Books, television programs, and the like are relatively expensive to produce. That cost serves as a screening mechanism: If you read something in a book, it means that someone thought it was important enough to spend thousands of dollars on printing. And before they spent that much money they probably took some care to check their facts. Unless a book is self-published, it generally reflects a publisher's judgment—corroborating the author's own—that the book has some truth and value.

Not so with the Internet. Because it's so quick, easy, and cheap to post, much more information is available on the Internet. Anyone can do it, no matter how ignorant or thoughtless they may be. They can do it on their own, with no need for anyone else to check their "facts." Since it doesn't cost them much, there's less reason to consider whether they're saying anything worthwhile. The volume of information placed online, even by commercial publishers, precludes the degree of fact-checking that's the norm in print.

TOO MUCH OF A GOOD THING

The biggest problem with Internet research is data glut. And the Internet has at least as much bad information as good. Worse, how something looks on the Internet is little indication of its accuracy. An expensively produced book or fancy-looking tour brochure isn't necessarily accurate, though it does indicate a substantial investment probably made with some care. A fancy-looking Web site, on the other hand, could be produced by an Internet self-publisher who knows nothing about travel. Our instinct to "judge a book by its cover" is nowhere else as dangerous as on the Internet. Slick-looking design is a poor indication of credibility and accuracy.

Similarly, books normally indicate the author, publisher, date, and place of publication. They don't have to, but most bookstores won't carry them if they lack this information. Web pages usually say little or nothing about their authorship or vintage.

Don't get me wrong: I'm not an advocate of Internet censorship. I'm glad that anyone can say anything online. But the anarchy and ease of Internet access requires a higher level of individual judgment and choice than do other media.

Enough caveats. We'll come back to the question of how to figure out what to believe. Let's move on to the nitty-gritty of travel planning, research, and resources online.

"Theater" vs. "Theatre"

I'm going to London on business next week, and I want to know what plays I can go to on a free evening. Type "London" and "theater" into my favorite search engine, and I get a list of 24,575 Web pages. Correct the spelling to the British "theatre," and I get a list of a different 99,075 pages. (Regional variations in spelling and terminology like this are common causes of failure to find what you want with an Internet search.) Some of these pages surely have what I want, but I can't possibly look at them all. And it's getting worse: these numbers are doubling roughly every six months. Where should I begin?

The Internet can't answer all questions, and it can answer any one question in thousands of ways. Your mission, should you choose to do your research online, is to find the right answers—and the ones to believe—from among those thousands. Skepticism and selectivity are the essential keys to success.

http://www.altavista.com
Spelling and "syntax" are crucial to effective search engine queries.

How To Find the Travel Information You Want on the Internet

OFFLINE INTERNET SEARCH TOOLS

Skip the Modem; Go Directly to the Phone

No telephone book or directory lists every e-mail or Web site address on the Internet. If you are looking for something specific, it's often easier to find the address offline than to try to search for it using the Internet alone. You can spend hours searching for someone's e-mail address or a Web site, or you can simply phone and ask. And there are real people—Internet research and travel professionals—who can save you time and aggravation with just a phone call.

Print References

Companies that have spent the money to make themselves available on the Internet want you to find them. Today, most advertisements, billboards, brochures, and business cards include e-mail addresses and/or URLs where you can get more information. If not, it's a sign the company doesn't take the Internet seriously. If you see a URL in an ad, brochure, or magazine that looks interesting, note it. It could be quite time-consuming to track down later—even simple URLs can be difficult to remember.

> **THE HUMBLE TELEPHONE**
>
> It's been taken as axiomatic for as long as the Internet has existed that the best way to find someone's e-mail address, if you have their phone number, is to call them. That's still as true today as it's been for 20 years.

Human Assistance

Obviously, none of this is relevant if you are searching for a concept rather than a specific person or company. Don't give up. You can't expect someone else to do all your research for free, but there's a good chance a librarian or travel agent may be able to point you in the right direction in a few minutes.

Neither librarians nor travel agents get the respect they deserve as information technology professionals. Travel agents were among the first and remain among the most computerized of workers. For people whose jobs have depended for decades on searching giant networks of airline computer reservation systems, formulating Internet queries is old hat—and easy by comparison.

Travel agents won't—and shouldn't—do your research for you unless you pay them an appropriate hourly fee. But if you have a regular relationship with a travel agent, or you have already paid them a service charge to assist you in planning a particular trip, it isn't out of line to ask them if they know where on the Internet to find specific information. Particularly if it's related to a destination or type of travel in which they specialize, there's a reasonable chance they'll already have it bookmarked. If it's going to take some digging, they'll tell you and set a price. It's up to you to decide whether it's worth paying to have someone do the research.

Librarians may know less about travel, but they know more than most about Internet research. The same electronic indices and searches used today on the Internet have been widely used at libraries for a decade or more. You can't get a degree in library science without taking graduate-level classes in search algorithms, Boolean query syntax, and effective strategies for using electronic indices.

And, of course, librarians—unlike travel agents—get paid to share their expertise, teach others their skills, and help others find what they want. In my book, librarians are the unsung heroes and most overlooked public servants of the Internet revolution. If you want to learn how to do Internet research, head to your local library. Many have free classes in Internet research and search engine usage.

WEB DIRECTORIES

What They Are

OK, but what if you *don't* know who has the information you want, or where to look on the Internet? What if your librarian or travel agent can't help?

The best place to start is a Web site called a "search engine" or "Web directory." Technically, a search engine and a Web directory are two completely different tools. But most people use the term "search engine" to refer to either, and some Web sites include both on the same page.

Yahoo.com is by far the largest and most widely used Web directory. Its major competitors include the Open Directory (**dmoz.org**), About.com, LookSmart.com, Go.com, Snap.com, and Ask Jeeves (**www.ask.com**).

Web directories are the most popular sites on the Internet. Like

A Directory of Web Directories

Compiling a million links to Web sites in tens of thousands of categories is an expensive task that few now sites want to start on from scratch, or feel they need to do themselves. Many other directory sites actually get their information from one of the larger sites. Search Engine Watch (**www.searchenginewatch.com**) maintains a fairly impartial and highly informative list of Web directories and search engines, with information about where they get their information and their size and popularity. Check it out before you start using multiple Web directories: there's no point trying several sites that are all going to show you the same set of links from the same underlying source.

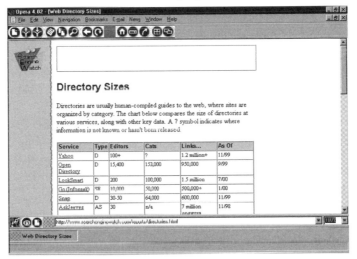

http://www.searchenginewatch.com
Numbers of editors and Web pages indexed in several Web directories

an encyclopedia of Web pages, a Web directory consists of URLs—sometimes with brief annotations—organized into larger, general categories, often followed by subordinate levels of smaller, more specific categories. Ideally, they compile for us a set of bookmarks or favorites on a common topic.

They're useful for finding Web sites of companies in a particular line of business—if you don't know the names of the companies in the field—or that (claim to) provide a particular kind of information. But you still need to evaluate those sites, and their credibility, for yourself.

What They Aren't

Many specialized directories relate to specific topics, including several devoted to travel. Unfortunately, travel is too broad for an amateur directory to cover thoroughly. And it's such a focal point for e-commerce that commercial directories often succumb to the temptation to sell "recommendations" to the highest bidders. Typically, amateur travel Web directories are limited to one or a few people's personal favorites. On commercial travel directories—even those maintained by otherwise-reputable news organizations—the listing for "travel reservations" or "lowest prices" generally goes to whichever online travel agency has bought that link.

I know of no specialized travel Web directory with any reasonable degree of both objectivity and comprehensiveness. Such a site probably would have to be operated as a fee-based subscription service by an independent nonprofit organization. Thus far, online travel consumers haven't demonstrated a willingness to pay a premium for unbiased links, recommendations, and advice.

> ### A LISTING IS NEITHER REVIEW – NOR RECOMMENDATION
>
> Don't mistake a listing in a Web directory for an endorsement, recommendation, or rating. Web directories are much too busy to carry out any meaningful evaluation of the sites they list. The more comprehensive the directory, and the more sites it lists, the less carefully they are reviewed.

Since Web directory access is free to the consumer, revenue must come from the same advertisers whose Web sites are often listed within the directory. Unlike newspapers—where "editorial" content and advertising are clearly separated—no major Web directory can promise an unbiased endorsement or rating of the sites listed. On the contrary, most directories openly advertise to have one's site listed first, or have competitors excluded from listing, for a price.

Use Web directory listings only as a starting point. While a great idea and a great commercial success, even the largest directory compilers don't have the resources to adequately complete the task.

Getting Around

As anywhere else on the Web, one click can take you from a page on Yahoo.com (or any other directory) to a page that looks similar but is actually on a different site with information from a different source.

Keep track of where you are. Always set your browser to display the full URL of the current page and the page to which a link will take you. You'll have at least a clue as to the source of the information you're viewing. In Microsoft Internet Explorer (MSIE), un-check "Show friendly URLs" in the "Advanced" options. In both Netscape and MSIE, un-check "Enable Internet Keywords."

Don't limit your search to the travel category of a Web directory. Like anywhere, many useful resources aren't intended primarily for travelers. Try searching under "Regions," "Countries," or "Geography." Or look under "News Media" and find the Web site for a local publication or broadcast outlet that includes a local events calendar. You could look under "Entertainment" for specific kinds of activities. In general, when looking for travel information in a Web directory, I look under "Travel" as a last resort.

Behind the Screens

Yahoo.com has about 150 editors and lists more than 1.2 million links. That means each editor is responsible for maintaining 8,000 or more links. If they check each link once a year, that gives them about 15 minutes to evaluate each listing.

Most Web directories have less money and smaller staffs than Yahoo. This translates to even less time on each site they list. Ask Jeeves, for example, has a staff of only 30 editors trying to maintain answers to seven million questions!

Web directories have little, if any, time to spend looking for interesting new sites. Most of their time is spent reviewing thousands of potential new sites that come in daily. Most major directories have backlogs of listing requests several months long. And since directory editors only have time to glance at content, attractive design becomes much more important than the content itself. A Web directory almost certainly hasn't checked any facts, compared any prices, or tried to buy anything from the site before deciding whether to list it. It's not as though they were selling advertisements in the margins of an encyclopedia or dictionary. It's more as though Merriam-Webster were selling the right to write the definition of "cola" or "beverage" to Coke, Pepsi, or the highest bidder.

KEYWORD SEARCH ENGINES

What They Are

Search engines are harder to learn to use, but they're much more

Operating Systems and Applications

This book isn't intended to be limited to users of any one platform, Web browser, e-mail program, or application. When I use the term PC ("personal computer"), I use it in its traditional sense of "single-user desktop microcomputer," not in the narrower sense of "Windows PC." I regularly use both Windows PCs (desktop and notebook) and PCs running MacOS (iMacs and iBooks). Other PC operating systems include Linux and BeOS.

Most people use either Microsoft Internet Explorer (MSIE) or Netscape Navigator as their Web browser, and Microsoft Outlook, Netscape Messenger, or Eudora as their e-mail client. There are alternatives, though: other Web browsers worth considering include Opera and Lynx (both for Windows, Mac, Linux, and other platforms), and iCab (for Mac only). I have MSIE, Netscape, Opera, and Lynx on both my computers, although I have Opera set as the default browser in Windows. Other important e-mail clients include Pegasus Mail (my default mail client in Windows) and Pine (available for Windows and Linux). This list isn't complete: new software is introduced all the time.

In this book, I've tried to strike a balance between recognition

powerful and useful than Web directories. It just takes practice. Rather than an outline or hierarchical "tree" of categories, a search engine lets you specify words or phrases and shows you any pages in its index that contain those words.

A search engine combines URLs and "spiders" or "crawlers"—essentially automated Web browsing robots—to compile indices of words that it finds on Web pages. Search engines don't pretend to judge or rate pages. They just serve up lists featuring a desired combination of words. When you realize how little judgment the human compilers of Web directories have, robotic search engines become an increasingly attractive alternative.

Search engine spiders start from the lists of URLs submitted by people who want their pages listed. They scan each page and index all the words, especially those in the title and headings. Then they check all the links on the page to see if they are already indexed. If they find a link to a page they haven't indexed already, they go to that page, index it, scan its links—and so *ad infinitum.*

The largest search engines are AltaVista.com, FAST Search

of diversity, advocacy for my own preferences, and acknowledgment of the dominance of both PC operating systems and Web browsers for which, at this writing, Microsoft has recently been convicted of abusing its monopoly power in restraint of trade. I try to give advice that will be useful regardless of what type of computer you have, and which operating system and programs you use—while realizing that most of you probably use Windows and MSIE or Netscape.

For the most part, I try to give general advice that will apply regardless of which specific platform or Internet software you use. To the extent that I talk about specific programs, however, I'll talk mainly (although not exclusively) about programs for Windows. To the extent that I talk about specific Web browsers, I'll talk mainly about MSIE, Netscape, Opera, and Lynx (each of which works similarly on different platforms). Realistically, those are what most people are using, and those are the programs with which I am most familiar and best able to offer advice.

I feel freer to suggest alternate applications than alternate operating systems. Whether or not it's worthwhile, changing operating systems requires a considerable investment of time (Linux or BeOS) and/or money (Mac). Trying out a new Web browser or e-mail program is much simpler and easier.

(**www.alltheweb.com**), Excite.com, Go.com, Lycos.com, Inktomi, and—with caveats—Google.com, NorthernLight.com, and Alexa. Inktomi provides its services only through other sites that pay to use its search engine, such as **www.iwon.com**. Alexa (a division of Amazon.com) is the engine behind both Netscape's "Smart Browsing/What's Related?" and MSIE's "Show Related Links" features, as well as services provided through a browser add-on you can download from **www.alexa.com**.

As with the Web directories, many other sites rely on one or another of these engines for their Web searches; some sites combine a directory from one source with a search engine from another. Websites change allegiance often: a site may provide search results from Lycos this week, and from Inktomi next week.

Getting Around

The key to using search engines effectively is understanding and learning to use so-called "query syntax". If you simply type a series of words into a search box, you'll be shown all Web pages in the

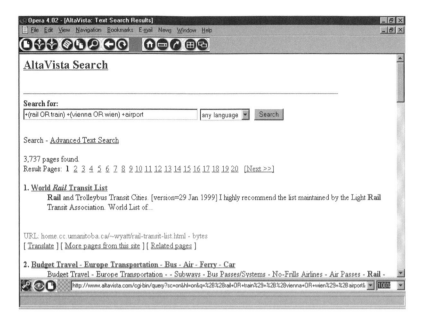

http://www.altavista.com

Is there a train to the airport in Vienna ("Wien" in German)? An all-purpose search engine won't necessarily answer your question directly. Often, as here, what it finds is a specialized directory that includes a link to the answer.

search engine's index that feature those words in any combination or order—probably not very useful.

The better search engines, however, permit you to:

- specify that certain words or phrases are required, not merely desirable;
- show only pages matching all of your criteria, not just one keyword or phrase;
- exclude pages on which other words appear;
- require that words appear as part of a particular phrase, or near each other;
- find pages containing groups of related forms of a word (e.g., "travel*" might turn up "traveler," "traveller," "traveling," etc.);
- show or exclude pages only from specific sites;
- show pages satisfying similar criteria (e.g., "sailboard" or "windsurfing").

Search Engine Pirates and Writers' Rights

Several search engines make their money from copyright theft. Alexa engages in the most systematic piracy, since it stores and provides copies on demand of every Web page it indexes, without paying a penny for any of them. Alexa even claims the right to control how the copies it distributes are used, even though it doesn't own them! Alexa supports itself by selling ads, but none of the advertising revenue goes to the authors or owners of the stolen material Alexa distributes. Google also stores and delivers copies of Web pages to which it doesn't have rights, but at least it doesn't yet sell ads (except for itself) on its pirated copies of other people's pages. In addition to providing links to Web pages, Northern Light provides lists of articles which it sells, to many of which Northern Light doesn't own the rights. If you buy a copy of an article in the Northern Light "special collection," be aware that you are probably buying stolen property for which the writer is not being paid. These companies also provide some legitimate services, but I cannot recommend doing business with thieves. It should be no surprise that well-known Web companies are stealing from writers: the *New York Times, Time, Lexis-Nexis, Newsday,* and *University Microfilms,* among others, have all been found guilty recently of wholesale copyright theft for placing work online without permission or payment to the authors or owners. As this book went to press, only the amounts of damages owed to writers by these companies remained to be determined. For more about these issues, see the Web site of National Writers Union (**www.nwu.org**), and their section on the case against the *New York Times* at **www.nwu.org/tvt/tvthome.htm.**

How do you specify all these things? Typically, you do so with so-called "Boolean operators" (AND, OR, NOT, NEAR) alone or combined with the following special punctuation:
- quotation marks (" ") around phrases or groups of words you want to appear in exact sequence;
- a plus sign (+) before required words or phrases;
- a minus sign (-) before criteria for pages to be excluded;
- an asterisk (*) as a "wild card" that matches any letter or letters, etc.).

Search Syntax: How to Find What You're Looking For

Nothing can do more to make it easier to find what you want on the Internet than learning how to use the search syntax of at least one major keyword search engine. With an unformatted string of words, you can expect a routine search to produce a list of tens of thousands of Web pages, most of them irrelevant. Worse yet, the most relevant pages aren't likely to be near the top of the list. With a little practice, however, you can format your search criteria to produce a much shorter and more relevant list of Web pages.

Look for a link on the search page to "Search Tips," "Search Syntax," or "How To Search" for instructions on how to format your query for a particular search engine. Fortunately, most of the major search engines use essentially the same query syntax, with only minor variations. Search Engine Watch has links to several good generic introductions to the commands and punctuation that work with most search engines at **www.searchenginewatch.com/facts**.

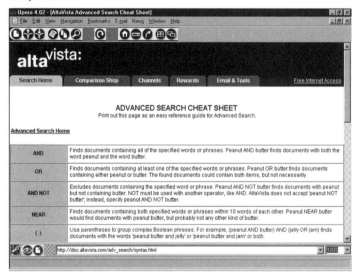

http://www.altavista.com
One search engine's explanation of its "syntax" for queries

Don't expect to get your query perfect the first time. And don't expect the most useful page to be the first one on the resulting list. You'll often need to refine your search—even a skilled searcher needs to reformulate their query a couple of times before they get a reasonably sized list. Try to focus on which words or phrases are most likely to appear prominently on the pages you are looking for, and least likely to appear in the same combination on pages you don't want. As an experienced professional, I consider myself successful if after two or three iterations I get a list of 100 or fewer "hits." It just takes practice.

A successful search (rather than find an exact match) may turn up a specialized site that discusses the topic you are interested in and has listings (and often reviews, although not necessarily objective ones) for sites within that field. There are niche "portal" sites like this for virtually any interest, activity, place, or business that some people—no matter how small or scattered—might have in common.

Impartial Information or Advertisement?

Almost all search engines show you links to their advertisers, along with links to index pages that match your request. Advertisers pay big to have their ads targeted to people who are searching for keywords relevant to their product or business, and likewise to have the ads look as much as possible like the answers to your search request. Usually they look a little different, but rarely are they plainly labeled, "Paid Advertisement" the way they would be in a newspaper. Learn to distinguish the advertisements and paid listings from the answers to your search request. If you can't tell which is which, find another search engine to use.

While most search engines make some distinction between ads and search responses (except those like GoTo.com that list *only* advertisements), none promise to list non-advertisers equally with advertisers, or not to exclude competitors. With travel, this is a particular problem. Most major search engines either have their own online agencies or get money for allowing other online travel agencies to be their exclusive or "preferred" travel providers. Travel information—especially about specific companies and prices—is one of the areas where you can rarely trust search engines to be impartial.

Search engines know that people come to them to search for

PAYOLA

One Web directory, GoTo.com, consists *exclusively* of paid listings from advertisers, in order of how much they've paid.

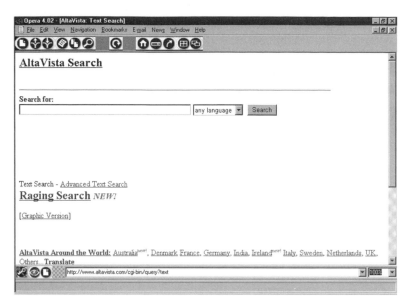

http://www.altavista.com/cgi-bin/query/?text
The "text only" version of a search engine is usually less cluttered and more efficient. Some of the white space on this page would be full of banner ads, except that I use a proxy server to filter them out and speed Web browsing.

other sites, but they make their money by getting them to look at advertisements or buy things while they are on the search site. Search pages are typically cluttered with advertisements and links to the search engine's partner vendors. They're deliberately designed to be as distracting as possible from the search. All you really need or want on the search page is a box to enter your query, a button to start the search, and a list of results. For those search engines that have one, the "text only" alternate search page is almost invariably faster to load and much more useful, with fewer advertisements, irrelevancies, and distractions. The advanced search page, which of necessity devotes more space to the search criteria, likewise has fewer ads and less junk.

Most people go to the MSN, Netscape, or AOL page every time they start their browser, because that's the way the browser was installed. It's easy, and usually much more useful, to set the "start page" or "home page" in your browser to your favorite search page. This way, it's a click away whenever you're browsing and want to look for something else. For what it's worth, the start page and home page in all my browsers are set to the AltaVista text search page **www.altavista.com/cgi-bin/query?text**. I don't know any higher praise I could give a Web site.

Behind the Screens

My final caveat on search engines: the best of them will, with skill and luck, take you to pages with links to other pages you've never heard of before. You'll find places that aren't in the search engines, and it's there you'll find what you want. Don't expect to find anything in one click. Search engines are a starting point, not a substitute, for surfing. The biggest search engines have indexed half a billion Web pages each. That's a lot, but still only a small fraction of all the Web pages that exist. A 1999 study (**www. metrics.com**) found that the best search engines had only indexed about 16 percent of all the pages on the Web. The majority of Web pages aren't indexed by any major search engine. Realistically, no search engine can keep pace with all the new sites: it can take from two to six months to index a new or revised site, even if the creator or sponsor submits its URL.

LOWEST FARES IN THE GALAXY

The descriptions that show up for each link in response to a search engine inquiry come from what the Web sites say about themselves, not from the search engine staff. (Search engine listings are compiled by robots, remember, not by people. No human being has probably ever looked at the search engine listing, much less verified if the description is true.) So if you see a link on the "search results" page that says, "ABSOLUTELY, POSITIVELY THE LOWEST FARES IN THE GALAXY," read it as though it were the headline in an advertisement, not a known fact.

FINDING INTERNET INFORMATION THAT HAS MOVED OR CHANGED

Whether you hear about a Web site or get its address from some other source, there's always a chance that when you type the URL into your browser you'll get either "404 not found," some other cryptic error code, or a page that isn't the one you were trying to find. What do "404 not found" and similar messages mean, anyway? And how do you get past them to find the page you want?

The exact error message you'll see depends on what software you and the Web server use, and how it is configured. But assuming the page once existed, one of three things is probably wrong. The first thing to do is to figure out which has happened.

#1: You've Entered the Wrong URL

If you typed the URL yourself, double-check it against your source. URLs can be case sensitive, meaning it matters which letters are or aren't capitalized. Follow capitalization exactly, even if it looks weird. URLs are arbitrary, cryptic, and devilishly difficult to proofread, so errors in printed URLs are common. Even the URL in a link on another Web page can be misspelled. (In most browsers, if you hold the cursor over a link it will show you the URL to which the link will take you.)

If a URL doesn't work, look for seemingly misspelled words within it, and try substituting correctly spelled ones. Particularly if it appeared in print, try substituting zero for the letter "O", or vice versa, as these are often transposed. Try substituting ".html" for ".htm" at the end, or vice versa. Try adding a slash ("/") at the end of the URL if there isn't one, or removing it if there is. (Usually these have the same effect, but not always.)

Be sure to type the entire URL, which usually but not always begins with "http://". URLs for secure parts of sites start with "https://"; some URLs start with "ftp://" and a few with other things. Don't assume that "Foobar" is always "Foobar.com": it might be Foobar.net, Foobar.org, Foobar.edu, Foobar.ca (in Canada), Foobar.co.uk (in the U.K.), or hundreds of others. Don't assume that the Web site for Foobar.com is at "http://www.foobar.com". It might be at "http://Foobar.com", "http://secure.foobar.com", or anything else you can imagine. One of the most common sites of this sort is the U.S. State Department's international travel Web site, travel.state.gov. It's arguably one of the best travel Web sites in the United States. But most people have failed to find it because the proper URL doesn't include "www." Until early 2000, when they added an "alias" to redirect visitors who got their URL wrong, typing "www.travel.state.gov" or "http://www.travel.state.gov" would only get you an error message.

A URL must be typed into your browser on one line, unbroken. In print, or in e-mail messages, URLs are often split over several lines. Make sure you included the entire URL, even if you have to cut and paste pieces from several lines of an e-mail message. Assemble them with no spaces; spaces are never allowed within a URL. Particular problems are caused by hyphens at the end of broken lines, especially in narrow newspaper columns. It's impossible to tell whether they are actually part of the URL (some URLs do contain hyphens) or whether they were inserted to show that the URL was being broken. Try reassembling the URL in your browser window both with and without the hyphen.

#2: The Site Exists, But the Specific
Page Has Moved or Disappeared

If you get an "Error 404" or "File Not Found" message, that's an indication from the Web server that the particular page you requested can't be found on that site. (There are a bunch of other standard-numbered Web server error codes, but "Error 404" is the only one most people need to know.) The good news in such a case is that you can't get this error message unless the Web server itself exists and is responding. The difficulty is in figuring out whether the page or information you want is no longer on the site at all, or whether it has simply moved to another URL within the site.

Most Web sites have internal indices and search tools, and/or a directory of the site (often labeled a "site map", although it's usually an outline rather than a map). Try to find some working page on the same site, as close as possible to the section that had the page you were looking for, and navigate from there. Like the files on your computer, the pages on a Web site are stored in folders within folders (directories within directories) on a Web server. Each "/" ("slash") in a URL represents a level in the folder structure, with the top-level folder ("root directory") for the Web site at the left. So you can often get closest to the area of the site where a missing page was located by working back up the URL from right to left, removing everything after each forward slash ("/"), one "/" at a time, until you get to the home page of the site.

Many Web sites, especially small personal ones, don't have their own domain names. John's Doe's personal site, for example, might be at www.foobar.com/doe, home.foobar.com/doe, www.foobar.com/users/doe, or www.foobar.com/~doe, among other common URL formats. Most of these personal sites are provided free to users of particular services. Those users often change service providers, so it's common for sites like this to move from host to host. If you find a dead link to a site like this in a search engine index, here's one way to find if it has simply moved to another host: copy as much as possible of the search engine's site description and try putting it into the search box (in quotes as an entire phrase) of some other search engines. With any luck, some other search engine will have indexed the page more recently, at its new location.

Search engines and Web directory compilers revisit a site rarely, if at all, especially if the site's maintainer doesn't specifically notify them of changes to URLs or request that they update their index. Good Web designers make sure that all the old URLs still work even if they add new ones or reorganize their site. But the world is full of bad Web designers, and millions of pages are moved to new URLs every day. One of the most common problems is that sites often move news stories and articles to a different URL when they are no longer current; the original URL then features a new story, not necessarily the one you were looking for. In other words, the link in the search engine's index is to a URL that always shows the current article, not the URL in the publication's archives for the specific article you wanted. In situations like this, go back to the search engine and look at the date the page was indexed. (Better search engines include this in their summary of each page.) Then return to the Web site, and search its archives for that date.

#3: The Entire Site Has Moved or Disappeared

If you get a "Cannot Connect To Server' or "Site Not Found" message, that means the entire Web site is either unavailable or defunct. (Unfortunately, in most cases MSIE gives exactly the same error message, or redirects you to the MSN search page, regardless of whether the server doesn't answer or answers that it can't find the specific page you requested. Most other, better browsers give a clear indication of which happened, which is more helpful in deciding what to do.) One thing to do is to try again the next day. Web servers, especially those of smaller, amateur, and nonprofit sites, often go down for a few hours at a time, but rarely for more than a couple of days. If it doesn't work three business days running, the site is almost certainly dead, renamed, or relocated.

There are services (including Alexa.com and Google.com) that will provide you with copies of Web pages from their archives that aren't available from their original sites. Understand that these are stolen copies made without the permission of the authors of the content, and for which the rightful owners aren't paid. A Web site may have paid to use an article for a limited period of time, but by making pirated copies of the page available forever, these "archive" or "cache" sites can deprive the author of the opportunity to get paid for long-term reuse, no matter how many people read the bootleg copies from the archive. Even if you don't mind receiving stolen property or depriving authors and designers of their livelihoods (Web site investors may be getting rich, but pay for freelance writers who contribute to Web sites is often dismal), you might want to think twice before relying on material that is by definition out of date, or that might have been removed from its original site because it was inaccurate or misleading.

At some point, you just have to give up and look for another source. Don't despair: there's rarely only one good site on the Internet for information about a particular subject. And for every site that disappears, a dozen new ones are created.

USENET NEWSGROUPS

Recently, I was on a panel of experts on travel and the Internet. After we answered questions from the audience about the Web for about an hour, I finally got a chance to say, "But actually, the most valuable things on the Internet for travelers are Usenet newsgroups, not the Web." All my fellow panelists immediately agreed—despite our very different perspectives on some of the other topics we discussed. Lots of Internet "old-timers" (myself included) value Usenet newsgroups as epitomizing the noncommercial values of the Internet. Today's Internet community is too often drowned out by a flood of advertising. Unlike some other older features of the Internet such as "gopher" (see below), Usenet newsgroups have in no way been replaced or rendered obsolete by the emergence of the Web.

FROM 50 TO 50,000

Travel has been a major topic of Usenet newsgroups from their earliest days. "Net.travel", the predecessor of the current "rec.travel.*" hierarchy of news-groups, was one of the first 50 of what are now about 50,000 Usenet newsgroups.

What Are Usenet Newsgroups, Anyway?

A newsgroup is a collection of messages on a common topic, to which anyone with access to the Usenet can contribute. Today, the Usenet is more or less synonymous with the Internet—if you have access to the Internet, you have access to the Usenet.

While a lot like a bulletin board, a newsgroup is actually much larger, decentralized, and open to many more people. When anyone on any connected system posts a message to the newsgroup, it is relayed throughout the Usenet so that eventually that message shows up on each system's news server. Each news server ends up with a copy of

MANY-TO-MANY COMMUNICATION

The Web is mostly, in practice, a form of "one-to-many" publishing or broadcasting. Someone puts something on a Web page, and then many people can see or read it. E-mail is mostly either one-to-one communication (private messages) or yet another one-to-many medium (e-mail newsletters and spam). Usenet newsgroups are significant and valuable as the only major feature of the Internet that is primarily devoted to "many-to-many" communication: open, participatory, collaborative, and shared.

each message on that topic from anyone on any system around the world.

In addition to the Usenet newsgroups that are relayed around the world, there are also private newsgroups that are hosted on just one server. These may require a password or they may be open to anyone who points their newsreader at that server. Many computer and software companies have a private news server for discussion of their products, for example. You can use the same newsreader programs to read private newsgroups, as long as you know the address of the server. But they don't have nearly the same wide reach and usefulness as the Usenet newsgroups.

Why the Usenet?

The power and utility of newsgroups stems from the vastly larger number of people who read and contribute to them. The result is a proportionately greater volume of topics and postings than would be possible for any single bulletin board, Web site, or chat room. If you want to find out if someone, somewhere out there, is interested in or has the answer to a particular question, your best chance of reaching that person is by posting a query in a relevant Usenet newsgroup. IMHO ("In My Humble Opinion," per Usenet shorthand), posting a question on a bulletin board site like Lonely Planet's "Thorn Tree" section is a poor use of time when you could communicate with a much larger community on a Usenet newsgroup.

Utilizing the Usenet

In addition to the several dozen "rec.travel" newsgroups, which have hundreds of new messages everyday, many other newsgroups are useful for travelers. There are newsgroups for almost any imaginable group of people with a common interest, identity, or sense of community. There are newsgroups for anyone and anything; if your interest isn't already represented, it's easy enough to create a new newsgroup.

There are "rec.*" or "alt.*" newsgroups for all sorts of sports, games, and recreational activities. Want to find out about sea kayaking opportunities in Baja California? Post a query in "rec.boats.paddle", and within a few days you'll probably get a batch of replies from fellow kayakers who've been there recently. Even if participating in a particular activity isn't the primary purpose of your trip, it can be a way to initiate an e-mail correspondence with someone in the place you are going who can give you a local's perspective on things to do.

Going abroad? Interested in the culture or society of the place you

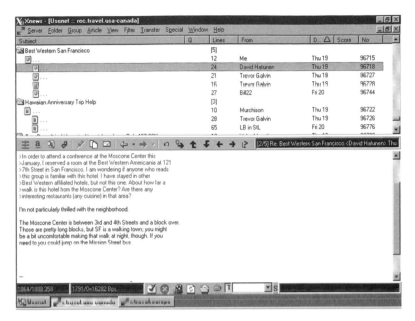

news:irec.travel.usa-canada

Usenet posting viewed in the Xnews newsreader. This is the sort of specific information about a neighborhood that would be hard to find a guidebook. If your browser and newsreader are already configured, you may be able to launch your newsreader by typing "news:" and the name of a newsgroup in a browser URL window.

---

will be visiting? There are "soc.culture.*" newsgroups for people who share an interest in dozens of different nationalities, ethnicities, and regional cultures around the world. These newsgroups are especially popular with foreign students and other expatriates who use them to connect with other people from their homeland while they are abroad. Many of these people are eager to help would be visitors, and can give a local perspective that you'll never find in a guidebook.

Newsreader Programs: To Use or Not To Use?

When you want to "read the news", you can use a newsreader program to contact your ISP's news server and retrieve whatever messages, in whatever newsgroups, interest you. You can read the messages from others, you can post a reply or follow-up message that can be read by anyone, or you can send a private e-mail message to someone who has posted in a newsgroup.

Newsreader Programs

I use different computers in different places for different things. I regularly use at least four newsreaders. Newsreader ratings are partly a matter of taste: Usenet aficionados seem to have even stronger and less consistent opinions about newsreaders than Web junkies do about browsers.

For what it's worth, I think the newsreader in the Opera browser, while limited, is one of the easiest Windows newsreaders with which to get started. Some of the most advanced browsers like Agent or Gravity are optimized for downloading multimedia postings (mostly erotica and boot-legged music) rather than the text discussions that are more likely to be relevant to travel. More powerful Windows browsers optimized for text include "slrn" (a port of a UNIX browser; my favorite but one of the most difficult to install) and Xnews. There's lots of discussion of the pros and cons of different newsreaders on (where else?) the Usenet newsgroup "news.software.readers".

Like the rest of AOL's features, their newsreader is relatively easy to learn, but limited. AOL uses a nonstandard proprietary format for newsgroups, just as it does for e-mail. So if you're on AOL, you're stuck with their newsreader and e-mail program unless you subscribe to a news service from another ISP.

Whatever ISP you are on, one possibility (if you get deeply into newsgroups) is a "shell" account that lets you run a news-reader program on a "host" computer that's connected directly to the new server. This enables you to search through messages much more quickly, since the searching is done on the host and only the messages that you want to read have to be sent to your computer. For text newsgroups, I use a newsreader on the host in a shell account whenever possible.

It's also possible to read newsgroup postings as though they were Web pages at archive sites like Deja.com, instead of with a newsreader program. That's an adequate way to get a feel for what sorts of things are said in newsgroups, without having to install any new software or learn how to use the newsreader components of your existing Internet software. But if you find yourself interested in newsgroups, or spending any time reading or participating in them, you'll find it well worthwhile

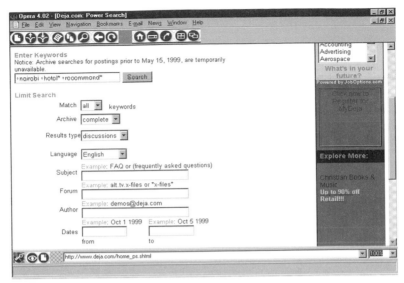

http://www.deja.com
Some of the options for searching the archive of Usenet messages at Deja.com. The query syntax is similar to that used by most Web search engines.

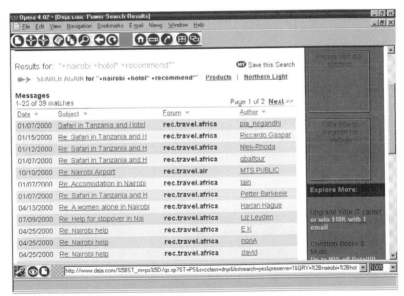

The result of the search in the previous illustration: 39 messages with recommendations (or advertisements) for hotels in Nairobi.

— ARCHIVED POSTINGS ———

The volume of postings in all the newsgroups is so great that even large ISP's delete new messages from their news servers after no more than a week or two. For the last few years, however, a couple of Web sites have been compiling and indexing archives of all newsgroup postings. If you want to see what's been said about a subject, or whether a question has been answered in the past in a newsgroup, you can search the Usenet archives on a site like Deja.com. Deja.com lets you search for all past postings from a particular e-mail address, as well as by keywords in the messages, which can be helpful in finding out about the tastes, interests, and experience of someone who is offering advice.

to learn how to use a newsreader program. Good newsreaders have elaborate filtering and scoring features that enable you to focus on messages that are likely to be of interest, without being overwhelmed by the volume of Usenet traffic.

The major Web browsers are all distributed as part of Internet software suites that include e-mail, FTP, and newsreader software as well. Microsoft Outlook can be used as a newsreader as well as an e-mail program, and Netscape can be used to read news as well as for e-mail and to browse the Web. You may be better off, though, getting a separate newsreader program. The Microsoft Outlook and Netscape newsreaders are afterthoughts to programs that are designed primarily for other uses, and are among the more difficult and confusing newsreader programs.

Graphical Web browsers all look very similar: a window that displays a Web page, surrounded by navigation buttons and scrollbars. If you're used to MSIE, Netscape, or Opera, you can sit down at a computer with one of the others and start using it right away. Newsreaders, on the other hand, have wildly different appearances and are optimized for different things. You can be highly proficient in using one newsreader and find another, equally good newsreader a complete mystery at first glance. Most newsreaders are harder to configure than a typical browser. Worst of all, the newsreaders that are most useful and efficient, once you get the hang of them, are some of the hardest to set up and learn. Be patient. Take the time to learn. Be willing to try several newsreaders until you find one you like. It will be worth it.

A Word of Caution

When you start posting to newsgroups, be aware that newsgroup postings are publicly accessible to anyone in the world, identifiable by your e-mail address, and archived for posterity. Don't say anything in

All the President's E-mail

Deja.com provides a powerful and useful, but sometimes frightening, "author profile" tool that enables you to search out all the messages ever posted from a given e-mail address. Enter **www.deja.com/profile.xp?author=president@whitehouse.gov**, for example, and you'll see all the newsgroup postings from the

president of the United States. (Try it, and you'll also see how many messages have obviously been posted with forged addresses.) I expect it won't be too long before some politician or public figure gets caught up in a scandal that hinges on whether a bunch of years-old anonymous postings in "alt.sex.fetish", or some such newsgroup, do or don't match their writing style.

a newsgroup, at least in your own name, for which you aren't prepared to be held accountable for the rest of your life.
If you're not comfortable with that, get another e-mail address to use
exclusively for newsgroup postings, and never put your real name or
anything that would identify you in your messages from that address.

True Story

One of my all-time best experiences using the Internet for travel planning came through one of these newsgroups. I was going to Bandung,
Indonesia. I had a question regarding contemporary Indonesian political perspectives. What did I do? After searching the Web and the
newsgroup archives to see if someone had already answered my question, I posted a query in the "soc.culture.indonesia" newsgroup: "Does
anyone know whether, or where, in Bandung I could find books giving
contemporary Indonesian perspectives on global politics?"

Several replies were posted in the newsgroup or e-mailed to me
privately. Typically, they were wildly contradictory. But one reply
came from an Indonesian graduate student at the University of Texas
who had grown up in Bandung. He gave me directions for a walking
tour of the English-language bookstores of Bandung. And, in case I
needed local assistance with translations, he gave me the name of
his high school English teacher and the address of his old school.

I hadn't meant to intrude on someone to whom I had such a
tenuous connection, but when I found myself walking past the
school, I decided to drop in and pass on greetings to the teacher
from his former student.

The teacher was initially quite confused (especially since I knew
almost nothing about his former student), but when I told him I was
interested in how his students viewed the history of their city, he
invited me to ask them my questions directly. Like many students of
English as a foreign language, they had few opportunities to practice
with a native speaker of English. Their instructor was delighted to
have me as a guest English conversationalist for his classes for the
day. I was delighted too: I couldn't have asked for a better opportunity to find out what I wanted to know.

The point of this story is that the person who made the high
point of my trip possible was someone I never would have found
without the Internet. Equally important, I never would have found
him on a travel bulletin board or Web site and I never would have
gotten the benefit of his advice if I hadn't been prepared to make my
own judgments about which authoritative sounding but conflicting
opinions to believe or to disregard.

BEYOND THE WORLD WIDE WEB AND USENET NEWSGROUPS: OTHER INTERNET TOOLS

"The Web" and "the Internet" are often used as synonyms. They aren't. To date, the "killer application" and most-used feature of the Internet has proved to be e-mail, which connects substantially more people more often than the World Wide Web. What's more, there are other Internet tools and services just as useful, in their own ways, to travelers. If you only use the Web, you're missing some of the better and more fun features of the Internet.

Mailing Lists

Mailing lists are similar to Usenet newsgroups as participatory exchanges of messages, but they are delivered by e-mail. There are some large-circulation travel discussion mailing lists, but I can't see much to recommend them over travel (or other) Usenet newsgroups.

E-mail Newsletters

E-mail newsletters are like magazines, newspapers, or catalogs, except that they are delivered by e-mail instead of by snail mail. They are most useful for informing you of potentially interesting things you

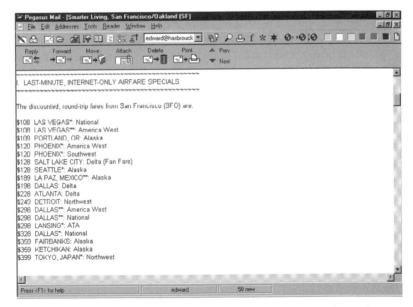

You can sign up with Smarterliving.com or other services to have them e-mail you a list like this each week with airlines' special fares for short getaways that weekend (or occasionally other times).

— I'm Going to Kansas City —

"Gee, since I can go to Kansas City (or New York, or Pudunk) for three days this weekend for $150 instead of the usual $250, I'm packing my bags." If this sounds like you, why not sign up for one of the e-mail newsletters that tell you about the airlines' weekly sales? The best-known of the bunch is SmarterLiving.com.

wouldn't have known to look for on a Web page, but want to know about when they happen.

Several online travel agencies and other Web sites have e-mail newsletters they send out weekly, or more often if there are shorter-lived special offers, to tell you about the airlines' weekly sales. You subscribe through their Web page, and tell them from which cities you are interested in fares. Every week, they send you an e-mail message with all the different airlines' special offers for that week from those cities.

Individual airlines also have similar mailing lists, but for most people it's more convenient to sign up with an agency or service that sends you a single e-mail message with all the different airlines' specials for the week from your city. You can also pay to subscribe to similar e-mail newsletters from "travel clubs" like BestFares.com, but they don't really give you anything for your membership or subscription fee that you couldn't have found free elsewhere.

Some other online travel agencies (notably Travelocity.com and Expedia.com) let you sign up for services that send you weekly advisories of the lowest fares between any two cities, or whenever the price between two cities drops below a specified amount. These advisories and alerts are limited to published fares, which aren't the only selling prices, so they don't really assure you of getting the best price or knowing about unpublished deals. But they can tip you off to fare wars you might not otherwise have known about.

Auto-Reply Robots

These are servers that send a specific document by e-mail in reply to a request also sent by e-mail. Some auto-reply robots send one canned message in response to anything sent to the robot's address. Send any e-mail message to faq@hasbrouck.org, for example, and the robot under my desk will send you back the latest version of my answers to Frequently Asked Questions about airfares. A company like Foobar.com often has a robot that responds to any message sent to info@foobar.com or brochure@foobar.com with a message giving general information or an electronic brochure about Foobar.com and its services. Other auto-reply robots can send different documents automatically, depending on what you put in the subject line and/or body of the message to the robot.

Auto-reply robots are mainly useful when you have access to the Internet but not to the Web. How could that be? In some poorly connected places, there isn't a continuous connection to the Internet. When you send an e-mail message from such a system, it's stored locally on a server. Periodically, the server connects to the Internet—perhaps with a daily long distance phone call in the middle of the night, or perhaps each time a low-altitude satellite passes overhead—and exchanges a batch of outgoing and incoming e-mail messages. This allows quite reliable e-mail communication with vastly lower transmission costs than would be required to keep the connection open all the time for Web browsing.

Several organizations operate robots that will retrieve any Web page and e-mail it to you in response to a properly formatted request by e-mail. You can get information about these services (from an auto-reply robot, of course) by sending an e-mail message to mail-server@rtfm.mit.edu with the following line, without the quotation marks, in the body of the e-mail message (you can put anything you like, or nothing, in the subject field; what matters to this particular robot is the message): "send usenet/news.answers/internet-services/access-via-e-mail"

If you have access to e-mail, you can thus retrieve almost any properly-designed "static" or informational Web page. Dynamic, interactive, or secure sites—including most shopping sites and all airline or other travel reservation sites—aren't accessible this way, unfortunately. And you'll only get the text version of the page, so if the page depends on graphics or isn't accessible with a text browser it won't be accessible by e-mail either. Still, e-mail to Web gateways are far better than nothing for the millions of e-mail users who don't have direct Web access.

FTP and Gopher

FTP ("File Transfer Protocol") and Gopher archives are generally handled by your browser. For most purposes you don't need to worry about how they differ from Web sites, and I won't discuss them in detail. It is occasionally important, however, to realize that they exist.

─ TYPE IT AS YOU SEE IT ─

If you see a URL that starts with "ftp://" or "gopher://", don't assume that it's a mistake or try to precede it with "http://" or "www". Just type it into your browser like any other URL, and go from there.

Personal E-mail

I mention personal e-mail last, but it's certainly not least in usefulness of Internet tools for travel planning and research. Never forget that the Internet is a communication medium that links real people. Those who post their travel experiences or recommendations in newsgroups or on personal Web pages are often willing, even eager, to correspond by e-mail about their trips. As a listener, you just have to remember that people you contact by e-mail may have changed or embroidered things to make a good story out of their experiences. Sometimes the people who talk most loudly are also those who exaggerate and invent the most.

— TRAVEL TALES —

People often get back from a trip to find that their friends aren't really that interested in hearing about their vacation. Other would-be travelers who contact them on the Internet are an ideal outlet for people's desires to tell their travel tales.

You can also get fee-based personal advice and consulting by e-mail. More and more travel agents offer travel planning assistance in exchange for service or consulting fees. If you prefer someone who isn't trying to sell you something at the same time that they are giving you advice, try Guidebookwriters .com (**www.guidebookwriters.com**). Unlike sites where visitors' questions are answered by unscreened amateur volunteers of uncertain qualifications, Guidebookwriters.com refers questions to a network of participating guidebook writers (including yours truly) selected by a committee of their peers for their expertise on specific places and topics. For a fee (typically $50-100 per hour), you can receive professional consultation, suggestions on your itinerary, or reliable answers to your specific questions.

How to Evaluate Internet Travel Information

The best thing about Internet research is that with only a little practice you can find more information than you could possibly use about almost any given topic—and much of it is fascinating, useful, and unavailable anywhere else. The worst thing about Internet research is that with only a little practice you can find more information than you could possibly use about almost any given topic—and much of it is propagandistic, misleading, obsolete, inaccurate, or simply unreliable and untrustworthy. How do you separate good advice from bad, and bargains from scams? First, be skeptical. Second, think critically. And third, evaluate the source of the information. Who wrote or said it? What did they base it on? Who paid for it or has an interest in it? How is it relevant to you, your style of travel, your budget, or your interests and tastes?

SOURCES OF TRAVEL INFORMATION ON THE INTERNET

On the Internet, the real source of information is often harder to find than it is in print publications. On many travel Web sites and newsgroups, most of the writers and articles are anonymous. The same company may have many Web sites to target different audiences; conversely, a single Web site often contains links that will take you to pages on many other sites. To figure out the source of the information on the page, you need to pay close attention both to where on the Internet that information is coming from, and to whatever fine print may give you clues as to who actually wrote or provided it. (For more on how to do this, see the advanced topic at the end of this section, "Finding the source of a Web page.")

Why does this matter? Knowing the source of a piece of information is essential to deciding how much to believe it, how much to rely on it, how much to trust it, and whether or not to send them your money.

- If you're looking for background information or specific facts, you need to find out who provided the information, or where they got it from. Is this what they saw last week, or a third-hand rumor they heard last year?
- If you're looking for specialized details, you need to find out whether the source actually has any expertise in the field. Is this current health advice from a professional, or something written by a local booster with no medical knowledge, trying to play down the health hazards to reassure tourists?
- If you're looking for ratings or recommendations of specific travel products, services, or suppliers, you need to know what

Looking Behind the Scenes

What might you find when you use the domain name to look up the owner of a Web site? Here's a look at a legitimate Web site, giving information excerpted (with permission) from one of the Moon Handbooks.

The home page features the reassuring Moon logo. But are the recommendations and advice those of the guide-book's author? Or are they paid advertisements placed by Adventurocity.com? Since the site doesn't say, you should assume they are ads. Neither the "About Us" nor the "Contact Us" pages give a name or address. And the Web-based e-mail form on the "Contact Us" page allows them to solicit e-mail without having to reveal *their* e-mail address.

Only with a WHOIS query can you find out anything about the real owners or backers of the site. Here's the actual result:

The "Hurricane Electric" contacts are merely those of Adventurocity.com's ISP—this is evident if you notice their e-mail addresses and try looking at **www.he.net**. That leaves Richard Green as the apparently responsible person—which he is, even though the Vancouver phone number in the domain registration didn't reach him or anyone who knew anything about him. I wasn't surprised; when I eventually met Rick Green, his business card gave no address, not even a post office box.

What does "TC" mean? Look it up in the ISO country-code database, and you'll find that it's the Turks and Caicos. There's nothing illegal, and nothing necessarily wrong, with incorporating your business in the Turks and Caicos (a tax haven in the Caribbean with 12,000 people and 16,000 corporations). Since you never have to set foot in the Turks and Caicos to set up a corporation there, there's no reason to rent an office, and a post office box is a typical Turks and Caicos corporate address. Perhaps for a Canadian expatriate, there are significant tax advantages to a Turks and Caicos corporation.

the relationship is between the source and the companies they are writing about.

■ If you pay by credit card, and complete the trip (or get your airline tickets in hand) before you pay your credit card bill: and you don't get what you were promised, you can get your money back through a credit card chargeback. If you are paying in advance, and won't take your trip until after you've

http://www.adveturocity.com

Post office box addresses, offshore corporate holding companies, and inconsistent or missing contact information should be red flags that make you wonder about whether and why these people might wish to remain anonymous. When it comes to anonymity and lack of accountability, offshore tax havens that don't require the disclosure of names of company directors or stockholders are the next best thing to cyberspace.

This is, in part, an unfair example. When I made these tests, Adventurocity.com was an unfunded startup at the beta test and demonstration stage. It didn't yet sell travel services or make reservations. But it's indicative, nonetheless, of just how little attention is paid to full disclosure.

paid your credit card bill, you need to know enough about the company to be confident of suing them successfully if something goes wrong.

Believing everything you find on the Internet would be a recipe for disaster. Even when it's not intended to mislead, there's a lot of plausible seeming, well-meaning, slick-looking misinformation and bad advice on the Internet. If you can't tell for sure where the information came from, assume the worst.

VERIFYING AUTHORSHIP OF POSTINGS

Newsgroups, bulletin boards, and chat rooms are full of uncensored, noncommercial advice from ordinary people just like you, right? Wrong. No Internet scam is more widespread than the posting of bogus testimonials, reviews, and recommendations by people with (undisclosed) financial interests in whatever they are touting.

On stock tip bulletin boards, that's illegal. In discussions of hotels, tour companies, and other travel services providers, it's just as unethical—but entirely legal. And it's easy. Anyone can get as many free and anonymous e-mail addresses from different providers as they want.

With more and more people using these sorts of accounts as their primary e-mail addresses, how can you tell which participants in an online discussion are legitimate? And even of those that aren't out-and-out frauds, how do you know whom to believe and rely on?

First, look at the message itself. Is it signed? Does it give you some way to contact the author? One of the largest problems with bulletin board systems is that frequently they don't even include an e-mail address for the poster. There are sometimes good reasons for anonymous posting. But anonymous praise or denunciation should be taken with the greatest skepticism. E-mail messages and newsgroup postings, on the other hand, generally include a "signature" at the bottom of their with the author's name, address, and sometimes other information.

─ **READER BEWARE** ──────

As you read a newsgroup or bulletin board message that looks like a testimonial, think about whether it sounds like something you would post if you had that sort of experience on a trip. If something sounds like an advertisement, it probably is.

If you aren't sure whether to take someone's advice, you can contact them directly. Send them a brief, polite e-mail message, or post a follow-up message in the newsgroup, with your specific questions. They aren't obligated to answer, of course, but they probably will. By corresponding with someone via e-mail, you can get a better sense of their knowledge, credibility, and travel style.

Many postings about travel businesses are from shills: people with an undisclosed interest in whatever they are promoting. Shills keep changing names and e-mail accounts so that their plugs appear

Authors' Personal Web Pages

Professional writers, especially freelancers, almost all have personal Web sites that they use to promote themselves and advertise their writing to publications that might hire them. If you're trying to figure out whether a place you read an article is a place for you, look at the author's personal Web site and you'll probably get a better sense of who they are, how they travel, and their tastes. (My own home page, if you want to apply that same strategy to this book, is at hasbrouck.org.)

http://www.southpacific.org
Author David Stanley's personal Web site for his Moon Handbooks to the South Pacific

to be coming from different people. If a short, polite message to the author of a relatively recent favorable posting gets no acknowledgment or reply whatsoever, the posting was probably from a shill using an account that they've abandoned.

Deja.com author profiles can also be helpful in evaluating newsgroup postings. If the only messages ever posted from a particular e-mail address are in praise of a particular business or product, it's almost surely the address of a shill. Conversely, you may find that they've complained in the newsgroup about every airline, hotel, or tour that they've ever been on.

If you have the e-mail address of the author of an interesting posting, try to see if they have their own Web site. Many online travelers, especially the sort who are active participants in Usenet newsgroups, put pictures and accounts of their trips on their personal Web pages. It's actually easy to find someone's personal Web pages through a keyword search on their e-mail address. Personal Web pages are unlikely to show up in Web directories like Yahoo. Use a search engine like AltaVista that indexes as many pages as possible.

CUI BONO: WHO BENEFITS?

Crucial to knowing what to believe on an Internet travel Web site is understanding from where the site's revenues come. Does the author(s) have a commercial interest or an axe to grind? Again, if they don't tell you, assume the worst.

One of the most common scams, for example, is for a tour operator or the owner of a group of hotels to put up an "informational" Web site about a destination. Because they can afford to spend money on search engine positioning, these are often among the first sites you find when you search for tourist information about a place. They may have some useful information, but it's incidental to their real purpose: getting you to choose your tour or hotel from among their offerings. Many of these sites try to bolster their legitimacy by calling themselves "The Official Timbuktu Travel Information Site," or the like. That may mean no more than that they are the official site of the Timbuktu Imperial Hotel. Typically, the domain name registration is an instant giveaway of such a scam.

Recently, I asked Sean Greene, president of the company that runs the adventure travel Web site Away.com, how he resolved conflicts between investors' demands for profits and consumers' desires for impartial information. He answered that there weren't any such conflicts—because investors weren't yet demanding profits. "What the financial markets are letting us do is invest in building great products" and provide valuable information for free, he said. Great idea, but the free ride won't last forever. Even as he made those remarks, Internet investors were starting to scrutinize the bottom line.

CREDIBILITY AND RELEVANCE
OF TRAVEL ADVICE

On the Internet, there is no journalistic standard requiring a clear distinction between advertising and editorial content, as there is in any reputable print publication. It's pretty obvious that things that look like "banner advertisements" are paid ads. It's less clear—usually not at all clear—whether hotels listed in an online guidebook are a function of the publication's judgment, or of which hotels paid to be listed.

Unfortunately, even those Web sites that don't currently accept paid promotional placements don't rule it out in the future. I know of no major travel Web site or online guidebook that promises in writing not to accept payment in exchange for listings or "recommendations" on the site, or to explicitly identify paid advertisements.

In the absence of such a commitment, you have to assume that everything you read on the Internet is a paid advertisement, unless it is credibly identified as the work of a specific writer or organization whom you trust and believe. This will only change if Internet travel consumers and Web sites visitors demand otherwise. There's no reason for Web sites not to follow the same standards of journalistic integrity taken for granted in all reputable print publications.

How do you figure out which advice is credible, well-founded, and likely to be relevant to you and your trip? Here are some general principles you can use to assess destination information and other travel advice.

Is the Information Firsthand?

Oftentimes, in an attempt to be helpful, people on the Internet will pass on information derived from other people's experiences, secondhand sources, or rumors. Sometimes that is indeed helpful, but only if the source is clearly identified.

"I've heard" or "I've read" should be taken as meaning, "Once upon a time there was a rumor somewhere that . . . " If they don't say what their own direct experience with the place, company, or topic is, ask.

How Recently Did They Visit?

The character of a tourist destination, the quality of a hotel, the nature of an operator's tours, all can change overnight. People often give undue weight to the experience of someone who has been there, even if they were there many years ago. Look for a mention of what year the person visited. If someone says they lived there, or grew up there, ask them when they last visited.

Up To Date?

Web pages don't necessarily give any indication of when they were researched, written, or updated. The best you can hope for, in most cases, is to find out approximately when a Web page was created or first made available. Look for clues on the page itself, in its URL (archival URLs from Web publications often include what is obviously some numeric form of the date), or in its HTML source code. If that doesn't get you anywhere, look up the page in a search engine.(Yes, I know that sounds weird, looking for a page that you've already found. But it works.) As a rule of thumb, you can guess that a well-linked page was probably made available on the Web between a week and six months before the date it was indexed by a major search engine like AltaVista—however, when the results go up on the Web, they may be based on research done years earlier. A writer may have spent six months researching a guidebook that was published a year later. A year after that, they may have been hired as a freelancer to provide destination information for a travel Web site based on that guidebook. That work may have taken another six months, with some telephone fact-checking and updating but minimal, if any, new field research. This is not an uncommon scenario.

Newsgroup archives and postings on bulletin boards are equally problematic. The messages themselves are usually dated, but posters rarely bother to mention how long ago their trip was. Be especially wary of relying on reviews and recommendations of specific travel providers more than a year old.

How Long Did They Stay?

This is kind of a trick question. You'd think that people who had been in a place longer would know more about it, and generally they do. On the other hand, "A nice place to visit" and "a nice place to live" are two different things. People who spent a long time in a place—especially if they lived there, rather than just traveling through—may have lived very differently than you will as a tourist. Ask them how they liked it when they first arrived and how long it took them to get used to the place.

Don't assume that travel writers spend a lot of time getting to know each place they write about. Professional travel writers are experts at collecting the essential information about a place quickly, so that they can move on to the next. Someone who writes a book about a country or region probably spent at least several months there doing research and probably had visited it before. But they may only have spent only a day or less in some places, particularly if a destination is less popular with tourists.

People who seem to have been everywhere probably weren't there for very long. If their travel purpose is to collect countries or sights, so as to be able to say, "Been there, done that," they probably don't make it a priority to hang around. Ask them specifically how long they've spent in the particular place or country you are interested in. They may have useful nuggets of practical information, but don't count on subtlety or depth of understanding.

How Does Their Style of Travel Compare to Yours?

This is probably the most important question to ask in evaluating why someone else did or didn't like a place.

The experience of travel for someone in a group or on a tour has little in common with that of an independent traveler. How did they travel? If they liked or didn't like the accommodations, are they talking about the $200-a-night hotels or the $15-a-night hostel dormitories? Did they do things you'd want to do? What was the purpose of their trip?

If they thought there was nothing to do, was that because there were no beaches? No museums? No cafés? No discotheques? No shopping malls? No hiking trails? No street life? What is their picture of an ideal day of traveling? If they loved the place, was it because of the food? The conversations? The music? The scenery? The social structure? The pattern of daily life? Was it "a great place to visit" for four hours on a cruise-ship port call? For a week's honeymoon spent entirely inside the grounds of a resort? For 10 years as a child living and grow-

> **DIFFERENT STROKES**
>
> The reasons some people would choose a destination are reasons other people would shun it, and vice versa. This is one of the strongest reasons not to rely on experts, no matter how well traveled and knowledgeable, in deciding where *you* should go.

ing up there? Even travelers with similar styles may be interested in very different aspects of places, and find the same place exciting or boring, wonderful or awful.

Travel writers, like journalists, often adopt a pseudo-objective voice that gives too little information about themselves for readers really to judge whether they would prefer the places writers love or

>>KEY THINGS
to Watch Out for on the Internet

Some of the Internet travel lies, scams, and shills to watch for:

- Advertisements and infomercials that aren't identified as paid ads and are mixed in with editorial content. Advertisements falsely represented as "recommendations."

- Undisclosed financial interests, sponsorships, and referral fees to Web sites for steering people to particular products or suppliers ("Payola," as they used to call it).

- Undisclosed provision of free or discounted trips ("junkets") to Web writers in exchange for favorable coverage.

- Newsgroup, bulletin board, and chat room shills. "Testimonials," and recommendations from family, friends, and others with undisclosed financial interests.

- Lowest-price "guarantees." No one can guarantee the lowest price, no one ever pays out on these "guarantees," and anyone who makes claims like this is suspect.

- Boasting and advice from know-it-alls, especially those who repeat rumors or second-hand stories as though they were their own experiences. Those who claim to have been everywhere and done everything probably haven't.

- Out-of-date information. If someone doesn't say when and for how long they visited a place, or if a Web page isn't dated, assume that everything they say might be obsolete.

- Sloppy research from writers and Web content providers who are required to write as though they know more than they do, or have been to places they haven't.

- Erroneous "reverse engineering" and speculation about the technical workings of the travel industry, reported as fact by people outside the industry.

- Rehashed secondary research misrepresented as personal experience; myths and rumors repeated as fact.

- Over-generalization from limited experience. Assuming that "I had a good [or bad] time there once" is the same as, "Everyone will always have a good [or bad] time there".

the ones they pan. The perfect trip is different for everyone, and there's nothing like travel itself for making one aware of the diversity of humanity.

Every guidebook I've read describes Tashkent, Uzbekistan, as completely without touristic interest—a big, industrialized city; a center of education, administration, technology, and commerce; not a "living museum" of medieval architecture like Uzbekistan's tourist magnets, Samarkand and Bukhara. Too modern. Too fast-moving. Too aware of the rest of the world. Too much of an ethnic mix to give one a proper sense of "pure" Uzbek culture. The descriptions in the guidebooks are all accurate. Most tourists don't like Tashkent, for just these reasons. For all these same reasons I knew that Tashkent was the place for me. It took me several years to get there, but when I did, I found it was everything I had hoped for—a cosmopolitan, mélange. It's your trip. Make your own choices.

When someone tells us about their trip face-to-face, we filter our interpretation of their advice through our impression of the person's appearance. And we do so, typically, without conscious thought. On the Internet, we have no such clues. The only way to find out about someone's tastes or background is to ask and to pay deliberate attention to whatever clues they give us.

Spamming For Scams
If you get unsolicited bulk commercial e-mail (spam) from a company you've never contacted before, assume it's a scam. I get lots of travel spam, and it's invariably for some sort of scam. Legitimate travel companies don't want, and can't afford, to alienate hundreds of people with spam. Travel scammers are fly-by-night operators. They'll change their name before their next scam anyway, so they care less if they ruin the reputation of the disposable dummy company they're using for their current scam.

I never buy anything from spammers, anyway, on principle. Boycotting spammers won't stop them, but buying from them will only insure their survival.

Same Old, Same Old
Most Internet scams that are specific to travel are the same travel scams that one finds in the offline world. Probably the most widespread travel scam is a notice that you've been selected to receive free accommodations that are available only as part of a package with overpriced airfare, or free airfare available only as part of a package with overpriced accommodations. "Selected" implies

that you've won some sort of prize, but of course everyone whose address the scammers can find is "selected". The scam is that the component of the package for which you have to pay is so grossly overpriced that the total cost to take advantage of the "free" offer is more than what the whole package would normally have cost.

The second major class of travel scams (often combined with the first) are those in which you are urged to pay long in advance for certificates or vouchers for future travel. The idea is to make sure that you've already paid your credit card bill, and thus forfeited your right to contest the charge, before you discover that the company that took your money has skipped town and their vouchers are worthless. Any situation in which you won't either use the travel services or receive tickets from an airline or cruise line for more than a month after your payment should be viewed with great suspicion.

Yet a third offline scam that seems to be propagating the Internet is that of worthless memberships in travel clubs. Travel clubs promise that membership will make you eligible for special deals not available to nonmembers, but rarely are they any cheaper or genuinely restricted to members. Variations on this theme include discount airfare clubs that first sell you a worthless membership card and then make more money by referring you to discount travel agencies of their choice, air courier associations, and card mills that sell worthless "travel agent ID cards."

Here's the reality: airlines don't give travel agents contracts for discounts that are only for members of certain clubs; all the courier companies care about is that you have a passport, not a club membership; travel agents don't get as many discounts as most people think; and real travel agent credentials require proof of full-time employment and earnings from an accredited travel agency.

THE INTERNET RESEARCH PROCESS

Offline, for all but the most popular destinations, you're lucky if you can find two or three current guidebooks that mention the particular topic or detail you're interested in. Often you'll only find one. Online, there are many more sources and thus more difficulty in choosing between them.

One of the joys of Internet research is being able to find many different people's opinions and points of view. But the lack of gatekeepers and quality control that makes that possible also means that you can't take everything you find for granted. It might be authoritative, but it equally well might be propaganda from someone with an axe to grind, or the ravings of a nut.

Fortunately, on the Internet it's easy to compare multiple sources and to solicit confirmation (or repudiation) of advice you've been given. The research process is more likely to involve several rounds of queries and replies than simply looking something up, and accepting the first answer one gets.

Combining Research Tools

Suppose, for example, you are trying to find a good hotel in your budget range in a place with which you aren't familiar. What process might you follow? First, use a search engine or Web directory to locate some sites with listings and reviews of hotels. If there are no negative reviews, it's probably an advertisement.

Next, you might post a query in an appropriate newsgroup or two. You'll probably get several suggestions from readers of the newsgroup(s). Keep monitoring any newsgroup you post to for at least a week after posting your query. It can take a day or two for new postings to propagate around the world, and answers to come back. Only the most active participants keep up with a newsgroup every day. From these suggestions, you choose a few of the most promising sounding, and do some more research on them. Look them up in the newsgroup archives on Deja.com to see if others have posted messages about their experiences. Use a search engine to locate their Web sites. Look them up in online guidebooks. Use an online mapping site to figure out where they are, and what's nearby.

If you have specific questions, of course, you can e-mail them directly to the people who posted the recommendations. Be polite, and be sure to thank everyone who responds, even if you don't find their answer useful. Don't get carried away, though, with obtaining endless opinions. What makes a good trip is an intensely personal decision, and making that decision depends on knowing yourself and your own tastes. In the end, you have to rely on your own common sense and judgment.

What Kinds of Travel Research are Best Done on the Internet?

You can find information on the Internet about almost any aspect of travel and any question you might have in planning a trip. The AltaVista search engine has 50 million Web pages in its index mentioning some form of the words "travel" or "tour," another 10 million on "vacation," "holiday," or "cruise," five million more on "hotel," and yet another two million on "airfare" or "airline." The size of the Web is currently estimated at about a billion Web pages. This means more than five percent of all Web pages are travel-related.

The volume, comprehensiveness, and searchability of the information available on the Internet—the very reasons that make it such a powerful resource—makes the Internet itself, not a book like this, the best place to locate specific Internet resources. Check the Practical Nomad Web site at **www.practicalnomad.com**, for more details about specific Web sites and resources.

Because of the profusion of results when you search on broad general topics, it can be harder to find a good overview of the most popular things to see and do in a major tourist destination. Since printed guidebooks and tourist literature are generally directed at the most common types of tourists and interests, they may be best suited for this kind of mainstream information.

— THE NET IS GOOD FOR NARROW QUESTIONS

In general, the more specialized your interests, the narrower your question, and the fewer people who would be interested in the answer, the more likely it is that the Internet is the best way to find the answer.

That said, following is an attempt to survey some of the aspects of travel and categories of travel information that can best be located on the Internet. This isn't a comprehensive list; its intended merely to assist you by suggesting things you may not have thought of.

BACKGROUND INFORMATION FROM AND ABOUT DESTINATIONS

The most useful travel resources may be those not primarily intended for travelers. Online guidebooks for travelers, like printed guidebooks, focus on travel-specific information like lists of hotels and restaurants and directions for getting around. Other topics get short shrift.

The best printed guidebooks are often those with extensive sections of background information about the culture, history, people, and character of life in a place. But that might mean 100 pages in a good print guidebook, or a few dozen Web pages in an online guidebook, on a destination about which there are tens of thousands of Web pages on non-travel sites. In this section, we'll look at what some of those sites might be.

Local Publications From Your Destination

It's rare for a daily or weekly newspaper in an American city not to have a Web edition. Often one of its features is a section of background information about the area where the publication circulates. This is typically quite self-serving: one of its functions is to convince potential national advertisers that the publications' readers are free-spending and attractive customers. But it's useful anyway.

http://www.estado.com.br/english/english.html
This is the English-language online edition of the daily
0 Estadao *of Sao Paulo, Brazil*

Many newspaper and regional magazine Web sites have sections specifically intended as travel guides for locals and visitors alike, or relocation guides for people new to the area. These can be extremely useful in giving you ideas about local events, attractions, and things local people do and go to for fun in their spare time that don't make it onto the radar screen of visiting travel writers. They'll also give you an excellent glimpse of local values, issues, and ways of life. I always make it a point to read the letters to the editor and the op-ed columns, and to look at what's considered front-page local news.

In a resort or vacation area dominated by tourism, reading local publications in advance on the Web gives you a window into how tourists are perceived by locals, and which of the things that tourists do may be resented. Let these be among your guides to responsible tourism.

Local Web Portals In Your Destination

Many local Internet Service Providers (ISPs), particularly in smaller cities, try to attract business by emphasizing their local roots and community involvement. One tool they use is to promote themselves as a

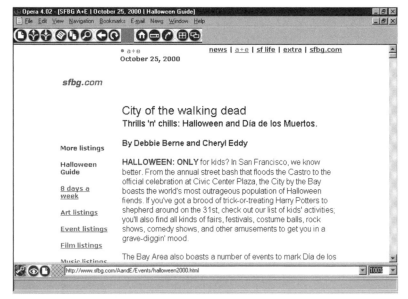

http://www.sfbg.com/AandE
Local portals and Web sites for local publications like this one for the San Francisco Bay Guardian *often have more detailed listings of local events than any travel site.*

portal and starting point for local or regional Internet resources, with pages of links to local resources. Other local information portals are provided by local public libraries; real estate and relocation agencies; historical societies and museums of local and regional art, history, and culture; and a variety of community organizations allied with local governments and/or chambers of commerce. None of these, of course, are likely to tell you what's *not* to like about the place.

Academic Web sites

For deeper background you can find Web sites devoted to academic research, including American regional and ethnic studies; regional geography, land use, urban sociology, cultural studies, literature, and planning; and national and international studies. Academic research centers, specialized departments, and individual scholars who've devoted their lives to studying and understanding particular places often have non-commercial home pages devoted to links and recommended reading lists about the places they know best. Quite often,

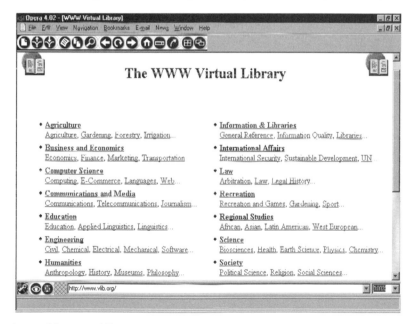

http://www.vlib.org

The "International Affairs" and "Regional Studies" sections of the volunteer-compiled "World Wide Web Virtual Library" include links to a wide variety of specialized sites and directories, including many personal sites of academic experts.

the world's most knowledgeable expert on a place has made a personal Web site with their personal recommendations of the best Internet resources regarding that place.

Tourist Boards and Travel Information Centers

Official tourist boards and travel information centers are generally sponsored by governments and/or chambers of commerce. They've been around for years as kiosks by the side of the road and in transportation centers like airports and train stations. Sometimes you could get them to mail you a packet of information, but only if you could find their phone number or address. Now, on the Internet, even the small ones from less visited areas are easy to find. They are a good place to start if you want to know what the main attractions are in a region; where most of the tourists go and what they do; or where to find a directory of local resorts, hotels, and tour operators. Local tourist boards can be especially useful in locating local guides, outfitters, and tour operators—often the same ones with whom big-name companies subcontract for local services. Their whole point is to get you to come visit, so they'll give you little in the way of warnings about potential problems.

http://visitmt.com
Like the state governments and Chambers of Commerce that run them, state and local tourist boards' Web sites are a mix of boosterism and helpful advice from locals.

Tourist boards are also a useful source of logistical information. Will I need a car? Which roads are open year-round? Only in summer? Is there a place in this area where I can pay to take part in a certain activity? Does any company offer tours to nearby places of historical interest? Is the birthplace of my hero open to the public?

Even better than tourist boards' Web sites is the fact that tourist boards are generally available by e-mail to answer your individual questions. I've mentioned newsgroups as a source of first person advice. But newsgroup participants are volunteers, and anything they do is done as a favor. Tourist board staff get paid to answer questions, so you don't have to feel that you're wasting their time. For them, there are no stupid questions; it's their job to answer them all. Try to find the answer on your own, first. If you can't, don't hesitate to e-mail the tourist board. They'll probably thank you for asking. If it's a question of general interest, they'll probably add it, along with the answer to the FAQs on their Web site.

Climate, Weather and When to Visit

Let's be clear: climate and weather are two different things. "Weather" refers to atmospheric conditions—temperature, sun, wind, rain, clouds, humidity, etc.—at a particular place and time. "Climate" is the pattern of weather over a period of time, usually based on observations over many years. If you want to know, "Did it rain in Florence yesterday?" or "How likely is it to rain in Florence tomorrow?", you are asking about the weather or the weather forecast. If you want to know, "How likely is it to rain during my weeks stay in Florence next July?", you are asking about the climate.

Weather forecasts are useful, at best, for predicting conditions no more than a few days in advance. Further ahead than that, one has only climate patterns to go by. At the last minute, packing for a trip of no more than a couple of days, weather forecasts are useful. Planning for a trip further in the future, climate data is essential to knowing what sort of weather to expect.

This distinction is important because weather and climate information is found in quite different places on the Internet. There are lots of weather Web sites, and it's easy to get detailed forecasts of tomorrow's weather in any city or town in North America large enough to have an airport, or in any major world city. Oddly, many of these weather sites have no climate information at all, and even on the best of them it's very limited.

It's understandable that a newspaper doesn't have room to print

What You Need to Know Before You Go

For a beach resort, the likely temperature, hours of sunshine, and rainfall (or lack thereof) may be the only important factors in when to visit. For sightseeing, however, it's often equally important to know about local holidays, festivals, and other special events that can bring unexpected crowds or cause the attractions you want to visit to be closed. Printed guidebooks mention these, but the exact dates often vary from year to year. Many religious holidays and festivals, for example, are determined by calendars other than the Gregorian calendar used in secular affairs in the United States. Knowing to expect particular complications with travel in predominately Islamic countries during Ramadan isn't very useful if you don't know where in the Gregorian year Ramadan will fall.

Fortunately, this niche has been well filled on the Internet, with sites that provide tables of holidays and festivals around the world, indicating on which ones businesses are typically closed, and giving the expected dates of "floating" holidays (Hajj, Passover, Easter, Lunar New Year, Carnival, etc.) for years to come. Most tourist board Web sites also have information on upcoming national holidays and major festivals.

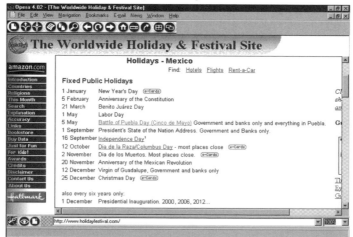

http://www.holidayfestivalcom
Holidayfestival.com has a comprehensive directory of government and religious holidays around the world.

climate tables along with the current weather and short-term forecast for each place. On the Internet, however, it would be almost trivially easy to link the weather forecast with a comparison to the average for that place at that time of year, and to provide a searchable database of typical weather conditions for any given place and season. When you make a reservation in March for a flight to Florence in July, what use is it for the online travel agency to show you today's weather in Florence, as many do? Why not show you the typical climate in Florence in July, when you plan to arrive? Ideally, it would enable you to compare the typical conditions in two different places.

Whatever the reasons, few major weather Web sites does any of this yet. Government meteorological agencies are the source of almost all climate data, but they don't tend to make it available in a user-friendly form. The domain name "climate.com" has been registered for almost five years without being used for anything, which would seem a pretty good indication of the disinterest of cyber-entrepreneurs in this field. For now, the best online climate data is found either buried in the background-information sections of online guidebooks, or in the online brochures from tourist boards and chambers of commerce—not on most weather sites.

If you can't find climate or weather information for the specific place you are going, you'll have to extrapolate from somewhere nearby. Try to find a detailed topographic or climate-zone map to help you. Places 50 miles apart can have a completely different climate if they are at different elevations, on different sides of a ridge or valley, or are closer to or farther from features like coastline that affect local weather. In some places there are even different microclimates close together. Don't over-generalize from limited information about the weather at the airport (the usual monitoring station for city weather forecasts and climate records). Temperatures in my neighborhood are routinely 10°F higher than across town at the beach, just five or ten miles away.

SPECIAL-INTEREST TRAVEL

If you want to sign up for a standard tour to a popular vacation destination, any all-purpose travel agency can probably help you. If you want something more uncommon, exotic, or personalized to your particular interests, you'll have a better chance of finding it on the Internet.

Highly specialized travel agencies and tour operators were the first to get on the Internet, and with good reason. The Internet makes it possible for the smallest agency or operator to offer its particular expertise to a global clientele. Perhaps equally important, the Internet has made it possible for people everywhere to find such niche travel services providers without spending a fortune on national or international advertising.

A typical travel agency's raison d'être used to be that it was the de facto airline ticketing office in its neighborhood. Overnight couriers, 800 numbers, electronic tickets, and, at least in some part, the Internet have made the travel agency obsolete as a mere ticketing service. The travel agencies that are surviving this transformation of the industry are those that offer added-value advice and expertise. More and more often, that comes through specialization in a certain type of travel, a certain type of traveler, or certain destination or activity.

Old-fashioned directories of travel agencies are designed to help you find a travel agency near you. On the Internet, that's about as stupid as it gets. The whole point of the Internet is that it frees you from the need to use a travel agent near you. The Internet allows you to take advantage of the expertise of a specialist accessible by e-mail, even if they are in another time zone or on another continent.

As I've already mentioned, there are Web sites, newsgroups, and Internet communities for people interested in everything from snowboarding to chess to West African music. If there's a group of people who engage in some

— SCATTERED COMMUNITIES — OF COMMON INTEREST

Not every town, or even every big city, can support travel agencies or information centers for all of the myriad tastes people have in travel. On the Internet, even the smallest and most scattered communities of common interest can find or create their own place to exchange ideas and share experiences. And if there's a specialist in your kind of travel anywhere in the world, you can find them on the Internet.

Zeroing In

Printed maps are much better than a computer screen or computer printout of a Web map for general orientation. However, only on the Internet can you get maps or door-to-door directions to specific addresses of homes, businesses, or places of interest.

activity, there's a place on the Internet where they talk about it—and where enthusiastic, even evangelistic, volunteers make themselves available as guides and advisers to newcomers to their avocation.

A major theme of special-interest sites is typically, "Where are the best places for...?", and some of the most common questions are "What are the conditions for [activity] in [place]?" The best place to find people with the answers is through a newsgroup or the Web site of a club in that specific region.

Often these amateur, club, and hobbyist Web sites and mailing lists have more impartial (and sometimes more expert) reviews of destinations than commercial sites. Just check carefully to see if someone who always recommends Brand X skis on the rec.skiing newsgroup is really a Brand X employee. (This is normal, and usually considered acceptable as long as they disclose their self-interest.)

SHOVELWARE

Some of the most comprehensive-seeming travel Web sites are "shovelware" (as in, "assembled with shovel" rather than by intelligent selection) into which the compiler has shoveled everything they can find about a topic or destination—the good, the bad, and the ugly all thrown together indiscriminately.

DETAILS

Printed brochures and guidebooks are limited by size, weight, and the cost of printing. Brochures and guidebooks therefore confine themselves, of necessity, to the information relevant to the largest numbers of readers. Not so the Internet. You *should* be able to find much more detail online than in print, even on questions of less general interest.

Or you can look for a set of "answers to frequently asked questions" (FAQs) that might answer yours. Great effort is put into

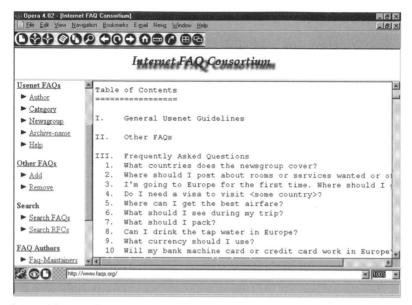

http://www.faqs.org
Some of the Frequently Asked Questions about travel to Europe that are answered in the FAQ in the "rec.travel.europe" newsgroup. Before you ask a question in a newsgroup, always check whether it is answered in the FAQ.

compiling FAQ's for newcomers to Usenet newsgroups and visitors to Web sites. Indeed, the FAQ is arguably the most influential new literary format to have originated on the Internet. Respect the effort that FAQ maintainers—most of them, at least on Usenet newsgroups, unpaid volunteers—have put into trying to help people like you.

Before you e-mail a question, or post it in a newsgroup, look for the FAQ to see if your question is answered there. Asking an answered question in the FAQ will provoke answers ranging from a curt, "Read the FAQ," to the ruder "RTFM" ("Read the F——ing Manual"). FAQ's from all the Usenet newsgroups are available at **ftp://rtfm.mit.edu** or most accessibly at **www.faqs.org**.

TIME-SENSITIVE INFORMATION
The Internet excels as a resource for time-sensitive or rapidly changing information, though just because things on the Internet *can* be updated frequently doesn't mean they are. That said, the Internet is really the only place where you have a chance of finding specific

details regarding what is happening today, tomorrow, or on the specific date you plan to be somewhere.

Some of this information can be found in current local newspapers or television and radio broadcasts. But that does you no good if you're trying to get the information before you arrive—unless, of course, you can find the Internet versions of those local print or broadcast information sources.

Weather, traffic, and transit information obviously has to be up-to-the-minute to be useful. Other kinds of timely information well-suited to the Internet include:

- **current events** that can affect travel (natural disasters, political and economic events, transit and other service disruptions, etc.);
- **travel conditions** in rapidly-changing places (the pace of change in the Third World, for example, is much more rapid than in the United States);
- **arts and entertainment** (performances, festivals, sports events, etc.);
- **guidebook updates** (any decent guidebook should have its own URL where you can find errata and corrections, links to Internet resources mentioned in the book, and updates to key things that have changed since the book went to press).

INTERNATIONAL INFORMATION

For a variety of reasons, the Internet is the logical first place to turn for information about all aspects of international travel.

Within the United States, most travel companies have toll-free telephone numbers; if they don't, you can still call them for pennies a minute. Unless you are committed to doing as much as you possibly can on the Internet, on principle, it's often easier and faster to pick up the phone than to try to find an answer on the Web or to wait for one by e-mail. If you want a printed brochure, they'll be happy to mail you one, and you'll have it within a week.

Internationally, it's another story. Phone calls to some parts of the world can cost two or three dollars a minute if you aren't on a special calling plan, and you may never be awake during their business hours. If no one is available who can help you when you call, they probably won't call you back from another country: you'll have to keep trying (perhaps in the middle of the night) until you get the

The Volcano Report

In two weeks, I'm going on vacation in Ecuador. Before buying my tickets, I want to find out whether the volcano overlooking the city of Quito has been erupting lately. Last year clouds of volcanic ash—which is highly abrasive and damages jet engines—closed the airport for several weeks. Travelers on flights to Quito ended up landing in Guayaquil instead. Guidebooks mention the volcano, but can't say anything about what's happened in the year or more since they were researched. What's the situation now?

In a Web directory, I find a set of links to online editions of Quito newspapers. One of them, *El Comercio* (**www.elcomercio.com**) has a prominent link on its home page to the daily volcano report. Click on it, and I get to a page (in Spanish), with yesterday's pictures from the volcano observatory.

But I don't read Spanish. Should I give up? No. Cut and paste the text of this Web page into the Babelfish translator (**babelfish.altavista.com**), select "Spanish to English," click "Translate," and voila!

"Diagnosis: the volcano continues with a state of low seismic activity. There were four small transmissions (19:45 and 23:09 of antier and 01:27 and 12:38 of yesterday). The greater one moved 3 centimeters square."

Not perfect, nor entirely grammatical, but more than adequate

right person. They might not be willing to spend the international postage to mail you a brochure, or will only send you their lightest-weight (and least detailed and informative) introductory flyer. Even if they send it by airmail, it might take two weeks to arrive (a week to get to the United States and another week in the U.S. postal system). By surface mail, it could take two or three months.

Domestic telephone directories are readily available, and domestic directory assistance is cheap and fairly reliable. International telephone directory assistance is expensive, even when it fails—as it often does—to find the number you want. Fishing expeditions, repeated wrong numbers, and long periods of time on hold are, of course even more expensive when you're calling internationally. It can sometimes take quite a while to figure out whether you've gotten the wrong number or just someone who doesn't speak English.

The first thing I say when I'm calling internationally is always,

for my purposes. I can make my reservations without worrying too much that my flight will be diverted.

http://www.elcomercio.com
"Alerta": the daily volcano report for the Tungurahua and Pichincha volcanos from El Comercio *of Quito, Ecuador.*

"I'm calling from San Francisco", or wherever. If the city you're calling from isn't instantly and universally recognizable, just say (verbatim), "I'm calling from the USA. America." (Saying the name of the country like this may sound peculiar, but it works. Saying "America" to mean "USA" implies a hegemony of the USA over the Americas which, while true, is resented by people from other American countries. But "America" or "USA" are comprehensible to speakers of more languages than "United States". Expatriates from the USA sometimes say, "the States", but no one else does.) "USA" is more understandable than "United States". This dramatically reduces the likelihood of being placed on hold, transferred to voice-mail, or told to call another number. Still, there's nothing like knowing you're paying a dollar a minute to listen to Muzak on hold, or to a radio station giving the current Singapore traffic report, as I've been forced to do at times.

http://www.franceguide.com

The French Government Tourist Office has information in French, German, and Italian as well as separate English-language sections for visitors from the U.S., Canada, and the U.K.

Fortunately, English is the international language of tourism. *Someone* at any tour company or hotel in the world can read and write basic tourist pidgin English, and even small companies in poor countries find it worthwhile to have their basic brochure translated into English for their Web site. But there may be only one person in the organization who reads and writes English, and they may not be available at the moment you call. On the telephone, there's no certainty that you'll get through to someone who speaks any English at all.

Most non-native speakers can understand, and make themselves understood, much better in writing than in speech. On the telephone, they can't supplement their words with gestures. Written communication has a much better chance then speech on the telephone of succeeding across a language barrier. An e-mail message can be passed on to the person in the organization with the best English skills—they can answer, at their leisure, with the aid of a dictionary.

Online Translation and Language Resources

Notwithstanding the advantages of information in English, the Internet has valuable resources for communicating with people who don't know your language. Internet language tools include online translators for Web pages, newsgroup postings, e-mail messages, or printed materials in other languages, as well as language learning tools to help prepare you for basic communication in other languages.

Several Web-based services provide automated translation of Web pages and other text. The two leaders are Systran Software, Inc. (**www.systransoft.com**) and the **www.freetranslations.com** site run by Transparent Language, Inc. (**www.transparent.com**). Both of these sites are run by companies that sell translation software you can run on your own computer. They provide free translation of Web pages or short text through their Web sites as a demonstration of (and advertisement for) their technology. If you like their translation software, and want to use it when you aren't connected to the Internet, you have to buy it. Most people, however, don't need to download it; for translating Web pages, their free online services are really just as useful.

With these Web services, you can either enter the URL of a Web page you want translated, or cut and paste the actual text you want translated into a form. Specify the languages from which and to which it is to be translated (e.g. "Portuguese to English"), click "Translate," and you'll have a crude, robotic translation in 10 to 30 seconds or so.

Systran licenses its software to many other Web sites; it's actually better known as the engine behind AltaVista's "Babelfish" service, babelfish.altavista.com, than in its own name. (The free, downloadable "AltaVista Power Tools" package of add-ons for MSIE 5 for Windows can add a "translate the current Web page" button to your MSIE browser toolbar that uses the Systran translation engine through AltaVista's Web site.) If the meaning of a translated document or Web page isn't clear, it's often helpful to get several different translations to compare.

TRANSLATION, PLEASE

Don't freak out if the home page of a tourist board Web site (or, for that matter, any other Web site) isn't in English. If worst comes to worst, you can use one of the online translation services mentioned above to get a crude translation. But that's rarely necessary. Look for a link somewhere on the home page with the word "English" or "USA", or with an icon of the U.S. flag or the Union Jack (U.K.) to symbolize the English language. It's unusual to find a tourist board site that doesn't provide a version in English.

The Web Really is Worldwide

They don't call it the World Wide Web for nothing. Most Internet users are in countries outside the United States, and the percentage of Internet users in the United States is expected to continue to decline for several years. (That should come as no surprise: the United States has less than five percent of the world's population. Even looking just at comparably wealthy parts of the world, the EU alone has more people than the United States.) Here are some tips for interpreting information from other countries and making your queries and postings comprehensible to people in other countries.

- Never assume anything about where someone is physically located, or where they are from, unless they tell you explicitly. You never know whether, or when, the person answering your query—even about travel within the United States—will be someone from the other side of the world who happened to visit the place you are interested in. A Web address (URL), e-mail address, or e-mail signature reveals nothing whatsoever about a physical location. Most e-mail addresses are ".com" addresses that could be anywhere in the world. Even in national top-level domains, it's common to have an e-mail address, and even a signature line at the bottom of one's e-mail messages, associated with a different country than wherever one may happen to be at the moment. An expatriate may have their mail delivered to a forwarding service or corporate head office in another country; someone at "chicago.edu" may be on sabbatical or doing field research 10,000 miles from the University of Chicago. All this holds true for yourself as well: no one can know where in the world or in what country you are, or where you will be leaving from on your trip, if you don't tell them.

- Respect non-native speakers of English. If they've learned your language better than you've learned theirs, or you haven't learned theirs at all, they've come more than halfway to meet you. Make every effort to try to be understood and to understand and not to fault them for mistakes.

- Avoid abbreviations and acronyms. You'd be surprised how often an abbreviation or acronym has more than one usage.

- Avoid using words that have different meanings in different variants of English (U.S. English, British English, South Asian English, etc.). Avoid sports or other metaphors specific to particular cultures. Avoid slang. Use simple, unambiguous language.

- Identify jokes and attempts at humor with "joke" or some similar, explicit label. Humor is hard to translate, and a misunderstood joke may offend or confuse the reader.

- Specify times of the day in 24-hour time ("09:00-17:00", not "9-5", "9 a.m.-5 p.m."). Outside the United States, all timetables are in 24-hour time. "a.m." and "p.m." are rarely used, and the abbreviations for them vary. If you have any doubt whatsoever whether or not someone is using -12 or 24-hour time, ask.

- Specify time zones (important if you are trying to arrange a voice phone call) by the name of the largest or best-known city in that time zone, not by time zone name or abbreviation. Locally-used time zone abbreviations like "ET", "EST", or "PDT" are not internationally standardized nor recognized. Does "Central Time" mean Central North American Time, Central European Time, or Central Australian Time? "Chicago time" leaves no ambiguity. To be doubly sure, add a reference to the positive or negative offset from the universal standard, Greenwich Mean Time: "Chicago Time (GMT -6)". Specifying the offset from GMT also eliminates any uncertainty over daylight savings time (usually referred to internationally as "summer time"), which is in effect on different dates in different places. If your computer is set correctly, you can look up the difference between your local time zone and GMT in the "Day/Time" section of the Windows "Control Panel".

- Never write a date in numbers only. Always spell out the name of the month. In most of the world, "8/6/2000" means "8 June 2000". In the United States, it usually means "August 6, 2000". If you write a date in numbers, no one can tell which you mean.

- Whenever possible, specify precise dates (month, day, and year). Usages like "this week", "Tuesday next", "the third week in November", or "this coming July" can often be misunderstood (especially by non-native speakers of English) as meaning the day, week, or month before or after what you intended. In different places and cultures the week is considered to begin on Friday, Saturday, Sunday, or Monday. Instead, say, "July 2001", "the week of 19-25 November 2000", etc.

Continues on next page

- Always specify all units of measurement. If you're comfortable with them, use metric units whenever possible. Everyone in the world outside the United States uses metric units except when dealing with people from the United States who don't understand the metric system. If you must use U.S. units (feet, miles, gallons, degrees Fahrenheit, etc.), it's imperative always to specify what units you're using. Confusion is especially likely to result when you're talking about temperature, since the temperature units in both Celsius and Fahrenheit are called "degrees", and have the same abbreviation, even though they are completely different. "Gallons", "tons", "miles", "ounces", and several other non- metric units have different meanings in different contexts, and should be avoided for that reason as well.

- Always specify the currency you are using whenever you mention any prices. Using "dollar" or "$" without specifying which country's dollar you are referring to, or assuming that "dollar" always means "U.S. dollar", is perhaps the most common "ugly Americanism" of Internet usage. It leaves everyone uncertain of your meaning, confuses most readers, and annoys even those who guess correctly what you mean. It's perhaps most resented by Canadians, although it's also offensive to Australians, New Zealanders, Singaporeans, and many others. Similarly, "Pounds" can mean "U.K. Pounds" or "Irish Pounds", "Francs" can mean "Swiss Francs" or "French Francs", and so forth.

  If you know them, and can use them correctly, the three-letter International Standards Organization currency codes such as "USD", "CAD", "GBP", "INR", "JPY", and so forth are the best

But look at which translation engine is actually used, or you may waste your time getting translations from four different Web sites that all use the same translator.

Automated translation is difficult and imperfect at best. Don't expect grammatically correct or entirely comprehensible results. What you can expect is something that will give you the general outlines of the meaning and many of the details, interspersed with literal translations of slang and metaphor, and occasional completely untranslatable words.

Because most people in the United States don't have software installed to display characters or alphabets other than those used for English, and because of variations in how non-alphabetic writing

choice. These are specified in ISO standard 4217, and can be found on most currency-exchange Web sites. If you don't know the ISO 4217 currency code, spell out both the country and currency name. (The only acceptable, widely-recognized non-ISO currency abbreviations are "US$", "C$", "A$", "NZ$", and "S$", but the ISO abbreviations are preferred in global usage.) Avoid culture- specific and slang currency terms like "buck", "dime", "sterling", etc. Even if there is only one country with a currency unit called the "Baht", it's better to say "Thai Baht" than leave some portion of your readership scratching their heads as to what you mean.

- Write telephone and fax numbers, including those in the United States, in the complete international "plus" format, including the country code as well as the area code or city code. Whenever possible, include a local number as well as a toll-free number, since toll-free numbers (including 800, 888, and 877 numbers in North America) generally can't be called from other countries.

- Specify the country whenever you are talking about a place. Do you mean Delhi, New York, USA, or Delhi, India? If you don't say, no one can tell. Don't assume people will deduce correctly from the context whether you mean San Jose, California, USA, or San Jose, Costa Rica. Just because you've never heard of a place in another country with the same name as a U.S. town or city doesn't mean it doesn't exist. In the United States, many place names are found in more than one state, so specify the state as well.

- Never underestimate the potential for misunderstanding, either by yourself or by others. Don't guess what someone means, or what they think you mean. If you have the least doubt, ask.

systems are represented electronically, these services have largely been limited to languages written in the Latin alphabet. Systran, for example, currently translates in either direction between English and French, Spanish, Portuguese, Italian, and German. Languages with alternate alphabets like Russian, Hebrew, Hindi, and Greek will be next. Automated translation to or from non-alphabetic languages like Chinese is unlikely to be available for a few more years.

The Internet doesn't provide the depth of language teaching resources that are available in print or on tape. But if you're taking a short trip to a place where you're not fluent in the local language, the Internet may well provide as much language information as you need or are able to use.

Many travel and language Web sites include short written vocabularies of key words and phrases for travelers. And more and more language Web sites include audio files so that you can click on words and phases in different languages and hear how they are pronounced. The "Travlang" Web site at **www.travlang.com/languages** has vocabularies for a couple of hundred basic and travel words, written and spoken, for more than 70 languages. Many national tourist boards have written and spoken basic travel vocabularies in the national language(s) on their Web sites as well.

Foreign Tourist Boards

Most countries (except the United States) have some sort of national tourist board or government ministry for the promotion of tourism, and many of these have offices in the United States. Some are larger and better funded than others, but all of them exist precisely to serve potential visitors like you. They'll tell you why you might want to visit their country and give you information that will help you have an enjoyable trip.

Maintaining and staffing an office in the United States, much less paying for a toll-free telephone number or detailed printed literature, is beyond the financial means of many countries. Even for wealthier countries and those that most want visitors from the United States, cost has been a major limitation on how much information their tourist boards have been able to provide.

All that has changed with the Internet. Some of the countries that have done the best job of putting information for travelers on the Internet are those that couldn't afford to either put any of it in print or maintain an office in the United States. I wouldn't even think of visiting any other country without checking out what's available from their tourist board. And the first place I look for that is on the Web.

Some of the less helpful tourist board offices will do no more than refer you to operators of package tours, but the services of the tourist boards themselves are free. The best of them have Web sites with a profusion of useful maps; climate tables; train, bus, and ferry schedules; hotel, restaurant, sightseeing, and shopping guides; schedules of holidays, festivals, and special events; peculiarities of local modes of travel, accommodations, customs, religious practices, and taboos; cultural and historical background information; suggested itineraries; and practical tips for independent travelers.

If you can't find a Web site for the national tourist board, try to find one for the country's national airline. Failing that, look for a link to tourist information on the Web site of the country's embassy or consulate in the United States or any English-speaking country. If all else fails, try to find the national government's Web site, and look for either a ministry of tourism or a section of tourist information under either the ministry of foreign affairs, economic development, industry, or some such name.

Information from governments is, of course, propaganda, but unlike a lot of other Internet propaganda you can usually tell from whom it is coming and whose interest it is intended to serve. Just don't expect it to compare the country's advantages and attractions impartially with those of other countries, or to give balanced treatment to the problems of travel in that country.

Passport, Visa, and Immigration Information

Traveling across national boundaries inevitably raises questions regarding passports, visas, and entry/exit requirements.

Requirements for travel documents and border crossings are discussed in detail in my other book in this series, *The Practical Nomad: How to Travel Around the World.* Overall, customs and immigration are less of a problem than most Americans imagine. Rarely is it impossible or prohibitively expensive to get the necessary documents for an international trip you want to take. It's just bureaucracy.

For information on visa and other entry requirements, you need to consult the government of the country you want to visit. Visa and other entry and exit (customs and immigration) requirements from many countries are found on the Web sites of their national governments (usually in a section under "visitor information", "immigration", or "foreign affairs") and/or on the Web sites of their consulates or embassies. There are several sites with links to consulates and embassies, but none of them come even close to being complete, and most of them mix up links to unofficial information sites with actual government sites. You're better off searching directly for the national government's visa and customs and immigration Web site, which in most cases is linked from the national tourist office's Web site.

It's not always obvious to first-time international travelers, or to those who simply haven't needed a visa before, that your own country's government has no role whatsoever and can offer no assistance in obtaining permission for you to visit other countries. If you are a citizen of the United States, don't rely on the U.S. State Department to tell you whether you need a visa to some other country, or appeal to them for assistance if some other country turns you away. They have no authority over such matters and will not be able to help you. Because of the frequency with which it is asked such questions,

Passport and Visa Information

Complete and up-to-date information for citizens of the United States on all aspects of how to obtain or renew a passport, including downloadable application forms and lists of offices where passport applications are accepted, is available from the U.S. State Department at **travel.state.gov/passport_services .html**. Information for citizens of some other countries on how to obtain passports is available from those countries' governments' Web sites.

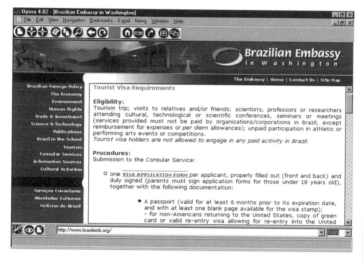

http://www.brasilemb.org
The embassy or consulate of the country you wish to visit is the authoritative source for entry requirements. Visa rules, procedures, and application forms are available from many embassies and consulates on their Web sites.

the U.S. State Department has compiled a summary of other countries' entry requirements for U.S. citizens. It is useful but not authoritative, has no official weight, is often out of date, and should never be relied on without confirmation directly with the government of the country you want to visit. The same goes for information on visas and entry requirements from guidebooks or any other secondary sources.

All representatives in the United States of foreign governments must register with the U.S. State Department. So the U.S. State Department does have, and makes available on its Web site, the only complete list of foreign embassies and consulates in the United States. Unfortunately that list doesn't yet include links to embassies' or consulates' Web sites, just their addresses and phone numbers.

It's also essential to realize that the requirements to enter a country can and often do vary depending on your citizenship. The requirements for a Canadian citizen, a Mexican citizen, and a Japanese citizen to enter the United States are quite different. The same goes for the requirements for citizens of each of those countries to enter, say, France.

When you read something published in the United States, you probably take for granted that it is written for U.S. citizens. So if it says, "You don't need a visa to visit France, that probably means, "A U.S. citizen doesn't need a visa to visit France." Most such statements also refer to strictly tourist visits of short duration. Most countries require visas for business travelers even from countries whose citizens don't require visas as tourists. Almost all countries require visas for longer-term visits, even purely touristic longer-term visits.

On the Internet, you can't make any such assumption. Something that says, "You don't need a visa to enter Australia", might turn out to be written for citizens of, say, New Zealand, whereas U.S. citizens do need visas for Australia. On the Internet, information about visa or entry requirements must explicitly identify the citizenship of the people to whom it's referring or it's completely useless.

Accordingly, if you ask a question on the Internet about visa or entry requirements, you must specify your citizenship, and preferably should specify the purpose (tourism or other) and duration of your intended visit. Don't ask, "Do I need a visa to visit Japan?" That doesn't give anyone enough information to give an answer. Instead, ask, "I'm a citizen of the United States intending to visit Japan as a tourist for three weeks. Do I need a visa?"

Political and Safety Information

Governments of several countries, including the United States, provide background materials and advisories to assist their citizens who are traveling to particular other countries. While they are often skewed by the political perspectives and perceived interests of the U.S. (or whichever other) government, they also can contain valuable advice from local U.S. embassy and consular officers in a country as to what sorts of problems are most often reported to them by visiting U.S. citizens.

Deep Background

The most detailed background information about other countries available from the U.S. government is contained in the book-length *Country Studies* and *Area Handbooks* produced under contract to the Library of Congress. The complete text of all new volumes in this series is gradually being placed on the Web at **lcweb2.loc.gov/frd/cs**.

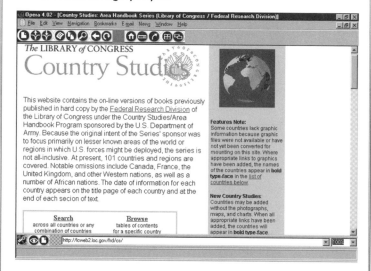

http://lcweb2.loc.gov/frd/cs
Encyclopedic Country Studies *by the Library of Congress have the most detailed information available from the U.S. government about other countries. The full text of the entire series of more than 100 books is available and searchable online.*

Consular Information Sheets (for all countries) and *Travel Warnings* (for countries with special problems), are available on the U.S. State Department's Web site at **travel.state.gov/travel_warnings.html**. The U.S. State Department also has *Background Notes,* summarizing information on different countries, available at **www.state.gov/www /background_notes**.

Other countries that provide similar travel advisories on the Web include Canada, the United Kingdom, and Australia. Obviously, all of these countries (and the United States) have a considerable amount in common in their political points of view, but comparing their different advice about travel to the same country can give you at least some better perspective than just reading the advice from the U.S. State Department.

There are also some private "travel safety" and "travel hazards" Web sites put up by security consultants, but I've found them even less useful or relevant for tourists. Security firms make their money on consulting and services, mostly for the ultra-rich and for expatriate corporate executives (in many countries these two groups are largely synonymous). The hazards and worries facing resident managers of transnational corporations often bear little relation to the kinds of risks facing ordinary tourists.

HEALTH INFORMATION

Insurance and Travel
The most important health information for travelers pertains to what to do if you become ill or injured, especially whether or not you need to contact your health insurance company or health maintenance organization before you seek treatment. If your insurer or HMO has a Web site, check to see if they have information on how to contact them internationally, in what circumstances treatment or expenses have to be pre-authorized, and a directory of participating or preferred health-care providers (if applicable) in the place(s) where you'll be traveling.

Remember that you generally can't call 800, 877, 888, or other toll-free numbers from outside the country. If you're going to be traveling abroad, be sure to get a local number to call, preferably one you can call collect. Rules, procedures, and forms for health insurance claims often vary when you're in another country; some insurers and HMOs even have a special kit of instructions and forms for international travelers to use. If you're going abroad, check for this in advance.

In case you either don't have travel coverage through your regular insurance, want specialized or additional travel coverage, or don't have health insurance at all, an increasing number of companies sell travel insurance on the Web.

Government Travel Health Advice
For international travel (and, occasionally, domestic travel) the U.S. Centers for Disease Control (CDC) provides a very thorough set of

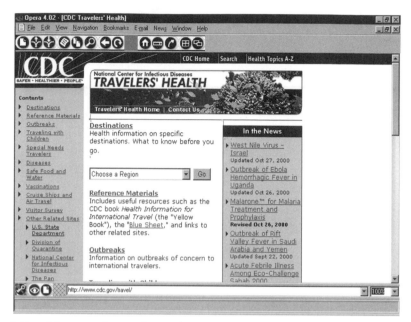

http://www.cdc.gov/travel
The travel advice section of the Web site for the U.S. Centers for Disease Control.

informational and instructional bulletins about the health risks of particular countries and regions. Contrary to widespread belief, immunizations are rarely required by any country's laws. The real question is not, "What shots are required?", but, "What shots or oral vaccines are recommended?" CDC bulletins do include recommendations by country for both immunizations and other preventative measures such as those against malaria (for which there is no vaccine).

Despite occasional criticisms, the CDC is very highly regarded for the professionalism and political neutrality of its advisory services. All CDC travel information is available on their Web site at **www.cdc.gov/travel**.

General Travel Health Advice

A variety of general health advice for travelers is available online. Use care, and look carefully at the qualifications of the source: some travel sites distribute medical myths, falsehoods, or information that isn't kept up to date. In my opinion, the best general primer on travel health is *Staying Healthy In Asia, Africa, and Latin America*, most of which is available online at **www.moon.com/staying_healthy/**. (It's published by Avalon Travel Publishing, the same company that publishes this book.) I've carried a copy in my luggage on each of my trips outside the First World, and found it useful in preparing for overseas trips as well.

Finding Travel Clinics or Doctors While Traveling
Whether you want a specialist in travel medicine for advice, inoculations for a trip, or an English-speaking doctor while you are abroad, you can find them on the Web. Both U.S. and international professional associations and consortia of specialists in travel medicine have searchable directories available online.

PERSONAL ADVICE, EXPERIENCES, AND RECOMMENDATIONS
Perhaps the greatest advantage of the Internet over print and broadcasting is the personal advice, experiences, and recommendations from individual people. You aren't limited to reading what they have to say: you can respond, ask questions, share ideas, and engage in discussion. That's the whole point of the Internet being an *interactive* medium.

Travelogues and Trip Notes
Never is it more apparent how differently people travel than when reading collections of personal accounts. Lots of people post travelogues or notes from their trips on personal Web pages, newsgroups, or travel bulletin boards. Several services, such as Trip Journal from AirTreks.com (**www.tripjournal .com**), provide Web-based customizable pages that are specially designed for sharing travel experiences. In addition, several rating sites (most of them inspired by the success of reader ratings and reviews of books on Amazon.com) give visitors an opportunity to rate and post comments on hotels, hostels, cruise lines and ships, tour operators, and so forth.

Finding travelogues about specific places on the Web can be

TRAVEL EXHIBITIONISM

Most people who bother to write up accounts of their travels and post them on the Internet are in some sense travel exhibitionists: they take pleasure in knowing that people have actually bothered to read their journal or look at their picture. So if someone's "What I did on my vacation" Web page, or Internet version of their vacation slide show, leaves you with questions to which you can't find the answer, feel free to e-mail them. They'll probably be glad to hear from you.

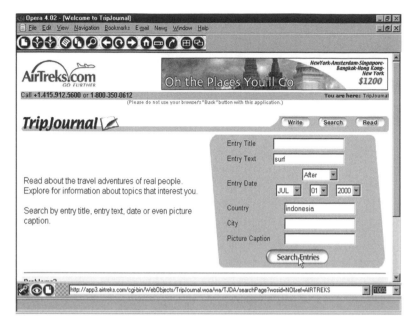

http://tripjournal.com

Several sites including Tripjournal.com have searchable archives of travelogues that let you find out what other people's trips were like. Here I'm searching for surfers' accounts of their visits to Indonesia.

a hit or miss affair, even with skillful use of a good search engine. They exist on different Web sites in different formats with different titles. Trip Journal is a searchable index of words in journal entries, but only for journals posted on that one site. Searching newsgroup archives on Deja.com for accounts of travel to particular places is equally problematic. Travel-Library.com, the archives of the rec.travel newsgroups has an archive of selected travelogues of general interest originally posted to travel newsgroups.

Local People in Your Destination

Local people are typically local boosters and enthusiastic local volunteer guides and travel advisers. Expatriates (foreigners who live in your destination) are some of the best sources of travel information and advice if you can find them—and if they are willing to help you. As foreigners, they too understand the needs of those who are newly arriving as tourists. Yet as people who live there, they often know a lot more than even the best guidebook or travel Web site writers. Long

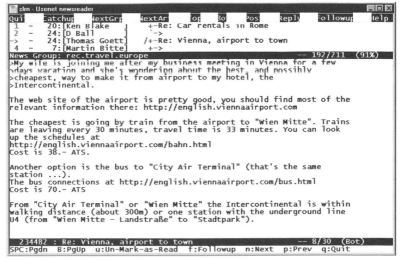

news:rec.travel.europe

If you can't find the answer on your own, there's probably someone on a Usenet newsgroup who can point you in the right direction. This is how a message looks in the "slrn" newsreader.

after they return, expats often retain an interest in the place where they lived, and remain eager to talk about it to anyone willing to listen.

Expatriates in popular tourist destinations are often tired of being asked for help by tourists. In places where tourists have a bad reputation with locals, expats often go out of their way to distance themselves from tourists and places where tourists congregate. In really remote areas, it can go either way: isolated expats may be glad to hear from, or get a visit from, other people from "back home". But Peace Corps workers in many countries, who are often the only foreigners around, sometimes get very tired of being presumed upon for hospitality or guidance by every other backpacker who passes through town. Expats find themselves in a place for some reason other than helping tourists or visitors. Respect that, and take any help they choose to give you as a gift.

You're less likely to find expatriates on travel newsgroups than on their own newsgroups and Web sites specifically about expatriate living. Major expat portal Web sites include ExpatExchange.com, iAagora.com, and EscapeArtist.com, among others. Each of these includes links, sections, and/or bulletin boards focused on particular countries and regions around the world. Some expats specifically iden tify themselves on these and other Web sites as people willing to answer questions about living in particular countries. Don't bug them with questions you could have answered by reading a guidebook, but don't be afraid to ask specific questions that guidebooks don't answer.

Immigrants and People From Your Destination
Immigrants, expatriates, and visitors from a country often regard themselves as de facto ambassadors for their homeland. It's surprising—although it shouldn't be—how often even refugees and exiles will enthusiastically encourage would-be travelers to the place they have left. Although there are lots of places to meet such people, online and offline, by far the most likely places on the Internet to find them are on the various soc.culture.countryname and soc.culture.regionname newsgroups. These function as, among other things, a place for homesick and geographically scattered immigrants, expats, exiles, refugees, foreign students, and travelers abroad to stay in touch. For many people isolated abroad, these newsgroups are the primary link to a sense of home. Even "lurking" (reading and following a newsgroup without posting anything yourself) in such a group can give you many insights into the values, cultures, and issues of a place.

LOCAL TRANSPORTATION INFORMATION
I'll talk about long distance transportation ("big-ticket" travel purchases) in the next chapter. Local transportation, however, is also an area where the Internet is especially useful. Whether on foot, by public

transportation, or by private car, the Internet is the best way to figure out how to get from Point A to Point B in a strange city or town, before your arrive.

For driving, a wide range of Web sites can provide customized road maps and/or driving directions based on the address you will be starting from (the airport, for example) and the address you want to go (say, your hotel or the location of your business meeting). These are great for figuring out how to get to a specific spot, although much less useful for general orientation.

The same map Web sites are also useful for walking directions and finding cross streets for a particular address. Realize, though, that their cartography is designed for driving. There may be no sidewalks on a major road, or no way to cross a highway on foot; conversely, there may be pedestrian only routes that don't show up on online maps.

For general orientation, you may do better with the maps in online guidebooks to highlight key tourist attractions. However, even the best home computer printers can't match the information density of good printed maps. If you want a general-purpose map to carry around, you'll probably be better off buying a printed one.

For the United States, comprehensive street level mapping and street address indices are available on the Web. The main Internet mapping sites are all based in the United States, and their international coverage is spotty. You may have to try several sites to find one with a decent map of a city outside the United States where you are going. Or you may find that the maps of a non-U.S. city available on Web sites based in the United States are inadequately detailed for your purposes. For maps of other countries, you'll generally do better on Web sites based in those countries.

Mass Transit

Local and regional public transportation systems (buses, subways, and so forth) in the United States have put most of their route maps and timetables on the Web. The more sophisticated local transit Web sites can provide customized directions by public transportation from one address to another, or customized schedules for a particular route and date. If you know it, you can search for the name of the transit system in the place that interests you. If you don't know the name of the transit system, you can find it through topical Web directories or through an online guidebook. In addition to official sites run by transit agencies, there are a wide variety of amateur transit-fan hobbyist sites. These are often interesting, and sometimes have useful details not found on official sites, although they aren't as likely to have up-to-date schedules.

How to Ask for Advice or Recommendations

Asking for advice is harder than it sounds. It's not just the (characteristically male) failing of being unwilling to ask for help. It's also about how you frame your question.

Every day there are messages in newsgroups and on travel bulletin boards from people asking for advice, especially recommendations of where to stay and what to do. Most of the questions don't give enough information for even the most knowledgeable respondent to give a useful answer.

Keep in mind as you frame your question that the people who read it won't know anything about you except what you tell them. They won't know where in the world you are coming from, what your budget is, or what your tastes are.

You don't need to preface your request with your life history, but you'll get more useful feedback if you give some idea of the nature and purpose of your trip, what kind of person you are (and what kind of group you're traveling with), and any specific requirements, features, activities, or amenities which are important to you.

Descriptions like "affordable," "budget," "tourist-class," or "good" (or for that matter "bad") mean different things to people with different budgets and standards. Even pseudo-numeric ratings like "four-star hotel" are really no more than subjective opinions, with no universal meaning. Proximity to clubs and nightlife may be viewed as an asset by holiday-makers who like to party, and as a drawback by families with small children. Hotels well situated for travelers doing business downtown are often in dreadful locations for vacationers, and vice versa. If you have business or plan a visit to a specific spot, say so.

Because people's standards of "expensive," "cheap," and the like vary so greatly, it's essential to give specific prices or ranges. Because the Internet reaches people everywhere in the world, it's essential to specify the currency. If you're going to Singapore, are you talking about prices in Singapore dollars or US dollars? If someone in Canada is talking about prices in the United States, are they talking about prices in Canadian or US dollars? People in most other countries are usually more careful than people in the United States to specify the currency they are using, but you never really know unless the currency is made explicit. On the Internet, you cannot assume that someone is from the United States. The Internet is global; there is no "default" nationality.

"Can anyone recommend a good place to stay in Atlanta?" is a typical but useless request. If someone answers, "You should stay at the Hotel Recommended," what does that tell you about the place? Almost nothing. Did they stay there themselves, or did they merely see it mentioned in a guidebook once upon a time? They don't say. More importantly, is it a place that someone like you is likely to enjoy? You have no idea.

If you're going to take the time of everyone who reads a newsgroup to read your question, take the time to frame it carefully. A well-worded query might look like this: "Our family will be passing through Atlanta in July, and we'd like to stop for a day or two to see some of the historical sites associated with the civil rights movement. We'll be traveling by car, but we'd prefer to stay somewhere near the Martin Luther Ling, Jr. Center, which is our primary destination. There will be four of us, including children ages 7 and 11. Normally we stay in motels along the highway for (US) $70-$90 for a room with two double beds, but we expect to have to pay more in a big city. A swimming pool would be a plus, but isn't essential. Can someone recommend a family-friendly hotel comparable in quality to a typical Holiday Inn that they have stayed in within the last year, in this part of Atlanta, where we could expect to find a large room for no more than $120 per night?"

There's no need to bother someone who's recommended a hotel to find out about specific services or amenities: if you want to know whether it has a swimming pool, it's better to look that up on the hotel's Web site, or contact them directly, for the most accurate and timely information. They might have had one when your informant stayed there, but it could be open only seasonally, or closed for maintenance, when you plan to visit. But don't be afraid to follow up, politely, by e-mail or a private follow-up posting, if you have other questions to which you can't find answers elsewhere. ("Is that neighborhood one where you think a mixed race family would feel comfortable on the street?") Often people who respond to an initial request for recommendations will volunteer advice about other things. ("If you are interested in ... you might also want to visit ... And by the way, there's a great place for traditional Southern breakfasts around the corner at the Foo Diner. It looks like a dive, but inside it's spotlessly clean and the food is excellent.") The more you reveal about yourself, the more likely you are to get appropriate suggestions in reply.

Transportation to and from airports is covered on some general travel information Web sites. More detailed and more comprehensive information on airport transportation options is generally found on airports' own Web sites. To find an airport's Web site, use a search engine to look for the full name of the airport as a phrase. Or check the directories of airport Web sites on general-purpose Web directories or on special-purpose aviation Web directories like Landings.com (**www.landings.com**) and Aerolink (**www.aerolink.com**).

Local transportation connections to and from Amtrak and Greyhound stations are among the most conspicuous absences from the Amtrak and Greyhound Web site. Where this information is available at all, it's available on Web sites for local transit agencies in places also served by Amtrak or Greyhound.

ONLINE BROCHURES

By now you probably think I'm terribly down on advertising. Not so at all: I just think we need to know when we're reading propaganda, or *whose* propaganda it is. Like all travelers, I often go looking for propaganda: brochures and other advertisements from travel companies. When you want travel propaganda, the Internet is a great place to find it.

It's much easier and faster to look up a company's online brochure than to look up their phone number or address, call or write them, and wait a week for a brochure to arrive. If you decide the trip isn't for you, you don't have any paper to recycle. Printing and distributing brochures is expensive, so travel companies can put much more detail in their online brochures than in even the fanciest and most elaborate printed brochure. If you come across a printed travel brochure or advertisement that leaves you in doubt about some detail, check the company's Web site and you'll probably find the answer.

Hotels, tour operators, outdoor outfitters, and cruise lines all have online versions of their brochures. Online ticket sales Web sites, whether from travel agencies or airlines, railroads, etc., are a form of interactive online brochure. But we'll deal with them separately, in more detail, in the next chapter.

SHOPPING FOR TRAVEL BOOKS, GEAR, AND EQUIPMENT

I'm the kind of person who likes to touch and feel things before I buy them, and I think that's particularly important with most travel gear. That said, I also realize that some of the best travel clothing and

Gear Online

There are far too many online sellers of travel goods, clothing, gear, and accessories for me to begin to list them here. My favorite is Recreational Equipment, Inc., **www.rei.com**, which I like because as a nonprofit membership cooperative they offer much better and more impartial comparative information on different brands and models than any for-profit retailer. A life membership in REI is only $15; at the end of each year, any "profits" are distributed to the member/owners in proportion to their purchases. Typically, in recent years, this rebate has been about 10 percent, so membership pays for itself fairly quickly.

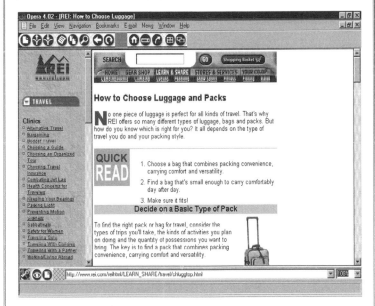

http://www.rei.com
The REI co-op's Web site includes lots of "how-to" advice like this on choosing travel gear, as well as useful specifications charts for comparing products and models.

equipment is available from only a few specialty stores. If there isn't a travel store you can visit in person, or a store that sells gear for your particular activity, you can find whatever you want on the Internet.

There are a wide variety of special-purpose online retailers of gear and equipment for particular kinds of travel, travelers, and travel and leisure activities. Newsgroups for specific interests or activities often include lists of specialty suppliers of equipment for those activities. Those newsgroups are also a good source of feedback about those suppliers. It's a good idea to search the Usenet archives through Deja.com or a similar site for reviews or warnings about a company before you buy.

LOCATING PRINT AND OTHER OFFLINE RESOURCES

All of the Internet tools I've listed above are useful not just for locating other Internet resources but for locating offline sources of information. Don't rule out the possibility that the best result of an Internet search might be finding a book that you can get at a library or bookstore. Or the phone number or address of someone you can call or write for more information. The Internet is only useful, in the end, to the extent that it contains information about the real world. Your trip will take place in the real world, not on the Internet, and sometimes so will your research and planning.

ADVANCED TOPIC: FINDING THE SOURCE OF A WEB PAGE

Finding the real source, company, or person responsible for a particular Web page can be surprisingly difficult and technical. But it can also be essential to knowing whether you can rely on that page to be accurate or impartial. If you are looking at an interesting Web page, and you want to find out where it came from, where do you start? Here are some techniques for digging below the surface.

Read the Fine Print on Web Pages

First, look on the page or section you are interested in for the name of the author or source. Ideally, the source will be named; their name will be a hyperlink to their personal home page or to a page that gives you an idea of who they are and how they travel. (I'll talk more about how to evaluate the credibility and relevance of the sources, once you know who they are, below.)

Amateurs often sign their pages, and give credit where credit is due. Most commercial Web sites don't say who wrote them, or from where their information came from; you'll probably have to look deeper to find out the real source.

Absent a clear link to information about the author or source, try to find a general description of where the material on the page, section, or Web site as a whole came from. Look for an "About Us", "About This Site", or "Contact Us" page.

Different states may have different disclosure laws. For example, California law requires certain minimum disclosures from any Web sites that accept business from customers in California. If they are selling anything (not just travel), they must have their legal name and physical address on the page with the "buy" button. If they are a travel agency, they must have their California Seller of Travel (CST) registration number on every page that advertises specific prices.

There's more to a Web page than meets the eye. If you can't find any indication of who wrote a page or when they wrote it, try looking at the HTML source code. In most browsers, you can see the source code by choosing View/Source from the main menu. Most of it is gobbledygook if you're not a Web designer. But often you'll find comments near the beginning or end of the page of code that indicate the author, copyright holder, and the date the page was created or revised. (Dating Web pages is one of the most important, and difficult, aspects of Internet travel research.)

Don't overlook the "Investor Relations," "Corporate Information," "Media Information," or "Press Releases" pages. That's where you have the best chance of finding out who really pays for listings on the site, or who profits from it. The SEC does a better job of enforcing its requirements for disclosures to investors than the FTC, the DOT, or state and local consumer protection authorities do in enforcing their (largely non-existent) requirements for disclosures to consumers.

There's a clubby sort of insider attitude that makes businesses willing to say things in financial prospectuses about their real motives and sources of money that they'd really rather their customers not read. Yet Internet businesses are so focused on raising money from investors that they put their prospectuses and business plans on the same Web sites as their advertisements and information for customers. Perhaps they are correct to assume that customers won't bother to read them. But if the door to the corporate boardroom is open, why not go in and see what they say about themselves before you buy from them, or rely on their advice? I'm not saying you have to read a Web company's prospectus before you buy anything from them, but if you are trying to figure out whether a listing of a "recommended" hotel is a heartfelt opinion or a paid advertisement, it may help.

Domain Names and What They Mean

Meaningful top-level domains that are restricted to particular types of organizations:

.int = international organizations (Many international organizations including the United Nations have .org domains. But all .int domains are international organizations. These include both non-profit and for-profit entities, although most transnational corporations are in the .com top-level domain. Among significant occupants of the .int domain are the EU (although there is a proposal afoot for a new .eu top-level domain) the World Health Organization, **www.who.int**, and the airline communications cooperative SITA.)

.edu = postsecondary educational institutions in the United States (Academic organizations in other countries are in their geographical domains, such as ".ac.uk" for those in the U.K. Elementary and secondary schools in the United States are in the .us domain.)

.gov = civilian divisions of the federal government of the United States (Other countries' governments are in their geographical domains. Logically, the U.S. government ought to be ".gov.us", but it isn't. Local and state government agencies in the United States are in state domains within the .us domains, such as.ca.us for California. But the .us state domains also contain private, commercial, and nongovernmental organizations and individuals.)

.mil = U.S. military (Other countries' military agencies are in their geographical domains.)

.aero = airlines, airports, and other companies accredited by them.

Twenty years ago I worked briefly as a runner on the trading floor at the Chicago Board Options Exchange. I watched the behavior of the market-makers and read a dozen different discarded financial and general newspapers daily. Ever since, I've regarded financial reporting as more frank and revealing, in a peculiar way, than much mainstream journalism. The need to anticipate monetary consequences enforces a certain sort of honesty in even the most optimistic financial reports.

Look at the URL of the Current Page

The URL—the address of the Web page—can help you figure out where it came from, but only if you know the URL. Make sure your browser is set always to display the full URL of the current Web page. In MSIE for Windows, choose View/Toolbars/Address Bar (make sure "Address Bar" is checked) from the main menu. To ensure that you see the actual address of the page, you also need to uncheck "Show Friendly URLs" in the "Advanced" section of the "Internet Options" menu (reachable from the tools menu in MSIE, or from the Windows Control Panel). In Netscape for Windows, select View/Show/Location Toolbar from the main menu.

Look for Frames Within Web Pages

See if the information you want is in a frame within the page. Frames are rectangular regions within a Web page that can each display information from different sources. Each frame actually has its own URL, and it's possible for information from one site to be displayed in a frame on another site that misleads casual viewers as to its true source.

Frames aren't part of the HTML standard, and whether they are a good or a bad idea is a matter of considerable debate. Websites that frame information to make it look like they provided it, when it's actually from another source, have also been accused of copyright infringement. For better or worse, though, many sites use frames.

Some browsers such as Opera have an "Always Show Frame Border" option that makes it easier to tell if a Web page consists of several frames. Unfortunately, neither MSIE nor Netscape gives you this choice; both these browsers permit borderless frames that can't be detected except by viewing the page properties or source code.

For example, this page makes it look as though my article is from About.com. Actually, my article on "Eco-tourism and independent travel" is from the Moon Travel Handbooks Web site (**www.moon.com**); About.com is merely displaying it in a frame on their page.

How do you find out what's really going on? In a well-designed browser, the URL of the frame would be displayed when you moved the cursor over a frame. But no browser yet does that. In MSIE for Windows, alternate-click anywhere on the frame, then choose "Properties" from the context menu to see the URL of the frame (left-click if you are right-handed, or control-click if you're using a Mac with only one mouse button). In Netscape for Windows, alternate-click on the frame, then choose "View Frame Info."

How to Find Out Who Owns a Domain Name

In most cases—especially the most common cases of .com, .net, and .org—domain names reveal little or nothing about the site. You need to find out who owns it. That means asking the registrar for that domain.

Each domain name registrar maintains a "WHOIS server" that will tell you "who is" the owner of any domain name it has registered, and the contact information they provided with their registration. You can request this information from the WHOIS server with a special "WHOIS" program; most registrars also provide a Web site through which you can make WHOIS queries. Most registrars throughout the world provide English-language versions of their WHOIS query pages in addition to those in local languages.

If you're browsing the Internet, you obviously already have a Web browser, but not everyone has a "WHOIS" program (one is included in Windows 2000 and Windows NT, but not in Windows 95/98 or the Mac OS). It's worth the time and effort to download and install one, though; many good ones are available as freeware.

With a Web browser, it's at least a three-step process:
1) Find the registrar for the top-level domain. (There are several regional WHOIS servers that aggregate information for groups of countries, but there are still about a dozen top-level servers to try, depending on the top-level domain.)
2) Go to the registrar's Web site, and find their WHOIS query page.
3) Use the form on the Web page to make your WHOIS request.

What Can You Tell From a Domain Name?

So you have the URL of either the frame, or the entire page if it doesn't have frames. Now what?

Look at the domain name in the URL. (e.g., in "www.example .com/gobbledygook/session", the domain name is "example.com") Usually, the domain name tells you who owns the site on which the page is located.

If it's a personal Web page, or a site without its own domain name, the domain name says little or nothing about the site. If you've found something interesting at www.foo.com/users/~bar/, domain name research will tell you only about "foo", and nothing about "bar" (except that "bar" uses "foo" as their Web host).

There are many different competing registrars for the generic three letter top-level domains. For these, start at **www.crsnic .net/whois**. This will tell you which registrar registered a particular .com, .net, or .org domain name, and the addresses of their Web site and WHOIS server.

Good WHOIS programs take care of finding the correct registrar automatically, making the process much more manageable. Just enter the domain name, and click on "query". The WHOIS program automatically will find the correct server to start with and follow its redirection instructions until its get to the server with the information on the domain name you want.

Look in any shareware or freeware archives for a variety of downloadable WHOIS programs. (A well-designed Web browser would include WHOIS lookups in its context menu of information about the page being viewed, but so far as I know none yet do. For now, you'll have to use a separate program.) For Windows, good free WHOIS programs include the simple and straightforward "WsFinger" and the much more powerful but slightly more complicated "Sam Spade". Most high-end WHOIS programs are bundled with other tools that can prove helpful, with skill, in tracking down spammers and diagnosing Internet problems. The best, but not cheapest, of these is Visual Route, **www.visualroute.com**.

All this may sound complicated, but really it's not. Once you've downloaded and installed a WHOIS program, all you need to do is enter the domain name ("foobar.com"), and click on "whois".

In theory, the top-level domain (.com, .org, .edu, .gov, .country-code etc.) should tell you whether or not a site is commercial (usually restricted to the .com top-level domain) and in what country it is located. However, the recommended protocols for domain registrations are rarely followed or enforced.

What to Look for in a Domain Name Registration
A WHOIS query won't tell you anything a Web site shouldn't tell you on its own: the name of the owner (person, company, or organization) of the domain name, their mailing address, their phone and/or fax numbers (if they chose to provide them to the registrar), the names of the contact people for the domain (including their e-mail addresses),

and the date the domain name was reserved (the "Record Created On" date), as well as some geekier technical info. Many Web sites *don't* volunteer this information, and it's common for a Web site to have a domain name that obscures who's really behind it.

A WHOIS lookup is an important reality check. I wouldn't think of buying anything, making reservations, or relaying on advice from an unsigned Web page without it.

Among the most useful features of WHOIS lookups are the reliability of the names and addresses. Internet businesses' most important assets are often their domain names. Dot-coms are meticulous in ensuring that their domain name registrations reflect their actual legal ownership. If they don't pay the annual bill for their domain registration, they will lose it. And if their registration address isn't accurate, they won't get their registration bills.

So unless they are incompetent, out of business, or have absconded, you can be confident that messages sent to the registration addresses—especially the primary address for the registrant, and the e-mail addresses of the contacts—will actually reach some person responsible for the domain. They may not answer you, but they will get your message.

What matters most is the *owner* of the name, usually listed first. There may be as many as four individual contacts for the domain, but most of these are typically associated with the ISP that hosts the domain or connects it to the Internet.

When someone decides to set up an Internet business, the first thing they usually do is register the domain name. It's not uncommon to find that even after they've raised the money to hire a staff and open an office, the registration still shows the name, home address, home phone number, and personal e-mail address of the founder of the company, as well as an indication of the founding date. Very useful if you have a complaint and are getting the runaround.

The address in the domain name registration is a good, although not certain, indication of where you'll have to go to sue if you have a legal or financial dispute with the company. And the degree of openness in the domain name registration can be an important indication of how open they are in general, and thus of how accessible they are likely to be if you have problems.

A Buyer's Guide to the Virtual Travel Bazaar

Buying Airline Tickets on the Internet

The virtual travel bazaar is huge, and growing as fast as anything on the Internet. Online travel purchases in the United States alone grew from $1 billion in 1997 to $2-3 billion in 1998, $5-10 billion in 1999, and a projected $10-20 billion in 2000. Travel is the oldest and largest sector of the online economy, with airline tickets consistently the largest-selling single product or service category on the Internet.

But are these billions of dollars being spent wisely? Are travelers getting the best deals online? In many cases, no. Both the airline industry and the Internet marketplace are more heavily stacked against the online ticket buyer than most consumers realize.

Airline ticket Web sites, even those operated by independent travel agencies, depend on and are limited by information provided by the airlines themselves. And the airlines, of course, have no interest in getting you lower prices or giving you the information you would need to find them. Whether you research ticket prices on your own or through a travel agency; on the Internet, on the telephone, or in person; you are compelled to use tools and rely on data provided by the airlines in a format carefully optimized to serve their interests, not yours. From the airlines' perspective, the "best fare" is the highest fare you are willing to pay, not the lowest. It takes skill to use

>> KEY ADVICE
About Internet Travel Reservations and Purchasing

- Don't assume that tickets or other travel services will be cheaper on the Internet. Always compare prices from online and offline sources. Online robotic reservations and ticketing have more advantages in convenience and sense of being in control than in price.

- There is no magic URL. Different sites, sources, and tactics may be best for different trips. No one Web site consistently has the best prices, even for similar trips.

- Don't expect Internet travel robots to do your work for you, or find you the best price. They are designed to get as much of your money as possible, not to help you pay less.

- Not all Web sites or online travel agencies have the same information or access to the same prices. Use sites that offer real alternatives and have access to different types of prices.

- Don't waste time "comparing" prices from sites that all have the same offerings. Web sites that look different may rely on the same data, or may even be different virtual doorways into the same online travel agency.

- The better you understand your own travel preferences, the better the chances that you will find what you want. Do you really want the cheapest ticket even if it's for a three-stop flight at 3 a.m.?

- The bottom-line price for confirmed reservations, including *all* charges. Most advertised prices are substantially less than what you'll really have to pay and many advertised prices aren't available at all.

- Read all the rules. Understand what you are buying, and from whom, *before* you buy.

- Some of the best travel deals you can find online may be with travel agencies you have to e-mail or phone for prices and reservations. Online travel agencies aren't all just robots.

- Avoid e-tickets as much as possible. Insist on paper tickets whenever they are available, even if they cost a few dollars extra.

these or any tools to extract information designed to be hidden, and to serve a purpose exactly the opposite of their designers' intent.

Almost all "independent" airline ticket sales Web sites are operated by agents for the airlines. That travel agents are "agents of the airlines" is more than a figure of speech. Unless you pay them a service charge or consulting fee to work for you, a travel agent works exclusively for the airline, and is legally obligated to do their best to get the best deal possible *for the airline.* The people and Web sites that appear to be advocates for your interests are actually working for the other side.

The ease of use of travel Web sites leads many travelers not to think about, or realize, the difficulty and complexity of the task they are undertaking in trying to be their own travel agents. It's one thing to know how to click on the "Find Best Fare" or "Buy" buttons. It's quite another to know how to tell whether the "best" fare the robot chooses for you is really the best for *you,* or to know how to do some of the less obvious things that a travel agent would otherwise do for you, perhaps without you even realizing what they had done.

All these things make it difficult, but not impossible, to be your own travel agent. As with anything, if you want to do it yourself, and do it well, you have to learn how. Knowledge is the key to power and the prerequisite to informed choice.

ADVICE FOR THE DO-IT-YOURSELF TRAVEL AGENT

"Wait a minute," I hear you saying. "Why should I have to learn all this? Isn't the Internet supposed to make it easy? Aren't there Web sites that will find the best deals for me?"

To make a long answer short, "No." The single most common and costly mistake in buying tickets on the Internet is to rely on a single Web site or "best fare finder" robot to find you the best deal or to protect your financial interests.

The Internet makes it technologically possible for you to get access to airline databases, make your own reservations, and purchase tickets without ever talking to a ticket clerk or travel agent—just as the Internet makes it possible for you to place your own "buy" and "sell" orders for stocks without talking to a human stockbroker. But the Internet no more eliminates the need to understand airline pricing and ticketing than it eliminates the need to understand the stock market—at least if you don't want to waste your money or risk getting scammed.

Origins of Travel E-commerce

We tend think of "e-commerce" as being only a few years old, and having originated on the Internet. But e-commerce in travel, especially airline ticket sales, is decades old, and went through several generations of development before moving to the Internet. Today, travel agencies are often caricatured as old-fashioned. In reality, they were part of the first major e-commerce system.

Consider what happened as much as 25 years ago when you wanted to buy an airline ticket. First, you went to the nearest node on the global real-time network (the world's largest) of airline computers. That node was a terminal in a local travel agent's office, on a local area network linked to a larger network of networks. There, an agent sent a series of messages requesting information about current availability and prices, which were routed from one computer host to another, and answered in the same way by the airline. Then you gave your credit card number to the agent, who entered it into the terminal. A message came back in a few seconds confirming the transaction, and the agent printed out a transaction confirmation ("ticket") on a local printer connected to the network but controlled by the remote host.

No products or money changed hands. The actual services were provided at a completely different place and time from the electronic sales transaction. Neither you nor the agent knew or cared in what geographic location the charge was processed to your credit card and the reservation entered into a database of flights. Every salient feature of the sale (queries, offerings, payment) was accomplished through real-time network messages back and forth.

Many people think that travel Web sites are designed to help them get the best deals and find the lowest prices. But that's not true. With rare exceptions, they are designed to maximize the profits of airlines and travel agents by getting you to pay as much as possible for your tickets. It's possible to use them to find good deals, but only if you know enough about what you're doing to beat the designers at their own game.

"So what?" may be your retort. "I don't want to be a travel agent—I want to have the computer do it for me. How much skill

If that isn't e-commerce, I don't know what is.

In 1986, airline ticket e-commerce took a further step forward when Sabre (then a division of American Airlines) introduced "EAAsy Sabre". EAAsy Sabre (later "Easy Sabre") allowed travelers to make their own flight reservations electronically. It used a simplistic (by contemporary standards) gateway that simply translated between Easy Sabre commands and formats and a limited subset of Sabre commands and displays. But at its best, it gave skilled travelers more information and more powerful tools than any contemporary airline ticket Web site. At first, Easy Sabre was accessible only through Compuserve and other proprietary online systems, and couldn't issue tickets automatically. You could make reservations through Easy Sabre, but you had to call or visit an airline or travel agency to buy tickets. Later, Easy Sabre was made accessible over the Web, and upgraded to permit automatic ticketing. Finally, in 1999, Easy Sabre was merged with Travelocity.com, Sabre's more recent Web-based travel agency, and the Easy Sabre interface closed down.

The problem for airlines, CRS's, and travel agencies isn't how to create an e-commerce system. They already have one, and they don't have the luxury newcomers to e-commerce have of creating systems from scratch. The problem for the airline ticketing industry is how to shift their existing worldwide e-commerce system, through which they process hundreds of billions of dollars a year worth of tickets, from their own network infrastructure and protocols onto the Internet, without disrupting their ongoing operations or having to replace their billions of dollars of installed network hardware.

does it take to be a travel agent, or to be my own travel agent? Don't travel agents rely on computers for all their information, anyway?"

Travel agents get much, though not all, of their information about airline prices from computerized sources—just like currency traders, air traffic controllers, librarians, and stockbrokers, to name a few. However, that doesn't mean that any of these jobs are unskilled or could easily be done by robots, or that you could do them yourself successfully as long as you had the same computerized tools. Few people would set out to be their own carpenter, plumber, or electrician

Travel Agents and Information Technology

Travel agencies have been leaders in computer use and networking for decades. The local travel agency in your town was probably the first local business to have a real-time connection to a global computer network, and travel agents were the first professionals all to have computers on their desks. The first local area network in most towns was at the travel agency office. For years civilian global real-time computer networking was the exclusive province of airlines and travel agencies. Only sometime since 1990 has the network of airline computerized reservation systems (CRS's) been surpassed by the Internet, its only real rival, as the world's largest interconnected computer network.

Oddly, that hasn't translated into respect for travel agents' technical or professional skills. Perversely, many travelers assume that because travel agents use computers, the computer is the real source of all their knowledge and advice. Every travel agent can tell horror stories of customers who routinely treat them like dispensable robotic extensions of their computers. Every day, people ask me, "Can you check the computer for the best price to...?" or "Doesn't the computer have the answer?"

Like other travel agents, I take pride in the fact that computers can play chess as well as people, but computers can't yet do my job (and aren't likely to be able to any time soon). Airlines have made determined efforts to automate the interpretation of fare rules, and airfare search software has long been a leading goal of artificial intelligence researchers. But no computer program can yet reliably determine the price applicable to a particular itinerary (specific set of flights), much less which alternatives might better suit a traveler's desires. No airline has been able to replace its "rate desk" with machines, even though they could save huge amounts of money if they could find a way to do so.

without first learning of the skills those professions require. Yet few travelers appreciate the complexity of travel agents' work or the skills their work requires. Good travel agents are skilled information technology professionals.

The bottom line is this: if you don't understand what is going on, you have no way to tell when you're being ripped off. Much of this chapter is therefore a primer on how to be your own travel agent.

TRAVEL SCHOOL 101: FREQUENTLY ASKED QUESTIONS ABOUT BUYING TICKETS ONLINE

Are Tickets Cheaper On the Web?

Unfortunately, there is no simple answer to this question. You can't assume everything is cheaper if you buy it on the Internet, or that you will get lower prices by cutting out the middle person.

This leaves the question of whether there are lower prices online or offline. As of now, there are far more prices for tickets that *aren't* available on the Internet, but that are available from offline sources (i.e. by visiting or telephoning a storefront travel agency or airline ticket office), than there are prices that are available only on the Internet. This is changing, but slowly, with the balance unlikely to tip for at least several years.

There are at least several thousand possible prices for any given itinerary. Most of these prices are set by individual travel agencies, not by the airlines. Even the most exhaustive search, involving multiple Web sites, phone calls, and pavement pounding, will reveal at most a few dozen of those possibilities as suggested options.

Put aside any notion of, "I want to see all my options." You do *not* want to see all your options. Technology doesn't currently exist to display them all; if it did, it would take you years to review them all. The whole point of a human or robotic travel consultant is to *reduce* the choices to a manageable number.

The important question, then, is not "Are there better prices on the Internet?" The question is, what are your chances of finding them?

The answer is simple: your chances of finding just the right set of tickets will be greatest if you *always* look both on and off the Internet. Beyond that, there are few, if any, simple answers. Airfares have the most complex and volatile price structure of any product or service in the world, and there is no simple way around it.

Am I More Likely to Find the Best Deal Online or Off?

As of this writing, that's impossible to predict. It depends on the skill of your travel agent and their understanding of your priorities, as compared with your own do-it-yourself skills. On your own, you'll be

Cutting Out the Person in the Middle?

Online travel agencies' commissions on sales of tickets at published fares are capped by most U.S. airlines at a maximum of $10 per ticket. Even for automated Internet travel agencies, the costs of sales and customer service exceed $10 a ticket. A significant percentage of Internet ticket buyers call or e-mail the agency—or, if they buy the ticket directly from the airline, the airline—with questions or problems. Internet travel agencies need large numbers of qualified travel agents, and have associated office and overhead expenses, to handle phone calls and e-mail messages from customers with problems, cancellations, refunds, and changes to reservations and tickets, none of which can be handled robotically.

At a maximum cost to the airline of $10 per ticket, online travel agencies are almost certainly airlines' cheapest distribution channel. Offline travel agencies and airlines' own Web sites (which have to be supported by airlines' own customer-service call centers and ticket offices) come next in order of increasing cost. Airlines' 800-number telephone call centers are still more labor-intensive and expensive. Staffing their own airport and city ticket offices is clearly the most costly way for airlines to sell tickets, given the cost of labor and office rent in the necessary prime locations.

No online travel agency is making a profit selling tickets at published fares. Travel agencies like Travelocity.com and Expedia .com sell tickets at a loss. They hope to make up the deficit in commissions on car rentals, hotel bookings, tours, cruises, or sales of other products.

Airlines point to the commissions they pay travel agents as proof that eliminating travel agents would save consumers money. What they don't do is give real or comparable figures for their costs of selling tickets themselves, versus selling tickets through travel agencies.

Airlines' figures for "commissions paid to travel agencies" include large sums that are actually rebated to travelers. The majority of tickets on some international routes are sold through so-called "consolidators" at less than the airlines' official fares. But regulatory rules, require the airlines to pretend that these tickets are sold at the official fares, thus artificially inflating airline figures for both sales and commissions.

For example, if the official fare is $1,000, an airline may charge a travel agency $750 for a ticket that is sold to a traveler for $800. In fact, the airline has made an $800 sale, on which the agency's real commission was $50, or 6.25 percent. But the transaction will be shown on the airline's books as a $1,000 sale of which $250, or 25 percent, was paid to the travel agency as "commission". The additional $200 of sales and commission volume is an accounting fiction: neither paid by the passenger nor received by the travel agency, and in no meaningful sense a "cost" to the airline.

The same rules that forbid airlines from selling tickets at prices below their published tariffs, and that enable travel agents legally to sell tickets for less than the lowest prices available from the airlines, make it impossible for airlines to collect or publish accurate information on travel agencies' selling prices or profits. Airlines know that their figures are inaccurate and misleading, but it is in their interest to exaggerate how much they pay travel agencies.

Companies in most industries would be overjoyed to have outsourced their distribution as successfully as the airlines. Airlines have minimal fixed costs or overhead for ticket sales through travel agencies, especially online travel agencies, which is important for profitability in a cyclical industry. Airlines pay only below-cost per-transaction commissions. Switching from selling tickets primarily through travel agencies to selling most tickets directly will require airlines to expand their brick-and-mortar and/or online sales infrastructure and hire additional staff, at considerable expense.

The question is not whether airlines will save money by vertical integration and taking distribution in-house. All evidence is that they won't. The real question is why they consider it worth the additional cost to build their own ticket distribution system to replace travel agencies. Presumably, they believe they will make more money that way. It's unlikely that airline sales representatives or Web sites will convince more people to fly than do online and offline travel agencies. That leaves only one logical inference: airlines believe that getting rid of travel agencies, and selling tickets directly, will somehow enable them to get people to pay more for tickets.

So, let's go back to our original question: will cutting out the person in the middle save you money? Airlines' own behavior is evidence of their belief that getting rid of the agencies in the middle—whose primary role is to facilitate comparison shopping between airlines—will cost you money.

– Low Price vs. Convenience –

The "best" deal is not necessarily the least expensive. It's important to keep in mind that a large percentage of air travelers are business travelers for whom price is a relatively low priority after convenience, schedules, travel time, time spent shopping for tickets and making reservations, and frequent flyer mileage credits. If most ticket Web sites aren't optimized for price alone, that is at least in part an accurate reflection of many travelers' preference for faster, more direct flights at more convenient times on preferred airlines, even if those cost more.

dependent on tools that are considerably more limited than those available to travel agents, and that give access to a much smaller set of possible prices than are available through offline sources.

For now, let's suppose that the only thing you care about is price. If that's the case, the largest factor is whether your trip is within North America or farther afield.

Travel Within North America: (within the United States, Canada and the Caribbean) you can probably do as well or better for yourself online as through any offline source. If you are patient, willing to invest time in searching and comparing prices from multiple sites, and place a low valuation on your time, you can probably get at least as low prices as any but a few of the best offline travel agents. Consider also that most competent offline travel agents charge fees for arranging tickets like these.

For Round-Trip International Travel—short stays with fixed dates: (from the United States to Western Europe or other relatively close or common international destinations) you stand about equal chances of getting the lowest prices online or from offline travel agents, depending on your luck, the timing of your purchase, and the current state of airline fare wars.

For Round-Trip International Travel—longer stays with flexibility: (from the United States to other continents, and less common destinations) you are most likely to find the lowest prices offline from specialized travel agents if you need flexible tickets, one-way tickets, and/or assistance with complicated or multi-destination trips. Many of these agents are accessible by e-mail, but most don't offer automated online booking.

Is This Situation Changing?
Yes, more discounted prices are being made available on the Internet.

And yes, independent Web sites are beginning to develop software designed to serve travelers rather than airlines. But both of these trends are moving slowly.

The biggest disparity is between domestic tickets within the United States and international tickets. Internet-based ticketing services already work far better, and are far more likely to find consumers the best prices for domestic tickets. Consumer-service Web sites could soon become the best source of low prices on domestic U.S. tickets, eliminating the need to compare offline prices in most cases.

Because of the deregulation of U.S. domestic airfares since 1978, there are relatively few unpublished fares. Most discounted domestic prices are available through centralized and interconnected computerized reservation systems (CRS). The key issue, then, for most domestic ticket pricing is the effectiveness of automated consumer CRS-interface software versus travel agents with their access to CRS.

Today's Internet-accessible automated price optimization ("lowest fare finder") software is, on the whole, poor. That's not surprising: almost none of it is designed by people with any real financial interest in reducing the prices you pay. And the task of developing such software is far more complex than most people outside the discount airline ticket industry realize. Every travel agency I know of that has tried to develop fare search software has found that it took longer than expected, cost more than expected, surprised the software developers with its subtleties and pitfalls, and frequently didn't work at all.

Teaching a computer to find the lowest-priced ticket is like teaching a computer to play chess. While this is a large problem, it is nonetheless a soluble one. The extremely poor performance of current pricing software (from the customers point of view), coupled with the fact that most domestic U.S. discounted prices are already available in computerized form, creates an attractive niche for upstart Web-based buyers' agents and their software developers. I predict that niche won't remain empty for long, and the pricing software available to consumers for domestic U.S. tickets will improve rapidly. As it does, Web sites that offer such software will soon become the least expensive sources for most U.S. domestic air tickets.

International tickets are another story. Because of the continued regulation of international ticket prices by national governments, international treaties, and an international airline price-fixing cartel, most discounted international ticket prices are set not by the airlines and not in any centralized way, but by individual travel agencies.

The problem for international tickets on the Internet is not the

Which Side is a Travel Agent On?

It should be obvious that, when you want to buy a ticket (and pay as little for it as possible), the airline is not your friend. What about the travel agent? Which side are they on: yours, or the airlines?

An "agent" is someone who works on someone else's behalf. A travel agent can be a "seller's agent" (working for the airlines, for a commission paid by the airline), a "buyer's agent" (working for the traveler, for a consulting or service fee), or a "dual agent" (working for and paid by both the supplier and the consumer).

Traditionally, travel agents have been exclusively seller's agents, answerable exclusively to the airlines and other suppliers of travel services. Such an agent's sole goal, and legal duty, is to get you to pay as much as possible. All agencies who sell tickets at published fares without charging additional service fees (which includes all major Internet published-fare travel agencies) are strictly seller's agents. They are not on your side. Most even tell you so, explicitly, if you read the fine print: "This travel agency acts solely as an agent for suppliers of travel services," or words to that effect.

Buying airline tickets from an agency that is solely an agent of the airlines is like buying a house from a real estate agent who works exclusively for the seller. Don't do it if you can avoid it, at least if you care about price and value.

The way to insure that a travel agency has accepted at least some obligation to work for you, and not just against you, in dealing with the airlines, is to insist on using an agency that charges service fees or sells discounted tickets (making them either a buyer's agent or, more often, a dual agent).

Travel agents who sell discounted tickets include a *de facto* fee for their services in the markup from their costs to their retail prices. They are thus either buyer's agents, dual agents, or not agents at all but "principals" to the sale. Their exact legal status is unclear, but they certainly aren't purely seller's agents.

Agency law also affects what rights you have if you have problems with a travel company, as discussed in more detail in the chapter on consumer protection. You have far more rights in a dispute with a buyer's agent, or a dual agent, than in a dispute with a seller's agent.

price-search software but the raw data: *most* discounted international ticket prices are set by individual travel agencies and are not available in any electronic format. That too is changing, but more slowly, since it requires major investments in automation by tens of thousands of individual discount travel agencies around the world. Large discount ticket wholesalers are switching rapidly to distribution of their prices in electronic form, rather than printed tariffs. But each is using their own proprietary and incompatible format.

The few centralized electronic compilations of discounted wholesale prices for international tickets contain only summary fare and rule information, making them insufficient for use by pricing robots. They are intended only to assist consumers or travel agents in figuring out which discounters to telephone for more information. None of them is a comprehensive source of all the details needed to make a reservation, verify the price applicable to a particular reservation, or purchase a ticket.

Given that most discounted international ticket price data is not and will not soon be available in any electronic form, even the best international price-search software will remain limited in what it can do. For discounted international tickets, it will remain necessary to compare both online and offline prices until the majority of discount prices are available in an automated form accessible through a common interface.

Which Web Site Has the Lowest Prices?

There is no magic URL. I'm sorry to disappoint those readers who hoped that the secret to success in finding cheap tickets would be a single, magic URL identifying the best air ticket site on the Internet. But such a site, and such a URL, doesn't and *can't* exist.

Web sites change, prices change every day, and travelers' preferences change. At any given moment, different travelers have different priorities. No one site consistently offers the lowest prices even for the same sort of traveler and trip. There are, however, several specific places to shop, and I'll discuss those at length later in this chapter (including, of course, their URLs).

How Can You Tell if Tickets Will be Cheaper Online, or Which Online Source Will be Cheapest?

The only way to know which will be cheaper is to compare prices from alternative sources online and offline. There is no magic shortcut.

Comparison shopping—keeping an open mind and an open eye—are the keys to success for price conscious shoppers on the

Factors to Consider in Deciding Whether to Shop Online or Offline

■ How important is price to you? The more important price is to you, the more important it is for you to compare prices for each trip both on and off the Internet. It could be as costly a mistake not to use the Internet as to rely on it exclusively.

■ Do you have a strong preference of airline? If you don't care if other airlines might be cheaper, you might as well buy all your tickets from your preferred airline's Web site. It might not be cheap, but it will be simple, and they'll probably give you extra frequent flyer mileage credits or other bonuses for your loyalty.

■ How frequently do you travel? The more often you travel, the more time and effort it's worth investing in learning how to be your own travel agent on the Internet.

■ How experienced a traveler are you? Are you likely to benefit from advice from a professional travel adviser?

■ How skilled a computer user are you? Buying tickets on the Internet isn't hard, but mistakes do get made by Internet novices. Errors can be impossible, or costly, to correct once you push the "buy" button.

■ How important to you is a sense of being self-sufficient and in control? Control freaks are likely to be happier with online buying, and frustrated in working with offline suppliers.

■ How complicated a trip is this? Robots can't yet deal with the more complex trips, especially those that involve personalized arrangements or visits to more than one place. Keep in mind, though, that the Internet isn't inhabited only by robots: The Internet is usually the best place to find a specialist in your interests or type of travel.

■ How willing are you to do the work for yourself? If you want to let someone else take care of everything, find a travel agent to do it (although, once again, you might find that agent on the Internet, and deal with them by e-mail).

Internet just as they are in any other product or service marketplace. It's important to be sure that you are evaluating real, comparable, distinct alternatives. Here are some of the most common mistakes to avoid in this sort of comparison shopping:

Don't waste time "comparing" prices from sources that don't offer real alternatives. This includes getting prices from several different Web sites that all rely on "private label" versions of the same online travel agency, or getting prices from different online agencies that all use the same CRS to select options from the same set of published fares. For example, Yahoo Travel, AOL Travel, and Preview Travel are all just different gateways to Travelocity.com; there's no point checking prices with more than one of them. There's not even that much point to using more than one published-fare site or travel agency at all, even if they use different CRS's to suggest options. But it's especially pointless to compare offerings from several online agencies that all use the same CRS to suggest options from the same set of published fares. Asking different travel agents about *published* fares for the same trip is about like comparison shopping for a car by asking different dealers what they say the list price is. Unless they sell for less than the list price, they'll all give you the same answer.

Don't base your decision on comparing apples and oranges. There's more to a ticket than price. In order to make an informed judgment about which tickets will be better, you need to know the price, dates, airline(s), flight departure and arrival times, stopovers and connections, and rules for cancellations, refunds, and changes. A cheaper ticket may be much worse, but if all you ask about is price, you won't find out until it's too late. Get the *full* details before you push the "Buy" button. If a Web site, airline, or travel agency won't show you a written itinerary and all applicable rules before you buy, go someplace else.

Don't be misled by bait-and-switch advertisements or prices for which no seats are available. I'll talk about consumer protection rules in a later chapter, but one of the most important things to realize is that there is no meaningful restriction on airlines or travel agencies who advertise prices that aren't available. Because of the separation of pricing and availability information by the airlines, there's no way any travel agency can determine, when they decide to advertise a price, whether any seats will actually be available for that price. This makes it almost impossible to distinguish deliberate bait-and-switch ads from ads for seats in booking classes the airlines

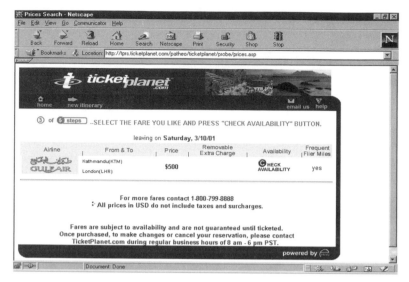

http://tprs.ticketplanet.com

*Hidden charges and "bait and switch" tactics are common online.
Ticketplanet.com's $500 one-way price from Kathmandu to London
looks good. But...*

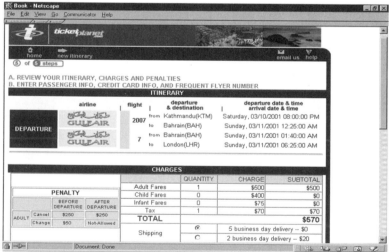

*...When you actually try to buy it, the real price turns out to be $570
including $70 "tax." Actually, there is no tax on tickets on this route.
But calling part of the price "tax" sucks shoppers in by making the initial
price look lower. Always compare final confirmed totals including all
taxes, surcharges, fees, and ticket delivery.*

have later chosen not to make available. The only way to know if a price is real is to make reservations. Seeing a price in an ad or on a Web site does not mean that you can buy a ticket for that price. The only guarantee of availability is a confirmed reservation in a specific name, with an itinerary and a total price in writing (including all taxes, fees, delivery charges, etc.).

Make sure you include all the "extras" in the prices you compare. Advertised prices are usually for nonrefundable, nonchangeable tickets for travel on certain days of the week, in low season, for stays of 7 to 30 days. High season or peak-day (usually weekend) travel, changeable or refundable tickets, or a shorter or longer stay can raise the price substantially. Hidden surcharges and fees—either buried in the fine print or revealed only on the last page before the "Buy" button—are among the leading complaints against some online travel agencies. Airlines typically advertise "half round-trip" fares; the actual round-trip prices are double the numbers in these ads. Keep in mind also that most ads exclude some or all of the taxes and airport fee; on domestic tickets within the United States, all but about $12 is usually included in the advertised price. Taxes on international tickets can add $100 or more to an advertised round-trip price for the United States. Make sure the prices you're comparing include any seasonal, day of the week, or length of stay surcharges; service or rush fees; or additional charges for "processing and handling," ticket delivery, etc. The numbers to compare are the answers to the question, "What is the total amount that will be charged to my credit card?"

STRATEGIES FOR BUYING TICKETS ONLINE

There are different optimum strategies for buying different kinds of tickets. If price is your main concern, here's my advice for where and how to look for tickets. It depends on where you are going:

Tickets Within or Between the United States and Canada

For domestic tickets within the United States, domestic tickets within Canada, or "transborder" (as the airlines call them) tickets between the United States and Canada, the best prices on scheduled airlines are generally available online.

That doesn't, however, mean you can find them in any one place on the Internet. If you want the best deal for a flight itinerary within North America, you should do all of the following:

Are Online Travel Agencies Biased?

Most travel agencies (other than discounters and agencies that charge service fees) are biased toward airlines and other suppliers of travel products, and against consumers. There's an additional question, however, of whether agencies, or their Web sites, are biased toward *particular* travel services vendors. If a travel Web site lists one airline first, is that because that airline is the best choice for you, or because it's the best choice for the agency?

In most cases, any bias in online displays of airline prices and options is accidental. But that is changing for the worse. Just as a skilled salesperson in any shop will suggest that you buy the product on which they make the most money, so travel agencies have every reason to program their computers to suggest the choices on which they make the largest commissions.

To date, most online travel agencies have relied on simple-minded interfaces that merely display whatever options a CRS suggests, in the order they are listed in the CRS. As online travel agencies become more focused on profitability, and have time to develop more of their own software, they can be expected to add modules between the CRS's and their Web sites to rearrange or filter the choices you are shown to steer you to those on which the agency will make more money. That could mean favoring airlines that give the agency a higher commission in exchange for steering business to them. Or it could mean simply selling prioritization in displays, just as Internet search engines do.

In the past, CRS's were accused of biasing their displays to favor the airlines that owned them. This gave the few airlines that own the major CRS's oligopolistic power to impede new airlines' efforts to make themselves known to consumers. In response to antitrust complaints, the Federal government adopted regulations

Check Web sites of all the airlines serving the route, directly or with connecting flights. If it survives federal antitrust scrutiny, the Orbitz.com Web service (discussed further, below) should eliminate the need to check individual Web sites for participating airlines. Not all airlines participate in Orbitz.com (visit **www.orbitz.com/about /charter.html** for current list), so you'll still need to figure out whether any non-Orbitz.com airlines serve the route you are interested in, and check their Web sites separately.

for airline-owned CRS's in the United States that prohibit them from deliberately biasing their flight or fare displays to favor specific airlines.

Bizarrely, the CRS regulations don't restrict what information CRS's provide directly to the public, only what they provide to travel agencies. One Justice Department enforcement lawyer conceded to me, when pressed, that the only way a consumer could be assured of getting an unbiased display from the CRS was, literally, to go to a travel agent's office and look over the agent's shoulder at their CRS display. That's not feasible, of course, and even experienced travelers wouldn't understand the formats used in CRS displays anyway.

It's completely legal for travel agencies, including CRS- owned travel agencies (such as Travelocity.com and Trip.com) to bias their displays to favor choices that are more profitable for the agency over those that are cheaper or better for travelers, or to sell positioning to airlines that want to pay to get their fares or flights listed first. It's actually surprising that they haven't done so sooner; I can only take that as a sign of their focus on market share rather than profits. I'm sure it will be happening by the time you read this.

You could only trust an online travel agency to give you an unbiased display if they made a contractual promise, in their terms and conditions, to display flights and fares in the exact order in which they are ranked by the CRS. No online travel agency does this, and none is likely to unless consumers demand it. (Orbitz.com claims that it is "contractually" committed to an unbiased display. But they're talking about Orbitz.com's promises to participating airlines not to favor one or the other—promises allegedly contained in contracts which have not been made public—and not about anything in Orbitz.com's contract with consumers.)

Compare as many different online agencies selling consolidator tickets from different sources as you can find. At a minimum, this would include the big four online retail agencies for consolidator tickets on domestic U.S. flights: 1travel.com, Cheaptickets.com, Hotwire.com and Lowestfare.com. Each of these four has significantly different deals with different airlines.

If you can't find any ticket from any of these sources at an

acceptable price, consider an offer to Priceline.com. If you do this only as a last resort, when there's no other acceptable alternative, you have little to lose. But Priceline.com's deals are similar to those of other major domestic consolidators, so the odds that they will find it profitable to accept an offer for a price less than those set by their competitors are poor. Expedia.com offers a "Flight Price Matcher" service that's an imitation of Priceline .com. Because their contract-price sales volume is smaller, and they have less buying power with the airlines, Expedia.com's costs—and thus the offers they are willing to accept—are probably higher. So I'd try Priceline first, and Expedia.com's "Flight Price Matcher" only if my offer was rejected by Priceline.com, as my absolute last option. I haven't heard of anyone who has had an offer accepted by Expedia.com's "Flight Price Matcher" for less than an offer that was refused by Priceline.com.

International Tickets

For round-trip international tickets, check the Web sites of all airlines serving the route (as many of them as possible through Orbitz.com, as well as any non-participants in Orbitz.com, and compare prices from as many consolidator agencies selling tickets to that region of the world as you can find.

Most agencies selling consolidator tickets don't have automated reservations and ticketing Web sites. You might use the Internet to find them, and perhaps to view their online advertisements and brochures, but you'll need to e-mail or call for flight availability. And most consolidator ticket agencies, including in many cases the best and cheapest, have minimal if any Internet presence.

You can find agencies selling international consolidator tickets most quickly and easily offline, not on the Internet. Start with the Sunday travel sections of the *New York Times, San Francisco Chronicle,*

Miami Herald, Los Angeles Times, and the major international gateway city nearest you. Look for small ads from agencies selling discounted tickets to the part of the world where you want to go. Call, phone, or e-mail them for prices for your itinerary. Advertised prices mean little or nothing: the only prices that mean anything are those for which space can actually be confirmed on a schedule, route, and airline acceptable to you. They often have Web sites, but usually these are little more than online brochures or expanded versions of their print ads.

Since agencies that sell consolidator tickets never tell you who their wholesale suppliers are, it's impossible to know if several agencies are really getting their prices from the same supplier. You can waste a lot of time "comparing" prices from different retail agencies who all buy their tickets on the route you are interested in from the same consolidator—but there's no way to avoid this or to know for sure what's going on.

The longer you are staying, the more unusual your destination, and the more complicated your itinerary, the less likely it is that the best price is available directly from any airline, and the less need there is to check published fares with airlines before starting your search for consolidator prices. One-way international tickets (which might be expected to be simpler, but are actually harder to find at a discount) are almost always cheaper from consolidator agencies than directly from the airlines.

Tickets For Flights Within Other Countries and Regions

Air passes, special fares, or discounts are offered to foreign visitors for travel within many countries and some multi-country regions. These fares are sometimes substantially cheaper, and usually less restrictive, than tickets available for purchase separately.

Sometimes these are special published fares; sometimes they are consolidator discounts offered through travel agents for domestic flights ticketed in conjunction with international flights on the same

---

KOREAN AIRLINES TO BRAZIL —

With airline Web sites, make sure you consider all possible airlines. It's often less obvious which airlines might serve an international route than a domestic one. Would you think to check with Korean Airlines for cheap, nonstop flights from Los Angeles to Sao Paulo, Brazil? With Varig Brazilian Airlines, or Malaysian Airlines, for cheap nonstop flights from L.A. to Tokyo? Or with Kuwait Airlines for cheap nonstop flights from Chicago to Amsterdam? Often the cheapest airline is the least obvious, for precisely that reason.

airline. This is one reason it is often advantageous to use a country's own national airline to fly to a country where you plan extensive domestic air travel.

The common denominator is that, with few exceptions, tickets at these prices must be purchased outside the country, usually at the same time that you buy your international tickets. If you don't find out about them (or how expensive tickets are locally) until you've bought your international tickets or until you've arrived in the country, it's too late to do anything about it.

The other common denominator of these prices is that they aren't available through automated online travel agencies. Air passes and visitors fares and discounts have extremely idiosyncratic rules that CRS and other automated pricing systems don't generally bother to implement. For the most part, you can get these prices only by buying your tickets through a human travel agent (on- or offline) who specializes in the country or region of the world you want to visit. This means you should avoid robotic online ticket sales sites if your trip will include flights within other countries or, in most cases, any international flights between or within other parts of the world.

AUTOMATED PUBLISHED-FARE INTERNET TRAVEL AGENCIES

The largest and best-known Internet travel agencies, at least in the United States and Canada, are those specializing exclusively in sales of tickets at published fares. These include independent Internet-only travel agencies such as Travelocity.com and Expedia.com, Internet travel agencies run by CRS such as Trip.com, and the Internet services of major offline travel agencies like American Express (GetThere .com/ITN) and Rosenbluth International (Biztravel.com).

These agencies offerings are limited to published fares and are primarily useful for business travelers or relatively upscale leisure travelers (those more concerned with convenience and schedules rather than with price). Lower prices are usually available directly from the airlines or from discounters.

I discuss some specifics of selected online travel agencies below. Developing the software for such a service is extremely expensive, and very few agencies or Web sites have bothered to do so on their own. Most "portals" and other Web sites that sell airline tickets are using a private-label version of one of these or a few other similar services.

Because they lose money on ticket sales, published-fare sites are eager to sell you, or help you reserve, other more profitable travel

Types of Internet Airline Ticket Sources

Automated published-fare Internet travel agencies
- Travelocity.com
- Expedia.com
- Trip.com (Galileo)
- American Express (GetThere.com/ITN)
- Biztravel.com (Rosenbluth International)
- Amadeus.net

Automated online consolidator ticket agencies
- 1travel.com / onetravel.com
- Cheaptickets.com
- Lowestfare.com
- Priceline.com
- Hotwire.com

Student/teacher/youth fare specialists
- Council Travel
- STA

Online ticket purchases directly from airlines
- Individual airline Web sites
- Orbitz.com

Sources for flights from outside the United States and Canada
- Flights from the United Kingdom (Farebase, Teletext)
- Flights from Europe (TISS, ebookers.com)
- Flights from Australia (Travel.com.au, Cyber Air Broker)
- Multi-stop international tickets (AirTreks.com)

products and services like car rentals and hotel reservations. They are even more eager to expand into the really high-margin travel products like cruises and package tours, although they've had limited success in these areas thus far.

If you just want to buy an airline ticket, you may find it annoying to be prompted with questions about whether you need a rental car or hotel. If you're a typical business traveler who does want these other services, all of the online agencies listed below excel at integrating and automating the process of reserving a basic itinerary consisting of flights, rental cars, and hotels.

All of these services are oriented toward customers in the United States. They vary in their willingness to accept business from customers in other countries. Yes, this is stupid, especially on the Internet where geographic location shouldn't matter. But that's the way they have chosen to do business. If you aren't in the United States, check the fine print carefully before you waste time reviewing options that they won't let you purchase.

Travelocity.com

Travelocity.com (**www.travelocity.com**) was created by the Sabre CRS as a Web-based successor to its original online travel agency, Easy Sabre. Sabre, the most widely used CRS in the United States, was then owned by AMR, the parent company of American Airlines. But in 2000, Sabre became completely independent of AMR (and thus of American Airlines), and Travelocity.com became a separate company from Sabre. Seventy percent of Travelocity.com is owned by Sabre, and the remaining 30 percent is publicly traded.

Travelocity.com includes the former Preview Travel, with which it merged. "Private label" versions of Travelocity.com include AOL Travel, Yahoo! Travel, and many others.

Because of its close relationship with Sabre, Travelocity.com has been able to integrate its software more closely with the CRS than any competing online travel agency. Although its offerings are limited to published fares, and its price optimization is dependent on the CRS, Travelocity.com has been able to offer some innovative and unique flight and fare selection options based on low-level access to Sabre data.

Sabre's (and thus Travelocity.com's) price optimization is, for example, significantly better than Worldspan's, and thus Expedia.com's. Similarly, although Travelocity.com's car and hotel prices aren't necessarily the best available, its interface and tools for reserving them are better than most of its competitors. As published fare online travel agencies go, Travelocity.com is clearly the pacesetter and first place to look.

If you make reservations through Travelocity.com or any other Sabre travel agency, you can view your itinerary at Sabre's "Virtually There" Web site (**www.virtuallythere.com**) by entering your last name and the six-character "record locator" for your reservations. This is good if you've misplaced your printed itinerary, but at present is dangerously insecure. Anyone who sees your name and record locator on an itinerary (through a window envelope, for example, or over your shoulder in an airport check-in line) can find out your home address, the exact dates you'll be away, where you are staying, etc. Properly secured, it could be a great feature, and hopefully Travelocity.com will have secured it before you read this. If they haven't, don't make use of any site that makes reservations in Sabre until they do, unless you want every detail of your trip to be public. Galileo has a similar service at **www.viewtrip.com**, with the same security vulnerability.

Expedia.com

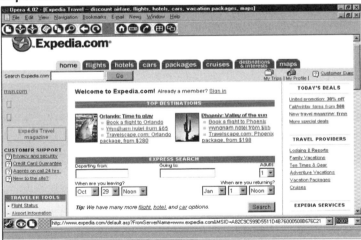

Expedia.com was started as a division of Microsoft. In its ignorance of the travel industry, Microsoft "thought that selling travel would be a simple software problem", according to Expedia.com Marketing V.P. Erik Blachford. They were unprepared for the degree of specialized technical knowledge required for airline pricing, reservations, and ticketing. When I asked him at an industry conference why Expedia.com (which has boasted of its desire to "serve consumers") offers only published fares, for example, Blachford replied that offering any consolidator prices on Expedia.com had proved, "too difficult". Too difficult for Microsoft? "You heard me. Too difficult." In late 1999 Expedia.com was spun off as a separate company, but 85 percent of Expedia.com is still owned by Microsoft, with only 15 percent publicly traded. So Expedia.com still functions as part of Microsoft, with fairly typical advantages and disadvantages for a Microsoft company.

Separately from its CRS-based system for buying tickets at published fares, Expedia.com offers a "name your price" imitation of Priceline.com, "Flight Price Matcher." Like Priceline.com, Expedia.com's Flight Price Matcher sells consolidator tickets without allowing you to know the airline, route, or schedule before committing to buy. You give the cities, date and price. If your offer is far enough above Expedia.com's contracted wholesale price with the airline, they issue you a ticket on whatever airline, route, and schedule is available for their lowest cost on your desired dates. No matter how far below your offer their cost may be, you still get charged as much as you offered.

Trip.com

Trip.com is the retail travel agency division of the Galileo CRS. Trip.com started as an independent Internet travel agency, but was bought by Galileo in early 2000. Galileo, the number two CRS in the United States, evolved from United Airlines' in-house reservations system. (In the United States, Galileo's CRS is better known by its trade name of Apollo.) Today, Galileo International is a largely-independent company: 73 percent of the stock in Galileo is publicly owned, with United Airlines still owning 18 percent and other airlines the remaining nine percent.

Trip.com was founded explicitly as a service for business travelers. Not surprisingly, it offers much better schedule, route, and airline-choice optimization than price optimization. No Web site with only published fares is a good choice for budget travelers, but Trip.com and Biztravel.com are the worst. Trip.com's added-value services are all oriented toward business travelers: real-time tracking of flight delays, its own site specific frequent-buyer program, lists of currently-available frequent-flyer mileage bonuses, and so forth.

American Express Travel

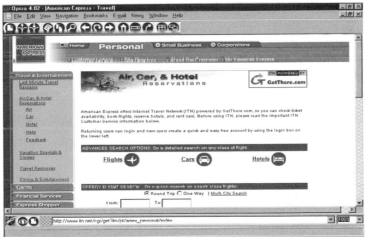

The Internet division of the American Express travel agency (**travel .americanexpress.com**) uses the airline reservations and ticketing system from GetThere.com, the "Business Travel Solutions" division of the Sabre CRS.

GetThere.com's main strength has been its systems for dealing with the special fares that corporations negotiate for their employees. Before it was bought by Sabre, GetThere.com had its own Internet travel agency (the Internet Travel Network, ITN.net), and a close relationship with Sabre's rival CRS, Galileo. Shortly after the Sabre acquisition, it was unclear which CRS would be used by the American Express Travel site. But for customers who don't work for a company with special negotiated fares, AmEx Travel isn't likely to have anything to offer that you couldn't get from any published-fare agency.

Tickets online from AmEx Travel will mostly be of interest for business travelers who also use other AmEx services, or whose employers use AmEx as their corporate travel agency. If you buy your tickets online from AmEx Travel, and charge them to your AmEx card, you can get travel reports integrated with your AmEx card billing statements. AmEx's goal is to use their Web site to offer individuals and small businesses some of the "travel management" services previously available only to large corporate travel accounts. AmEx Travel online also has one of the better automated services for keeping track of your frequent flyer mileage in multiple programs (for flights bought from them, of course) on a single statement.

Biztravel.com (Rosenbluth International)

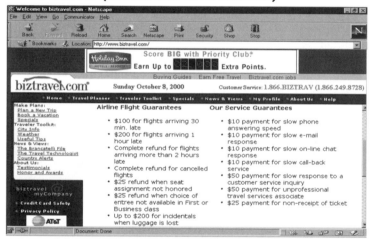

Biztravel.com is the online retail division of Rosenbluth International, one of the world's oldest and largest corporate travel agencies. Biztravel.com began as an independent Internet travel agency, but was bought by Rosenbluth in 1999.

Biztravel.com relies on the Worldspan CRS (owned by Delta, Northwest, and TWA) for price and flight availability information, as does Expedia.com. But Biztravel.com's user interface is narrowly focused on business travelers' concerns with schedule, route, and airline—not price. I'm no fan of Microsoft, or of Expedia.com, but Expedia.com offers significantly better access to Worldspan's (limited) price-optimization tools than does Biztravel.com.

For its intended clientele of business travelers, Biztravel.com may have the best array of special services of any online ticket-sales service: real-time flight tracking, automatic frequent flyer mileage tracking and reports, and so forth. Lots of Web sites have summaries of airlines' limited-duration airfare specials, but Biztravel.com has one of the few summaries of frequent-flyer mileage bonus specials: "Continental Airlines: Receive double OnePass miles when you travel from Sacramento via Houston by July 2," and all the other major airlines' current offers of this sort.

Biztravel.com's biggest advantage may be its offer of refunds to customers whose flights on certain airlines are late (up to $100 for flights that arrive more than 30 minutes late, up to $200 for flights more than one hour late, and a full refund of the price of any ticket for a flight that arrives more than two hours late or is cancelled entirely). Not all airlines are included in this offer, and "flight delays or cancellations due to aircraft mechanical problems are not included." Still in its infancy, it's too early to tell whether this will prove a successful long-term drawing card for Biztravel.com, or an unaffordable and therefore short-lived gimmick.

Amadeus.net

Amadeus.net (**www.amadeus.net**) is a Web interface to (surprise!) Amadeus. Amadeus is the largest CRS in the world in numbers of travel agencies and international reservations, although it's a distant fourth in the United States to Sabre, Galileo, and Worldspan. Sixty percent of Amadeus is owned by Air France, Iberia Airlines of Spain, and Lufthansa; 40 percent is publicly owned.

Traditionally, CRS didn't sell tickets or compete with the travel agents to whom they provided information and electronic connectivity. Amadeus.net isn't a Web site for any one travel agency, but a portal through which reservations can be made in the Amadeus CRS for ticketing through any travel agency that uses Amadeus. There's an index of Amadeus travel agencies by location on the site. Before you can make reservations or check prices, you have to register with Amadeus.net and create a profile that includes your choice of which travel agency you want to issue your tickets. You can check availability of seats, but that's useless unless price is no object.

The main reasons to use Amadeus.net are either that your favorite travel agency uses Amadeus, or simply to get other CRS suggestions. If you don't actually intend to buy your tickets through an Amadeus travel agency, it doesn't matter which agency you designate. You can use Amadeus.net to see which flights and prices Amadeus suggests, and then make your reservations for those flights through another online agency that permits automated ticketing.

Amadeus owns 20 percent of ITA Software, the company whose pricing and flight-suggestion software has been licensed by Orbitz .com. If and when it is deployed by both, as is likely to happen eventually, one can expect Amadeus.net and Orbitz.com to suggest pretty much the same published fare and flight options. Amadeus.net, however, doesn't list the airline-direct specials that will be available through Orbitz.com.

If you choose to make your reservations through Amadeus.net, you can have them issued either by the agency you designate or by the airline directly. One advantage of this otherwise cumbersome system is that it enables you to hold confirmed reservations without paying for them immediately. The drawbacks are the lack of automated ticketing, and the fact that because relatively few travel agencies in the United States use Amadeus, the agency most convenient to you may not be able to issue tickets from reservations you have made through Amadeus.net.

GENESIS

A new CRS dark horse called GENESIS is being developed by a cooperative of travel agencies. It's not yet clear what form Web access to GENESIS will take, or if it will be available to the public or only to travel agencies. But it's the first CRS built around Internet protocols and architecture, and the first CRS not to start out under airline ownership. GENESIS is largely a result of travel agencies' disenchantment with airlines, which doesn't necessarily matter one way or the other to consumers. (Although travel agents who are mad at airlines are more likely to side with travelers.) But with so few CRS's controlling access to flight and fare information, any new choice is to be welcomed. Check it out through links at **www.ustar.com**.

AUTOMATED ONLINE CONSOLIDATOR TICKET AGENCIES

Building a robot to connect a Web site to a CRS is reasonably straightforward. Building a separate system to store consolidator prices and their rules, and integrate them with flight and availability information from the CRS, is fundamentally more complex and expensive. And travel agencies that sell consolidator tickets are, especially in the United States, considerably smaller and less well funded than more mainstream agencies catering to people who don't balk at published fares. It should come as no surprise, then, that agencies that sell consolidator tickets have been slower than pub-lished-fare agencies to implement automated online ticketing, and that a much smaller percentage of consolidator ticket sales than of published-fare ticket sales has moved to the Internet.

Here are the major *automated* Internet consolidator agencies, especially for domestic flights within the United States. Many more consolidator agencies, especially for international flights, are accessible by e-mail and have brochures and advertisements on the Web, but they don't have fully robotic ticket sales Web sites.

1travel.com / onetravel.com

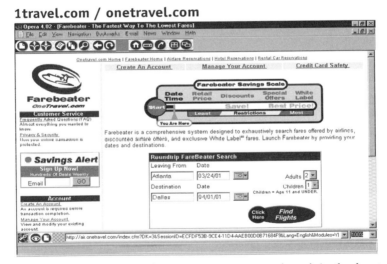

1travel.com (**www.1travel.com** or **www.onetravel.com**) is the least-known of the major online domestic U.S. consolidators, but offers the widest array of choices and, as of now, the only integrated com-parative display of published fares and consolidator prices. Of course, they list only their own consolidator prices, so some other consolidator agency might have a lower price. But at least you don't have to check a separate published-fare site to see how their consolidator prices compare to current published sales. They also offer (in the same integrated comparison), so-called "white-label fares" that offer many of the advantages of tickets from Priceline.com without the drawbacks of hidden prices or unforeseeable schedules. These "white-label" prices are listed with the route, approximate schedule, and price—everything except the airline name.

As a privately owned, profitable, company, not a money-loser supported by venture capital or an IPO, 1travel.com hasn't had as much money to spend on a slick user interface as its competitors, though the Amadeus CRS has a minority stake in 1travel.com. At this time, it isn't yet apparent what changes that might bring.

1travel.com's advantages are its uniquely wide range of offerings and its unique ability to compare prices from multiple sources. Its big disadvantage is the difficulty of finding what you want on the site. To search for the lowest available price from the main home page, for example, you first have to select and request a price for whenever flights are suggested as most direct. Then, by asking for "Farebeater" options, you can get a list of lower prices available on indirect flights or through "white label" prices.

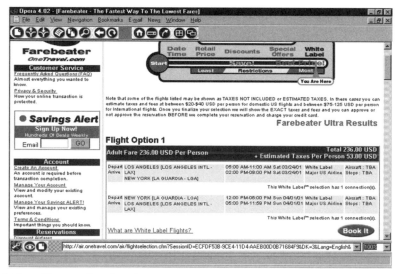

http://www.farebeater.com

Once you click your way through to "Farebeater Ultra", 1travel.com's airfare search at Farebeater.com includes "White Label Fares" with the price, approximate times, and number of connections, but not the airlines or exact schedule.

If you are just interested in flight prices, there's a more direct gateway to 1travel.com's airfare section at **www.farebeater.com**. This isn't a different company, just another domain name the same company uses. Once you get the initial set of "Farebeater" suggestions, choose "Farebeater Ultra" unless you are in terrible hurry. It takes 1-2 minutes instead of seconds, but it queries many more possibilities.

Cheaptickets.com

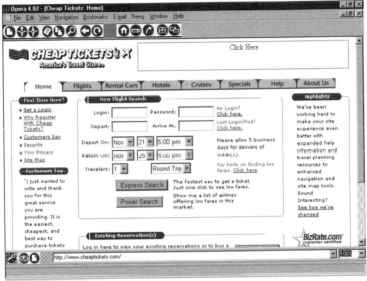

Cheaptickets.com is a well-established no-frills travel agency selling a mix of published fares and consolidator tickets, mainly for domestic U.S. travel. Although the company was renamed "Cheaptickets .com, Inc.," it still makes most of its sales from its storefront offices and 800-number call centers. That's actually good for online customers; Cheap Tickets' offline sales give the company much larger volume, and enable it to negotiate better deals with the airlines. Prior to the advertising-driven growth of Priceline.com, Cheap Tickets was probably the largest retail consolidator of tickets for domestic flights within the United States.

Be sure you are clear on what the *total* charges will be before you click on the "Buy" button. I've heard several complaints about unexpected surcharges and fees from Cheaptickets.com's telephone and Web customers. The Cheaptickets.com Web site lists only their consolidator prices; it's up to you to check a published-fare site to see if a published sale fare might be lower.

Lowestfare.com

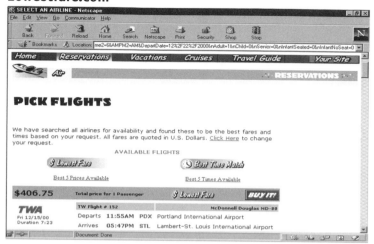

Lowestfare.com sells both by phone and over the Web. The agency is owned in part by Carl Icahn, former CEO of TWA. In exchange for loans he made to bail out TWA, Icahn is able to buy all TWA tickets at a certain percentage discount from the published fare. This deal will expire in 2003, and TWA has no interest in renewing or extending it.

In late 1999, with money raised from its IPO, Lowestfare.com bought the U.S. division of Jetset Tours, a major wholesale-only consolidator of international tickets from the United States. Thus far, few of Jetset's prices have been made available through Lowestfare.com. Like most wholesale consolidators, Jetset Tours has a policy of never selling directly to the public. Offering their tickets at retail through Lowestfare.com will require a change in that policy, potentially alienating the retail travel agencies who are Jetset Tours' established customers. But once Lowestfare.com starts offering the full range of Jetset Tours' consolidator prices, it could become one of the best online sources of discounted international tickets from the United States.

For now, Lowestfare.com is of interest mainly for domestic U.S. travel: if TWA has the lowest published fare for your route, you can probably get tickets cheaper through Lowestfare.com. On many TWA routes Lowestfare.com has waivers of advance purchase and minimum-stay requirements, making them an especially good choice for last-minute, short-stay, and business travelers.

Priceline.com

Priceline.com is a retail consolidator ticket agency with the huge disadvantage that they don't reveal their prices. Don't confuse Priceline.com

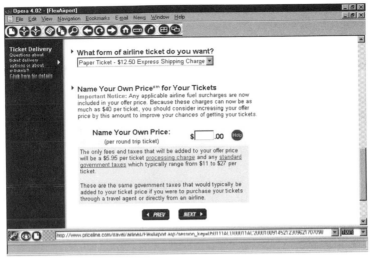

with an auction or discount site, or confuse offers to Priceline.com with "bids." Priceline.com says itself that it is not an auction and not a discounter. You aren't "bidding" against anyone except yourself.

Priceline.com has contract prices with airlines similar to those of other consolidators. "Name your own price" is just a pricing mechanism. It ensures that you pay as much as you are willing, and no less. If you offer $50 more than Priceline.com's contracted cost, or $500 more, the airline (in most cases) gets the same amount. Priceline .com pockets the difference.

Priceline.com will buy you whatever ticket is cheapest for them, regardless of which airline it is on, the route, or the time of day. All you know when you commit to buy a ticket for a specific price from Priceline.com is that they will give you a ticket on some airline between those cities sometime on those dates. You can expect to be on whatever flights are least popular and thus have seats available for the lowest cost to Priceline.com. Often the least popular flights are the least convenient, such as those very early in the morning or late at night.

Individual offers to Priceline.com are not sent to the airlines, nor are they individually evaluated by the airlines. Airlines aren't set up to work that way, and their sales through Priceline.com aren't nearly large enough to justify completely restructuring their pricing and yield management system.

Offers you make to Priceline.com are evaluated only by Priceline .com, to see if you have offered enough over Priceline.com's contracted cost to make it worth their while. In most cases, airlines don't even know how much you have paid, or how much Priceline.com has made on your tickets.

Priceline.com is not a discounter. If some people have gotten good deals through Priceline.com, that's mostly because Priceline.com has chosen to accept offers for less than their cost. That can't last. Eventually, Priceline.com will have to start rejecting all but the profitable offers.

If you're willing to accept some uncertainty in return for a better price, my strong recommendation is to look at Hotwire.com or the "white label" prices from 1travel.com (which tell you the price and dates, but not the airline) before you make an offer to Priceline.com. Make an offer to Priceline.com only as your absolute last resort, if there's no ticket available from any other source that is at all acceptable to you.

Hotwire.com

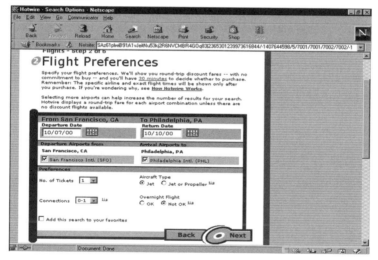

Hotwire.com is an Internet-only travel agency launched in August 2000 to sell tickets on unnamed airlines. (Hotwire.com is no relationship to *Wired* magazine's "Hotwired.com" site.)

Hotwire.com lets you choose how many times you're willing to change planes and whether you're willing to fly on turboprops or redeyes—but not which airlines or what time of day. In return for being willing to accept flights on any airline at anytime of day, Hotwire.com offers prices 30-50 percent less than the lowest published fare, even for trips without a Saturday-night stay. Unlike Priceline.com and its ilk, Hotwire.com gives you a specific price *before* you decide to buy.

Hotwire.com is modeled on, and competes mainly with, 1travel.com's "white label fares." There are two main differences between these two agencies: Hotwire.com has "white label" prices from more airlines, but 1travel.com sells tickets at published fares, and at consolidator prices on named airlines and known schedules, in addition to its "white label fares." A third, less significant difference is that 1travel.com gives you an approximate time of day (a four- or six-hour time window) for a "white label" flight, while Hotwire.com will only tell you whether or not it is an overnight flight.

In exchange for being given part ownership of Hotwire.com, more airlines are offering "white label" prices through Hotwire.com than through 1travel.com. I always check both, but with more airlines participating, Hotwire.com is more likely to have a "white label" price, especially to or from smaller cities.

On the other hand, Hotwire.com offers tickets *only* to people who are willing to accept a ticket (for a known price) without knowing the exact airline. 1travel.com is likely to remain the most diverse—though by no means complete—integrated array of different types of prices, and lets you compare published and consolidator prices. Before buying from Hotwire.com, it's essential to check a published-fare site to see if some airline has a sale fare that's cheaper than Hotwire.com—and that will let you know the schedule before you buy.

Unlike Orbitz.com, Hotwire.com was founded by venture capitalists, not the airlines. But several airlines own minority interests in Hotwire.com, as they do in Priceline.com. The combination of joint ownership by multiple airlines, and a business model that hides prices from public or governmental scrutiny, makes both Hotwire.com and Priceline.com ideally suited as a vehicle for airline collusion on prices. Either agency's airline owners could, for example, be agreeing on a minimum selling price for tickets on the specific route, for example. I have no knowledge of whether they are or are not: part of the problem is that it would be impossible for any outsider to tell. Unlike Orbitz.com, however, Priceline.com and Hotwire.com have thus far escaped the antitrust scrutiny they deserve.

STUDENT AND YOUTH FARE SPECIALISTS

Student and youth fares are the best-known and most widely available of a class of published fares called "status fares." By restricting eligibility for these fares to people who can prove they have a certain status indicative of limited willingness to pay—such as students or professors—airlines are able to offer these discounts with little risk

– STUDENT FARES

Not all airlines offer student or youth fares, and the rules and their prices vis-à-vis consolidator tickets vary. On most airlines, you must have a current, valid International Student Identity Card (ISIC) at the time of ticketing and when traveling on tickets at a student fare.

that they will be used by people who would otherwise have paid higher fares.

Because they're published fares, student and youth fares should—in theory—be available directly from any published-fare source. In practice, most student and youth fares aren't programmed into CRS's and aren't available from online travel agencies or airline Web sites that rely on CRS's for price information. Almost all student and youth tickets are sold by a few travel agency chains specializing in the student and youth market.

Some airlines have made teachers at post-secondary educational institutions eligible for the same fares as students, although rules on faculty eligibility for special fares vary. Like their students, professors may find student fares better or worse than consolidator tickets, depending on their itinerary.

No airline allows elementary or secondary school teachers to use student fares. The exclusion of teachers in lower grades is unfortunate and unfair (fairness being of course irrelevant in setting fares), since they get paid less than college or university professors for higher-stress work, with few compensations except for the longest vacations of any major job category in the United States. A pity—certainly students at all levels would benefit if their teachers had more international travel experience.

There are two main online student and youth travel agencies in the United States. The first is **Council Travel** (**www.counciltravel .com**). As the travel agency division of the Council on International Education and Exchange (**www.ciee.org**), it has long been the largest student travel specialist in the United States. Council Travel has alliances with independent student travel agencies in countries around the world.

The second is **STA Travel** (**www.sta.com**), a global student travel agency. STA Travel originally was based in Australia and called Student Travel Australia; it has its own offices in the United States, United Kingdom, Australia, and more than a dozen other countries. For links to STA Travel offices worldwide, see the head office Web site at **www.statravelgroup.com**.

Both Council Travel and STA Travel have facilities on their Web sites for automated booking and ticketing of student and youth fares.

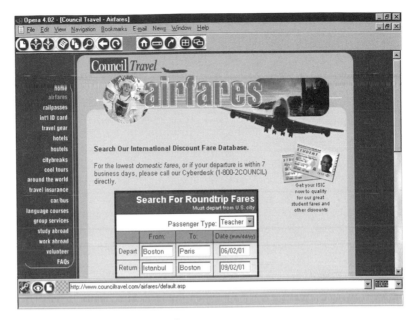

http://www.counciltravel.com
Specialty agencies like Council Travel and STA have prices for students, teachers, or anyone under age 26 that are sometimes better than those available through all-purpose agencies. Not all student deals are available online—note here, for example, that you have to phone for airfares within the U.S.

Council Travel also provides for automated sales of faculty fares, and some consolidator prices available to everyone. But neither site displays general published fares.

Student, youth, and faculty fares are not necessarily the lowest fares, much less the tickets sold at the lowest prices. For international travel, consolidator tickets are often cheaper, and more flexible, than student-fare tickets. Student tickets are available on fewer airlines than consolidator tickets, and more often on the airlines that are more expensive in the first place.

Student, youth, and faculty fares are an excellent value in some cases and relatively poor value in others. If you qualify for fares of these special types, you should always check them out before buying tickets at regular published or consolidator prices. Always compare prices from sources whose offerings aren't limited to these special fares.

ONLINE TICKET PURCHASES DIRECTLY FROM AIRLINES

Individual Airline Web Sites

Offline, more tickets are purchased through travel agencies than directly from the airlines. Airlines have only a few storefront ticket offices in the largest cities, while travel agencies have tens of thousands of locations, including ones in every small town, office park, and shopping mall. For most travelers, the convenience of dealing with a local travel agency, and of one-stop comparison shopping, are worth a travel agent's service fee.

Online, it's the reverse: most online ticket purchases are directly from airlines, through their own Web sites, even though almost no online travel agencies charge service fees. On the Internet, geographic location and local offices are irrelevant. And airlines offer a wide array of incentives on their Web sites to get you to buy your tickets directly from them, rather than from an online travel agency.

Special Airline-Direct Internet Fares

Almost all airlines offer some special fares exclusively to people who buy tickets directly from their own Web sites. These are generally thought of and described as Internet specials, but they are also airline-direct specials and aren't available from any Internet travel agency. That may change in the future with Orbitz.com, as discussed below.

Each airline has a slightly different system for these special offers. But whether through competition or collusion, they have evolved to a fairly similar plan: once a week, the airline announces a set of sale fares between specific cities for tickets purchased that week on the airline's Web site.

Most of these special fares are available only for weekend travel, typically on routes where most of the traffic is business travel on weekdays, and weekend flights have lots of empty seats. So most of the weekly specials announced on Tuesday or Wednesday are limited to travel departing that Friday or Saturday and returning the following Monday or Tuesday. Typical prices for

— **E-MAIL NOTICE OF SPECIAL FARES**

The best-known of the services sending weekly e-mails outlining the airlines' special fares is "Smarter Living" **www.smarterliving.com**. Each week, I get one e-mail message from Smarter Living listing all that week's special fares from San Francisco or Oakland airports, summarizing the travel dates for which each is applicable, and giving a link to the pages on the airline's Web site where each can be booked.

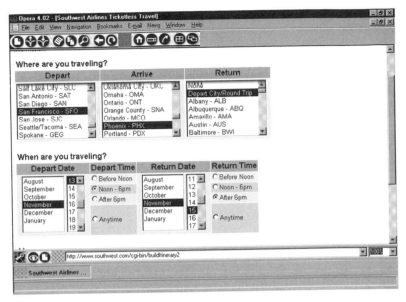

http://www.southwest.com
*Southwest Airlines' Web site doesn't waste any space on ads for
other companies, doesn't require cookies, doesn't make you register,
and collects only the information needed to issue your tickets.
Maybe that's part of why it's the most successful airline ticket sales
Web site in the U.S.*

these specials are about two-thirds of the lowest regular published
advance-purchase round-trip fares. Useful if you're after a spur-of-
the-moment weekend visit. Not useful for much else. Different
routes are discounted each week by each airline, depending on
which of their flights on the coming weekend have an especially
large number of unsold seats. You can never count on when one of
these deals will be offered on any particular route.

The success of these special fares in filling empty weekend seats
on specific flights and routes has led the airlines gradually to expand
them: along with their special fares for travel that weekend, many
airlines' weekly sales include flights on a few routes for a wider
range of future dates, if tickets are purchased that week only, directly
from the airline's Web site. As with the weekend travel specials, the
rules are usually highly restrictive, and routes and travel dates
offered each week are unpredictable. If there happens to be an offer
like this available at the time you are shopping for tickets, and with

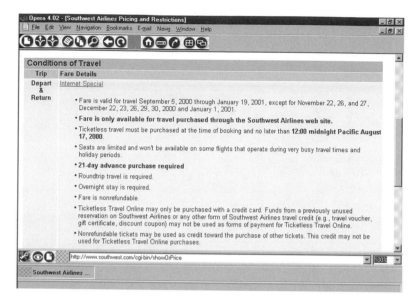

Conditions of Travel

Trip	Fare Details
Depart & Return	Internet Special

- Fare is valid for travel September 5, 2000 through January 19, 2001, except for November 22, 26, and 27, December 22, 23, 26, 29, 30, 2000 and January 1, 2001.
- **Fare is only available for travel purchased through the Southwest Airlines web site.**
- Ticketless travel must be purchased at the time of booking and no later than **12:00 midnight Pacific August 17, 2000.**
- Seats are limited and won't be available on some flights that operate during very busy travel times and holiday periods.
- **21-day advance purchase required**
- Roundtrip travel is required.
- Overnight stay is required.
- Fare is nonrefundable.
- Ticketless Travel Online may only be purchased with a credit card. Funds from a previously unused reservation on Southwest Airlines or any other form of Southwest Airlines travel credit (e.g., travel voucher, gift certificate, discount coupon) may not be used as forms of payment for Ticketless Travel Online.
- Nonrefundable tickets may be used as credit toward the purchase of other tickets. This credit may not be used for Ticketless Travel Online purchases.

http://www.southwest.com
Read, print a copy, and make sure you understand all the fine print before you click "buy".

seats available for the route and dates you want, great. If not, look elsewhere. Waiting and hoping for one of these sales for a specific route and travel dates is usually a poor strategy.

Since each airline has its own specials on different routes each week, the key to taking advantage of the deals that might interest you is being alerted to them as soon as they are announced. Each airline has an e-mail list to which you can subscribe through their Web site to be notified of their specials each week. But if you live near an airport served by many different airlines, you might have to wade through a dozen different e-mail messages each week from different airlines to see of any of them are for flights to places you are interested in going.

Any of several Internet travel agencies and independent third party services will send you, by subscription, a single weekly e-mail message summarizing that week's airline direct-sale Internet specials for whatever cities you have told them you're interested in. These bulletins are just informational (and advertising for the other services of the agencies that send them). Internet travel agencies can't sell you tickets at these prices directly—the point is that you have to buy them directly from the airline on the airline's own Web site.

Advantages of Buying Direct from the Airlines

Airlines want you to buy tickets directly from them, not through travel agencies, and to do so on the Internet. A large proportion of airlines, especially smaller, newer, no-frills, and discount airlines, are willing to bribe you in some way to do so.

Usually, these bribes take the form of extra frequent flyer mileage credits. The exact bonuses vary from airline to airline, and from time to time, the typical bonuses have been either an extra 5,000 to 10,000 frequent-flier miles per ticket, or double frequent-flier mileage for tickets bought directly from the airline through its Web site. The bonus is as much for buying tickets directly from the airline as for buying online; you can't get these bonuses by purchasing tickets from an online travel agency.

Not all airlines offer these bonuses, but enough do that it's always worth checking the airline's own Web site before buying a ticket at a published fare from any other source. This doesn't apply to consolidator prices, since by definition they aren't available directly from the airline, online or offline.

Orbitz.com

Sometime in 2001, a group of major U.S. airlines plan to launch a joint ticket sales Web site called "Orbitz" (**www.orbitz.com**). As a condition of participating in Orbitz.com, airlines must agree that they won't offer any lower fares through any other Web site—although they can still offer lower consolidator prices through any number of travel agents, online and offline.

An antitrust complaint, filed by the Association of Retail Travel Agents (ARTA), is pending. It argues that Orbitz.com is an attempt by the airlines to compete unfairly with travel agencies. But that isn't likely to stop Orbitz.com entirely, even if it may prompt minor changes to the plans.

Orbitz.com is owned by United, Delta, Northwest, Continental, and American Airlines. Several dozen other U.S. and foreign airlines have committed to participate in Orbitz.com. In some sense Orbitz.com will be just another Internet travel agency, competing primarily with Travelocity.com and Expedia.com. Even before the site was launched, it's airline owners had announced their intention eventually to sell the site to public stockholders. For now, Orbitz.com is

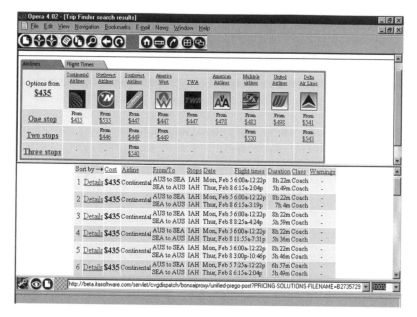

http://beta.itasoftware.com

Orbitz.com plans to use an airfare comparison screen based on this beta version from ITA Software. It makes it easy to compare those options it includes, but it will only show prices available directly from the airlines that own Orbitz—not the larger number of often-lower consolidator prices.

owned and controlled entirely and directly by the airlines. It is a portal Web site through which airlines sell tickets directly to the public, rather than a travel agency.

The most important difference between Orbitz.com and other travel agencies is that the airlines participating in Orbitz.com have promised to make all their direct-sale and "Internet special" fares available through Orbitz.com. That means it won't be necessary for consumers to check individual airlines' Web sites for weekly specials on participating airlines: on Orbitz.com, they'll be integrated with the displays of regular published fares.

Orbitz.com won't be a one-stop shop for the best air fares. At press time, none of the airlines known primarily as low-fare airlines (Southwest, American Trans Air, Airtran, etc.) had joined Orbitz.com. And while participating airlines have promised to offer all their published fares through Orbitz.com, they can still offer non-cash incentives (frequent flyer miles, upgrades, etc.) for buying tickets directly from their individual Web sites.

Perhaps more importantly, Orbitz.com will offer only "publicly-available" (i.e. published) fares. Like the airlines' own Web sites, and like the published fare online travel agencies with which it is intended to compete, Orbitz.com will not list any consolidator ticket prices. As a creature of the airlines, it probably couldn't even if it wanted to, which it doesn't.

The Association of Retail Travel Agents (ARTA), which filed an antitrust complaint against Orbitz.com, argues that Orbitz.com is an attempt by the airlines to use their oligopoly power to compete unfairly with travel agencies. Others see Orbitz.com as an oligopolistic venture by larger high-fare airlines.

In response, Orbitz.com claims that it will offer superior comparisons of published fares from participating airlines. Instead of relying on a CRS for fare information, Orbitz.com will use a completely new flight and fare comparison and optimization system developed by an independent company, ITA Software.

ITA Software claims categorically that Orbitz.com "will find the best choices for you" and "optimizes all fare and flight options". That's nonsense, since their software doesn't ask most of the questions, and isn't capable of taking into account most of the factors, that would be needed for real optimization or to determine which option you would really find "best". Their claim to evaluate "all fares" is deceptive at best, since for every published *fare* there are hundreds or thousands of lower unpublished consolidator *prices* that won't be available through Orbitz.com. Orbitz.com says that "other travel sites contain bias", but Orbitz.com is inherently biased toward airlines that pay to participate over those that don't, and toward published fares over consolidator prices. Orbitz.com is no less biased than its competitors.

ITA Software and Orbitz.com say they will "allow travelers to make...decisions based on all the facts and available options." That's nonsense, too, even within the domain of published fares. The whole point of their system is, of necessity, to eliminate most of your options and reduce the millions of possibilities to a manageable few to show you.

Nevertheless, ITA Software has come up with a user interface capable of showing fare comparisons better than anything available from the CRS's. On the one hand, that's an enormous accomplishment. On the other hand, it was relatively easy to do better for consumers than the CRS's, since CRS's were never trying to optimize their systems to serve consumers.

If you can look beyond the hype, Orbitz.com will have some advantages over individual airline Web sites. Orbitz.com is never likely to be a very good choice for price conscious travelers looking for tickets on international routes, where consolidators often have lower prices than published fares. And it may not get participation from some important low-fare U.S. airlines. But largely because of the advantages of ITA Software over the CRS pricing software used by Orbitz.com's published-fare competitors, Orbitz.com will probably become the best single comparison shopping Web site for tickets at published fares on major airlines for domestic flights within the U.S.

It's important to keep in mind three things when shopping at Orbitz.com: 1) not all airlines will pay to participate, 2) airlines can still offer non-cash incentives for buying tickets directly from their Web sites (frequent-flier miles, upgrades, etc.); and 3) Orbitz.com will offer only published fares. Orbitz.com has no information regarding domestic or international consolidator ticket prices.

Orbitz.com will use the Worldspan CRS, owned entirely by Delta, Northwest, and TWA (though not the same ones who started Orbitz .com). However, Orbitz.com will use a completely new flight and fare comparison and optimization system developed by an independent startup company, ITA Software (now 20 percent–owned by another CRS, Amadeus).

Despite its shortcomings, Orbitz.com will have some significant advantages over individual airline Web sites. Largely because of the advantages of ITA Software over the CRS pricing software used by Orbitz.com's published fare competitors, Orbitz.com will probably become the best single comparison shopping Web site for tickets at published fares on major airlines for domestic flights within the United States.

SOURCES FOR FLIGHTS FROM OUTSIDE THE UNITED STATES AND CANADA

Most ticket sales Web sites based in the United States are focused largely on customers in the United States. Some refuse to accept business from customers in other countries; others simply don't have much to offer them. Customers outside the United States need to look elsewhere if they want good deals.

The United States has the world's largest domestic airline system, and most air travel by people from the United States is on domestic routes. Because of the deregulation of domestic airfares within the United States, consolidator prices are a relatively minor factor in domestic U.S. air travel. Most travel agencies in the United

States only sell tickets at published fares, and online agencies are no exception. All of the largest online travel agencies in the United States are published-fare only agencies.

Outside the United States and Canada, most air ticket sales are on international routes dominated by consolidator pricing. U.S.-based online travel agencies like Travelocity.com and Expedia.com have had little success in trying to market tickets at published fares to travelers in other countries where virtually all travel agencies offer lower consolidator prices. Successful online travel agencies in other countries have all found it essential to incorporate consolidator pricing on international tickets.

Flights From the United Kingdom

The United Kingdom has the world's largest consolidator ticket market. Thus far, its scale and complexity have defied full automation. Most of the better prices on flights from the United Kingdom are available only from offline travel agents or tour operators, not from automated Internet travel agencies. The value of the Internet for tickets from the United Kingdom is in giving access to comparative information about consolidator ticket prices from multiple sources. This can greatly simplify, if not eliminate, the process of phoning around to different agents.

Two useful resources can also help you compare prices from different agencies. **Farebase (www.farebase.co.uk)** is an independent information service that lists prices from dozens of consolidators of international tickets originating from the United Kingdom. It is supported by thousands of retail travel agencies in the United Kingdom who subscribe to it as their source of consolidator prices. If you like a price, and want to find out if and when seats are available, Farebase will forward your inquiry to a subscribing agent in your area. The prices shown on the Farebase Web site are retail selling prices, and include the retail agent's markup but *not* the taxes.

The consolidators who distribute their price lists through Farebase are wholesalers, not retailers. You can't buy tickets directly from them, even if you can find them, and they aren't identified on the public Farebase Web site.

For travelers in the U.K., Farebase is a resource unparalleled anywhere else in the world. Unfortunately, Farebase only lists prices for flights originating from the U.K., and Farebase subscriber agencies generally aren't set up to accept business from customers located outside the U.K.. But if you are planning a side trip from the

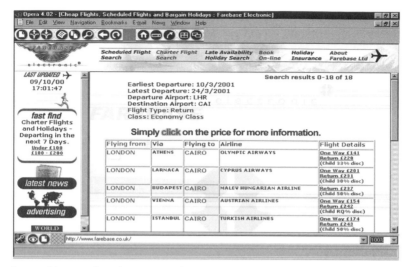

http://www.farebase.co.uk

*Farebase is an independent service that allows you to search a
database of discount prices from dozens of U.K. consolidators.
It's too bad there's nothing like it for prices from the U.S., where
consolidators are harder to find.*

http://www.teletext.co.uk/holidays

*Teletext.co.uk provides an Internet window into current U.K.
discount travel ads.*

U.K. you can use Farebase to get a general sense of what kinds of prices *might* be available for purchase once you get to the U.K.

Teletext is a system in the United Kingdom for piggy-backing text information and advertising onto television broadcasts. With a special converter, you can display selected Teletext pages on your TV. What's this got to do with the Internet? The same travel (and other) information that's available to Teletext subscribers in the U.K. is now available for free to anyone on the Internet through the Teletext Web site at **www.teletext.co.uk/holidays** (follow the "TV text ads" link).

Because Teletext advertisements can be updated electronically and almost instantaneously, Teletext is the main advertising medium for last-minute travel discounts in the United Kingdom, as well as for many other ads from consolidator ticket agencies, charter flight operators, and tour companies. Keep in mind these ads were designed to be read on a low-resolution television screen—that's why they look so strange. Some of the abbreviations, travel jargon, and Briticisms may be unfamiliar to American readers, and phone numbers in Teletext ads are presumably in the United Kingdom. Prices can be assumed to be in British Pounds (GBP), for flights from London (frequently from outlying airports like Stansted or Luton rather than from Heathrow). Some of the abbreviations, travel jargon, and Briticisms may be confusing or ambiguous to American readers. Phone numbers in Teletext ads are presumably in the U.K. and some of the phone numbers are "freephone" numbers that you can't call from outside the U.K. Most Teletext advertisers have no idea that their ads can be seen on the Internet by customers abroad, and would have no idea what to do if you called them from the United States to try to book a flight or purchase a package holiday. As with Farebase, Teletext ads are mainly useful to customers abroad for information about what might be available once they get to the United Kingdom.

Flights From Throughout Europe

The Internet, and the deregulation of airfares within the EU, are transforming air travel in Europe. Of all the world's airlines, the one that sells the highest percentage of its tickets on the Internet is U.K.–based Easyjet. And the two leading online travel agencies in Europe are both pan-European, multilingual, consolidator ticket agencies. Their home pages are in English, but you can switch immediately to the major Western European language of your choice. Both agencies below sell tickets in and from the British Isles and continental Europe, but from the United Kingdom you'll probably get better deals from local offline agencies (as discussed in the preceding section). Both of these agencies specialize in consolidator prices; you'll need to check alternative sources to compare published fares.

Flights.com (formerly TISS.com) began as a global marketing consortium of independent travel agencies in different countries around the world. Reservations made through the Flights.com Web site were referred to the Flights.com affiliate in the customer's country of residence. Eventually, Flights.com opened some of its own ticketing offices, and then began to acquire its affiliates in targeted countries. Today, it's a hybrid of Flights.com–owned and independently-owned agencies. Before you buy a ticket arranged through the Flights.com Web site, be sure you know who is responsible (in case you encounter a problem). Flights.com has associates scattered around the world, but is based in Germany and strongest in Western Europe.

Ebookers.com (www.ebookers.com) began as the online division of "Flightbookers," an otherwise unremarkable offline consolidator ticket agency in London. Ebookers.com has expanded across Europe by buy-

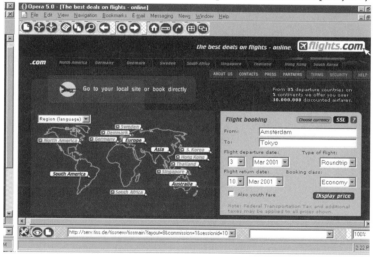

http://www.flights.com

ing an existing travel agency in each country where it wants to operate. Their strategy is to acquire a presence and a local ticketing and customer service center, in each major Western European country.

Flights From Australia
Travel.com.au (www.travel.com.au) is a start-up that offers both auto-

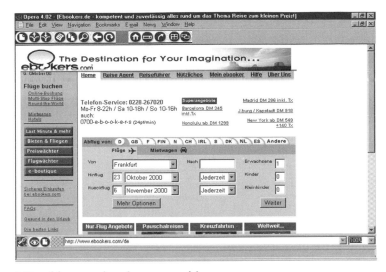

http://www.ebookers.com/de

mated booking and ticket purchasing through their Web site, and access to human travel consultants by phone or Internet or at their storefront offices. They appear to have at least some consolidator prices as well as published fares. Their focus appears to be on booking tours and packages, not just airfares. Travel.com.au also owns and operates Travel.com in New Zealand.

Cyber Air Broker (**www.airdiscounter.com**) is a service of Phil Travel, an established Sydney agency specializing in consolidator tickets worldwide. They offer the widest range of consolidator prices of any online agency in Australia. They've had repeated delays and problems getting their automated Web-based booking facility to work, so you may have to e-mail or call to find out if listed prices are actually available on an acceptable schedule for your trip.

Flights From Other Countries

While the wholesale market in international consolidator tickets is global, there is no one retail travel agency that's best for simple one way or round-trip tickets from everywhere in the world. In most cases, you need to find a local agency.

In addition to Flights.com, which has a spotty network of affiliates around the world, there are two major consortia of retail consolidator ticket agencies (note that these are *not* accrediting, certification, or bonding organizations): **The Association of Special Fares Agents (ASFA), www.asfa.net**; and **The Association of International Travel Agents (AITA), www.aita.org**. Each of their Web sites has listings and

Airline Ticket Auctions and Resellers?

Don't buy tickets offered through eBay, or advertised by private individuals (not travel agencies) in newsgroup postings or on Internet bulletin boards. Private buyers (and sellers) of tickets run the risk of not being allowed to travel, being charged full fare by the airline, and/or being arrested for fraud and theft of services.

People who've bought tickets they can't use or refund, or accumulated more frequent flyer mileage credits than they can use, frequently try to auction or sell them through eBay, newsgroup postings, or Internet bulletin boards. Almost all of these sales are completely and unequivocally illegal, and in violation of airline rules. Tickets thus sold are void.

No airline ticket can be issued without having a specific traveler's name on it. All airline tickets are nontransferable, Government issued photo ID is required on all flights. Once a ticket is issued, it can be used only by the person whose name is on it. Anyone who claims to have a "ticket" for sale, without a name on it, is a criminal, a fool, or perhaps simply ignorant.

Frequent flyer mileage credits are also generally nontransferable. You can redeem your frequent flyer miles for a "free" ticket in a friend's name, but you must certify that they did not pay you for that ticket. If they did, it is void.

A variety of discount coupons and vouchers are issued by airlines for promotional purposes or as compensation for denied boarding, flight delays, etc. Sometimes these don't have a name on them, but almost invariably the fine print includes the rule, "Void if sold".

There simply isn't any legitimate way for a private individual to end up with valid tickets, legally salable, that are usable by any buyer.

A few airlines occasionally have held auctions of tickets on specific routes. These auctions have been infrequent and unpredictable, and the numbers of tickets sold have been tiny. For the most part, auctions of tickets by airlines have been a publicity gimmick, not a useful option for travelers.

But these ticket auctions by airlines, despite violating IATA and tariff rules, have been more or less legitimate—unlike most private auctions and sales of airline tickets.

links to their members, by country. If you don't find any agencies associated with any of these groups in the country where you are (e.g. Japan), that's probably because local regulations restrict discounting. You might still be able to import tickets at a discount from an agency in another country.

Multi-Stop International Tickets

The more complex your itinerary, the harder it is for a robot to figure out the best price. Some itineraries are too complicated for a CRS to come up with any price, even a high one. Airlines send these to human experts on their "rate desk" for manual pricing. Most online travel agencies either can't deal with them at all, or can't price them optimally. The only online travel agency that allows automated online pricing for customized international itineraries, without limiting the number of stopovers, is AirTreks.com (**www.airtreks.com**), where I work.

Some other agencies have online catalogs of sample multistop prices, but none of them allow interactive customization. Even AirTreks.com doesn't (yet) provide completely automated booking or ticketing for multistop itineraries. For complex trips, however, most people want to work with a human consultant by e-mail or phone before they buy their tickets.

HUMAN TRAVEL AGENTS, VIA E-MAIL

Don't assume that buying tickets on the Internet has to mean dealing only with robots, or giving up personal service from a human travel consultant. Don't think the big-name fully automated agencies are your best or only choice. There's nothing inherently superior about robots. They aren't necessarily cheaper, and they don't necessarily give you better advice.

For every travel agency with a fully automated Web-based reservation and ticketing robot, there are hundreds of agencies and human travel agents whose services are accessible by e-mail. Personal service and consulting by e-mail can offer you the best of both worlds: advice from a real person, freed from the necessity to do business with an agency in the same city, town, or time zone. Many of these have Web brochures that describe their services, qualifications, and areas of expertise, so you can often find them through careful keyword searches. Like most providers of professional services, though, the best way to find good travel agents is through referrals from satisfied clients.

ADVANCED TOPIC: HOW AIRLINE PRICING, RESERVATIONS, AND TICKETING WORK

The process of getting prices, making reservations for flights, and buying airline tickets is far more complicated than it appears. For those who are interested, here's a brief picture of the steps in the process, and what goes on below the surface of a seemingly simple ticket sale.

Much of the rest of this section is a primer in how to be your own travel agent. Consider it a sort of Cliff Notes for Travel School 101. This may, of course, be exactly what you hoped to avoid learning. Feel free to skip the section, or just the sidebars, if you don't want to deal with the technical details or don't care about the reasons for my advice.

How Do I Evaluate a Ticket Site, Or Know Which Site To Try?

The same factors determine which Web sites are best for you as determine which offline ticket sources are best for you. Being able to offer the best deals depends on: 1) to what set of prices a site or other travel source has access (especially prices not available elsewhere); 2) what tools they have for identifying the best price for a particular trip, at a particular time, according to your priorities; and 3) what tools they have to help you find the best time to buy your tickets. These are the factors you should look for and evaluate in deciding which sites are promising ones to try.

Access To Prices

You might assume that all travel Web sites have access to the same underlying database of available tickets and prices. But they don't. Airline ticket pricing is surprisingly decentralized, with prices being set not just by airlines but by individual travel agencies around the world. Even of those prices that are available somewhere on the Internet, many are available only from a single airline or agency source or site.

Not all air ticket prices are available on the Internet. The universe of prices—as represented in the diagram on the facing page— includes some that are available only on the Internet, many that are available from both online and offline sources, and many that are available only from offline sources.

As the diagram indicates, there is little overlap between most of the different groups of prices. This is one of the biggest reasons why no single site or source is consistently the best for a wide range of destinations and type of tickets.

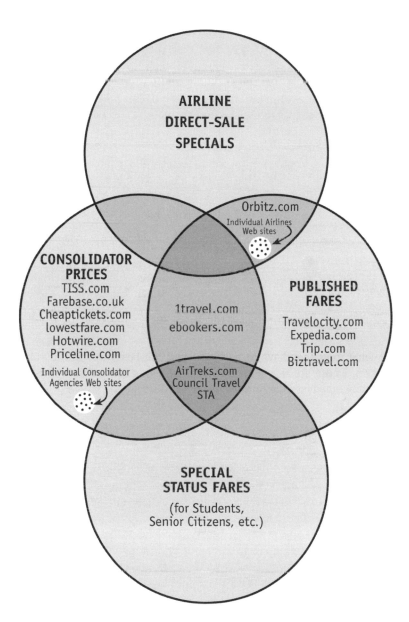

**AIRLINE
DIRECT-SALE
SPECIALS**

Orbitz.com
Individual Airlines
Web sites

**CONSOLIDATOR
PRICES**
TISS.com
Farebase.co.uk
Cheaptickets.com
lowestfare.com
Hotwire.com
Priceline.com

1travel.com
ebookers.com

**PUBLISHED
FARES**

Travelocity.com
Expedia.com
Trip.com
Biztravel.com

Individual Consolidator
Agencies Web sites

AirTreks.com
Council Travel
STA

**SPECIAL
STATUS FARES**

(for Students,
Senior Citizens, etc.)

*The universe of airfares include several different types of prices, as
shown above. Different Web sites include different types of prices,
and many sites list prices of only one type. No single Web site
includes all major types of ticket prices.*

So one of the first things to figure out about any site is this: from where does it draw its pool of prices? At present, there are three main sources of prices: published fares, consolidator prices, and airline direct-sale specials. The ideal Web site would offer comparisons of prices from all three sources, including not just one but a wide range of consolidators and many different airlines' current direct-sale specials. No such site yet exists, but you should look for several things.

Published Fares

Published fares are the official prices that are filed with and approved by governments, published in printed and electronic tariffs, and available for sale from any airline or accredited travel agent. Most airline ticket sites—except those that advertise themselves specifically as discount ticket sites—rely exclusively on the airlines' electronically-filed tariffs as their sources of price information, and thus give access only to published fares. That's about like offering a comprehensive database of automobile manufacturers' list prices, without including any information about the selling prices set by individual dealers, which can be significantly more or less than list prices. Don't be misled into thinking that published-fare sites give access to all prices or that the lowest official fare is necessarily the lowest available *price.* It is, nonetheless, essential to consider published fares, since much of the time for travel within the U.S. they are the only available option, and during sales they are sometimes the best deal even for international round-trips. So it's equally problematic that most consolidator Web sites don't include published fares.

Consolidator Prices

These are prices below the airlines' published fares that are set by individual travel agencies. For technical reasons related to the fact that domestic airfares in the United States are unregulated, consolidator prices are available primarily on international routes. For tickets from or within the United States, there is not yet any single or comparative source for prices from a wide range of consolidators. While more and more U.S. consolidators are making their prices available online, most of those prices are available only from individual consolidators' own Web sites. Some published-fare sites have added links to consolidator prices, but almost all such links turn out to be links to a single preferred consolidator (to which you might more easily have gone directly). Equally importantly, most consolidators do not yet make airfares available through any online source. The largest drawback to relying on online sources for ticket pricing is the possibility (for international tickets, the probability) that the lowest available price is from a consolidator accessible only by reading ads in the newspaper, calling travel agents on the phone, or visiting their offices—and nowhere on the Internet at all.

Airline Direct-Sale Specials

These "Internet specials" have rules that make them useless for most travelers, but when they are offered for a route and dates that you want, they are usually the cheapest way to go. Some of these are available only on the Internet, but what really distinguishes them is that they are available only if you buy tickets directly from the airline. For this reason, sites other than those of the specific airline making the offer can't sell tickets at these prices. It is possible, however, for other sites to index these prices, include them in price searches, and offer links to the airline sites through which you can reserve and purchase them if they are available and what best fits your budget and needs. Since one of the points of these prices for the airlines is that they only offer them directly, and pay no commissions to travel agencies for selling them, there's no money in it for other sites to refer people to the airlines (whose direct sales compete with those sites), and very few do. But inclusion of these airline-direct specials in price searches is definitely a feature to look for in a discount ticket site.

The bottom line here is that no matter how many millions of different prices are accessible through any given Web site, there is no single source for comparison shopping of all possible airline ticket prices. Claims by any Web site to be able to search "all available fares" or to "guarantee the lowest fare" are false and misleading at best, out-and-out lies at worst.

The only way to find and compare prices is either to pay a travel agent to use their expertise to choose options for you, or to do it yourself by reviewing prices on multiple Web sites from multiple sources of different types. Nor is it enough to compare prices from multiple sites if they are all published-fare sites with access to only the same limited subset of possible prices. At a minimum, you need to research at least one published-fare site, direct-sale specials from the airlines that serve your route, and prices from several consolidators specializing in your particular type of trip.

Access To Tools

Whether or not a site has access to a price becomes moot if it does

Why "Best Fare" Buttons Don't Find the Best Fare

Almost no serious effort has gone into price-optimization software developed to serve the interests of buyers rather than sellers. Instead, most Web sites' owners have focused their software development on the visible features of the user interface, and on tools to make it easier to buy, rather than to make it easier to find lower prices.

Because software development is being carried out to save Web sites' owners money, not to save travelers money, the situation is getting worse. Effective price-optimization software, like chess playing software that considers very large numbers of possible moves, places heavy demands on expensive computer resources. Operators of ticket Web sites, like all travel agencies, must pay per-inquiry fees for access to airlines' and computerized reservation systems' fare and seat-availability information. Newer, more sophisticated, "front-end" interfaces are thus being used to further *reduce* the number of inquiries made, the number of possibilities considered, and the amount of pricing and availability information revealed to each traveler—and thus the computer costs and CRS fees paid by the Web sites' operators.

not bring that option to your attention within at least the first few dozen possibilities it suggests.

Many sites have a "Find the Lowest Fare" button to click, and some even purport to offer a "guarantee" to find the lowest available fare. What does that mean? Few if any sites explain what their tools really do or how they work.

At best, such a tool will find the lowest fare of those available through that site, and I know of no one who has collected on any site's low fare guarantee if they found that a lower price was actually available elsewhere. Since prices change instantaneously and continuously, it would be impossible to prove that another offer was actually made at the same instant. A site's operator can always claim that the lower price wasn't actually available at the instant that they guaranteed that some higher price was the "lowest available." And all such guarantees I've seen are limited to guaranteeing the lowest published fare, which offers no guarantee that there won't be a consolidator price available somewhere else that is lower. (Technically speaking, a fare is an official price, and consolidator tickets show the official fare, if they show any dollar value at all, even when they are sold at a lower price.)

Most sites' "Best Fare Finder" tools can't be relied upon to find the lowest prices, even on their own sites. The dirtier secret, though, is that most don't even try. Sites operated by airlines, or by agents of the airline, have no interest in getting you the lowest fare. If giving you the opportunity to push a "find the lowest fare" button makes you more willing to pay whatever price you are offered after you push that button, fine. It's a useful sales tool for them. But few sites work as agents of customers or have any interest in investing in the development of software tools that would divert potential buyers of more expensive tickets to less expensive tickets.

Preference-mapping and price-optimization software distinguish one ticket-sales site from another in their ability to serve domestic U.S. travelers. For domestic tickets within the United States, the lowest price that fits your requirements is usually a published fare. There are relatively few consolidator prices for domestic tickets, and the airline direct-sale specials are usually so limited and restricted in available dates, etc. as not to be useful for most trips. And most major sites derive their information about published fares and seat availability from the same sources.

Preferences: What's the "Best" Ticket?

You may think your preference is simple: "I just want the cheapest price." But most travelers who say they want the lowest price don't really want the lowest conceivable price if it's for a ticket with too many other drawbacks (inconvenient times, long layovers, multiple stops etc.) Even for budget travelers and simple trips, preference structures are often surprisingly complex.

Most Web sites have only a single set of assumptions as to what your preferences are, and use the same preference profile for all visitors to the site. Worse, they rarely tell you what that profile is. How much weight is given to convenience of schedule, how much to price, and how much to airline preference? Rarely do they say. Often that's because they haven't constructed their own model of travelers preferences, or paid any conscious attention to what assumptions are embodied in the software used by their Web site. Typically, they rely on the tools provided by a computerized reservation service (CRS) to select which options to display and in which order.

A logical airline preference system, for example, would allow you to specify that frequent flyer mileage on Airline X is worth one

What's Your Preference?

What's the "best" combination of flights and price for you? Consider all of the factors that might go into your judgment:

- **Price.** Price is the most unambiguous, if complicated, criteria: there might be millions of possible prices, but at least each of them has a specific dollar value.
- **Travel dates.** Even business travelers who think of their travel dates as inflexible might be willing to stay over a Saturday night if it would save $1,000 on their airfare (and especially if their employer were willing to split the savings with them). Retired people traveling to visit friends or family may be willing to fly a week or more earlier or later for a better price. Someone looking for a weekend getaway may be willing to travel on any weekend during a two-month period—but only on a weekend. No one model can account for all these types of travelers.
- **Departure and arrival times.** Some people prefer to fly during the day; some people prefer night flights. And different people would put different dollar values on these preferences.
- **Total travel time.** This is fairly straightforward to calculate in hours, but harder to calculate in dollars. A business traveler might be willing to pay $200 per hour to get where they are going faster. A family of five traveling on vacation might value their time at $50/hour for the whole family, or $10 per person per hour.
- **Number of landings and takeoffs.** Most people prefer nonstop flights. But some people prefer to be able to get off the plane periodically, especially on very long flights. Some people don't care whether they spend their time on the ground or in the air, if it takes the same total amount of time to get where they are going.
- **Number of times you have to changes planes.** Because of fraudulent and deceptive practices by the airlines, it can be difficult to tell from an itinerary whether or not you will have to change planes. What's shown as a single flight and number may actually involve a change of planes and even a change of terminals. One major reason airlines label connecting flights as a single "through" flight is to trick flight-selection software into ranking these flights as "direct" flights, ahead of honestly-labeled connecting flights on other airlines.
- **Frequent flyer mileage.** It's actually fairly easy to calculate the value of frequent flyer mileage credits. First, figure out what ticket you'd be most likely to use your frequent flyer mileage for.

Then divide the amount you would normally expect to pay for that ticket by the number of frequent flyer miles you'd have to redeem for it. Typical values range from 0.5 to 2.0 cents per mile of frequent flyer credit. Multiply that by the length of the flight, and you know how much extra it's worth paying to fly on an airline that gives you mileage credit in that program. ($10 to $40, for example, for a round-trip ticket to a place a thousand miles away.) Most people don't think that systematically, and are willing to pay more for tickets that earn frequent flyer miles than the mileage is actually worth.

■ **Airline preferences.** Opinions of airline quality are highly subjective. How much more would you be willing to pay to fly on a particular one of your preferred airlines rather than a random airline? What's important to you: Perceived quality of service? Perceived safety? Seat pitch? Overhead bin size? Food? To complicate matters, most people have some airlines they would pay money to avoid, some airlines they would pay extra for, and a third group about which they are indifferent.

■ **Airport preferences.** Many cities and regions are served by more than one airport. Would you rather pay more to fly from or to a more convenient airport, or pay less to fly in or out of a less convenient one? How much more or less? If you won't have a car, or someone to meet you, you may be willing to use an alternate airport, but only if it's served by public transit, and only during the hours that public transit is available.

■ **How likely are you to cancel or change your plans?** The best-laid travel plans go awry more often than most people expect, for reasons that can be impossible to anticipate. How much extra would it be worth paying for refundable tickets or tickets that would cost less to change? Obviously, those valuations depend on how likely you are to want to make changes.

■ **What kind of trip is this?** You may have very different preferences for your business and pleasure travel, or for trips alone, with a partner, or with children. In order to accurately satisfy your desires, a flight selection robot would need to allow you to specify several different sets of preferences, and choose the one you wanted to use for each trip.

In short, which are the best flights, at the best price, for you is what a mathematician would describe as a problem in linear programming (a systems analyst might call it multi-variable optimization) rather than a simple ranking. Whatever you call it, it's not as easy a task as it looks at first glance.

cent per mile to you (because you need 25,000 mileage credits to get a ticket for which you would regularly pay $250), and would take that weighting into account in choosing which flight and fare options to show you. For a 5,000 mile round-trip coast-to-coast journey, you'd be willing to pay ($.01 x 5,000) = $50 more to fly on Airline X.

Instead, the most you can hope for from an online travel agency is that they'll let you indicate that you "prefer" a certain airline or airlines, without any opportunity to put a price on the preference. If you indicate a "preferred airline," that probably means that no other airlines will be shown at all, no matter how much cheaper they might be.

Similarly, rather than allowing you to specify how much you would be willing to pay to get to your destination more quickly, in dollars per hour, they simply rely on an arbitrary threshold value set by the CRS. This might determine, for example, that any connections more than two hours long would automatically be excluded, regardless of how much cheaper they might be.

When one Web site or online travel agency finds a set of flights and prices dramatically different than another, it's often because they are using different CRS's whose programming incorporates different assumptions about these sorts of criteria. Whatever is going on, they almost certainly won't tell you what their preference system is. If they rely on a CRS's "show the lowest fare" or "show the least expensive flights" function (as they usually do), they probably don't know and couldn't find out the underlying assumptions about your preferences even if they tried: no CRS I've spoken to is willing to say what criteria or process are actually used by their "best fare finder" command.

Tools For Finding the Tickets and Prices That Best Fit Your Preferences

Assuming that two Web sites have access to the same prices and flight availability information (which is true for pretty much all sites whose offerings are limited to published fares), and assuming that they don't have a sufficiently sophisticated preference model simultaneously to weigh and balance different factors that contribute to your choice (which is true of all sites in operation as of mid-2000), the only fundamental difference between them is what happens when you push the "Find Flights" or "Find the Best Fare" button.

Because the number of flight and fare possibilities is usually too large to permit an exhaustive search, successful airfare optimization software must rely on a selective search process that mimics, and incorporates the insights and methodology of human pricing experts. By and large, the experts at getting travelers lower prices don't work for the airlines or (largely airline owned or dominated) computerized reservation systems. Even if airlines and CRS's were motivated to do so, they wouldn't know where to begin in trying to build an automated "expert system" to identify which fare and flight options would best serve travelers' needs and desires.

Online travel agencies, assuming they wanted to switch from being airlines' agents to being travelers' agents, would face a different problem: the difficulty and cost of access to the necessary data.

As discussed in more detail in the section below, there is no simple database of available tickets with price tags on them. A travel agent, or for that matter an airline, must determine from separate data sources whether seats are available in a particular "booking class," and what price applies for those seats in that booking class on that schedule and route.

Information on published fares is readily available to travel agencies through the CRS's. Unpublished prices aren't publicly available or listed in CRS's. But travel agencies can, and a few do, assemble their own searchable databases of unpublished ticket prices available from their own unpublished deals with airlines and from other agencies.

Getting information on whether seats are available for these prices is another matter. CRS's have databases of which flights the airlines have told them have space available in which booking classes. But these are comparable to archives of "cached" copies of previously-retrieved Web pages: useful, but not a reliable indication of what you'd get if you requested the same page right now. Travel agencies, including online agencies' robots, have no direct access to these databases anyway. In order to find out whether an airline is willing to confirm seats for a particular fare on particular flights, a travel agency must send a query to the airline or CRS about availability on those specific flights, and wait for a response before they can send a query about another set of flights. Travel agencies are charged by CRS's for each query.

It's a fairly classic case of, "Those who know, don't say, and those who want to say, don't know." Those people who determine whether to confirm seats for specific prices on specific flights (or who set up the robots that do so) are the airlines, and they have no reason to reveal their internal decision-making process to their customers.

The CRS's have the most information of anybody but the airlines, but they are also the people most beholden to the airlines. Each time a

Too Many Questions? Or Too Few?

Most ticket-sales Web sites ask both too many and too few questions.

Travelers often complain about how many questions online travel agencies insist that they answer before they will show them any information about flights and prices. This resistance to being interrogated is quite justified: most of the information required on Web site "registration" forms is for the sites' use in marketing, not for helping you find what you want.

Yet, as I hope the earlier discussion of factors in choosing flights and fares made clear, different people have very different preferences. There is no "best" option for everyone, and no way to tell what's "best" for you without knowing your preferences and criteria.

If a travel agent—online or offline—doesn't ask you about your preferences, that means either (1) that they are making assumptions without asking or (2) that they aren't taking the factors they don't ask about into account at all in choosing which options to suggest.

A human travel agent may be able to make some reasonable assumptions from your appearance, what you say about your trip, the sort of neighborhood the agency is located in, what sort of customers typically contact them, and so forth. Sizing up customers, and figuring out what they want, is a key skill for travel agents. Experienced professionals become experts at guessing how travelers would answer questions that haven't even occurred to them, and defining preferences that their clients couldn't articulate explicitly or quantitatively.

An online travel agency, on the other hand, especially a robotic one, doesn't know anything about you that you don't tell them explicitly. Online travel agencies thus must choose between

reservation is made through a CRS, the airline pays the CRS $3 or so for each flight segment. With online travel agencies' commissions capped at $10 per ticket, the CRS gets paid more than the online travel agency for a typical four-segment round-trip on connecting flights.

Travel agencies and consumers are reduced to playing a sort of "20 questions" with the airlines, either directly or through a CRS, to find out what's really available. If they tried to ask about seat avail-

the risk of driving away business by asking lots of questions about your preferences before they answer any of their would-be customers' questions about flights and fares; making a set of one-size-misfits-all assumptions about what people want (which airlines they do and don't like, the relative importance they place on time versus money, and so forth); or foregoing any attempt at an overall ranking of choices.

Almost all current online agencies have chosen the last option, and given up on any attempt at overall prioritization. It's more important to them to ask marketing questions, rather than questions that would help them better serve you. And it would be too difficult and expensive for them to take all your preferences into account, anyway, even if they asked enough questions to find out what they are.

Instead of trying to consider many factors at once, they allow you to select options according to only one variable at a time. You can, on the best airline ticket Web sites, request a display of the flights with the lowest fares, or the most direct flights, or the flights on a specific airline. What you can't yet do on any Web site is request a set of options that takes into consideration your preferences of airlines, schedules, price, or any other set of multiple criteria.

There can be tens or hundreds of thousands of possible flights for even a seemingly simple trip. With so many choices, the best option—if all the things that are important to you are taken into account—may not be in the top choices ranked according to any single factor. The option that you would prefer overall, if you were aware of it, might rank 5th out of 10 airline options, 100th out of 1,000 fare options, and 1,000th out of 100,000 schedule options. You won't even know that this is a possible choice if the site only enables you to look at one factor at a time.

ability on every possible flight, it would take too long and cost them too much in CRS query fees. Their only hope is to emulate the behavior of skilled human travel agents, who selectively query the CRS for availability on the flights that they think are most likely to be available for the best prices.

Human chess masters, similarly, use their expertise to focus their analysis on a limited number of promising possibilities. Chess playing robots rely more on exhaustive brute-force evaluation of as many choices as possible. But CRS query fees, deliberate limitations of the types of queries CRS's allow, and the time CRS's and airlines take to respond to each query, essentially rule out such a brute-force approach to finding the best flights and prices for which seats are available. ITA Software (see below) claims to have done so, but they haven't offered any explanation as to how they could do so without generating too many costly CRS queries. It's likely that they actually rely on cached data from previous availability queries, not the real-time itinerary-specific availability queries for each and every flight possibility that they claim to use.

In theory, an online travel agency could charge service fees to cover the CRS and computer costs of providing a price-optimization system, but that appears highly unlikely to happen. Existing online travel agencies have been much less willing than offline agencies to charge fees to cover their costs, even though airlines pay them lower commissions than they pay offline agencies. So most online agencies will continue to use simplistic flight selection systems that minimize the costs to the agencies, rather than maximizing value to consumers.

Systems For Tracking and Comparing Prices Over Time

Among travelers' most common questions is, "When is the best time for me to buy my tickets?" Unfortunately, neither human nor Internet travel agents can give you a definitive answer to this question.

Prices vary substantially with time, in ways that are extremely difficult for even experts to anticipate. The seemingly random character and bizarre rules of airline ticket sales are no accident: airlines try very hard to make their sales unpredictable. If everyone knew tickets would be on sale for less tomorrow, no one would buy them at today's higher prices. It doesn't help that airlines refer to most of their prices as "discount" or "sale" prices. "The sale ends tomorrow" means little or nothing when you know there'll probably be another sale starting the day after tomorrow. The question is whether today's, tomorrow's, next week's, or next month's sale will offer the lowest prices for travel on your desired dates. If you expect that a later sale will be cheaper than the current one, there's the additional question of whether you can expect seats to be available when that lower price (space permitting) is offered. Keep in mind that there's no meaningful guarantee that space will be available for an airline's advertised price.

How, then, can you make any intelligent decision about whether to buy tickets now or wait and hope for a better price later, closer to your travel date? Obviously, the airlines are no help. They'll always deny that any future sale is contemplated. They are probably being honest, the people you talk to at an airline almost certainly aren't the ones who set prices. And because of complaints that airlines were using announcements of future price changes as signals to each other in jointly setting prices, U.S. airlines are currently forbidden to announce most price changes in advance. One option is to consult a human travel agent who regularly sells tickets on the route in question, and has a feel

BUYING TICKETS IN ADVANCE—

In general, the further in advance you buy your tickets the better price you'll get. And you can expect to have to pay substantially more if you buy tickets less than two weeks in advance for almost any trip. But that's because of advance purchase requirements, and because the lowest-priced seats on the cheapest airlines are usually the first to sell out, not because the prices (if space is available) are any lower further in advance.

for trends in prices and availability of seats. The advantage to this is that travel agents who make many reservations and sell many tickets on a particular route can offer advice about both prices and availability of seats. The disadvantage is that no one travel agent can closely track fares and availability on more than a handful of routes. If you're going someplace to which they don't sell tickets regularly, a travel agent may not have much more idea than you do what a "typical" price is, or how far in advance to expect the cheap seats for your dates to sell out.

The alternative is an Internet service that shows you trends in prices over time. Some online travel agencies including Travelocity .com and Expedia.com offer features that will track prices on a specific route, or e-mail you when those prices change by more than a certain amount or percentage.

The advantage to these price tracking services is that, being automated, they can track prices even on obscure routes, and can automatically notify you when prices drop. The disadvantage to Internet price tracking services is that they only track fares, not availability of seats. There are thousands of fares between any two airports, all with different rules, most of them not applicable to any given trip, and none with any guarantee that seats will be available. So a graph of the lowest of these fares in effect on each date may indicate little or nothing about the trends in average amounts that travelers are actually paying. The graph can be greatly distorted by a sale fare that applies only to very limited travel dates for which very limited space is available.

Finally, a graph of published fares, or even of average prices paid by customers of a published-fare-only Internet travel agency, says nothing about trends in unpublished prices. For the same reasons that no one has comprehensive comparative information about any aspect of unpublished prices, no Web site is able to offer a meaningful comparison of current unpublished prices with those at other times. Fortunately, however, unpublished prices are more stable than published fares, and less prone to short-term sales. If you're buying tickets at unpublished prices, when to buy your tickets is a simpler question: buy them as far in advance as any unpublished prices are available.

When To Buy

What about published fares? How should you decide when to buy your tickets? Unless you have a relationship with a skilled human travel agent who regularly works with travelers on the particular route you're interested in, you have to guess. And once you've bought your tickets, your decision is made. Put it out of your mind. There's usually nothing you can do if a lower price is offered later. In theory, airlines will sometimes allow you to exchange a ticket for a cheaper ticket for the same flights and dates, if a lower price is offered. In practice, the circumstances in which this is allowed are extremely restricted: among others, seats must be available for the new, cheaper fare on the exact same flights as the original tickets.

No law requires airlines to reissue tickets for lower fares, or restricts what they can charge for this. Don't assume it will be possible unless you've been told so, in writing, before buying your tickets. Having a ticket reissued for a lower fare, when possible, is usually subject to an airline penalty of at least $75. Travel agencies, including online agencies, can add whatever service fees they like as long as they are disclosed up front (typically in the fine print). If the airline charges $75 to have a ticket reissued, and the travel agency charges $25, the fare has to drop by at least $100 before there is any chance that you might be able to get some money back. You can always ask the agency or airline from which you bought your tickets if they can be reissued for a lower fare, but usually it's a waste of time.

Airline Tickets As a Commodity? Not.

The first temptation of people outside the airline or travel industry is to conceptualize air travel and air tickets as a commodity like pork bellies or coal: transportation from Point A to Point B. They imagine that airlines have, in effect, put a price tag on each seat on each flight. Finding the cheapest ticket, they conclude, is a matter of finding the lowest price tag on flights corresponding to one's desired trip. While a large task, this would be a straightforward one, comparable to what is done by any search engine in looking through a large database of possibilities.

No major airline works anything like that. Why not? There are many reasons, but perhaps the most significant is that a seat on a particular flight may be sold as part of any number of different journeys, for which different prices are appropriate. Someone on a flight from Dallas to Atlanta may be traveling on a one-way ticket from Dallas to Atlanta. But more likely they'll be taking that flight to connect with one or more other flights to or from someplace else, and/or as part of a round-trip. On the same plane, one person might be traveling from Dallas to Raleigh by way of Atlanta, returning four days later. Another might be on their way back from Atlanta to Austin, on the return leg of the trip that began three weeks earlier. It's quite possible that no two people on that plane will be traveling on the same itinerary.

For reasons of supply and demand, the price from A to C, via B, is not necessarily the sum of the prices from A to B and B to C. And the price of a round-trip ticket is usually less than twice the price of a one-way ticket. Given all this, there is no way airlines can put a single price tag on a seat. They don't, so there is no "database of ticket prices."

Instead, each airline has two independent systems: one for keeping track of prices (fares and rules), and another for keeping track of available seats. A "fare" is not a price for any specific seat on a specific plane. A fare is a price for a set of reservations satisfying certain rules. These rules define what route(s) you must follow, what airline(s) you must travel on, what season(s) or date(s) or times of day you may travel, whether you have to travel round-trip, how long you may stay, how far in advance you may buy your tickets, and many other conditions that you must satisfy in order to be eligible for the fare. If your reservations satisfy all the rules of the fare, you can buy tickets at the specified price. It's actually not uncommon for a fare to be published, and listed in all the online and offline databases of fares, even though there is no set of flights that satisfies the rules of the fare. Each fare (price and corresponding set of rules) is assigned a "fare basis code"—a string of letters and digits—which is shown on each ticket issued at that fare. The fare basis code on the ticket serves as a shorthand way of identifying the rules governing the use of that ticket, and is used to determine if the ticket can be changed, refunded, etc.

Airlines are the ones who determine the fares, and the fare rules. Their sole goal in setting fares and rules is to maximize their

Booking Class—Price Per Mile

One of the most important conditions of any fare is the "booking class" in which reservations must be made to qualify for the fare. Different booking classes are used to distinguish business-class or first-class reservations from coach-class reservations. More importantly, different booking classes are used within the same cabin on the plane and class of actual service, especially in coach, to distinguish reservations made at different prices. Typically, there are anywhere from 5 to 15 coach booking classes, designated by letters, even though people booked in class Q, Y, Z, or whatever are seated together indiscriminately in the coach/economy cabin.

Booking classes correspond roughly to different revenue levels (i.e how many cents you have paid per mile of flight). Many different fares, between many different places, may all have to be booked in the same class. But in general the airline tries to set up the fare rules so that all the tickets booked in the same class are priced about the same in cents per mile flown.

profits by ensuring that each traveler pays as much as they are willing. The more heavily booked a flight, the more demand there probably is for that flight, and the more the airline figures they can charge for the remaining seats. So as more and more reservations are made on a specific flight, the airline will refuse to confirm reservations in the lowest-revenue booking classes. When the flight is fully booked, or almost so, the airline will confirm reservations only in the booking class used for the highest fares.

Total ticket price would be a poor indicator of how much you are paying for a specific flight. One person might be paying twice as much for their ticket as a another person on the same flight, but the first person's ticket might include a connection to a much longer flight, and actually be much cheaper per mile. Managing availability by booking class, rather than by fare, is a clever way for airlines to control prices and revenues while maximizing their profits.

It's actually much more complicated than this: because of overbooking, the number of reservations an airline is willing to confirm varies, and doesn't correspond exactly to the capacity of the plane. For example, an airline will almost always confirm one or two more people in the highest-fare booking class even on a heavily overbooked plane. The price of "bribing" someone to take another flight, or in the worst case to compensate someone for being bumped involuntarily, is less than the profit from a full-fare ticket.

Usually, for convenience, the booking class in which reservations are to be made is the same as the first letter of the fare basis code. But there are many exceptions, especially for consolidator tickets. The same fare basis codes may permit reservations to be made in several different booking classes, or may require reservations for different legs of a set of connecting flights to be booked in different classes. This causes lots of confusion: there's no way to know if someone talking about "a Q ticket" is referring to a ticket for which reservations were made in booking class Q, or a ticket issued at a fare basis beginning with the letter Q. Most people don't realize that these could be different.

Airlines change the availability of seats in specific booking classes constantly, in response to changing booking levels on each flight. The only way to know for sure if seats can be confirmed in a specific booking class on a specific flight is to send a confirmation request to the airline for a specific number of seats. This is why all information about which fares and prices are "available" is inherently unreliable, and you can never be sure of what is available until you have made confirmed reservations.

In order to tell whether a particular flight can be used to construct an itinerary that will qualify for a particular fare, you need to know whether enough seats are available on that flight in the booking class required for that fare. CRS's and airlines permit travel agents to request availability and see how many seats an airline is willing to confirm in each booking class on a particular flight. Unfortunately, Internet travel services hide booking classes from their customers, so as to reduce the number of fee-based queries they send to the CRS's. Human travel agents can place you on a "waiting list" for a flight on which space isn't currently available, but that isn't possible through any automated Internet ticket sales site.

Pricing and Availability

Making reservations for a specific price isn't a one-step process. Many reservations on particular flights in particular booking classes doesn't qualify for any fare. And no seats in the proper booking class may be available to qualify for a particular fare. The trick is to find a set of suitable flights on which space is, when requested, available in the right booking classes to satisfy the rules of a desirable fare.

To search exhaustively for the lowest available fare, you would first need to find all the fares that might apply, if space is available, on your desired route and dates. Then you would need to ask the airline about availability for each combination of flights for each fare, starting with the cheapest. If no space was available on any of the flight combinations for the lowest fare, you would move on to the next cheapest, and do the same until you found seats available that qualify for some fare.

With thousands of possible fares, and millions of possible flight combinations for each of them, this would require a prohibitive amount of time and be prohibitively costly in CRS query fees. No travel agent or airline, and no Web site, actually does this.

Rather, smart human travel agents and the more sophisticated online travel agencies use an iterative and heuristic process: in other words, they make educated guesses about which flights are likely to have space available in which booking classes, and for which fares qualifying space is likely to be available, and prioritize their limited number of queries to CRS's or airlines accordingly.

Without access to complete fare rules, to displays of availability by flight and booking class, and the ability to make independent queries about availability and prices, there's no way you can do this yourself. It used to be possible, to a degree, with Easy Sabre, but no current online ticket sales system gives the public access to the necessary tools to really perform for themselves this central task of the travel agent. Your choices are limited to those suggested by whatever "travel agent emulation" robot an automated online travel agency provides.

Who Sets Ticket Prices?

There are two kinds of airline ticket prices: official fares published by airlines, and "consolidator" prices set by discount travel agencies.

Domestic U.S. airfares were deregulated in 1978. For domestic fares within the United States, since deregulation, airlines can publish pretty much any fares they want, and change them at whim. If they want to lower the fare, they publish a lower fare. Once published, a fare is available directly from the airline as well as from all its "appointed" agents, including brick-and-mortar travel agencies, online agencies, and those that sell both online and offline.

International airfares, on the other hand, remain regulated. International aviation treaties between most countries place restrictions on flights, routes, and fares; require that fares be filed with, and approved by, both governments before they take effect; and prohibit airlines from selling tickets at any prices except those in official tariffs (published and approved fares). Aside from national and protectionist purposes, these rules are intended to insure a degree of fairness: all passengers whose itineraries satisfy the same rules (origin and destination cities, routing, airlines(s), flight(s), booking class(es), duration of stay, season, advance purchase, etc.) are entitled to the same fare specified in the public tariff.

In accordance with those treaties, federal law in the United States (and the law in most other countries) forbids international ticket sales at off-tariff prices. The U.S. government is trying to renegotiate the aviation treaties to eliminate the requirement for government approval or publication of fare tariffs, so that airlines could charge each customer a different price. (Although, to protect U.S.-based airlines against foreign competitors with lower labor costs, the U.S. government wants to keep the protectionist rule against foreign airlines operating within the United States.) In the meantime, the United States can't repeal the law against off-tariff sales without violating reciprocal treaty obligations to other countries. This would jeopardize continued international air service with those countries that enforce IATA rules, local laws, and/or international treaties against off-tariff ticket sales. So the law remains on the books in the United States, but the government exercises its discretion not to enforce it. This is what gives consolidator (below-tariff) tickets their peculiar "gray market" status in the United States: officially illegal, but equally officially tolerated, and even officially declared a good thing by the federal government. Official fares published by the airlines thus give little indication of the actual prices at which agents sell tickets on those airlines, especially on international routes.

The differences between domestic and international airfares are largely due to the differences in how they are or aren't regulated. Unlike deregulated domestic U.S. airfares, international airfares are regulated both by international treaties and by an international airline price-setting association, the International Air Transportation Association (IATA).

It's worth noting that every U.S.-based airline operating scheduled international passenger flights has voluntarily joined IATA. U.S. airlines' invocations of "open markets," "free trade," and "open skies" can be dismissed as completely hypocritical and self-serving drivel until such time as they exercise their right to withdraw from IATA, as any of them could at any time. U.S. airlines are allowed to participate in IATA "traffic conferences" only because of a special exemption granted them from U.S. anti-trust laws which normally forbid such industry-wide price-setting.

Why do airlines join IATA? To keep prices, and airlines' profits,

Why Buy Tickets Online Even if They Aren't Necessarily Cheaper?

By now it should be clear that the cheapest tickets aren't necessarily available online, and that you aren't necessarily more likely to find better prices by buying tickets online.

Does that mean that there's no reason to buy your airline tickets, or to reserve and purchase other travel products, on the Internet? Not at all. Price may be the first thing on people's minds when they start shopping for tickets on the Internet, but there are plenty of other, more real, advantages to Internet travel shopping. For the most part, those who prefer buying tickets on the Internet are those who are not focused primarily on price, but on other factors.

■ **Convenience and speed.** Especially for frequent travelers who don't feel a need to do much comparison shopping, reservations can be made and tickets purchased online in a fraction of the time it would take to deal with a travel agent. It takes a little time to enter your personal information the first time you use a new ticket sales Web site, and to figure out how to use it. So occasional travelers, or those who care about price and thus need to check options from several different sources, may find it more convenient to pay a travel agent to do their comparison shopping for them. But once you have registered, created a profile, and gotten used to how a site works, it's the easiest way to arrange tickets for simple trips.

■ **(Perception of) Control.** Dealing with a travel agent or an airline in person or on the phone can be very disempowering. You always know that you don't have complete information about your choices. Someone else is always choosing which options to tell you about. You never know if there's some other choice you would have preferred, but that they didn't mention. Online ticket sales sites don't really put you in control, or show you all your options, either. You are at the mercy of hidden choices embedded in the logic of their programming. But they give you a very convincing, and gratifying, *sense* of having access to limitless possibilities, and of being in control. I suspect that this sense of empowerment is the strongest factor driving people to buy their tickets online.

Nothing wrong with empowerment. Just realize that in this case it's only a "feel-good" factor.

■ **Avoidance of service fees.** Competent travel agencies that provide human service have to charge service fees, or incorporate them in their prices. Someone has to pay for their services, or they couldn't offer them. More and more, the only way to buy tickets without being surcharged will be through online robots. Even airlines themselves are likely to start charging concierge fees for tickets purchased from human salespeople, whether by phone or at airline ticket offices. The clear precedent here is in banking: when ATMs were first introduced, banks had to pay people to get them to use ATMs. Once ATMs were well-established, banks started charging for teller transactions. Likewise with online stock trading. The same thing is already happening with airline tickets. As with bank tellers or stockbrokers, the question is whether the personal service and advice of a human travel agent is worth the price.

■ **Exclusive online offers.** Some prices are available only through online sources. These aren't necessarily the best deal, but if you don't check what's available on the Internet you won't find out about them at all. In the future, more and more tickets and other travel products will be cheaper and/or exclusively available online, so you will have to learn to deal with the online marketplace or miss out on these deals.

■ **Access to specialized products and services.** If you're going someplace, doing something, or have a special interest that's even a little out of the ordinary, you may not find any local travel agent with the necessary expertise to help you. The Internet allows you to tap the national or even global range of specialized travel agencies and travel services.

Even if the thing that first brought you to the Internet to shop for travel was the lure of, "Everything will be cheaper on the Internet," any of these reasons may be sufficient cause to keep doing your travel shopping online even when it sometimes costs more that way. If I seem pessimistic about getting the best prices on the Internet, that's not because I'm pessimistic about buying tickets online. I just think it's more likely to make more sense for travelers for whom price is a lower priority.

User Interfaces and Computerized Reservation Systems

Technically sophisticated travelers may wonder how what they see when they visit a ticket sales Web site compares with what they would see if they were able to look over a travel agent's shoulder. Most would be surprised at how much difference there is, not just in what the screen looks like but in what functional tools are available.

Human travel agents can use either a command-line or a graphical user interface to a CRS. The widest range of options in a fare or flight request can be specified as command line options. This should be no surprise: a graphical user interface (GUI) is typically easier to learn, at least for simple tasks. But a skilled "power user" (such as a travel agent who uses a CRS all day every day) can usually do more, more quickly, from a command line.

The graphical user interfaces (GUI's) available to travel agents implement only a limited subset of the command line CRS options. The GUI's to CRS's available to the public through ticket-sales Web sites implement an even smaller subset of command options.

Easy Sabre—the only command line interface to a CRS ever made available to the public—was discontinued precisely because it gave travelers more information than the airlines wanted, and enabled them to use more computing resources than the CRS that supplied Easy Sabre wanted. Those who used Easy Sabre shouldn't be fooled, however: it used a completely different command line format and syntax than travel agent's Sabre, and let you use only a few of the Sabre commands.

The limiting factor in how many customers can be served by an airline ticket sales robot, and how much it costs to serve them, is how much demand is put on the CRS computers by multiple, complex, or processor-intensive queries. Travel agencies, including online travel agencies, are charged by how many and what type of commands in queries they (or their robots) send to the CRS. The clear trend in ticket sales Web sites is to hide more and more of the price and flight optimization logic, and give travelers access to *fewer* tools, so as to limit the load on the CRS.

artificially high of course. International airfares are set by international agreement and regulated by the airline association, IATA. Most international airlines are closely related to, if not directly owned by, their national governments. Most governments in turn have an interest in protecting the profits of their national airline, and the IATA fares are therefore set artificially high.

As a condition of membership in IATA, airlines agree (voluntarily, remember) to sell tickets only at IATA-approved prices. IATA rules officially prohibit discounting, and in some countries these rules are actually enforced—one reason some countries have no local ticket discounters (although tickets originating in those countries can often be bought, over the Internet, from agencies in countries where off-tariff discounting is tolerated).

Airlines like IATA because it raises the prices paid by price-insensitive business travelers. But it's not the whole story. If airlines sold tickets only at IATA fares, they would have too many empty seats that might be salable at less-than-official prices.

The revenue-maximization problem for the airlines is how to get some money for seats that can't be filled at official fares, without destroying the benefits of belonging to IATA by allowing people who would be willing to pay full fare to get away with paying any less.

The system the airlines have developed for preserving IATA while actually selling discounted tickets at less than official fares relies on the intermediary of the travel agency, and the loophole that neither IATA nor international airfare treaties restricts how much commission an airline can pay an agent for selling a ticket. So the airline can pay a large commission to a travel agent, then turn its back and avert its eyes while the travel agent rebates some portion of the commission to the traveler.

All sales of international tickets on scheduled airlines at less than official fares are made through travel agencies, not directly by the airlines, and ultimately depend on rebating of commissions by travel agents to customers. This is how travel agencies can and do, quite legally, offer lower prices for international tickets than the airlines themselves.

Airlines know what is happening, of course, but they have to pretend they don't. In order to maintain plausible deniability and keep their hands clean with IATA and the governments of countries that enforce the rules against off-tariff discounting, airlines must maintain the fiction that all tickets are sold at official fares. Since airlines cannot admit that they are even aware of discounting, airlines cannot admit to any knowledge of agents' actual discounted selling

Airline Ticket Comparison Shopping Sites?

Two Web sites claim to offer one-click comparisons of other sites' airline ticket prices: QIXO.com and Farechase.com. An airfare search engine that frees you from the need to do comparison shopping on different Web sites would be a great thing. But these sites don't work well, and they probably can't work well without the cooperation of the Web sites from which they are getting prices—cooperation which they don't have and don't seem likely to get.

The model for QIXO.com and Farechase.com is Farebase.co.uk. Farebase gets prices in database format from a wide range of UK consolidators. Farebase compiles them into its own database, so its Web site puts no direct load on the consolidators' systems.

Farechase.com and QIXO.com haven't yet been able to get the cooperation of any of the online agencies or suppliers whose prices they want to redisplay. Published-fare agencies like Travelocity.com and Expedia.com are least likely to cooperate, since their prices are likely to compare unfavorably with those from consolidators. The sites that are happiest with QIXO.com and Farechase.com are some of the most disreputable and unreliable.

Since other agencies won't give Farechase.com or QIXO.com their databases, these "comparison" sites use a different technique.

prices. Strange but true: by the nature of the system of discounting, airlines do not usually know themselves which agents or at what prices their tickets are most cheaply sold (and couldn't admit to knowing even if they did).

All official fares are "published" in tariffs distributed electronically by IATA, the Airline Tariff Publishing Co. (ATPCO) **www.atpco.net**, and the computerized reservation systems (CRS) and airline databases such as Sabre, Apollo, Amadeus, Worldspan, Gabriel, and (in the works) GENESIS. By the very nature of the IATA system, airlines cannot admit any knowledge of the fact that agents are selling tickets for less than the official fares. So only published fares are shown in any CRS. No CRS—and no online travel agency or Web site that depends on CRS pricing information—contains any publicly accessible information on agents' actual discounted selling prices.

The glut of official international fare information available through online travel agencies that rely on CRS's, including Trave-

When you request a price from Farechase.com or QIXO.com, their robot logs into a bunch of other sites (impersonating a human user) and requests a price for your trip. When the answers come back from the other sites, they are compiled into one display.

This "screen scraping" approach is inherently slow, buggy, and vulnerable to disruption by even minor changes in the screen layout or user interface of the other sites. It also alienates the sites being searched: one query to QIXO.com or Farechase.com can result in hundreds of queries for the same itinerary to the same CRS, for which the other sites—not QIXO.com or Farechase.com—have to pay.

A site that doesn't want QIXO.com or Farechase.com to show its prices could either go to court to block them on grounds of copyright theft or virtual trespass (as eBay has done, thus far successfully, with auction comparison sites), give the comparison sites wrong answers, or simply block them from the site. Farechase.com and QIXO.com often are unable to get prices from most of the other sites they try to query. Even when QIXO.com or Farechase.com reports a price from another site, I've often been able to get a lower price directly from the same site.

locity.com, Expedia.com, and most others, is deceptively comprehensive-seeming and impressive. But it's fundamentally useless in finding discounted prices. If you want to pay less than the official international fare, you have to buy your ticket from an agent who gives discounts, not directly from an airline or other source that is limited to published fares.

Each airline has many consolidators. Different consolidators have different agreements with the airlines, based on sales volume and other factors. Airlines may offer different deals to different agents in the same country, or they may offer completely different deals along the same routes to agents in different countries. Each consolidator then sets their wholesale prices independently, based on their airline contracts and their own markup. Each retail agency that sells tickets from consolidators adds a different retail markup.

Like published fares, each discounted consolidator price corresponds to a set of rules governing the airline(s), routing(s), booking class(es), schedule, trip duration, advance purchase, etc., required for a set of reservations to qualify for that price. The rules of a consolidator price are a combination of the rules of the published fare at which the tickets are officially issued, as modified by the terms of the consolidator's contract with the airline. (Once issued, the ticket is governed by the rules of the fare shown on it, regardless of the typically lower price actually paid, except as modified by "endorsements" or rule codes written or printed on the ticket.)

The result of all this is that for each published fare there may be tens of thousands of different prices for otherwise identical tickets on the same route, issued by different consolidators and sold by different retail travel agencies across the country and around the world. *Most* ticket prices are set by individual travel agencies, based on their wholesale ticket sources and their sources' consolidator contracts with airline's local sales offices. The vast and seemingly definitive databases of millions of published *fares* accessible through airline and published-fare Web sites are but a tiny fraction—largely clustered toward the high end of the price scale—of the much larger universe of all published and unpublished airline ticket *prices*.

Disparities from country to country in discount ticket pricing are most important when you are shopping for complex and multi-stop international tickets. For more on how consolidators work, and the global wholesale market in discounted tickets, see my FAQs about discounted international airline tickets at hasbrouck.org/faq, and my other book in this series, focusing on international airfares and travel, *The Practical Nomad: How to Travel Around the World.*

Unfortunately, there is no single Web site or offline source—not even a bad one—for comparing prices from different consolidators in the United States. Many consolidators are strictly wholesalers anyway, and won't deal directly with the public. You can get consolidator tickets only through retail agencies that will make reservations for you, and have your tickets issued by a wholesale consolidator. Each consolidator, and each retail agency that sells consolidator tickets, has a completely separate system—not necessarily automated—for keeping track of their prices.

Farebase offers online access to prices from several dozen major U.K. consolidators. But the site doesn't enable you to check availability of seats—i.e., the prices you are shown may be sold out—and it refers you to local U.K. agents of varying competence, not the consolidators themselves. Most agents listed in Farebase won't sell to customers outside the United Kingdom. There's clearly a niche for a service and Web site like this in the United States, but none yet exists.

Reservations and Ticketing

People often speak of "booking a ticket." In reality, making a "booking" or reservation is entirely separate from buying a ticket. The term "booking" is a holdover from the days when reservations were literally written in a book with a page for the list of passengers on each flight, as is still done in some flights to the most remote places. It's possible to make reservations without buying a ticket, or to buy an "open" ticket without making reservations. It's sometimes possible (although difficult, counterproductive, and definitely not recommended) to make reservations through one airline and buy tickets from another, or to make reservations through a travel agency and buy the tickets directly from the airline.

Except with electronic tickets, the airline generally doesn't know if tickets have been issued for a particular reservation, or if reservations have been made for a particular ticket. Even when reservations are made, and tickets issued, by the same travel agency through the same CRS, they are reported and tracked through separate auditing channels. For years, travel agencies in the United States have reported their ticket sales to the airlines only once a week, on paper. Airlines are trying to force agencies to issue only e-tickets and to report sales daily, electronically, but agencies are actively fighting this.

Airlines' biggest reason for wanting to switch from paper tickets to e-tickets is to establish a positive one-to-one real-time correspondence between reservations and tickets. This will enable them to crack down on many tricks that enable people to pay less, such as buying a round-trip ticket for a one-way journey to avoid paying the higher one-way fare. With an electronic ticket, they can tell that you didn't use half the ticket. Under the terms of your ticket purchase contract, they can then bill you for the difference between the round-trip price you paid and the higher one-way fare for your actual trip.

At present, airlines can't tell when a travel agency has issued a ticket corresponding to a particular reservation unless an e-ticket has been issued. That makes it possible, in most cases, for travel agencies to hold reservations for at least a day, sometimes up to a week, before you have to decide whether to buy the tickets. This isn't possible online. Airline reservations and ticketing procedures, computer systems, and CRS's were designed for internal use, not for public accessibility. Airlines have been justifiably unwilling to allow travelers to make their own reservations and hold confirmed seats without paying for them at the same time. They are afraid of having people holding speculative, unticketed reservations that cause other people who are ready to pay to be told that no seats are available. So automated online

Electronic Tickets, Electronic Visas, and Ticketless Travel

While airlines are trying to promote e-tickets and ticketless travel as a convenience to passengers, e-tickets were developed and are being promoted solely to serve the interests of the airlines, not those of passengers. For your own protection, insist on paper tickets whenever possible. They may cost you an extra $10-20 per issued ticket (a few airlines and agencies already surcharge paper tickets, and others are expected to follow suit), but they are worth it. Most users of e-tickets don't realize their drawbacks, and wouldn't use them if they did. The tying of tickets to reservations, as discussed in the main text, isn't the only drawback to e-tickets. Here are some additional advantages of paper tickets, especially for international travel and travel anywhere outside the First World:

■ Flights may still operate when reservation computers are down, but only holders of paper tickets are transported, since e-tickets can't be verified offline. E-ticket holders get left behind.

■ For all tickets paid for by credit card over the Internet or by phone, airlines reserve the right to inspect the credit card and require the cardholder's signature when you check in. Because airlines only make occasional spot checks of credit cards, most people don't realize that this is possible. Many people purchase e-tickets for family members or business associates as a way to avoid the cost and risk of mailing tickets. But there's a risk in this: If someone else pays for e-tickets, and isn't present with their credit card when you check in, or if you buy your own tickets but don't have the credit card you used with you when you check in, you will be denied boarding unless you can come up with alternate payment on the spot. This isn't required with paper tickets. Spot checks of credit cards used to pay for e-tickets are rare, but they do happen. I've seen some very distraught travelers being turned away from flights paid for as e-tickets by spouses, colleagues, or other people who weren't there to show their credit card and sign a charge slip when they tried to check in.

■ For international travel, tickets are required by many countries (including, for most foreign visitors, the United States) as proof of onward or return transportation for immigration purposes. Since airlines can't usually see reservations or e-tickets on other airlines, onward or return travel on a different airline can only be demonstrated by a paper ticket. A traveler arriving in a country on one airline, and leaving on an e-ticket on another, is currently unable to provide any proof of onward transportation at check-in, and is likely to be refused passage.

Airlines are developing interline links, and connections to immigration authorities, for just this purpose. But early indications are not promising. The prototype "Electronic Travel Authorization" (ETA) system, including links to airline ticketing databases, was implemented in 1997 in Australia. Although the Australian government and the cooperating airlines assure travelers that they do not need paper proof of their tickets or ETAs, I've had several clients who found the ETA links down at their point of departure when they checked in for flights to Australia. They would have been refused passage had I not insisted, against government and airline advice, on providing them with paper copies of their ETAs.

■ E-tickets are especially disadvantageous in the event of a strike or operational problem affecting an airline. Normally, major U.S. airlines honor each others' tickets (even, in the interest of converting passengers' loyalties, inexpensive "nonendorsable" tickets that they are not required to honor) during strikes and the like. But they can't access, verify, or honor other airlines' e-tickets. As e-ticket usage has increased, each impending airline strike has prompted an increasingly overwhelming run on airlines and travel agents of passengers trying to get their e-tickets printed in order to be able to get them accepted by other airlines during a strike.

■ Changes to e-tickets can be made only through the airline. Holders of paper tickets can often make new reservations through a different travel agency or even through another airline (although they still have to deal with the original airline or travel agency to have the tickets re-issued).

travel agencies generally aren't allowed by the airlines to hold confirmed reservations for more than 24 hours without full payment. More often, they won't allow you to confirm reservations at all without paying for tickets at the same time you make your booking.

Arranging Ground Transportation Online

RENTING CARS

You can reserve rental cars on the Internet either directly from individual car rental companies' Web sites, or through general-purpose Internet travel agencies.

There aren't many third-party "consolidators" or discounters for car rentals the way there are for flights or cruises. All online and offline travel agencies get their rental car prices either directly from the car rental companies, or from the CRS's. Most name-brand car rental companies participate in all four major CRS's and supply them with essentially the same set of prices. All four major CRS's have equivalent tools for comparing prices from different car rental companies.

Because of differences in how and when prices are updated, it's sometimes possible to find a promotional price in one CRS that isn't listed by the others. But the differences are usually minor—much smaller than the differences between the prices of published airfare options suggested by different CRS's. Certainly there's no point at all to looking at prices from more than one online travel agency that relies on the same CRS.

Many special promotions and discounts for members of frequent flyer programs, automobile clubs, etc. are available only directly from the car rental companies, not through the CRS's. The problem is that the savings may not justify the extra time it takes to check prices from 10 different car rental companies' Web sites. Is it worth an hour's research to save $10 or $20 on a one-day rental? Even if you try, many car rental promotions and discounts aren't available on the Internet—you've got to phone. Obviously, comparison shopping is more important if you're renting a minivan for a week for a family vacation than a subcompact for a day for a business trip.

Don't Say I Didn't Warn You

I've had, and heard, about too many bad experiences to recommend trying to rent a car from a non-airport location (train station, downtown, etc.) or a one-way rental (pickup and dropoff in different places) without talking to a human reservation agent at the car company. Even if you get a confirmation from a CRS or over the Internet there's a good chance you'll arrive and find that the location doesn't exist, has moved, is closed at that time of day or on that day of the week, doesn't permit one-way rentals, or tries to charge you a higher price than what was confirmed. For example, you may be shown a $40 per day rate, and told that one-way rentals between those locations are possible, but not told about the $200 "drop charge" (if you don't ask) until you pick up the car.

Although car rentals would seem to be simpler and involve fewer choices than airline flights, both the CRS's and the car rental companies' own sites do remarkably badly at rentals that are even slightly unusual. Basically, the entire automated car rental system has been built around airline CRS's, and works well only for rentals in conjunction with simple airline flights. If you aren't picking up the car at an airport, and returning it to the same airport, forget trying to reserve it on the Internet.

A CRS or the company's Web site may indicate that there are no rental locations other than at the airport, or that one-way rentals are impossible. Not necessarily true. You can use the Internet or a CRS to get preliminary estimates. But go over all the details (pickup/dropoff times, dates, exact places, total charges and surcharges, etc.) by phone before you commit.

Finally, Priceline.com and Expedia.com offer car rental services similar to Priceline.com's airline ticket and hotel services. Properly designed, these services could work better for basic car rentals than for airline tickets or hotels. To many people, a car is a car, and all car rental companies are alike. Alas, it isn't quite so: there are too many potential unanticipated fees, conditions and surcharges for it to make sense to rent a car through Priceline.com or Expedia.com's "Price Matcher," or anywhere else where you have to commit your money before you know what the bottom-line total price will be.

BUYING TRAIN TICKETS AND PASSES

Train tickets are like airplane tickets, only simpler: rarely are there two different railroads to choose between on the same route or any prices from third parties different from those set by the railroads. Most major railroads use computerized reservations systems similar to those of the airlines. The Indian Railways (**www.indianrailway .com**), for example, have a computerized reservation system accessible, at least in part, on the Internet at **www.indianrail.gov.in**.

Railroad reservation systems and their Web interfaces vary more than do airline reservation systems. Pay close attention to the details when you're buying a ticket.

While rail fares are less complex than airfares, there often are more classes of accommodations on a train than on a plane. Be prepared for separate charges for: 1) transportation (the basic charge per person); 2) accommodations (a compartment, sleeping berth or premium seat); and 3) reservations. Some trains allow travel without reservations, if space is available, but most long distance and express trains require advance reservations.

It's not that simple, though. There are three major limitations to most automated online rail reservations and ticketing systems, including those for Amtrak, VIA Rail Canada, and most European rail systems.

First, almost all of these systems can handle only simple trips. Many are limited to basic one-way and round-trip reservations and tickets. If you want to plan a more complex itinerary—one of the big advantages of traveling by train is being able to stop along the way—you'll have to fill out a Web form or send an e-mail message for the railroad to process manually, or make your reservations by phone or in person at a railroad ticket office or travel agency. Amtrak's system is slightly better than some, and can handle up to three stopovers. But it can't handle trips that involve any travel other than by train (e.g., if you want to drive, or take a bus, between two of the stations on your rail itinerary).

Second, none of these systems include all fares. Worse, the fares that offer the best value and are most used by tourists and other budget-conscious travelers aren't available through the Internet robots. They'll give you a price, but it won't necessarily be the best available.

Almost all major rail systems have special passes for multiple journeys or unlimited travel in a specified period. Some of these, like the many varieties of Eurail and Britrail pass, Japan Rail Pass, Indrail Pass, and Amtrak's USA Rail Pass, are available only to foreign visi-

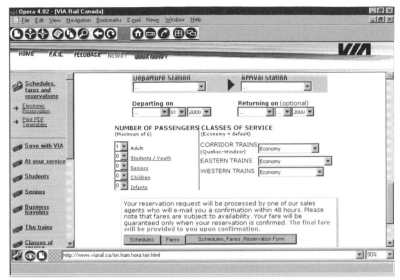

http://www.viarail.ca

For all but the simplest trips on VTA Rail Canada, you send your request to an agent by e-mail to get confirmation of the price and itinerary. It's not instantaneous, obviously, but it allows you to reserve complex trips and to get the full range of prices and services.

---

tors. Others, like the North American Rail Pass jointly offered by both Amtrak and VIA Rail Canada are available to local residents as well as foreign visitors. Many of these rail passes are bargains compared to point-to-point fares. (The North American Rail Pass, for example, is currently a steal at $459 for 30 days of unlimited train travel throughout the United States and Canada.) None of these are available through the Web sites of the railroads that offer them.

Many different online agencies sell Eurail and Britrail passes to North American residents over the Internet. But none of these online agencies provides an automated facility for making reservations for travel with your pass on specific trains. And you can't make reservations through any of the European railroads' own Web sites unless you buy your ticket through them (at the higher point-to-point fare, rather than the pass price). For now, if you want reservations for travel on a Eurail or Britrail pass you have to pay a travel agency a service fee to make them for you from North America, or wait until you get to Europe to make reservations.

An additional minor problem for travelers is the growing fragmen-

Total Fare: $256.00

Washington-Union Station (DC) to Philadelphia 30th St (PA) on Thursday (3/15/01)

108	Washington-Union Station, DC	Philadelphia 30th St., PA	3/15/01	3/15/01
	Full Fare Coach Seat		10:00AM	11:41AM

Philadelphia 30th St (PA) to New York-Penn. Station (NY) on Saturday (3/17/01)

124	Philadelphia 30th St., PA	New York-Penn. Station, NY	3/17/01	3/17/01
	Discount Coach Seat		4:56PM	6:15PM

New York-Penn. Station (NY) to Boston (MA) on Tuesday (3/20/01)

84	New York-Penn. Station, NY	Boston, MA	3/20/01	3/20/01
	Discount Coach Seat		12:30PM	5:20PM

Boston (MA) to Washington-Union Station (DC) on Friday (3/23/01)

67	Boston, MA	Washington-Union Station, DC	3/23/01	3/24/01
	Discount Coach Seat		8:45PM	6:20AM

Please be aware that Amtrak fares are subject to change without notice. It is possible that the only seat left at this fare is currently being booked by another customer. **In addition, this train may sell out and tickets may be unavailable at the time you choose to book.** For information on your departure and arrival station, click on the underlined station name listed above.

http://reservations.amtrak.com

Amtrak offers robotic online booking of all services, although some of the rail passes that offer the best value can only be purchased over the phone or at a ticket office.

tation of rail service. While Amtrak's steadily increasing ridership is proving the value of a unified national rail system, several other countries are moving in the opposite direction. The United Kingdom, Japan, and Australia, among others, have all recently taken major steps to privatize their railroads and break them up into separate regional companies. The results have been at least as confusing and disruptive for customers as the breakup of AT&T in the United States. While "British Rail", "Japan Rail", and "Rail Australia" still exist as brand names and marketing consortia, each now refers to the operations of numerous independent private companies. As one might expect, that's making it steadily harder to get comprehensive fare and schedule information or make reservations for travel throughout any of these countries through a single Web site.

Railroads, like airlines, are working to increase their revenues and profits by adopting increasingly complex fare structures. Like airline tickets, train tickets may have restrictive conditions and substantial penalties for cancellations or changes. Read the fine print before you buy.

Amtrak's Web site gets an "F" on this score, and may even be breaking the law: Amtrak will let you buy tickets online, but gives no online information at all about fare rules and restrictions. To be safe, you should assume that all tickets bought from the Amtrak Web site are completely unchangeable and nonrefundable. In reality, penalties for changing Amtrak tickets are usually less than those for changing airline tickets for similar trips. But to verify this, you have to call Amtrak or go to an Amtrak ticket office or brick-and-mortar travel agency.

On the plus side for Amtrak, their Web site handles discounts, promotions, and special service requests—such as discounts for senior citizens, and accommodations for people with disabilities—better than many airline Web sites. One of the most widely useful Amtrak discounts available online is the 10 percent discount on most Amtrak fares for members of the National Association of Railroad Passengers (**www.narprail.org**). A $28 annual NARP membership ($15 student/fixed income, $35 family) can pay for itself on your first Amtrak ticket.

LOCAL PUBLIC AND MASS TRANSPORTATION

Local public and mass transit is bewilderingly diverse: buses, commuter trains, subways and urban "heavy rail," streetcars and "light rail," airport shuttle vans and shared-ride taxis, passenger ferries, car ferries, water taxis, bicycle shuttles, dial-a-ride services, you name it. The lack of regional transit planning and coordination that's typical of most areas in the U.S. makes it difficult to figure out what public transit options might exist where you are going.

Does the Internet help you figure out how to get around by public transit? Sometimes, though not nearly as well as it should. Almost all transit systems have Web sites, and remarkably many of them have complete online route maps and timetables. Still, they have serious limitations.

Most transit Web sites aren't designed for visitors. Their purpose is to serve existing local transit users, and to get local automobile drivers out of their cars and onto public transit. With rare exceptions, transit Web sites assume that you are already familiar with the layout of the locality (neighborhoods, landmarks, etc.). Rarely do they give an overview.

Available Internet mapping is inadequate for the needs of transit users. Maps on transit Web sites rarely show every street, and all major "general-purpose" Internet map sites are actually automotive map sites that give no information about public transit. It's impossible to find a

RailFans

The most valuable Internet resource for rail travelers, whether in North America or around the world, is the worldwide fraternity of "railfans": amateur enthusiasts, chroniclers, and boosters of railroads, railroading, and all things related. They won't pay for your tickets for you, but they'll do just about anything else imaginable to encourage and assist you to take a train wherever you are going. They may seem a little over-zealous in the enthusiasm of their rail evangelism. But they are, as a group, deeply committed to helping fellow train travelers, willing to give endlessly detailed free advice, and by and large astonishingly professional in their expertise. A good many amateur railfan Web sites are better than the official ones for the same rail systems. When you can't figure out how to get somewhere by train, or if there is a train, you'll be grateful for their obsession with collecting timetables, mapping routes, and keeping track of changes in rail service. There's a huge network of railfan Web sites, newsgroups, and bulletin boards forming their own sub-culture community on the Internet.

http://www.trainweb.com
Railfan sites like TrainWeb.com provide links to a wealth of rail travel information and advice.

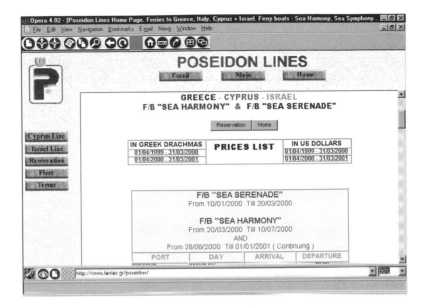

http://www.ferries.gr
How much does it cost to take a ferry from Greece to Israel? Most ferry lines provide route maps, schedules, and prices on their Web sites; some long-distance and car ferries let you make reservations online.

street-level map on the Internet for most locations that shows bus or rail transit routes or stops. Which streets have sidewalks? Which don't? Where is it possible for pedestrians to cross a major highway? Is there a bike lane? Are bicycles allowed on the shoulder? You won't find any of these things on most map Web sites. Even American Automobile Association (AAA) does a better job of providing for the needs of non-drivers in its center-city maps than most map Web sites.

Transit Web sites give, in general, remarkably poor information about prices and fare and pass options. Frequently there are multi-ride tickets, coupon books, daily or weekly unlimited travel passes, or special tickets or passes for passengers transferring from one transit system or mode to another (e.g., taking a bus to the subway). These are usually listed somewhere on transit Web sites, but rarely in a way that gives a visitor unfamiliar with the area any clear guidance in choosing which ticket or pass option will be cheapest.

The most common mass transit question from travelers is, "How can I get from the airport to where I want to go, if I don't rent a car?" Online travel agencies (which don't make any money on local transit)

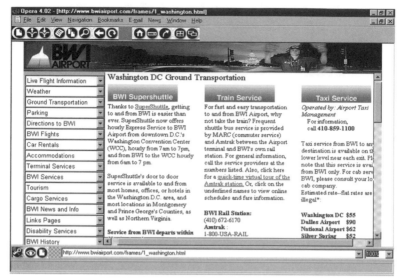

http://www.bwiairport.com

Flights from Baltimore-Washington International Airport (BWI) are often cheaper than those from the other Washington-area airports. But how do you get there from D.C.? Airports' own Web sites often have the most comprehensive information on local airport transportation.

and guidebooks often purport to offer airport transit information. Usually, however, I've found them to overlook some ways to get to and from the airport. I typically find more transit options and details on the airport's own Web site. The aviation portal Web sites Landings.com (**www.landings.com**) and Aerolink.com (**www.aerolink.com**) have particularly good links to airports' Web sites. Follow the "Airports" links on their respective home pages to their directories of airport sites by state (in the United States) and country.

Reserving Accommodations

Where do you want to stay? How can you find the place that's best for you, at the best price? Is the Internet the answer?

Maybe, maybe not. There are a wide variety of places for travelers to sleep, with equally varied pricing and distribution systems. The

Internet works well for some, poorly for others, and differently for each. Here's a survey of the major categories of accommodations for travelers, as they are represented on the Internet.

HOTELS, MOTELS, AND RESORTS

Everyone claims to have the lowest hotel rates. More than 30,000 Web pages refer to hotels, motels, or resorts and "lowest rates" or "lowest prices." Since they all have different prices, they can't all be the "lowest" anything.

Which of these sites, if any, can you believe? None of them, really, until you've compared prices for the same type of room at the same hotel on the dates you want. Even that will only answer the question for this one hotel, on this one trip. Next time, or for a different hotel or room category on the same dates, a different source or Web site might be cheaper. Hotel pricing is surprisingly decentralized, with different rates offered by the same hotel through different distribution channels. I'll get to different Internet hotel booking sources in the following sections, but no single source or Web site consistently has the lowest hotel prices.

Like airlines, it seems hotels set prices to try to maximize their profits. That means they want (1) to get each customer to pay as much as they are willing, and no less, and (2) to offer some people prices just low enough to fill all their rooms every night.

No hotel ever releases figures on how much the average guest actually pays for their room, lest that undercut their reputation and thus how much future guests would pay. I'd estimate, however, that a typical hotel guest pays 40-60 percent of rack rate at more expensive hotels, perhaps 70-90 percent of rack rate at bottom-end motels that play fewer price games. All claimed hotel discounts are calculated as discounts from the rack rate. Only during a holiday or special event, when every hotel in town is sold out, is it ever necessary to pay rack rate at a good hotel.

THE "REGULAR RATE" IS THE HIGHEST POSSIBLE

The price of a hotel room is "whatever the traffic will bear". But no hotel will ever admit that directly—that wouldn't be good public relations. If you ask, "Why are your prices so high tonight?", they won't say, "Because all the hotels in town are full, so we can get away with raising prices." Instead, they'll say, "This is our regular rate." True enough, but with hotels—as with airlines—the "regular" rate (hotels call it the "rack" rate, I don't know why) is actually the highest possible rate. Anything lower is a "discount" rate.

The big problem for a hotel is predicting demand for rooms, so as to set prices just low enough to fill every bed. Forecasting isn't an exact science, and most hotels have empty rooms on more nights than they are sold out. When that happens, hotels will take whatever they can get for a room as long as it's enough to more than cover their marginal costs.

— HAGGLING

I don't care if it's the Hilton or the Ritz, and I don't care what they claim about rates being non-negotiable. Someone on the premises is empowered to haggle, if you give them a face-saving way to do it. "Is there any discounted rate available?" "I was hoping you might have a promotional rate available," and "Can you think of any special rates that I might qualify for?", are appropriate lines to use in this game. If the desk clerk claims that rates are fixed, either the hotel is full, the clerk is ignorant, or they take you for a sucker.

If it's late in the day, they know they're going to have empty rooms and they know you have other choices—you can bargain with any hotel in the world. If there are obviously lots of vacant rooms, and other hotels nearby you could go to, try asking, "Could you possibly check with someone who might know if there's a better rate, or a less expensive room, available tonight?" before you give up and go elsewhere. The bottom-line best hotel prices, at times when rooms are empty, are usually those negotiated on the spot by travelers genuinely prepared to walk out if the price isn't right, and flexible enough not to mind having to try several hotels.

That's not to say that everyone should try this approach. It's risky: it might turn out that because of a convention you didn't know about, or some other unforeseeable reason, all the hotels are full. It may be worth it to you to pay extra for the certainty of a guaranteed reservation.

Frankly, I don't understand why people would feel more secure and confident reserving a hotel room sight unseen. To me, advance reservations in a strange hotel are the height of reckless travel risk-taking. I feel much more secure waiting until I can inspect the hotel, and the room, before I pay for it, even if that means arriving in a new city without reservations. But I realize that I'm in the minority on this question, at least in the U.S.

If you do make guaranteed reservations in advance, be realistic with yourself: there will probably be people who walk in that day without reservations and pay less than you. No matter what sort of price guarantee they claim to offer, no hotel reservation service—on or off the Internet—will give you any money back if you find a walk-in guest paid less than you did for a similar room.

Price aside, a wide range of subjective factors go into hotel choices and preferences. It would be nice to have an objective source of descriptions, reviews, and ratings, but that doesn't exist on the Internet. Descriptions of hotels on virtually all travel Web sites are written and provided by the hotels themselves, either directly or through CRS's.

Otherwise-reputable travel publications often sell hotel listings on their Web sites, or design their Web pages so that you can't readily distinguish the editor's choices from the paid ads. A "recommended" hotel is usually nothing more than a hotel that has paid to be identified as "recommended." Unless a Web site makes a written promise that it accepts no payments from listed hotels or travel service providers, take anything it says about a specific hotel or travel company as an advertisement, not an impartial rating, review, or opinion. In general, print guidebooks are less likely than are Web sites to take payments in exchange for reviews, although some bed-and-breakfast and small-hotel guidebooks sell listings.

Hotel Chains

Every significant hotel chain or franchise in the United States has a Web site for reservations. Even budget chains and smaller hotel groups that don't participate in CRS's, and thus aren't available through most online or offline travel agencies, usually have Web sites through which you can review hotel descriptions and make reservations. Because the hotel doesn't have to pay CRS fees or commissions to a travel agent,

Links in the Chain

A lot of brand-name chains are actually franchise operations, in which individual hotels or motels are independently owned. The franchisee (the hotel or motel) may have to pay the franchiser (the chain) a fee for each reservation processed through the chain's central booking service, online or offline. In such cases, the hotel may offer deals if you contact them directly that the chain doesn't know about or control, and that aren't available through the chain's Web site. If you know you want a specific hotel, and no other, contact the hotel directly even if it's affiliated with a chain.

and you don't have to pay a hotel broker's markup, bookings through a hotel chain's Web site typically entail the lowest transaction costs, and can sometimes offer the lowest prices when rooms are plentiful. Many shorter-term specials are available only from hotel chains or hotels directly, not through CRS's, agencies, or brokers.

The down side to hotel chain Web sites is that there are so many of them, and little way to anticipate which chain might have a good deal available in the place you are going, for the dates you will be there. You have to check all the chains that have properties in the area.

Computerized Reservation Systems (CRS)

Computerized reservation systems (CRS) are one step further removed from individual hotels than are the hotel chains, and CRS's typically offer a smaller range of prices that excludes some discounts. Just as only some of a hotel's local prices are made available through its parent company or affiliated chain, so only some of the chain's prices for the hotel are made available through CRS's.

Some travelers are concerned that airlines might charge higher prices for tickets bought through agents, rather than directly through the airline, in order to recover the cost of their commissions to travel agents. As I've said before, the structure of airline ticket pricing and regulation doesn't permit that. On the contrary, travel agents are able to offer lower air ticket prices than airlines. And travel agent commissions cost airlines less than what it would cost for them to issue tickets themselves.

Where travelers should be concerned about paying more if they book through travel agents is with hotels, tours, and cruises. Especially hotels. Almost without exception, and regardless of how vociferously both hotels and travel agents deny it, hotels set higher prices for rooms reserved through travel agents and through CRS's than for rooms booked directly with the hotel. The smaller the hotel, the greater the difference, but this is true even for big hotel chains. If the room is booked through a travel agent, the hotel

— **BOOKING ROOMS WITH A FLIGHT-BOOKING TOOL**

CRS's are mainly tools for booking flights, and most hotel bookings made through CRS's are made for air travelers. Frequent flyers sometimes forget that air travelers are a relatively small, privileged, and wealthy subset of travelers. Most travel in North America, whether for business or pleasure, is by car, and most Americans aren't really part of the "jet set". Hotels that aren't upscale enough to expect much business from air travelers have little reason to pay for CRS connectivity. Even name-brand chains of budget highway motels aren't in most CRS's.

has to pay a commission. If it's booked through a CRS, the hotel has to pay the CRS as well. Typical CRS fees are about $3 per reservation, plus the cost of maintaining the database of available rooms and prices in a form compatible with the CRS. For an independent hotel, getting connected to a CRS can be a considerable expense.

Hotel reservations made by a travel agency through a CRS—including reservations made through online travel agencies that rely on a CRS for hotel availability and prices, as most do—are those that are most costly for the hotel. Not surprisingly, the normal rates for hotels booked through online travel agencies are at or close to the highest "rack" rate.

All descriptive information about hotels available through CRS's is provided by the hotels themselves. A CRS might eventually ask a hotel to change an egregiously false claim, but I wouldn't count on it. Treat CRS hotel descriptions as ads, not guidebook listings prepared by an impartial writer.

CRS's can't be disregarded completely, however. Prices in CRS's are distributed electronically and can be changed and updated quickly, unlike, say, contracts between a hotel and a tour operator that needs to fix prices long in advance. If the hotel finds itself with too many empty rooms, offering a promotional price through a CRS is a fairly quick and easy way to unload them. It's common to find "promotional" hotel rates in a CRS that are never advertised anywhere else.

The bottom line is that CRS's are typically a poor source for times and places where most hotels are full, or expected to be, but sometimes the best choice on short notice when hotel bookings have fallen short of expectations. You have to check to find out which is the case for each trip. If the hotel couldn't anticipate the level of demand, you probably couldn't either.

Unlike airline tariffs, which are distributed to all CRS's through the same intermediaries (IATA and ATPCO), each CRS gets prices separately from each hotel chain. So there's considerably more variation between CRS's in hotel listings and prices than in air ticket prices. It's definitely worth comparing hotel offerings and prices from online services that draw their information from different CRS's. As a travel agent, I have terminals for two different CRS's on my desk. I'm much more likely to double-check hotel prices in both than to price an airline reservation in both.

Hotel Brokers

Hotel brokers (i.e., consolidators) negotiate contracts with hotels allowing them to offer rooms for less than the rack rate. Typically, they promise you a lower price than you would get if you book your room directly with the hotel (not always true), in exchange for paying for your room in full in advance, rather than paying only at the time of your hotel stay.

Sometimes hotel brokers have contracts permitting them to offer rooms at a certain retail price, of which they get a specified percentage as commission. Other times they actually reserve rooms themselves, and agree to pay a specified amount for them whether they fill them or not, in which case they can rent them for whatever they can get. You never know which is the case. The same broker may have deals of each type with different hotels, or may have both a commitment for a certain number of rooms and an option on more.

Hotel brokers are sometimes mistakenly labeled as discounters. But it's important to understand that a hotel room "discounted" from the rack rate is not necessarily any bargain. Hotel brokers generally have long-term contracts with hotels, so they are often able to offer rates below the rack rate even at times when the hotels are full, and people who book directly with the hotel are being charged rack rate. When there are lots of empty rooms, hotels may offer them directly to the public for less than the rates they've contracted with hotel brokers. Once again, there's no way to tell which will be a better deal without checking prices both directly from the hotel and from brokers.

Some hotel brokers advertise in their own names, have their own Web sites, and offer rooms directly to the public. Some are strictly wholesalers who offer rooms at a net price to retail travel agencies who then marks them up to you. Some brokers work both ways. Because hotel brokers get their contracts by promising to steer business to certain hotels, they generally offer substantially fewer choices of hotels in any given city than are listed in the CRS's. Since it's just as much work to book a cheaper room as an expensive one, hotel brokers mostly focus on middle to high-priced hotels, not budget hotels. Few hotel brokers deal with motels at all.

Most online travel agencies find it easier to partner with a hotel broker than to try to negotiate their own special rates directly with hundreds or thousands of hotels. Because you usually have to pay in full at the time you reserve a brokered hotel room, it's extremely important to know who you are paying (the agency, the broker, or the hotel) and who is responsible for ensuring that you are provided with a room. If the agency or broker takes your money, and the hotel has never heard of you when you arrive to check in (or has a reservation but says that it hasn't been paid for, as not infrequently happens),

The Worst Room for the Highest Price

Priceline.com and Expedia.com's imitative "Hotel Price Matcher" are hotel brokers, but with a different pricing system designed to get as much money out of you, and pay as little of it to the hotel, as possible. They negotiate net prices with hotels like other hotel brokers and booking services. But instead of adding their markup, and telling you a price, they make you name the price you are willing to pay, with a guaranteed offer. If you don't offer enough for them to rent you a room, with enough left over for them to make it worth their while, they turn you down. If your offer is profitable enough for them, they accept it. No negotiation. Their hope, obviously, is that you will offer more than whatever price they would have set.

Suppose one hotel has offered Priceline.com rooms for a cost to Priceline.com of $40, and another has offered rooms for a cost of $80. If you offer Priceline.com $90, you'll pay $90, no less. They aren't going to rent you the $80 room and make only $10; they'll rent you the $40 room, and make $50. No matter what price you offer Priceline.com or Expedia.com's "Hotel Price Matcher", you'll get the cheapest (and, presumably worst) room they have available in that category. Either way, you pay the same amount. Priceline.com or Expedia.com—not you—gets the benefit of any reductions they can negotiate in their cost, or any skill they can bring to bear on finding you a cheaper room. Offering Priceline.com or Expedia.com's "Hotel price Matcher" more money won't get you a better room or hotel if they have any cheaper rooms available in your selected category.

There's usually a reason why a hotel has so many empty rooms that they are having trouble selling them to people who know in which hotel they'll be staying. You can specify what category of hotel (3-star, 4 star, 5-star), but what does that really mean? Not much. The star ratings are assigned by the hotel brokers themselves, not by any impartial accrediting agency. To be fair, I haven't heard many complaints about people reserving, say, a 4-star hotel and ending up in a place they considered only 3-star. More often, you'll end up in a hotel with the facilities and amenities which are expected, but in an unattractive or inconvenient location within the area, or with some other drawback.

the hotel is not responsible. You have to pay the hotel, or find another hotel, and then try to get your money back from the agency or broker who you paid. If a hotel broker goes out of business after taking your money, and before paying the hotel, you're out of luck. This is one of the places where it's most important to deal only with an established, reputable company that you know where to find if you need to sue them in small claims court.

The best-known and probably the largest online hotel broker is Hotel Reservations Network (HRN). They operate several of their own Web sites (all with the same offerings), including **www.180096hotel .com**, **www.hoteldiscount.com**, and **www.hotelreservationsnetwork .com**. None of these sites are models of candor or full disclosure. In addition, many big-name online travel agencies supplement hotel listings in prices from the CRS with those from HRN.

Online Travel Agencies

Most online travel agencies rely on a CRS, perhaps supplemented by HRN or another big hotel broker, for their hotel listings, availability information, and prices. Claims to offer "special deals" on hotels are usually mere puffery.

The advantage of an online travel agency is the ability to compare prices and availability from a wider range of hotels than are available through any single broker or hotel chain. If you call, visit, or e-mail a travel agent, they can't afford the time to give you the descriptions of every hotel available in their CRS, or through hotel brokers they deal with. On the Web site of an online travel agency, you can spend as much time as you like reading about (and looking at pictures of) possible hotel choices. By the nature of their information sources, online travel agencies are best for large hotels affiliated with major chains, and worst for small, independent, and low budget hotels and motels.

Independent Hotels, Inns, and Bed-and-Breakfasts

It's easy to forget, in a world dominated by so few global brands, that most hotels and motels aren't associated with any chain. These include small inns and bed-and-breakfasts, most of the cheaper motels, as well as a growing number of independent city hotels.

In a backlash against formulaic modern chain hotels, there's been a resurgence of interest in distinctive and independent hotels. These include trendy new "boutique" and designer hotels, as well as renovated and modernized hotels in the rejuvenated downtown areas of larger and older cities, some of the key centers of urban tourism.

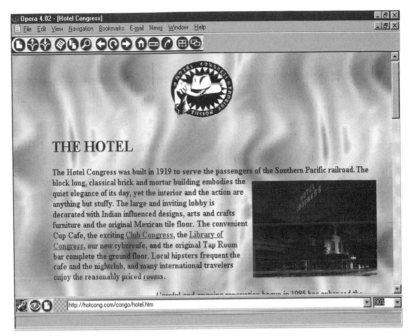

http://www.hotcong.com

Independent hotel Web sites usually have pictures of rooms and other facilities as well as descriptions of services and the neighborhood. As in this example, you usually have to e-mail for reservations, and shouldn't consider your reservation confirmed until you get an e-mail reply.

Independent hotels and motels are typically cheaper as well as more interesting than their chain competition. Brand names, and the television advertising that supports them, are expensive. Independent hotels spend their money on service instead of ads, and offer better value for the price. And lots of them have their own information and reservation Web sites.

How do you find these hotels and their Web sites, and tell the good from the bad? Ay, there's the rub! Plenty of independent hotels and motels are unrenovated flophouses, no-star dives, or in neighborhoods and locations you wouldn't want to stay. Part of the attraction of bed-and-breakfasts is their individuality. There is no simple source of objective ratings.

The most obvious source—word of e-mail and newsgroup postings—is virtually useless. Far too many of what purport to be reviews by hotel and resort guests are actually posted by shills: people who claim to be disinterested, but actually have an undisclosed connection (owner, employee, relative, friend, person who was given free lodging in exchange for a favorable review) to the hotels. The anonymity of the Internet has made shilling epidemic and ineradicable. And nowhere is it worse than in reviews of small hotels, inns, bed-and-breakfasts, and resorts—excepting writers getting their friends to tout their books on Amazon.com.

Hilton, Hyatt, and Marriot have more efficient, larger-scale ways to promote themselves than through phony testimonials for their hotels in travel newsgroups. Independent hotels are another story. A small hotel or inn's reputation on the Internet can be crucial to its financial success or failure. When a series of rave "trip reports" in a newsgroup or bulletin board can cause a bed-and-breakfast to be booked full of newsgroup readers for months, the temptation for struggling hoteliers is irresistible. You have to assume that any posting is an advertisement that originated with the proprietor.

HOSTELS

Americans are inclined to think of hostels as "youth hostels," and associate them primarily with Europe. But to do so would be a mis-

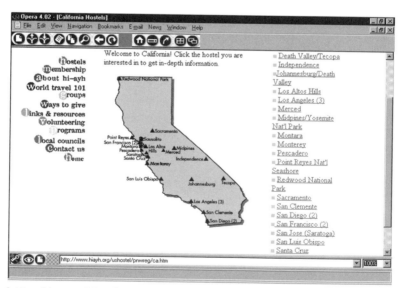

http://www.hiayh.org
Anywhere you're likely to go as a tourist, there's probably a hostel.

http://www.yha.org.uk

Hostel reservations over the Internet enable you to have a reliably clean, comfortable dormitory bed waiting for you—for a fraction of the cost of the cheapest hotel room. This hostel costs about $35 per person per night, including breakfast, in central London.

take: hostels offer a significant alternative for all travelers worldwide, not just young people and not just in Europe.

Hostels have no age limits. I regularly stay in hostels, even when I travel on business and I am well past my "youth". In at least one big-city hostel, most of the guests are business people, although that's certainly not the norm. More and more seniors stay in hostels as well. There are hostels throughout the world, including an extensive network of hostels in the United States and Canada. Most have dormitories (separate for men and women), but many have private rooms for couples and families.

Hostels are few outside the First World. But they offer the cheapest accommodations you can reserve in advance in major cities in the United States, Canada, Western Europe, Japan, Australia, and New Zealand. For $20 a night or so for a single person (less outside big cities), you can have a reliable clean bed waiting for you when you arrive in New York, Tokyo, Paris, or some similarly expensive city.

Beds or rooms in hostels worldwide can be reserved in advance over the Internet, usually by e-mail. Be warned, however, that some hostels have an e-mail address but don't check it as often as they should. If you don't get an answer to your reservation request within a few days, try again. If you still don't get an answer, contact the hostel by fax or phone instead. Don't assume your reservation is confirmed unless and until you get a definite answer.

Hostelling International

Hostelling International (HI) is the world's largest accommodation provider. The complete worldwide directory of hostels affiliated with the nonprofit International Youth Hostel Federation, and entitled to use the name Hostelling International, is available at **www.iyhf.org**. The main site includes links to affiliates in each country around the world, including the HI-AYH (formerly American Youth Hostels) Web site for hostels in the United States at **www.hiayh.org**. Listings of hostels each country are maintained by the national affiliates, and are organized slightly differently, All of the national HI affiliate sites that I've looked at include English translations of the essential hostel listing information.

HI doesn't (yet) have an automated central reservation system

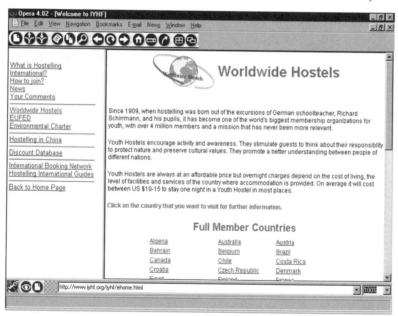

http://www.iyhf.org
The International Youth Hostel Federation has links to affiliated national hostel organizations with common standards around the world.

accessible over the Web. It's a bit odd: they have their own world-wide computerized reservation system, and a comprehensive Web directory of their hostels, but they haven't yet tied the two together. For now, make your hostel reservations by e-mail; reservation e-mail addresses and instructions are on the HI Web page for each country or hostel.

Private Hostels

There are many private and unaffiliated dormitories, hotels, and guest houses calling themselves "hostels"; the name "hostel," in itself, is no guarantee of anything. As long as they don't claim to be affiliated with Hostelling International, anyplace that wants to can call itself a hostel. Standards and services of private and unaffiliated hostels vary. Overall, in my experience, private hostels tend to have a younger, more party-oriented clientele. Guests at III hostels tend to be quieter, with less alcohol and a more diverse age mix.

There's no single source of information on private hostels, but the Hostels.com Web site (**www.hostels.com**) has the most extensive list of private hostels worldwide. "The most complete directory of hostels in the world," Hostels.com includes both III hostels and private and independent hostels. The emphasis, however, is over-

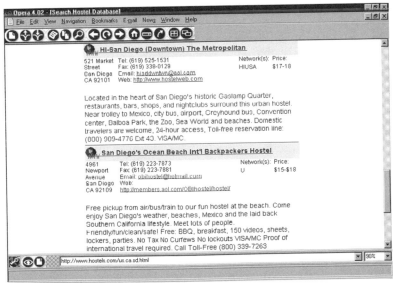

http://www.hostels.com
Hostels.com provides less detailed information, but lists a wider range of both Hostelling International and private hostels.

whelmingly on non-HI hostels; for HI hostels, you're better off going directly to HI's own Web site.

Hostels.com has information on bed availability and an automated online reservations system for a growing number of hostels. For those without automated reservations (yet), you can make advance reservations.

CAMPGROUNDS AND RV PARKS

I'm certainly not going to encourage you to carry a wireless Internet access device while backpacking. But whether you're a sunbird with a laptop computer in your RV, or planning a vacation trip to a popular national park where demand for campsites far exceeds supply, making campground or RV park reservations on the Internet isn't as crazy as it might first seem.

In the United States, the majority of designated campsites open to the public can be reserved in advance over the Internet. The only real difficulty is finding their Web sites, with campgrounds operated by a plethora of private companies and local, state, and Federal gov-

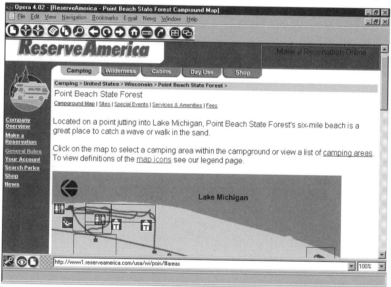

http://www1.reserveamerica.com

At Reserveamerica.com, you pick out and reserve a specific campsite. But even with the maps on the Web site, it can be difficult to tell which site you want until you've looked at the terrain.

ernment agencies from the National Park Service to the Army and the Bureau of Reclamation.

Some camping guides list Internet addresses for campground information and reservations whenever possible. Unfortunately there's no Web site that lists every campground in the United States, although there are several competing camping portal sites and directories such as that in the camping section of About.com (**camping.about.com**). Even government-run campgrounds on public land aren't listed, or available for reservations, through any central site. You'll have to do some searching, at least until a comprehensive site emerges.

Most campgrounds on Federal land are operated by the Department of the Interior (which includes the National Park Service, the National Forest Service, the Bureau of Land Management, and the Bureau of Reclamation) and the Army Corps of Engineers (which dams rivers and does other civil engineering). General information (but not reservations) about camping on Department of Interior and Corps of Engineers land is available on an unusual multi-department Web site (most Federal Web sites are strictly balkanized by department) at **www.recreation.gov**.

Campground reservations are handled through separate sites for different government agencies. The largest Federal campground reservation system serves the National Forest Service (but not the rest of the Department of the Interior) and the Corps of Engineers, with complete site maps, availability information, and automated reservations, at **www.reserveusa.com**. Like many campgrounds on Federal land, this site is actually operated by a private company under a franchise from the Feds. The same company has gotten franchises from at least 15 states to offer online reservations for campgrounds in state parks at **www.reserveamerica.com**.

The National Park Service has separate procedures for each park. Check the section for the individual park on the NPS Web site at **www.nps.gov** to see if camping reservations for that park are accepted over the Internet.

Canadian national park campgrounds don't yet accept Internet reservations, but details for those that do take reservations by phone, fax, or mail are in the reservation section of the Parks Canada Web site at **parkscanada.pch.gc.ca**.

VACATION RENTALS

Not everyone stays in a hotel or motel when they travel. For longer stays, you can rent an apartment or condominium, or even a house.

You can rent a place big enough to fit the whole family, cook your own meals, and generally settle in for a real vacation.

My impression is that more people would rent vacation homes, rather than staying in hotels, if they knew how. The Internet is making it easier, but it's still not simple. Vacation rentals are marketed through a wide range of online and offline channels: advertisements by individual private owners, mainstream apartment and home rental agencies, and specialized vacation rental and management companies. Search as many places as you can. No one Web site or newsgroup has emerged as the dominant or central place for matching homes for rent with extended-stay travelers, although in time I imagine one will.

Web site owners can't verify every listing they allow to be posted, and can't be held responsible for the accuracy of listings provide by owners or agents for rental properties any more than newspapers are responsible for the truth of classified ads. Every house or apartment has its drawbacks and less desirable features. Ask what they are. It's OK to say, "What are the most significant negative features of this rental unit?"

If you have specific concerns, make sure they are clearly addressed and resolved before you commit yourself to a rental. This isn't likely to be an automated process, nor should it be. You can review ads and descriptions on the Web, but you can expect it to take a certain amount of e-mail correspondence to work out details. Avoid any owner or rental agent who's reluctant to answer specific questions about the property or the rental arrangements.

HOME AND HOSPITALITY EXCHANGES

Home Exchanges

When it works, a home exchange is almost miraculous: You each get the use of an entire, fully furnished and equipped, home—probably much larger and more comfortable than any vacation home you could afford—and *neither of you pays a penny!* Nothing else comes close for value in long-term vacation (or other travel) accommodations.

Why doesn't everybody do this? The catch has always been the difficulty of identifying someone compatible and trustworthy, with the mirror image of your itinerary, wanting to travel between the same places, on the same dates, in opposite directions. That, however, is exactly the sort of matching task for which the Internet is perfect. Home exchanges have benefited more from the Internet than have any other

HOME   SEARCH LISTINGS   LIST YOUR HOME   ABOUT   CONTACT

HomeExchange.com

New York City, New York, USA

The Home
We often say, "we live in one of the top 5 neighborhoods in the world!" Our charming one-bedroom apartment is in the center of Greenwich Village. It sleeps 4, 2 in bedroom twin beds, 2 in living room fold-out sofa bed. A typical village apt., 12 ft X 16 ft living room has wood floors, ceiling-high windows which open onto

http://www.homeexchange.com/cgi-local/display.cgi?act=show&HomeID=6914518

http://www.homeexchange.com
The more attractive your home and its location are to potential visitors, the better your chances of finding someone with whom to trade.

---

kind of travel arrangement, and the numbers of home exchanges have exploded since they began to be arranged primarily on the Internet.

How easy it will be to arrange an exchange for your home depends largely on the attractiveness of your home and, more importantly, its location: is your home in a place lots of people would like to visit? If you live in an apartment in Manhattan, a house in San Francisco, or a vacation condo in Waikiki or Miami Beach, finding an exchange will be relatively easy. People with retirement apartments in resort areas often exchange homes for part of the year with people in a similar situation somewhere else. Homes, even nice ones, in areas without nearby tourist attractions are harder (but not impossible) to arrange to exchange. Most suburbanites include use of their car in the exchange, to make a home that's inaccessible by public transit more attractive.

Arranging a home exchange is usually a three-step process. First, you sign up with a home exchange matching service, and complete a profile of your home, when you want to travel, and where you want to go. Then, the service posts your listing in their search directory of available homes for exchange, and gives you access to

— Home-Swapping

You go on vacation from Point A to Point B. You leave your home empty in A, and rent a place to stay in B. Meanwhile, there's probably somebody else traveling from B to A, leaving their home vacant in B and renting a place to stay in A. Wouldn't it be nice if you could connect with each other, and arrange to each stay in each other's home? In a nutshell, that's a home exchange.

other members listings. When you find a potential match, you can contact them by e-mail to get to know each other, see if you think an exchange will work, and negotiate the details.

Listing your home with one of these services never obligates you to except an exchange offer. You can take as much time, and ask as many questions as you like, before you decide whether you're willing to let someone live in your home while you're not there. Of course, you'll be living in their house at the same time, so you both probably have the same concern for having your homes be well cared for. Mutual trust is essential.

There are at least three major worldwide home exchange matching services. Homelink (**www.homelink.org**) and Intervac (**www .intervac.com**) have both been around for decades before the Internet, matching home exchangers through annual book-length printed directories of members homes by location. Both now operate Web sites, but their fees (starting at $50 per year for Web access the listings, twice that for inclusion in the printed directory) still reflect the cost of publishing printed books. HomeExchange.com (**www.homeexchange.com**) is a newer, Internet-only service with membership starting at $30 per year and listings (but not members names, addresses, or e-mail addresses) available on the Web even to nonmembers.

Hospitality Exchanges

Hospitality exchanges are similar to home exchanges, except that they involve hosting people in your home while you are there, and staying with other people in their homes, rather than exchanging the use of your home while you want theirs.

As with home exchanges, hospitality exchanges are generally based on directories of members of a matching service. Also, as with home exchange networks, most hospitality exchanges now operate on the Internet. (You can find them with a keyword search for, "hospitality exchange.") You sign up as being willing to consider requests for hospitality by visitors. When a fellow member of the service wants to visit the place where you live, they can contact you and ask if you're willing to put them up on certain dates. You can always say no, without any obligation to give a reason, although of course the system works on mutual generosity and willingness to play host as often as you play guest. When you want to go somewhere, you can contact fellow members in that location to see if one of them might be willing to put you up.

Hospitality exchanges are not a substitute for other sorts of travel accommodations, and visits are generally limited to a few days. Guests are often expected to help with household tasks, although the norms of the relationship vary from one hospitality exchange service to another. Hospitality exchanges are mainly a way to meet people in a different place, and get experience of what their lives are like, rather than a way to cut the cost of travel. Many hospitality exchange networks are organized around "affinity groups" of people who share certain values or interests. It's not for everyone, but at its best a stay in a local person's home can be the highlight of your trip.

Booking Other Travel Services Online

Online travel agencies are eager to increase their sales of cruises, tours, and packages, because the profit margins for agencies on these travel products are higher than on airline tickets, hotels, or rental cars. The problem for Internet agencies has been that cruises, tours, and packages typically require advice and consulting that robots haven't been capable of providing in a way that can compete with human travel agents.

Automated sales of cruises, tours, and packages on the Internet are still in their infancy. It's far too early to predict which, if any, online agencies will prove best able to handle these types of reservations, or how they will do so.

Airline tickets are complex, too, as the discussion earlier in this chapter should have made clear. But most of the factors in choosing flights and airfares are readily quantifiable: flights times, numbers of plane changes, etc. can be represented, and compared, numerically. Not so most of the factors in choosing a cruise or tour. Computers have thus far done worst at problems that involve basing judgments on multiple, nonnumeric, subjective evaluations.

— FELLOW TRAVELERS

One of the most important factors in the choice of any cruise or group tour is your compatibility with the other people with whom you'll be traveling. On a tour, most of your time and socializing usually ends up being with the other people in your small group. On a cruise, the group of fellow travelers is larger, but even more isolated from contact with anyone else. In either case, getting along with the other tourists is, for most people, essential to having an enjoyable time.

Price is only one criterion, and probably not the most important, in choosing a cruise or tour. Price is an imponderable, anyway. Most cruise lines and tour operators have their own Web sites, but tours and cruises are re-sold by a multiplicity of agencies and wholesale brokers. Once again, no one type of Web site consistently has the lowest prices for cruises or tours. Comparison shopping on sites of different types (cruise lines or tour operators, automated online travel agencies, cruise or tour brokers, specialty travel agencies, etc.) is the only way to find who has the lowest price.

A human travel agent will try to steer you away from a cruise or tour on which they can tell you probably won't fit in or be happy (although, of course, their predictions aren't infallible). Cruise and tour booking robots aren't that smart, and will make reservations without question for a family with small children on a party cruise dominated by drinking and dancing singles.

Demographic profiles of cruise or tour customers are hard to come by, anyway, except through anecdote and experience. The age distribution of the passengers, for example, is one of the few facts about a cruise or tour that could be represented and compared numerically. Some cruises and tours are almost entirely for young people, some almost entirely for older people, and some have a wider spread of ages. Cruise lines and tour companies know what ages they expect, of course, and plan activities and services accordingly, but they never make that information public, lest it dissuade potential passengers of other ages.

Human travel agents talk with you, size you up, ask questions, listen to what you say about what you want, and learn from how you react to their initial suggestions. Ideally, a computerized travel agent would use "expert systems" that incorporate that process in their software.

Not surprisingly, the more promising developments in that direction are coming from pre-existing offline travel agencies that understand how to offer consulting and advice, not from online startup travel agencies that have been fixated on automation and the elimination of all access to human advice. Hopefully, over the next few years, we'll begin to see a new kind of online travel agency that combines the best of what automated "expert systems" and experienced human travel agents can deliver under the same virtual roof, with seamless integration of services delivered in whatever way works best: Web-based robots, e-mail, or phone call with a human agent. There are signs in the online travel industry indicating this is necessary, but it will take time.

As of now, the best you can hope for from a cruise or tour portal Web site is a referral to an appropriate tour operator, cruise line, or specialty travel agency for your needs and interests. There are at least half a dozen outdoor, adventure, active travel, and specialty portal sites, and even more cruise comparison and "review" sites. Some suceed, some fail, and services vary. But all of these sites face the same dilemma: travelers come to them for impartial, critical reviews of tours and cruises, but the sites get their revenues from tour operators and cruise lines in the form of commissions and referral fees. I'm not optimistic that any of them will transcend the role of advertising mouthpieces and hucksters for tour operators, outdoor outfitters, and cruise lines, or displace Usenet newsgroups as a forum for open discussion of travel companies' pros and cons.

eGulliver.com

Most cruise, tour, and specialty travel search engines are designed to lead you directly to a cruise line or tour operator. One important exception is eGulliver.com, an online directory of travel agents who can work with you by phone or e-mail.

The essential idea behind eGulliver.com is that expertise and understanding of your interests, destination, and type of trip are more important in choosing a travel agent than physical location. For ten years, I've been telling readers of my FAQ, "Find a specialist in your sort of travel. There is no one best travel agent for everyone or everything." As it turns out, eGulliver is the first online directory of travel agents that gets this critical point.

At eGulliver.com, you can search for a travel agent by specialization (destination, activity, "lifestyle," or other keywords). You can read travel agents' profiles (promotional self-descriptions) and credentials, and see how they've been rated by previous clients.

If you arrange your travel through an agent you found on eGulliver.com, the site gets a referral fee. Not surprisingly, the first agents to list themselves in the eGulliver.com directory have been those

http://www.egulliver.com

At eGulliver.com, you can search for a travel agent who specializes in your destination or type of travel, and who can work with you by e-mail or phone. You can also read travel agents' profiles and credentials, and see how they've been rated by previous clients.

who charge fees for their services (and to cover the cut they have to give to eGulliver.com).

eGulliver.com lists individual travel agents, not agencies. That's good, because different travel agents in the same office may be knowledgeable about very different places and styles of travel. But it makes it harder to get a sense of the overall quality and reputation of the agency, and it excludes some of the most innovative "bricks-and-clicks" travel agencies where customers don't necessarily deal just with a single agent.

One of travelers' most common complaints is that their local travel agent doesn't understand their needs and wants. And one of the most common questions is, "How do I find a good travel agent?" If you don't want to have your travel arranged by a robot, or you want comparative advice about the merits and demerits of different travel suppliers—and if you're prepared to pay for that advice—eGulliver.com may be one of the best places on the Internet to start.

Safe Surfing
and Shopping

Researching and arranging your travels on the Internet is not without risk: risk of invasion of privacy and misuse of personal information, risk of theft of credit card numbers or other data, and risk of getting ripped off.

How serious are these risks? Some are slight, some severe, neither in the ways most people expect. Are any of them sufficient reasons not to research or reserve your travels online? Rarely. Are these risks any different from those of arranging travel offline, or of buying things other than travel on the Internet? Yes, perhaps surprisingly so. And—the $64,000 question—what can you do about these risks? Quite a lot, mostly by using tools and techniques most people don't know or notice.

Concerns about the risks of using the Internet for travel planning arise both from its novelty and its power. And travel purchases entail greater commitments of our time and money than other common e-commerce purchases. When buying big expensive things in a new and novel way, using vastly powerful tools that we don't fully understand, a complete lack of fear and caution would be rash.

New Internet users, and first-time Internet shoppers, are often most concerned about the safety of their credit card information on the Internet. But the more people know about credit card security, the less worried about it they tend to be. The more people know about Internet privacy, the more worried about it they tend to be. The most recent surveys of travelers using the Internet show that privacy concerns are growing fast, and privacy invasion is now surpassing credit

It's the rare person who doesn't feel some trepidation the first time they authorize a charge of hundreds or thousands of dollars from a robotic salesperson, entirely on the basis of computer displays and without any tangible artifact—even a mail-order catalog—to hold onto as evidence that the seller has any more than a virtual existence.

card security as a reason people are afraid to make travel reservations and purchases online.

The Internet makes it easy for you to do many things that you previously relied on others to do for you. That's great. But one of the things you take on when you decide to "do-it-yourself" is the responsibility for looking out for hazards that others—such as travel agents and other professionals—protected you from when they handled your travel arrangements for you.

Internet companies, including online travel companies, don't want you to know what risks you take with your money and your privacy when you deal with them. If I talk at some length in this chapter about Internet consumer protection and privacy issues that aren't unique to travel, that's only because many important general principles of Internet consumer protection and privacy are so little known.

Privacy and Internet Travel Arrangements

People worry more often about theft of credit card numbers, but that's infrequent and has limited consequences by law. The real nightmare scenarios of the Internet all have to do with invasion of privacy. Information about you is most likely to be misused, not by unknown strangers, but by the travel and other companies to which you voluntarily provide it. That makes privacy more of a problem with travel than with anything else because travel planning necessarily involves revealing a more comprehensive and intimate personal profile than does anything else you're likely to do on the Internet, short of cybersex. And there are fewer legal protections— to wit, none—for travel information than for any other comparably revealing category of business information. You can protect your privacy, but only if you work at it.

WHY PRIVACY SELF-PROTECTION MATTERS

Privacy self-protection is important because:

- Travel reservations and itineraries contain some of the most detailed and intimate information about you and your lifestyle that you're likely to provide to any Internet service. Even travel research can reveal things about your interests, tastes, habits, and plans that you may rather keep private.

- People who get information about you and your travel interests and plans can spam you, harass you by phone with marketing solicitations, contact you at work about your personal travel, sell your travel plans to people who want to sell you other products or services, or anything else they can think of.

- Travel information has none of the special protections that medical, legal, and some other types of information have. Travel information is probably the largest and most personally revealing category of information that lacks legal privacy protection.

- By the time you get to a Web site's privacy policy, they may already know who you are, and everything you've ever revealed on any other Web site. If you don't like their policy, it may be too late to do anything about it. To protect yourself, you need to set up protections before you start browsing.

- Once your privacy is compromised, and someone finds out something you didn't want known, or uses the information in a way you don't like, there's nothing you can do about it. With rare exceptions, there's no way to get them to tell you what files they have, to delete information about you, or to stop them from using or selling that information.

- When Internet companies go out of business, they can be forced to sell their personal profile archives and logs to the highest bidder at the bankruptcy auction. Even if they were trustworthy, the new owners of your information may not be.

A surprisingly large amount of information can be revealed as you are browsing the Internet, without your knowledge and before you've even had a chance to read a Web site's privacy policy. To protect your privacy, you need to (1) read and evaluate each Web site's privacy policy before you deliberately provide them with any information about yourself, and (2) take technical measures (mainly in which browser you use and how your browser and Internet connection are set up, before you start browsing, to insure that you don't "give away" more information than you realize.

>> KEY ADVICE
About Consumer Protection, Privacy, and Security

- Always pay by credit card, even if it costs a few percent extra. Credit card chargeback rights are by far your strongest consumer protection.

- If you don't get what you paid for, question the charge immediately, in writing (not e-mail), with your credit card company.

- Unless you have to, don't pay your credit card bill for travel purchases until your airline tickets are in hand, or your trip is complete. If you have to pay your bill sooner, you must be much more careful about who you deal with.

- Don't do anything private or secure from a public Internet terminal if you can avoid it. Assume that anything you do at a public termninal is being monitored. If you have to use a password from a public terminal, change it as soon as you get home.

- Proofread your itinerary carefully, and read all the terms and conditions, before you click on "buy". Print them out or save them and back them up.

- Keep complete records of travel purchases for at least six months after the trip is complete and you've settled all the bills. Especially for international trips, duplicate charges may show up on your credit card bill months later.

- Protect your "cookies", passwords, and electronic signatures. Never allow passwords to be stored as cookies.

If you care about your privacy, you have to take your own measures to protect yourself, in advance. You might think you could rely on the law, but with the exception of certain specific instances as I'll list later, the law will not protect you. You have no right to personal information privacy under U.S. law.

The U.S. government considers any information you might reveal about yourself as a "purely voluntary and discretionary" gift. That's pretty hypocritical, given that the government requires the airlines to

- Don't consent to use electronic signatures if you have any choice. Limit your consent to electronic signatures to use with specific sites for specific purposes.

- Learn about the risks of privacy invasion before you start surfing. You can reveal much more about yourself while browsing the Web than you probably realize. Once someone gets information about you, it's usually too late to try to get it back or limit how they use it.

- Don't count on the government to protect your privacy. If you want privacy, take steps to protect yourself.

- Check your Web browser settings. You'll probably need to change them, or install a different browser, if you don't want everything you do on the Web to be tracked and logged, making your computer vulnerable to Web-based spying and data theft.

- Check the security of your Internet connection. Consider installing basic privacy and security software such as a proxy server and/or personal firewall to protect yourself and the data on your computer from Internet snooping and vandalism.

- Use an alternate e-mail address for all public postings to avoid getting your primary address flooded with spam.

- Read and evaluate any Web site's privacy policy before you buy anything from them or allow them to set or read cookies. Look closely for loopholes that will allow them to use the information they collect about you in ways you don't want.

- Don't do business with companies that don't respect your privacy. Tell them why you're taking your business elsewhere; if enough people do, maybe they'll change.

collect, and to turn over to the government, phone numbers and other personal information about passengers. You don't have to give your phone number or address when you make an airline reservation, but if you don't, that can be reason to make you "fit the profile" devised by the government, and be singled out for extra scrutiny or search of your luggage or person, or other harassment at check-in. (In case you're curious, the U.S. government also reserves the right to retain this information indefinitely, compiling a log of all your airline trips.)

— PROTECT YOURSELF

In the United States, there is no general legal protection for the privacy of personal information about you. If you don't take steps to protect your privacy on the Internet, you won't have any privacy.

Information of certain types, or maintained by certain entities, is protected by special privacy laws. For example, certain disclosures to doctors, lawyers, and clergy, are legally privileged (although not absolutely). In addition, there are Federal laws creating privacy rights, and legally recognizing your expectation of privacy, in personal information about you maintained by government agencies, banks, financial institutions, credit bureaus, and colleges and universities. Such laws also regulate, among other things, the use of driver's license information, telephone records, and records of cable and pay-per-view television and video rentals.

Unfortunately, there are no special laws for information about travel plans, Web browsing, or online shopping.

Travel records and Web browsing are two gaping holes in the piecemeal U.S. approach to data privacy law. Their intersection, Internet travel planning, is the goose that laid the golden egg of data mining, and the worst Internet privacy problem area for consumers.

The fundamental problem is that, except in the areas covered by special laws, U.S. data privacy law is premised on a lie. U.S. courts have held that you "have no expectation of privacy" in personal information that you provide to another person or business. That's obviously untrue. Whether you should have some rights to privacy may be debatable, but people do, in fact, have *expectations* of privacy when they give out information. U.S. law denies the reality of those expectations. People's natural privacy expectations are routinely violated, legally, and often without their knowledge.

— WEAK SPOT

Privacy is the Achilles heel of Internet travel planning.

It should be noted that there is nothing natural or inevitable about the lax approach of the United States to data-privacy. In the European Union (EU), for example, data-privacy law recognizes people's natural expectations of privacy. The recipient of personal information in the EU or about citizens of EU countries is presumed to have given an implied warranty that the information will be used only for the purpose for which it was provided. Just as the seller of goods in the U.S. is presumed to have given an implied warranty of the fitness of those goods for the purpose for which they were sold.

Moreover, in the EU, personal information remains the property of the person to whom it pertains, even if copies have been provided to others. Just as copyrighted information remains the property of the copyright holder, even if copies have been widely distributed. In the EU, as the legal owner of all personal information about yourself, you have the right to control how it is used. Under EU law, you must be informed, and give your consent, in advance, to any use or redistribution of your personal data.

U.S. businesses have denounced the EU Data Directive as a restraint of trade. All that it restrains, however, is the ability of businesses to use personal information in ways for which they have not asked permission and to which the subjects of the information would not consent if asked. The EU Data Directive allows any use of information for which businesses can obtain informed prior consent. It neither overrides nor precludes any explicit contractual agreements. The only real difference from U.S. law is that EU law enforces a more realistic set of implicit assumptions as to what people intend when they provide information to a business that doesn't commit itself to an explicit privacy policy.

— THE "GIFT" OF INFORMATION —

U.S. law treats information you give someone like any other gift. Once you "give" information about yourself to a person or business, they own that data. They can use it, rent it, sell it, publish it, broadcast it, or do anything they can think of with it. They don't have to ask you first, they don't have to tell you what they've done with it or to whom they've passed it on, and they don't have to show you the current contents of their dossier about you.

Negotiations between the United States (which opposes the EU Data Directive) and the EU have dragged on without agreement for almost two years, at press time, after the scheduled effective date of the EU privacy directive. It's still too early to tell exactly how it will be applied to e-commerce and other Internet contact between the EU and people and businesses in countries like the United States which don't meet the EU standard of data privacy protection. The directive provides for a prohibition on transfers of personal information from the EU to countries that can't guarantee the privacy of the transferred data, and some European privacy organizations have announced their intention to

— BIG BROTHER —

It's never mentioned in airline Website privacy disclosures, but under the little-known "Computer Assisted Passenger Screening" program, essentially everything that's entered into the airline computer or CRS about you is run through a US government profiling system each time you check in for a flight.

sue in European courts to enjoin personal data transfers to the United States.

Canadian data privacy law is closer to EU law than to U.S. law, and will probably be brought sufficiently close to the EU standards to permit continued personal data transfers between Canada and Europe.

— I Know What You Watched Last Summer

It's illegal for a business to reveal which television programs you watch, even if the cable company keeps logs for pay-per-view billing purposes, but legal to sell secretly-kept logs of which Web pages you view or what travel reservations you've made.

Some U.S. companies have been unwilling to commit to European standards of privacy protection for their entire operations, since doing so would require forgoing the lucrative potential revenues from sales of their customer data. This should give you pause: the fact that U.S. companies consider their potential profits from data mining to be greater than those from sales to customers in all the countries of the European Union is a good intention of just how extensively they expect to be able to market your personal data. This is probably the largest factor in the refusal of most U.S.-based Internet travel agencies (especially the larger ones) to sell tickets to customers abroad, except in those few countries where they have set up local subsidiaries isolated from their U.S. customer databases.

Some businesses in the United States have proposed a so-called "safe harbor" policy under which they would be exempted from most of the EU data privacy requirements if they agree to participate in a U.S. industry self-regulation system instead. Self-regulation in Internet privacy has not worked, and the "safe harbor" proposal falls

— Get It in Writing

Your only privacy rights in the U.S. are those created by specific contracts or promises or by laws in specific areas which unfortunately include neither travel nor Web browsing.

short of the protections required by the EU law. The "safe harbor" proposal has been denounced as ineffectual by privacy and consumer advocates on both sides of the Atlantic, and remains the subject of negotiation. If agreed to, it will surely be challenged in European courts as contrary to the EU law.

For the full text of the EU data privacy directive, see **europa.eu .int/eur-lex/en/lif/dat/1995/en_395L0046.html**. For background information, other links, and updates on the status of the Directive and implementing legislation by EU members, see **europa.eu.int /comm/internal_market/en/media/dataprot**.

In the United States, if you have no contract with someone, and they have made you no promises, you have no legal basis to object to anything they do with any information they can find out about you. Protecting your privacy is thus not a matter of asserting your general "rights" under the law but of making certain that you don't inadvertently disclose personal information to anyone, unless and until they have made a specific promise not to abuse that information about you.

WEB SITE AND TRAVEL COMPANY PRIVACY POLICIES

When it comes to data privacy in the United States, either in travel or on the Internet, all things not expressly prohibited are permitted. When you read the fine print, don't just look at what they say they will do. Look at what they say they won't do, and make sure the list of "don'ts" is complete. If every mode of misuse of your personal information that they could conceivably engage in isn't expressly ruled out, their privacy policy isn't good enough. And if you haven't read and approved their privacy policy, you shouldn't be giving them *any* information yet.

ONLINE TRAVEL RECORDS AND YOUR PRIVACY

What do travel companies know about you? What can they do with this information, and what can you do about it?

They know a great deal, and can do anything they want with the data they have on you, unless they've specifically promised you that they won't. They can use it themselves or sell it to anyone who will pay.

Will online travel companies sell this information? Of course, at least if they can get away with it.

Travel companies acknowledge that their customer databases are among their most valuable assets. Many of them say that, while the value of the data they collect has been "under-exploited", they expect that their profits from sales of user and customer data may eventually match or exceed their profits from commissions on reservations. That's not so surprising as most airlines cap commissions to travel agents on Internet booked airline tickets at a maximum of $10. Many Internet travel firms already make as much or more from advertising as from sales, and are desperate to find other ways to generate revenue from their existing transaction stream. Since the database is a byproduct of the bookings, at no additional cost, "data mining" and sale is one of their logical paths toward profitability.

What Travel Companies Know About You

Your name and the names of your family or other regular traveling companions. Your addresses. Phone numbers. Credit card numbers. Everywhere you went. When. How. For how long. With whom. Where did you stay? If you went there with someone, did you stay in the same room? Did you ask for one bed in the room or two? Did you reserve sports or theater tickets? To what performance or event? Do you smoke? Do you prefer the window or the aisle? Do you like high floors in hotels or low? What organizations do you belong to? What conventions do you attend? What are your hobbies or special interests, as revealed by what sorts of tours or cruises you take? All in convenient, computerized form, correlated by frequent flyer numbers. Travel companies have, when you think about it, an astonishingly comprehensive and intimate portrait of travelers' lives.

If a marketer has a set of Web browsing records about someone identified only by a numbered cookie on their computer, what they want is to link that profile to a name, address, phone number, and e-mail address. Travel reservation Web sites often require users to provide comprehensive personal profiles *before* they can make reservations. Thus they are a much more valuable source of this sort of personal data than other e-commerce sites that only require personal data when people actually make purchases. Frequent users of airline booking sites are often frequent fliers who charge all their purchases to credit cards affiliated with the frequent flyer program, making it possible to correlate their travel profile with even their offline purchases.

"We know everything you've ever bought from our site, and everything you've ever looked at, even if you didn't buy" says Travelocity.com president Terry James. A travel company might decide that if you spent an hour looking at their Web pages, you're a good prospect for a sales call. They are willing to pay well for sales leads with contact information derived from Web site profiles and browsing logs.

What might this lead to? Suppose you make reservations for flights to Florida for yourself and your family. Suppose the records of credits for your airline frequent flyer affinity card show a pattern of purchases that marketers defined as "luxuries". In combination, that

Discount Tickets to Sinville

Suppose you make reservations for a business trip, at a special "meeting fare" or discount that identifies you as attending a particular conference. Suppose you're trying to figure out what you'll do with a little free time between sessions, and happen on a Website for a restaurant or entertainment directory that includes a topless club. You aren't interested, but you look at the Web page—in amusement, curiosity, morbid fascination, or outrage—before moving on to browse descriptions of places more to your taste.

If the Website correlates your visit to that page with your reservation and the information about you it contains, your name and address might be sold to the nightclub as part of a list of people who (1) are planning to visit that city for that convention and (2) visited the page with the club's advertisement. The club, in turn, might turn out to be part of a company that owns a variety of sex-related businesses. In due course, you might start getting glossy envelopes at your home, bulging with descriptions of that company's full range of sex services, with cover letters beginning, "Since you expressed interest in one of our properties, Topless Enterprises Inc. wants you to know all about what we have waiting for you when you get to Sinville, and the special discount price we're making available to you and your group from the Straightlaced Corporation."

information—and your home and business addresses and phone numbers, the dates of your planned trip, and where you plan to stay—might be sold to timeshare condo developers in that part of Florida.

It's impossible to predict just what form the first big Internet travel privacy invasion scandal will take, but I think it's inevitable if people don't take steps to protect themselves against this sort of abuse. Let's move on to the techniques of Internet travel privacy, and of protecting yourself against them.

TECHNIQUES OF INTERNET PRIVACY INVASION

Understanding the dangers will help you understand what you need to do to protect yourself against them. Here are some of the forms of Internet privacy invasion to watch out for:

What to Look For in a Privacy Policy

■ "We will not give, share, rent, or sell any personally identifiable information about you to anyone else without your permission, or unless ordered to do so by a court. If we receive a court order demanding information about you, we will tell you."

■ "You may revoke your permission for us to use or retain information about you at any time. On demand, we will delete all personally identifiable information about you from our records, and stop any use of information about you to which you object."

■ "We will not give, share, rent, or sell any personally identifiable information about you to anyone else unless they agree to be bound by all of these conditions including this one."

The right to remove your information completely on demand, and the right not to have information given to anyone else without subjecting them to the same conditions, are the most essential things to insist on. Without them, none of the other rules really mean anything. Without them, if the site finds a way to twist its policy to do something you didn't anticipate and don't like, there's nothing you can do about it. Likewise if the site and its data about you are sold to someone with a different interpretation of the original privacy agreement. These principles are at the core of the EU privacy regulations, but no law requires them in the United States. You have to demand them yourself, and refuse to do business with anybody who doesn't agree to them.

Not many Internet travel companies in the United States have policies like these—nor will they unless their customers demand them. But there's nothing in this checklist that isn't legally required of all e-commerce companies in the EU, and that couldn't be done equally easily in the United States if the public insisted on it. Online travel agencies have already demonstrated their vulnerability to concerted consumer pressure on privacy issues: the same Websites that used to require you to register before you could check

Web Browsing Records

Browsing the Web is, in effect, a conversation between your computer's Web browser program and the Web site's server computer. Each time your Web browser requests a page from the server, it sends "headers" and possibly "cookies" that identify you, and tells the server where to send the page you want. Unless you take steps to

prices have almost all dropped that requirement in the face of public unwillingness to agree to it. If they want your business, give them no choice but to respect your privacy.

Note what doesn't appear in this checklist: the security of the site. "We use SSL, and your password is encrypted," is largely irrelevant. Security measures can reduce the (small) risk that someone unknown will get your information, but they do nothing about the (large) risk that the people you are (securely) sending your information to will misuse it. Security measures and privacy policy are quite different. Web sites typically munge the issues together so as to use a smokescreen of high security to distract you from their low respect for privacy.

Lots of privacy policies contain prominent "privacy certifications" from trade groups like TRUSTe and BBBonline, but these don't mean much either. Don't mistake these for a Good Housekeeping seal of approval for privacy policy.

TRUSTe is a self-regulation organization created by e-commerce companies as part of their lobbying against government protection of privacy rights. The purpose of TRUSTe is to reassure you, so you won't worry about privacy—not to protect you. TRUSTe's founders, sponsors, and financial backers include some of the leading developers of privacy invasion technology. BBBonline is a similar venture of the Better Business Bureaus, funded by many of the same corporate sponsors.

At best, a TRUSTe or BBBonline privacy "seal" indicates only that a Website has a privacy policy, and that it doesn't lie about what information it collects and what it does with that information. Neither of these seals means that a site has a good privacy policy, or even an adequate one. Like most self-regulatory organizations that are supposed to police the people who pay their bills, TRUSTe and BBB "enforcement" is a joke: they've even allowed companies that lied about their privacy policies to keep their TRUSTe and BBBonline seals.

limit the information that is sent to the server, it can log your every click from page to page or site to site. If you go to another site, or come back to the same one later, it can tell you're the same person, and can assemble a profile of all the sites you've visited, pages you've viewed, things you've bought, etc.

Even without cookies or referral headers, clever Web designers can use URLs themselves to transfer information about you to seemingly independent sites. There's no way you can tell how much information may be conveyed by a user ID or session ID in a URL, or whether the site that gets that ID uses it to get more information about you behind your back. Coded ID's are being hidden from browsers by attaching them to transparent images ("Web bugs") that you never see. Computer consultant Richard M. Smith has a good survey of some of these techniques on his personal site at **www.tiac.net/users/smiths /privacy**, including examples of a travel company using codes in URLs for banner ads to send your travel itinerary to an advertising and profiling company.

Monitoring Of Public Terminals

Everything you do at a public Internet access terminal, such as a cybercafe, can be monitored and recorded. There might be a log of every keystroke being kept in a hidden file on the terminal, or the computer on the proprietor's or system administrator's desk might be showing a mirror image of your screen. There's no way you can

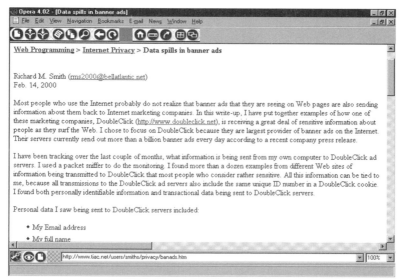

http://users.rcn.com/rms2000/privacy
Privacy consultant Richard Smith's Web site includes examples of personal information sent by travel sites to advertisers, including names, e-mail addresses, and trip destinations.

tell. Cybercafes should have their own privacy policies, but I've *never* been in a cybercafe with a posted promise to respect the privacy of patrons' online activities and I wouldn't trust one anyway.

Cookies

A "cookie" is a short coded snippet of text that a Web server sends you along with a Web page. Each time you go to that site, your browser sends the cookie along with its request for the next page. Cookies are the primary means by which the Web server can tell who you are, and distinguish one visitor from another. This is very useful to Web companies in building profiles of visitors.

Many sites rely on cookies for their "shopping basket", reservations, and purchasing features. That's unnecessary. Want proof that cookies aren't needed for e-commerce? Try Amazon.com, which does use cookies but doesn't require them for purchasing, or Southwest.com, the most successful airline Web site in the U.S., which doesn't use cookies at all.

For years advocates of cookies, mainly Netscape and Microsoft, claimed that cookies couldn't be used to correlate what you did on different Web sites. Eventually they have been forced to admit that that's not true: there are several ways that sites can use cookies to exchange information about you. If you've registered with a travel site that uses cookies, other sites you visit can get all the information you've given the travel site if it chooses to sell that information. The worst abusers of multisite cookies are Internet advertising brokers like Doubleclick.net. They want to know *all* the sites you visit, so that they can send you more highly "targeted" banner ads—for which they can charge advertisers higher prices.

Spyware

More and more programs are "Internet enabled". That's not necessarily a bad thing. But some programs send information about you over the Internet without your knowledge. For example, many downloadable shareware programs are now supported by advertising. Whenever you use the program, part of your display is taken up by ads downloaded from the Internet by the program. What isn't so obvious is that those programs send information about what you are doing with them to the advertising service. Once again, their goal is to build as much of a profile of your interests as possible, so as to send you targeted ads.

Worse, sometimes the part of the program that tracks your actions, and sends activity logs over the Internet, remains active even after you've uninstalled the rest of the program. Steve Gibson,

What Your Web Browser Says About You

Microsoft Internet Explorer (MSIE) and Netscape include features in their browsers which, unless you turn them off, can send Microsoft or Netscape a log of every page you view. They claim their purpose is to be able to help determine which other pages you might be interested in, based on where you have been in the past. Netscape's "What's Related?" and MSIE's "Smart Browsing" features both use software designed by Alexa (now part of Amazon.com) that keeps a hidden connection to Netscape or Microsoft open whenever you are on the Internet. For details, see the article, "What's Related? Everything but Your Privacy," **www.interhack.net/pubs/whatsrelated.** MSIE's "Page Hit Counting" is even worse; unless disabled, it lets Microsoft or other sites know what pages or files you've looked at, even those you looked at while you weren't connected to the Internet.

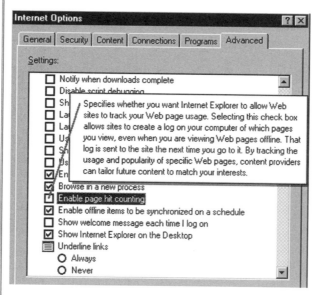

Among essential privacy settings hidden in MSIE 4 and 5's "advanced" menu are "enable page hit counting" and "install on demand". Shown above is Microsoft's own "What's This?" pop-up description of page hit counting. Didn't know they could do this, did you?

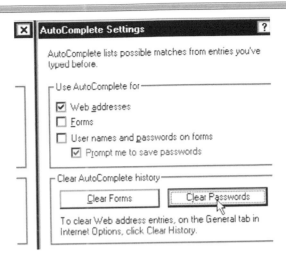

If you allow MSIE 5 to save your passwords, anyone who gets access to your computer can log into Web sites, view or change your reservations, or make purchases in your name.

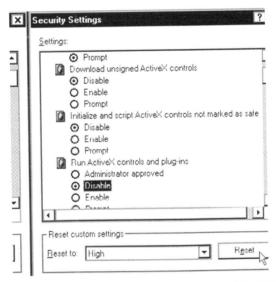

Set security to "High" for the "Internet zone" in MSIE 5. There's no in-between security setting for ActiveX: if you allow a Web site to run any ActiveX program, it can install, read, copy, change, or delete anything on your computer, leaving few if any traces.

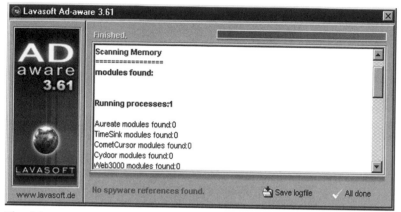

The Ad-aware program can detect and remove the most common "spy-ware" programs that are installed along with innocuous-seeming programs, but then secretly send logs of your Web browsing to advertisers.

who wrote one of the first tools to detect these programs, has christened them "spyware". You can use programs like Ad-Aware (**www .lavasoft.de**) and Zone Alarm (**www.zonelabs.com**) to detect and remove these programs from your computer.

Site Registrations

In order to make reservations or buy anything on the Internet, you have to give your name, address, and payment information. Once you've given that information, you have very little control over how it is used. Multi-site cookies and other techniques like uniquely coded URLs and referral headers make it easy for a site where you've registered to make that information available to other sites you visit, so that they can use it for profiling, junk mail, telemarketing, or spam.

Internet users are extremely reluctant to register until they are actually ready to buy. At one time, almost every airline ticket and reservations site required advance registration. In early 2000, both Travelocity.com and Expedia.com eliminated their registration requirements for browsing prices in response to heavy public pressure, although both still require cookies. Other sites were forced to follow suit if they wanted to compete. Similar gains are possible on other privacy and consumer protection issues, if Internet users assert their collective power through concerted collective action. Don't take privacy invasions for granted. Do something about them, and you might be surprised at how much it's possible to get them changed.

Newsgroup, Mailing List and E-mail Archives

Everything you post to a Usenet newsgroup is archived and available to the public forever after. In seconds, anyone who wants to can get a complete indexed list of all messages ever posted to newsgroups from any e-mail address.

Not all mailing lists or e-mail messages are archived. But what often happens is that one person on a mailing list keeps copies of all the messages, and months or years later puts that archive on the Web. You should assume that any message to a mailing list, and potentially any e-mail message to someone you don't trust, could eventually be made public on the Web.

Data Mining

"Data mining"—commercial exploitation of personal information about customers that they collect—is regarded by many travel sites as one of their major potential sources of income. Other sites and companies will pay well for information about you, such as your name, address, phone number and interests. Unless a site promises not to sell, rent, share, or give information about you to others, you have no control of where the details of your travel plans will end up. If the company that runs the Web site goes out of business, it could be forced to sell its customer data at the bankruptcy auction along with its other assets.

Spam

"Spam" (spammers prefer the more polite term, "unsolicited commercial e-mail") is, of course, the great plague of the Internet. Anyone who gets your e-mail address can send you spam, or give your address to someone else who will send you spam. Spammers generally hide their addresses, so it's very hard to find them or to know how they got your address.

HOW TO PROTECT YOUR PRIVACY

The following are some basic steps you can take to make yourself safer from Internet privacy invasion and misuse of information about you collected while you are browsing the Internet. Some require nothing more than paying attention to possible risks while using the Internet. Most involve changing some of settings of your Web browser, or using a different browser. And a few involve downloading and installing simple add-on privacy and security programs. Here's a privacy checklist for safer surfing.

All of these suggestions are corollaries of one general principle: don't give information (and make sure your browser doesn't automatically give any information) to people you don't trust. That's a function of which browser program you use, your browser settings, your Internet connection, and the care you take before you give out information about yourself. Keep in mind that once you tell a site something about yourself, you can rarely get your privacy back.

Read Everything Before Doing Anything

Before you fill out a registration form or let a site set a "cookie", read their privacy policy carefully. Privacy policies are written to look reassuring, while promising as little as possible. If you aren't completely satisfied that the site won't do anything you don't approve of, go elsewhere.

Don't Give Permission For Things You Don't Want

Don't be misled by promises that "We won't give information about you to anyone else." That doesn't stop companies from sending spam or making telemarketing calls on behalf of someone else who's paid them to do it. It's impossible to know in advance whether a company's e-mail "newsletter" will consist of one short message every six months, or daily messages filled with pages of ads from other people. Most abuse of personal information is done by people to whom you have knowingly provided it—but who use it in ways you didn't anticipate. The only way to protect yourself is to be sure that they promise to stop whatever they are doing on demand, no matter what you previously gave them permission for.

— UNCHECK THAT BOX

Many people give "permission" for spam, telemarketing, or junk mail without intending to do so. Look for a small box on Website registration forms that says something like, "Please send me information". Usually the box is checked; if you don't want to give permission for unlimited marketing harassment by all available means, you have to uncheck the box before you submit the form.

Consider Using a Different Browser

Microsoft Internet Explorer (MSIE) and Netscape Navigator are the best known and most widely used browsers. But both MSIE and Netscape have special built-in privacy invasion features not found in any other browsers I know of. Microsoft and Netscape are by no means the only browser makers. There are other equally good browsers, some of them smaller, faster, more reliable, and with more

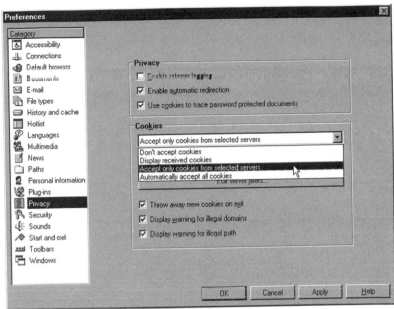

Opera is the only major browser that properly labels cookies and referral headers as privacy issues, rather than hiding them in "advanced" settings or giving no control of them at all.

features in addition to being better designed for privacy and security. You may not have heard of them, but you can download them from their publishers or authors, or from other shareware sites. If you spend several hours a week using a Web browser, a small investment of time, and maybe money, in a more efficient and secure browser could repay itself quickly. My current all-around favorite for general use in Windows is Opera, but I encourage you try out several and choose for yourself.

Disable "Referral Logging"

Neither Microsoft nor Netscape offers this option. "Referral logging" is always on in MSIE and Netscape, so to deal with this you'll need either to change browsers or use add-on software that removes the "referral" headers from your browser's requests for Web pages. Opera and Lynx, among other browsers, include options to disable referral hearers. Most proxy servers and firewalls intended for privacy protection can also remove referral headers. Referral headers tell each Web site which other Web site you went to previously, enabling them to track your movement from site to site and correlate different pieces of personal information that you provide to different sites.

Don't Accept "Cookies" From Unknown Web sites

Disable "cookies" except from specific sites that you've decided to trust. Opera 4, Netscape 6, and Lynx allow you accept cookies only from a list of specified sites. With earlier versions of Netscape, the best you can do is to set up two "user profiles", one for trusted sites (with cookies enabled) and another for general use with all other sites (with cookies disabled). For maximum protection against unwanted cookies, choose both, "Refuse all cookies" and "Warn before accepting cookies"; these are not necessarily redundant.

In MSIE for Windows, you can control cookie acceptance through the use of "security zones" in the Internet Options. Disable cookies in the security settings for the "Internet zone". Add only sites that you trust, and that require cookies, to the "trusted zone". MSIE 5 for the Macintosh (but not the Windows version) includes an easier to use site-specific cookie acceptance list.

If you need to enable cookies for a specific site, set your browser to accept only cookies that are sent only to that site's own server, not ones that can be sent to any site. That makes a slight difference, since there are ways for sites to exchange information anyway, but it helps a little.

If you don't like the way your browser manages cookies, you can install a separate privacy program to deal with them. The most effective cookie controls are provided by some of the personal proxy servers, as described below. There also stand-alone cookie management programs, but those I've tested are less effective than the cookie management features of good proxy servers.

Don't Allow Web sites To Run Unknown Programs

Web pages can contain embedded "scripts" and other programs that actually run on your computer. Once you load the page, the program is downloaded and starts automatically if your browser allows it. Then, if your browser permits it, it can do or send anything you could do or send from your keyboard. Obviously, it's crucial to make sure your browser keeps these scripts and other programs under control, so they don't send information out to the Internet without your knowledge or consent.

MSIE is probably the least secure browser on this score, making it uniquely vulnerable to privacy invasion, viruses, Trojan horses, and other Internet nasties. Virtually all independent security experts denounce Microsoft software as being designed without regard for security or privacy; almost any other operating systems and applications are more secure. The close integration of different Microsoft products (Internet Explorer, Windows, Outlook, Office, etc.) with each other and with the Internet makes it especially easy for programs hidden in a Web page to wreak havoc with your computer—or simply hide themselves and quietly send your every action across the Internet. But this isn't just a Microsoft problem: any software that allows Web pages to run programs on your computer makes you vulnerable.

To minimize these risks, disable "Downloading of active content," ActiveX, ActiveX scripts, Java, Javascript, "scripting languages," "Smart Update," and "AutoInstall." Set "Active content security" to "High."

Disable Automatic Sending of Your E-mail Address

If your browser offers this option, disable "Send e-mail address as anonymous FTP password." It's not anonymous if your browser automatically sends your e-mail address. If each copy of the file, such as a downloaded software program, contains a unique serial number (as it often does), all subsequent use of the software can be correlated with the e-mail address your browser gave out, perhaps without your knowledge, when you downloaded it.

Consider a Proxy Server and/or a Personal Firewall

Install a personal proxy server on your computer. The extra effort going into installing and configuring software will result in giving you fundamentally greater browsing privacy, vastly greater browsing speed and the ability to filter out annoying advertisements.

A proxy server sits between your Web browser(s) and the Internet. When you enter a URL or click on a link in the browser, it sends the request to the proxy server, instead of directly to the Internet. The proxy server evaluates the request, according to rules that you gave it, and decides whether to pass it on or not. You can set up your proxy server to ignore all requests for cookies, or for banner ads. Also, you can set the proxy server to remove "referral" headers and other identifying information before it forwards requests to Web sites.

Proxy servers do more than protect your privacy and security. Short of not loading any images at all, nothing will speed your browsing as much as a proxy server that blocks banner ads. In Europe, where most people pay by the minute for local phone calls to connect to the Internet, ad-blocking proxy servers are marketed primarily as tools to speed browsing.

Easy Ways to Protect Your Privacy

Check Your Web browser's Privacy Settings

The "default" settings of most browsers (the way the browser is set up when it is first installed) are the least secure and least private. You can easily change the settings of even bad browsers to make your browsing considerably safer and more private. But you have to take the initiative; if you do nothing, your privacy is at risk. Those who want to watch you are counting on your inaction. They know that few people even change the default home page (the page, if any, that is called up each time you start your browser), and even fewer dare change settings that are labeled "Advanced".

Browser privacy is similar to the situation with your phone number: it costs no more to have a listing in the phone book without your address or with only your first initial and last name. And for a small additional charge, you can have an entirely unlisted number that's much more private. But unless you specifically ask for something different, your listing in the phone book will have your full name and address.

Microsoft and Netscape hide most of the important security and privacy choices in the "Advanced", rather than the "Security", dialogs of their browsers. Presumably, this is to discourage novice users from turning off the privacy invasion features of these browsers. Don't be intimidated. None of these settings can damage your browser or your computer, and you can change any or all of them back if you don't like the results, or if you need to enable specific features to browse a particular ill-designed Web site.

Disable Microsoft and Netscape Privacy Invasion Features

If you use Microsoft or Netscape browsers, disable "What's Related?", "Show Related Links", "Smart Browsing", and (in MSIE) "Page Hit Counting". If you leave them on, these features make it possible for Microsoft and/or Netscape to maintain and receive logs of every site you visit and Web page or file you view, even when you aren't connected to the Internet.

Facing Page: *Don't be intimidated by the label "advanced": the settings on these screens in Netscape are basic to your privacy.*

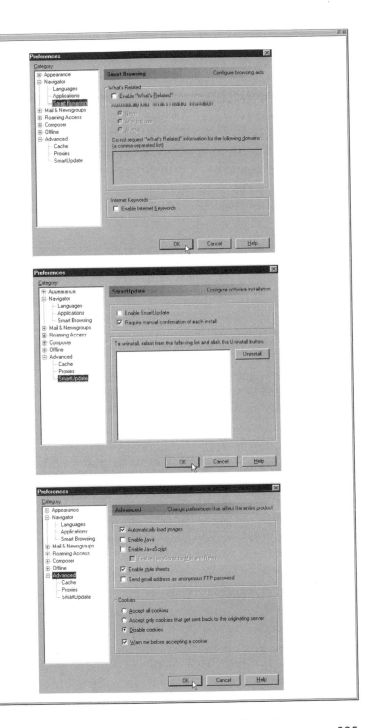

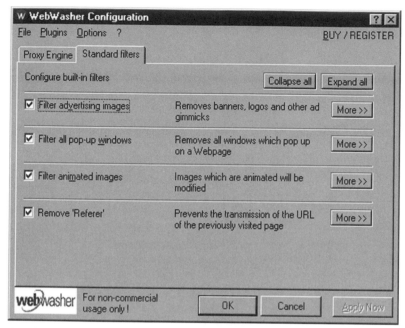

Free "proxy servers" like Web Washer, Proxomitron, and Junkbuster can eliminate many advertisements, speed Web browsing, and greatly enhance your privacy by reducing the amount of information about you that gets sent by your computer to each Web site you visit.

My current preference for Windows (it's also available for Linux and several other platforms, although not for the Macintosh) is the Internet Junkbuster Proxy, **www.junkbuster.com**. Unfortunately, the initial installation and setup of the Junkbuster proxy requires manual copying of files into different directories and editing of configuration files in a text editor. There's a version of the Junkbuster proxy for Windows that's easier to install (although you still have to configure it manually) at **ourworld.compuserve.com/homepages/gtschech/ijb95_en.htm**.

Some Windows programs that perform most of the same functions and have graphical, menu-based user interfaces and one-click installation include Proxomitron (**proxomitron.tripod.com**), AdSubtract, **www.adsubtract.com** (formerly called InterMute), and Web Washer, **www.Webwasher.com**. Proxomitron (my favorite of these three) is slightly more privacy-oriented; AdSubtract and Web Washer are designed primarily to speed Web browsing by eliminating unwanted banner ads and annoyances. Since most shareware download sites are supported by banner advertising that these programs are designed to block, they won't list them. You'll probably need to go directly to the programs' own sites to download them.

None of these programs (yet) gives optimal privacy protection with its default settings. Whichever you use, you'll need to review the options it offers and do some manual reconfiguration after you install it. Check around, this software niche is being driven, fast, by Internet users' growing recognition of privacy risks and growing desire for a software equivalent to the "mute" and "fast-forward" buttons on TV's and VCR's.

Most Internet connection sharing software (except Microsoft's built-in Internet Connection Sharing) includes elements of a personal firewall and/or proxy server. Personal firewalls are also available separately, especially for people with "always on" DSL or cable modem Internet connections. The exact features of these programs and other personal firewalls are beyond the scope of this book. My most important advice,

IF THEY DEMAND UNNECESSARY INFORMATION, LIE

As a last resort, you can always register with a Website as Mickey Mouse or your dog, give 555-1212 (directory assistance) as your phone number, and give a nonexistent address. I'll leave it to you to decide when that's ethically appropriate. But I will note that even paid consultants to the privacy invasion (direct marketing) industry have been known to recommend giving bogus information if a site asks for more information than you think appropriate.

however, is not to rely for your privacy or security on a program you don't understand. If you're not sure what you are doing, it's easy to configure even a very good program in a way that leaves you vulnerable. Privacy and security are definitely areas in which to call on your most knowledgeable and paranoid friend for assistance in setting up your system.

Use an Alternate E-mail Address for Public Messages

Use an alternate e-mail address for all postings to Usenet newsgroups, bulletin boards, mailing lists, or chat rooms. Spammers "harvest" e-mail addresses from all these places. Any e-mail address that appears in these places will get more spam. To avoid the spam, you can either get a different, but valid, address for these uses, or "munge" your address by changing your address in a way that a human reader will understand, but a spam robot won't. For example, "My address is edwardnospam@hasbrouck.org. Remove "nospam" to contact me".

Unless you want to be known, and are *really* sure you want whatever you are saying preserved in your name for posterity, use an anonymous address. Free providers of anonymous Web-based e-mail accounts are discussed in the chapter on using the Internet while traveling.

Don't Do Anything Private from a Public Computer

Public Internet access terminals in cybercafes, libraries, etc. are inherently vulnerable to electronic eavesdropping. To date, it's been rare, but you'll never know when it is happening. If you want to do anything private—including anything that requires entering a password you wouldn't give out freely to total strangers—don't do it from a public terminal if you have a choice. For more on laptop computers and handheld Internet access devices, see the chapter on using the Internet while traveling.

Of course, you may not be able to afford that choice: the price of privacy is the cost of bringing your own computer. If you can't afford a portable computer, there may be times when you have to use a cybercafe for something private, or that requires a password. If that happens, be as cautious as you can. If there's a choice, use the cybercafe that seems most trustworthy. (No, there's really no way to tell except your intuition.) If you have to use a password at a public terminal, change it as soon as you get home.

Reveal no more than necessary, and think about the consequences if what you are doing turns out to be monitored. If someone gets your e-mail password, they can read and delete your e-mail, and send mail that appears to be from you. That's bad, but probably not a disaster. If someone gets your password to a travel site, they can cancel or change your reservations, or perhaps make charges to your account. If they get your online banking password, or anything that's considered an electronic signature, they can do much more serious damage.

PRIVACY COMPLAINTS AND ENFORCEMENT

— IT'S HARD TO ENFORCE — NON-EXISTENT LAWS

In theory, the U.S. Federal Trade Commission is in charge of enforcing Federal privacy laws. The problem is that there aren't any meaningful Federal Internet privacy laws.

Privacy protection is a do-it-yourself endeavor, not a matter for the police. In the United States, the collection, distribution, sale, and misuse of personal information and Internet activity profiles is, in most cases, perfectly legal.

The power of the Federal

Trade Commision (FTC) on privacy issues is effectively limited to cases of fraud, where a Web site or Internet-based service lies about what information they collect, or how they will use it, or breach of contract if they violate their stated privacy promises. If they say nothing, or you haven't yet agreed to anything, they can do anything they want.

The FTC doesn't seem to have tried very hard, anyway. Fines for flagrant violations of written promises have been minimal, and all the worst offenders are still in business.

Security and Credit Card Numbers

Surveys show that consumers' greatest fear of online purchasing is fear of sending credit card information over the Internet. This is also the most common reason why even people who use the Internet to check prices often prefer to complete their purchases by phone, fax, or in person.

Is this fear justified? So far as I can tell, it is not. I've never heard of anyone whose credit card number was stolen and used to defraud them as a result of an Internet purchase. Without exception, every expert I spoke with dismissed the chances of a credit card number being intercepted in transmission over the Internet, and used to defraud the cardholder, as negligible. Consumer groups have raised many issues about potential fraud and invasion of privacy on the Internet, but the security of credit card number transmission is not one of them. Indeed, if your primary concern is the safety of your credit card numbers, that would be a compelling reason to use your credit cards *only* over the Internet.

That doesn't mean that there is no risk to giving out your credit card number over the Internet. The point that the computer security and fraud experts are making, however, is that:

- The actual transmission of the credit card number over the Internet is the safest part of the process.
- There is at least as much risk of fraud or theft of personal information in face-to-face, phone, or fax transactions as over the Internet.
- The cardholder has minimal, if any, liability for unauthorized use of their credit card or card number, regardless of how someone obtains it.

It's natural, of course, to be afraid to send our credit card numbers, the closest equivalent to the vaunted "digital cash" in the present American payment system, off to who knows where by such intangible and impersonal means as the Internet. How, then, can we do so safely and without undue fear?

Most of the real dangers of fraud are unrelated to the technicalities of how credit card numbers are transmitted. The possibility of fraud—and how to avoid it—crops up often throughout this book. But since fear of sending credit card numbers over the Internet is so strong and so widespread, this section will focus on a few simple, specific things you can do to protect yourself against credit card number theft and resultant fraud.

SECURE BROWSERS AND WEB SITES

The most basic technical precaution is to use a secure browser and to make online purchases only from secure Web sites.

One of the standard "protocols" for transmitting information over the Internet is something called the "Secure Hypertext Transfer Protocol", represented in URLs by "https". Browsing the Web using https looks just like browsing using the regular Hypertext Transfer Protocol ("http"). But in the secure form of the protocol, as one would expect from its name, all data sent between your browser and the Web site, in both directions, is encrypted.

Current versions of the four most important browsers (Microsoft Internet Explorer, Netscape Navigator/Communicator, Opera, and Lynx), include some version of the "Secure Socket Layer" (SSL) required for secure http. You don't have to do anything to turn it on; when you browse a secure Web site, the encryption is automatic. You can disable SSL in your browser's security or cryptography settings, but in that case you won't be able to visit secure sites at all. It's impossible to browse a secure site without having the entire transaction securely encrypted.

You can tell you're browsing a secure site because (1) the URL begins with "https" or "shttp", (2) your browser shows a security icon in the status bar (MSIE and Netscape both use a stylized padlock that appears closed when you're browsing a secure site, and appears open or disappears entirely when you're browsing an ordinary, insecure site), and (3) unless you disable it, a window pops up to notify you whenever you enter or leave a secure site.

The exact level of encryption varies, depending on the browser and server software you and the Web site are using. Web browsing is, in effect, a conversation between your browser and the Web site's server. Whichever is less secure is the limiting factor.

The nature of the Internet complicates the task of data thieves. Breaking messages into many small pieces, sending the pieces out of sequence and by different routes, and interspersing small pieces of one message in a large stream of unrelated data, are standard techniques for foiling code breakers. On the Internet, all messages are sent that way. No one knows or can predict how any message will be broken into packets, or what path any packet will follow. Even if someone intercepts and decodes one packet, it's likely to contain only part of the information they need to do any damage. Ten thousand unrelated packets from other conversations may go past before the next packet in your message goes, even if it passes the same point in the network where one packet from your message was intercepted.

I go to such lengths to explain browser security not because I think it's a big issue but because I know it's such a big bugaboo and barrier for Internet buyers. I don't think it should be an issue at all. There has been no documented case of theft of credit card numbers from secure browsing sessions.

But I also recognize that your skepticism is justified. Microsoft and Netscape don't make their money on browsers—they give them away. They make their money selling server software and the biggest buyers of server software are people trying to sell you things over the Internet. Their profits, and their ability to pay for more Microsoft and Netscape server software, depend on your willingness to send your credit card number over the Internet. Improving the *perceived* security of online credit card transactions is one of the highest priorities of browser and server designers.

Can the codes used for secure browsing be broken? Yes. Any code can be broken, just as any safe can be cracked, with enough time, talent, and tools. All that physical or virtual security measures can accomplish is to keep out the less skilled or less well equipped

Electronic Signatures

On June 30, 2000, the Electronic Signatures Act was signed into law, making "electronic signatures" legally equivalent to written signatures. Electronic signatures are being touted as providing heightened security and making possible a more secure system for online shopping. In reality, the Electronic Signatures Act could prove to be the greatest setback for consumers in the history of e-commerce, increasing the damage potential of identity theft and shifting the effective burden of proof in disputes between consumers and online merchants.

What's an electronic signature? The law doesn't say. The idea is that you would use some sort of software to "sign" a message electronically. Your electronic signature would be legally valid—to the same extent as a written signature—in proving that you, and no one else, had "signed" the message.

No one yet knows exactly how this will work, and the law doesn't include any technical specifications. One of many criticisms of the Electronic Signatures Act is that it allows the substitution of electronic for written signatures, without any requirement that an electronic signature actually be secure, reliable, or resistant to electronic forgery.

Electronic signatures were developed to solve the problem of credit card fraud by customers against merchants. This type of fraud is a huge risk for merchants, and they are, naturally, extremely eager to see consumers forced to use electronic signatures to identify themselves. But electronic signatures will do nothing to make e-commerce more secure for consumers, and there's no reason for you to prefer prefer Web sites that use them. On the contrary, consenting to give electronic signatures the same legal status as physical signatures will significantly reduce your protection against unauthorized charges.

The essence of the new Federal law is to direct courts, banks, and credit card chargebacks departments to accept an electronic signature as proof that you authorized and are responsible for a charge.

At present, if the merchant doesn't get a physical signature on a charge slip, they have to prove in some other way that you actually authorized the charge. You are not responsible for unauthorized charges, no matter how much information about you a thief has.

Legal recognition of electronic signatures as equivalent to physical signatures could effectively shift the burden of proof for disputed charges from the merchant to the consumer: if someone uses your electronic signature, it will be up to you to prove it wasn't really you.

Electronic signatures were not a consumer protection initiative. The point of electronic signatures is to add a means by which the merchant can verify the customer's identity and, later, prove that a charge was authorized by the cardholder. That's great for merchants, but what will it mean for consumers?

In order to provide any real security, the password or key to any electronic signature will have to be too long to be conveniently written down, memorized, or typed in each time it is used. You'll either have to store the key in each computer you might wish to use for online purchases, or carry it around on a floppy disk. Anyone who can steal or get access to a disc or computer with your digital key stored on it will be able to create perfect forgeries of your electronic signature on electronic purchase orders charged to your account.

A floppy disk, obviously, is larger, more fragile, and harder to carry securely hidden than is a credit card. Even "safe" inside your computer on its hard disk, an electronic signature file is vulnerable to anyone with even brief access to the computer (a nontrivial problem even in your home, much less in an office), as well as outright theft of the computer.

Some people have proposed "biometric" passwords, such as voiceprints or electronically scanned fingerprints. But these have their own vulnerabilities: How can you prevent anyone who has a digital copy of a voice recording or fingerprint scan from using it in place of a "live" recording or scan? And once they've scanned you once (and kept a copy), how can you prove whether they've actually scanned you again for a subsequent purchase, or simply used another copy of the first scan?

It's still too early to tell how the Electronic Signatures Act will change the way airlines, online travel companies, and credit card chargeback departments do business. The law is vague, and how it will be interpreted and implemented probably won't be known for years. It's not clear if you'll have a real choice, but if you do, don't consent to recognition of your password as an "electronic signature" within the meaning of the Electronic Signature Act, or as a legal equivalent of your written signature.

intruders, and to make entry slow and difficult enough that the real professionals will take on easier targets.

Browser security meets that test. It's simply not worth the time and computer resources that a thief would need to decode even the lowest levels of secure browser packets. Decoding would be difficult, at best; it's impossible to tell in advance which packet might be one of the tiny fraction that contains a credit card number or a fragment of one; and there are so many easier means of obtaining credit card data as to make Internet credit card number theft unattractive to thieves.

COMPARING INTERNET AND OFFLINE TRANSACTIONS

Why are thieves so unlikely to waste their time trying to tap and decode secure browser sessions? Compare what happens when you use your credit card to buy things by phone, fax, or in person.

If you order by phone, there's no way you can tell who might be listening in, or whether you can trust the person who takes your order. Telephone calls are vulnerable to interception anywhere along the wire. Telephone orders are taken and processed by everyone from minimum-wage clerks to maximum-security prisoners. More and more U.S. businesses, including some airlines and some travel agencies, are using prison labor for their order-taking, telemarketing, reservations, and ticketing call centers. It's impossible to get the work done without giving low-level employees access to as many credit card numbers as they may figure out how to abuse.

If you use a cordless phone, both sides of the conversation are, quite literally, *broadcast*, unencoded, to anyone in the neighborhood. Cordless-phone eavesdropping is the simplest way to steal a person's credit card number. All it requires is the patience to wait nearby with a scanner until they purchase something over their cordless phone.

Faxed orders are even more vulnerable to interception than phone orders. Any phone line can be used for phone ordering, so businesses' phone orders may come in over any of dozens of lines, sometimes through digital switchboards that would require more specialized equipment to tap. Most fax machines, on the other hand, require separate lines, almost always standard analog lines, so it's usually possible to intercept all of even a good-sized business's faxed orders by tapping one or two dedicated fax lines.

Fax taps are also much less labor-intensive than voice wiretaps. Just connect a fax machine to the tap, or play the intercepts back through one, and then flip through the printed faxes to find the filled-in order forms. These give not just card numbers but billing addresses, phone numbers, and facsimile signatures. Fax ordering is used especially often by businesses that sell to other businesses, where the orders are charged to corporate cards with higher credit limits and less closely scrutinized bills than personal credit cards.

Even if you order in person, and even if your credit card never leaves your sight, as it usually does, for example, in a restaurant, and you leave nothing behind in writing, the person who takes your order has ample opportunity to memorize your card number and expiration date.

No matter how you place your order, the merchant eventually has to get an approval for the charge from the bank that issued your card. E-commerce servers for Internet purchases generally connect to the bank through a digital link with the same security—or greater—as secure browsers. In most cases of orders by other means, the merchant either telephones for an approval—with all the interception risks of another phone call—or uses a "Verifone" terminal—the familiar countertop unit with the keypad, card reader, and receipt printer—to get the approval. Verifone terminals, like fax machines, use dedicated analog phone lines and transmit information to and from the bank in a standard,

FEAR NOT THE ONLINE PURCHASE

I regularly make purchases from one Silicon Valley business that takes nearly all of its orders by unencoded e-mail. Yet most of its customers are computer geeks, hackers, and engineers. Even unencoded e-mail is at least as safe as any of the other ways that consumers regularly give out their credit card numbers. Online purchases through secure browsers are by far the safest ways of all to use your credit cards.

unencoded format (ASCII at 1200 baud). Secondhand Verifone terminals cost little more than fax machines, but aren't even necessary for interception or decoding, since the format is compatible with any standard modem. Even large-scale telephone order centers generally obtain their credit card authorizations over standard dial-up modem connections.

At the end of each day, when the merchant closes their "batch" of charges, all the credit card numbers, approval codes, and amounts are retransmitted in sequence. Tap the credit card processing phone line for those few minutes, play a recording of the tap back to a PC's modem, and a thief will have a neat file of details on every charge by that merchant that day.

Given all these factors, it's hard to understand why people who are reluctant to send their credit card number over the Internet, even encoded, would *prefer* to transmit that credit card number by such less-secure means as phone or fax. The more people know, the less confidence they have in the security or privacy of phone conversations. The more people know about the Internet, the more confidence they have in the security of Internet data transmission.

RESPONSIBILITY FOR UNAUTHORIZED CHARGES

"Wait a minute," you say. "You were supposed to be reassuring me, and now you've just told me that my credit card number is readily available to anybody who wants it. Where's the security?"

Well, suppose someone gets your credit card number. What can they do with it? The real protection against credit card fraud is *not* in the protection of your credit card number, but in the substantial legal and practical protections credit card customers have against being held liable for unauthorized charges.

At *worst*, under U.S. Federal law (15 U.S.C. section 1643, **law .house.gov/uscsrch.htm**), holders of credit cards issued in the U.S. are liable for a maximum of $50 per credit card, regardless of the volume of unauthorized charges. The $50 limit applies only if your card is used before you have taken reasonable steps to notify the card issuer that your card number might have been stolen. In practice, in order to keep your good will as their customer, most credit card issuers won't charge you even the $50 that they are allowed.

Under the same section of the law, the burden is on each merchant to prove that you authorized each charge they make to your credit card account. The fact that someone knows your credit card number is not considered proof of your authorization. If your card number was used without your permission by a criminal, or if you authorize the charge but the merchant can't prove it, it's the merchant, *not* you, who takes the loss. Consumers' direct losses to credit card fraud are trivial, merchants lose billions of dollars a year to credit card fraud by dishonest customers.

WEB SITE REGISTRATIONS

Many Web sites require you to "register" by filling out a form and perhaps accepting a "cookie" before you can make purchases. Travel Web sites, in particular, usually require you to complete a profile and provide your credit card number before you can make confirmed reservations.

Many travelers consider these requests to be intrusive. Why should I have to provide my credit card number before I even know how much a ticket might cost, much less whether I want to buy it? Once I give them my credit card number, how do I know they won't use it without my approval?

They can't charge your card unless they can *prove* that you authorized the specific charge. Giving a Web site your credit card number doesn't give them permission to charge your card. The reason they want your card number in advance is not to charge it without permission, but to separate serious customers, "bookers", from Web window-shoppers, "lookers".

Travel reservation Web sites use complex and expensive software running on unusually large server computers. These connect to even larger and more complex CRS's, the world's largest integrated real-time databases, that provide the airline reservation and pricing information. Browsing a Web site may be free for you, but it's an expensive toy to play with, and somebody has to foot the bill. The Web site is charged by the CRS for each query you make, whether or not you buy a ticket. That's on top of the cost of running their own Web server.

One of the key factors for the profitability of an airline reservations Web site is then the ratio of lookers to bookers. It's certainly the first issue that executives of big Web based travel agencies talk about when they get together. If you aren't ready to buy, with your credit card ready, they don't want you running up their computer and CRS bills by making unproductive reservations. So they often require you to register and provide your credit card number as a way to "qualify" their potential customers and drive away the idle browsers.

That all makes sense. Their purpose isn't to provide a source of

Read Before You Click "Okay"

When registering to use a Web site, one of the greatest dangers is of inadvertently waiving your rights or pre-authorizing charges while registering to use a Web site. Typically, you'll be presented with a small window in which you can see only the start of a long, legalistic document, under which is an "OK" or "Accept" button that you have to click to register. Or there'll be a line in fine print at the bottom of one or another screen, stating that by registering you agree to accept the site's terms of use. No matter how much of a nuisance it might be, it is absolutely essential in any such case to read all of the terms carefully before proceeding.

I know: everyone knows you should read the fine print, but no one does. Don't blame me, though, if you get in trouble because you didn't read what you were agreeing to before you clicked "OK".

The language to look out for is a clause stating that by registering you authorize or agree to be responsible for any purchases or charges using your password, account, or electronic signature. The word "authorize" should be a special red flag, since that's the word used in the federal credit card law. So should "consent to use of an electronic signature", since such consent makes your password legally equivalent to your written signature as proof of your authorization. If you agree to terms like these, you could be considered to have waived your right to contest unauthorized charges made by anyone who has your site password. Site passwords are far too insecure for that to be safe.

Courts have been—quite justifiably—reluctant to enforce such "click-wrap" agreements on purchasers of software, on the grounds that people aren't really expected to read them and that a waiver of your rights has to be made "knowingly". The same

free information on fares and schedules, their purpose is to sell stuff. It's a nuisance for you to have to go through the registration process the first time you use the site, but that's the point. If it isn't important enough to you to take the time to register, they see that as a sign that you aren't a serious customer. And registration is no nuisance at all to regular customers, since they already registered the first time they used the site.

So there's no reason not to register with any sites you want to

arguments ought to apply to click-through agreements in site registrations. But you can't count on it, and you shouldn't accept such terms just because the courts *might* find them unenforceable. I recommend strongly against completing any registration that requires such a pre-authorization, waiver, or consent to use of electronic signatures.

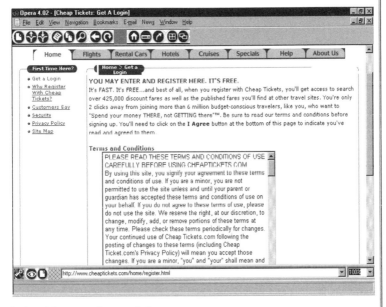

http://www.cheaptickets.com
If you click through pages like this without reading them, you could find out later that you've agreed to fees or rules you didn't know about and wouldn't have wanted.

use, *if* they have an acceptable privacy policy, nor any reason not to give them your credit card number. The things to watch out for are (1) sites that use registrations and/or e-mail addresses for telemarketing or spamming and (2) sites that try to get you to waive your consumer rights or pre-authorize charges as a condition of registration.

Telemarketing and spam are impossible to avoid completely, but there are a few things you can do to reduce them. To minimize telemarketing calls at my home, I always use my business phone number on site registrations, warranty cards, sales slips, and the like. Most telemarketers call outside of business hours, and give up if they get the switchboard of a business. If someone has little reason to need your phone number, you can always give a fax number as your phone number. Telemarketers will only get noise in their ears if they call a fax number; someone who *really* needs to contact you will figure out what it is, and send you a fax.

To minimize spam, many people "munge" their e-mail addresses in site registrations and newsgroup postings. For example, I might use, edwardnospam@hasbrouck.org, instead of my actual e-mail address, edward@hasbrouck.org. A human being will figure out that they should remove the "nospam". Spam robots won't, and will waste their time, not yours, misdirecting their unwanted messages to the virtual dead letter office.

This is fine when registering for purely informational sites, but I don't recommend this for travel reservations and other e-commerce sites from which you actually intend to make purchases. Many e-commerce sites use the e-mail address you give them when you first register as the address to which to send confirmations of your online purchases. Giving an anti-spam address may keep you from getting confirmation notices or follow-up e-mail messages advising you of schedule changes.

PROTECT YOUR COOKIES AND PASSWORDS

Protect your Web site login names and passwords as well as you can. They probably can't be used to make charges that you'll have to pay. But they might be used to view your stored profiles, personal information, and travel history and plans; to make or change reservations in your name; or to cause you a wide variety of other nuisances. **The vulnerability of Web site and online account login names and passwords, and the cookies or files in which they are stored,** *not* **the transmission of credit card numbers, is the primary hazard of reserving or purchasing travel online.** The main threat is the extreme ease of privacy invasion and identity theft. An identity thief can learn far more about you, and do you far more damage, with a Travelocity.com or Expedia.com user name and password than with all your credit card numbers put together. Also, once you consent to electronic signature use, there's no limit to what an identity thief can do.

Sad to say, this advice is of limited value, since there is no easy way to store your site passwords securely yet have them readily available when you want to use them. Any really secure way of storing them involves either an encryption key too long to memorize, portions of a key stored on separate disks, computers in separate locations, or a disk with the key kept physically secure in a safe deposit box. None of these is really practical.

A variety of identification technologies have been proposed, but all have problems. Smart cards are vulnerable to loss or theft, like any physical key. "Biometrics" like fingerprints or voiceprints are vulnerable to spoofing. How can you tell the difference between a digitized voice password and a perfect digital copy of a recording of that voice password?

In practice, most people allow their Web site login names and passwords to be stored on their computers in "cookie" files. Unless you have changed your Web browser's default settings, you probably won't even know when a Web site stores information on your computer as a cookie, nor when it reads your computer's cookies. Since most consumers are unaware of cookies, how they are used, or the threat they pose to their privacy and security, businesses and Web designers are under no public pressure to limit their use.

Cookies aren't the only way to do most of the things Web designers use them for, although that's outside the scope of this book. Cookies are an especially poor choice for travel sites, since cookies reside only on the computer on which they are set, and travelers are likely to access their accounts from different computers in different places. Each browser program stores its cookies separately, so cookies received while using one program don't work when you're using another browser, even on the same computer. No one browser is best for everything. Moreover, many public Web access terminals—in cybercafes, libraries, and airports—are configured not to accept cookies. Otherwise, each user of such a terminal would have access to information about prior users through the cookies they had left behind.

Most "shopping basket" e-commerce systems that I have seen rely on cookies or on similar and equally problematic capabilities of Java. The notable exception, and the clearest proof that cookies are unnecessary for e-commerce, are Amazon.com and Southwest Airlines, neither of which requires cookies for purchasing. Most travel reservations and e-commerce sites require that you enable or accept cookies, at least temporarily, while you are actually making reservations or purchases. That's likely to continue until you, the traveling and ticket buying public, demand that they use a better system.

Storing your Web logins and passwords as cookies spares you from having to re-enter them each time you want to login to a site. But that also means that anyone else using your computer, or who gets access to your computer for long enough to copy your cookie file(s) onto a floppy disk, can impersonate you on those sites. Depending on the site, impersonating you might enable them to learn the details of your past, present, and future travel plans; make, change, or cancel your reservations; or send messages in your name. Your stored credit card number, profile, and travel history are only as safe as the cookie or user name and password that someone needs to have to log into your account on a reservations Web site.

You can set most browsers to delete the cookies from your computer each time you're done browsing, or use a "cookie manager" program to do that. But if you don't allow your passwords to be stored as cookies, you have to find some other way to store your passwords securely yet accessibly.

In theory, you could store your cookies and/or login names and passwords in code, using any of various encryption programs. Aside from the inconvenience and complexity of setting this up, it would make *all* your passwords available to anyone who learns your master password to the encryption program. And if the master password is short enough for you to remember and use, it will be short enough for someone else who sees you enter it to memorize. The "Microsoft Wallet" for storing credit card numbers that is being distributed with Microsoft Internet Explorer suffers from this typical and fundamental flaw, and should not be used. Anyone who sees you type the password to open your Microsoft Wallet or use it, and later has access to your computer, can open your electronic "wallet" and find out *all* your credit card information at once. Programs that store complete financial profiles with one password, like Quicken or Microsoft Money, all have the same weakness.

If you do a lot of travel planning online—or, for that matter, a lot of Web browsing of any sort—you'll soon end up with a fairly long list of Web sites and corresponding user names and passwords. Sure, you can use the same user names and passwords with many sites. But that just makes it easier for anyone who finds out any of your passwords to impersonate you to all those different sites.

Most people who don't like cookies keep a list of URLs, login names, and passwords in their address book, calendar, or electronic

Shoulder Surfing

"Shoulder surfing" for passwords and account ID's is easier than you might think. With practice, shoulder surfers can memorize remarkably long passwords even from across a room. Call me paranoid, but a couple of years ago my telephone credit card number—14 random digits unrelated to my phone number, in the middle of a total of 36 digits I had to dial to place the call—was stolen by a shoulder surfer while I was using a pay phone at O'Hare Airport in Chicago. I dialed quickly, from memory; I blocked the keypad as best I could with my body while dialing; and no one was using the phones on either side of me. I learned of the virtual theft the next time I tried to make a call, and couldn't. My credit card number had been blocked by the phone company on suspicion of fraud. In less than 24 hours my number had been used to make more than $1,200 of calls to and from 20 countries on five continents.

It didn't cost me a penny, and it only took one call to the phone company to get all the unauthorized charges removed from my bill and a new telephone credit card issued. But since I was still on the road, it was a considerable inconvenience not to be able to make credit card calls until I got home and got my new card number. Had it been my password to the Web site I used to make my travel reservations, though, it could have been a real disaster. Had it been my electronic signature—or the password they needed to get it—they could have done anything in my name.

organizer. Occasionally they get really clever and store them in a personal code. Believe me, any code simple enough for you to use easily will be equally simple for a thief to figure out, although it's better than nothing. This avoids some problems—such as those of leaving cookies on an office computer accessible to many other people when you're on break—but only at the expense of increasing the potential cost of losing your notebook or organizer.

Do you keep a current, frequently updated copy of your notebook, address book, Filofax, or a disk with a backup of your electronic organizer—along with the backup of your computer's hard disk—in your safe deposit box in case your home burns down? You probably should. However, it could be extremely inconvenient not to have access to your reservations while in the middle of a trip if you lose your organizer with your password to the reservation Web site. A stolen laptop computer can cause serious problems on a trip. But electronic organizers and address books lost, stolen, broken, or ruined by water (left in a pocket and put through the washing machine, for example, or dropped in a toilet or sink, etc.) are much more common data loss disasters for travelers. Make several sets of backups of them—often. Carry one set of backups separately in your luggage and leave another at home.

Consumer Protection Law and Online Commerce

REGULATE THE INTERNET? NOT.

Don't count on the government, or on Internet self-regulation, to protect you as an Internet consumer. At least in the United States, there are almost no consumer protection laws or regulations specific to the Internet. Government regulation of the Internet has lagged far behind the growth of e-commerce and of Internet scams and fraud. The only functional method for Internet users themselves to regulate or police the Internet against consumer fraud is that old standby, "caveat emptor"—let the buyer beware.

U.S. Government Policy Toward the Internet

The U.S. government created the Internet, and only recently began to privatize it, so it's more natural than some would claim to expect the U.S. government to regulate Internet commerce. Initially the U.S. government presumed that the Internet was its private preserve, a position deeply resented both by Internet civil libertarians and by Internet users and system operators in other countries. During the Clinton administration, though, there was a dramatic reversal of U.S. Internet policy.

The turning points seem to have been the privatization of the Internet backbone (formerly operated by the National Science Foundation under rules prohibiting its use for commercial purposes) in 1995. Now the official line is that the public will best be served by complete privatization of the Internet (a massive giveaway of taxpayer-financed infrastructure) and a hands-off attitude by government.

"Laissez-faire" libertarians argue that self-regulation by the Internet "community" will fill the gap left by the absence of government protection for Internet users. Whatever one might hope for, they haven't done so yet, and Internet self-regulation remains a pipe dream. At its best, it could only be a rating system limited in its sanctions to ostracism, blacklisting, and noncooperation. Self-regulation does nothing to help consumers who are wronged by businesses who don't regulate themselves.

Monitoring and Enforcement

Any government would have a hard time regulating the Internet. The key problem isn't so much figuring out what constitutes online criminality—there are some good laws already on the books, some specific to the Internet and some that apply in any forum—but the special difficulties of monitoring and enforcement on the Internet.

The nature of the Internet makes it hard to monitor for criminal activity. The Internet is new, large, diverse, decentralized, rapidly growing, and constantly changing. Each of these attributes complicates life for would-be Internet police. Shifting resources from other enforcement areas wouldn't solve the problem, since e-commerce and Internet advertising have been added to, but haven't replaced storefronts and print and broadcast advertising. Huge increases in staffing, budgets, and monitoring technology would be required to enforce even existing truth-in-advertising, disclosure, or other consumer protection laws in e-commerce.

─ **FRAUD SQUAD** ──────────

Try calling your local police department, and asking for the e-commerce fraud squad. You're lucky if one even exists in your town or city. It would cost far too much, and there isn't enough public pressure for it. As a result, existing laws are enforced only haphazardly against Internet businesses, in the rare cases when they are brought to regulators' attention by public complaints or spot checks.

Jurisdiction Over the Internet

1) **Where is cyberspace?** Internet enforcement is complicated by the question of "jurisdiction": the territorial boundaries of which courts and enforcement agencies have the authority to govern, regulate, and punish activities in which, usually geographically defined, places.

Since a Web site, an e-mail address, or a newsgroup posting has no single physical location, it's tempting to believe that jurisdiction would pose intractable problems for any attempt at Internet law enforcement. If you buy an e-ticket with a credit card over the Internet from a travel agency in cyberspace, to the police of which nation or state do you complain if you show up for the flight and the airline has never heard of you?

Deplorably, even the "legitimate" e-commerce industry has capitalized on false claims about the impossibility of establishing jurisdiction over Internet offenses as an excuse—thus far, largely successful—to avoid being held to the same honesty, fairness, and consumer protection standards that apply to every other form of business. Lack of enforcement and falsely presumed lack of jurisdiction enable e-commerce businesses to do things they couldn't hope to get away with in any other medium. I've said it before, and I'll say it again: caveat emptor.

2) Who's minding the store? In the U.S., the largest share of responsibility for enforcing travel consumer protection laws lies with the Aviation Consumer Protection Division **www.dot.gov/airconsumer/** and the Office of Aviation Enforcement **www.dot.gov/ost/ogc/org /aviation/index.html** of the Department of Transportation (DOT). "We regard our rules as applying equally to the Internet as to print advertising," spokesperson Bill Mosley of the Office of the Secretary of Transportation told me, "but it's not like anyone here is working on [the Internet] full-time. We don't have the staff for anything like that. When one of the attorneys has time, the enforcement office does scan the Internet periodically. We've obtained a couple of consent agreements by Internet travel advertisers to desist from false or misleading advertising since the first such agreement with an airline in 1995," Mosley said.

With airline tickets the largest category of e-commerce—more than ten billion dollars a year and growing—and Internet advertising, and without even one full-time DOT watchdog for the entire Internet, it shouldn't surprise anyone that DOT has caught less than one Internet travel scammer a year

The DOT appears to have adopted the narrowest possible interpretations of the applicability of its general rules to Internet travel bookings. For example, when I asked a DOT spokesperson whether they considered that laws requiring certain information to be made available at "places" where airlines sell tickets required that same information to be made available on airline Web sites where tickets are sold, the response was, "Gee, we've never considered that. No one ever asked us that before." Eventually they called back to say that no, they wouldn't try to apply that law to airline Web sites, and that they

Jurisdiction Problems No More Complicated Online than Off

From an In-Flight Airphone while above the clouds over I know not what state, I call the toll-free 800 number of a merchant whose catalog is sent from a return address in Minnesota. Depending on the current call volume, calls to that number may be routed to any of several states. This time, my call is answered by someone in Nebraska (although I have no way of knowing that) who takes my order and credit card details. My gift is then shipped from a regional warehouse in Maine to my mother in Massachusetts. Eventually a credit card bill is sent to my home address in California, and I pay it by writing a check from a bank account in New York which I put in a mailbox in Oregon in an envelope addressed to a post office box in Nevada.

The interesting thing about this scenario is that there is a well-developed, reasonably effective, and surprisingly unambiguous set of standards for determining in which place (probably Delaware or some other state with similarly pro-business, anti-consumer laws) I am entitled to sue if I think I've been ripped off. It's generally determined by technicalities unrelated to the physical site (if any) of the transaction or the location of either of the parties at the time of entering into the contract, such as my legal residence and the places of incorporation and registered business addresses of the merchant, the bank that processes their credit card charges, and the bank that issued my credit card.

There's no reason that the same principles couldn't be applied with equal ease to Internet transactions. They have been, in some cases, such as those of gambling Web sites hosted outside the United States, but whose credit card charges for gamblers' losses are processed through customers' card accounts with U.S. banks. In other cases, jurisdictional problems have been, not an insurmountable barrier, but a convenient excuse for overworked regulators and enforcers who don't want to be held responsible for monitoring the entire Internet, and an equally convenient delaying and diversionary tactic for electronic flimflam artists.

won't require an airline that sells you an e-ticket online to tell you the rules of your ticket until you present yourself for check-in!

The DOT's difficulty in fulfilling its responsibility to protect Internet consumers against deceptive, misleading, and illegal actions by airlines is apparent if one compares other Internet enforcement agencies. As early as fiscal year 1998, the Federal Trade Commission dedicated the equivalent of 66 full-time employees (compared with the DOT's less than one) to electronic commerce and Internet-related issues. The FTC's Bureau of Consumer Protection spent approximately 16 percent of its staff and budget monitoring consumer protection concerns related to electronic commerce and bringing a wide range of e-commerce enforcement actions. (See **www.ftc.gov/os/1998/9804/blileyt .htm**.) But airlines, railroads, and cruise lines, which are among the largest U.S. e-commerce companies, are mostly exempt from the FTC's realm of authority and subject only to that of the DOT.

Federal law has also been interpreted to exempt airlines from all state and local laws against deception, fraud, false advertising, unfair business practices, and pretty much anything else. In legal terms, it "preempts" all other regulation of the airlines, making it a matter of exclusive Federal jurisdiction. Many states argued against this interpretation, and have lobbied Congress to change the law. (See **caag .state.ca.us/piu/airlines.htm**). For now, state attorneys general can only denounce, not prosecute, airline activities that would be illegal if engaged in by any other business.

The outrage of state and local law enforcers at the combination of federal preemption of state regulations and Federal inaction focuses especially on airline advertising of fares and flights. Particular areas of concern are: the non-availability of advertised fares; failure to disclose fare restrictions; code sharing; the advertising and sale of flights operated by one airline when in fact they are wholly or partially operated by another; the labeling of connecting flights that involve plane changes and sometimes even airlines as "direct" flights.

APPLICABLE CONSUMER PROTECTION LAWS

Even if they aren't consistently enforced, it's worth knowing what laws are on the books. Since the authorities responsible often aren't taking the initiative, these laws aren't likely to have any meaning unless consumers call attention to violations and demand their enforcement or initiate lawsuits themselves. Your complaints to dishonest businesses are likely to carry more weight if you can cite specific laws that they are breaking. Some existing laws provide useful guidance in what you should look out for and how you can protect yourself.

Truth In Advertising

Thus far, the biggest problem I've seen on the Internet has been false and misleading advertising. With more and more information on the Internet, and less and less of it anything *but* advertising, systematic monitoring of truth in advertising on the Internet is a virtual impossibility (pun intended). Don't count on anyone having vetted the ads you read on the Internet for even the most minimal level of honesty.

A wide range of national and local laws already forbid false and misleading advertising. Local laws don't apply to the airlines, but they *do* apply to tour operators, hotels, rental car companies, and, in some cases, travel agents and agencies. Their value to you as a consumer is that if you can show that you relied upon false or deceptive advertising when you entered into a contract, you can have it declared null and void. You are then entitled to get your money back and/or sue the advertiser for damages caused by their fraud.

Aside from some of the airlines' own practices, the most widespread and effective in misleading people, are the misleading advertising claims by almost all the major online travel agencies to offer—indeed, "guarantee"—the lowest fare for your trip. Any such claim is complete nonsense, as those who read the "Internet Shopping" chapter will recognize.

There is no single "lowest fare". No one airline or agency always offers lower fares than every other, has access to every source of discounted tickets, or consistently finds the lowest

SAVE THAT AD

It's important to save copies of any Internet advertisements that you rely on in making reservations or purchases. It isn't enough to bookmark the URL. Print the page, or save it along with any significant graphics to a disk—and back it up. There's no guarantee that an online ad won't have changed or disappeared long before you find out that the hotel, cruise, or tour wasn't as promised, and try to complain. If you can't prove how the hotel was described, what services were specified, or at what price, you won't be able to prove that it wasn't as described, and your complaint will go nowhere.

even of its own fares. And none of them even offer a real "guarantee". Just try asking for the difference back if you find that the person sitting next to you on the plane paid less for their ticket!

What can you do about it? Just don't believe the hype. If you don't want others to keep on being misled, make your complaints known to the advertisers and to industry and government regulators (ASTA, the Better Business Bureau, the local fraud squad, the state

Open Access to the Internet

Print advertising is subject not only just to greater post-publication legal scrutiny than Internet ads but also to advance screening by publishers of the periodicals in which it is to appear. Most major newspapers and magazines don't want their reputations associated with obvious bait-and-switch or similar scams, and refuse to publish ads they think are obvious con-game come-ons. Many consider it their business to protect their readers against deception, and have staff assigned to investigate complaints against their advertisers.

Most ISP's, on the other hand, don't seem to care. ISP's aren't—and shouldn't be—responsible for what their subscribers say, and even the sleaziest e-con artists can have their pick of ISP's for less money a year than the smallest one-time ad in a big-city daily paper. Even if one ISP gets overloaded with a flood of complaints, and kicks them off, they can always find another. It's not like daily newspapers, where there is usually only one game in town.

Attorney General, the U.S. Department of Transportation) and deregulators (the Congress) whenever you see bogus lowest-fare claims or phony "guarantees".

Required Disclosures

In addition to the general principles not to lie, cheat, steal, or deceive, the laws in some places require Internet travel advertisers to include specific additional information in their ads. Exactly which laws apply depends on ambiguous, or at least as yet unresolved, jurisdictional questions, as discussed above. But since an advertiser who wants customers in one jurisdiction has to comply with its local rules, and since it would be more trouble than it would be worth to provide the required disclosures only to customers in those places, it's worth knowing what you are and aren't entitled to be told by Web advertisers in some key places.

Fares, Rules, and Conditions

The Federal Aviation Act 49 U.S.C. 41510, (**law.house.gov/uscsrch .htm**), requires all U.S. airlines and foreign airlines serving the U.S. to publish—either electronically or in print—complete "tariffs" of their fares and rules. Regulations under the Act further require that, "Each carrier shall post and make available [its tariffs] for public inspection...at each of its offices, or locations at which tickets... are sold" (14 CFR 221.171). In addition, 14 CFR 253.5 provides that passengers have the right, upon request at any location where the carrier's tickets are sold...to receive free of charge by mail or other delivery service the full text of the airline's conditions of carriage." The complete text of the Code of Federal Regulations can be searched at **www.access.gpo.gov/nara/cfr/cfr-retrieve.html**.

The only reasonable interpretation of these rules, as they apply to ticket sales directly by airlines on the Internet (especially e-tickets), would be that in such cases the airline Web site is the "office or location at which tickets are sold," and thus that airlines are required to provide their complete tariffs and tariff rules, and a means to request their conditions of carriage by mail or e-mail, on their ticket-sales Web sites.

Unfortunately, the Department of Transportation, which is responsible for enforcing the Federal Aviation Act, has not adopted this logic. DOT has not yet taken action to enforce these requirements on airline Web sites. I know of *no* public Web site that provides access to any airline's complete tariff or rules. Few airline Web sites include their conditions of carriage or a request form for them.

Why, then, do I mention this at all?

First, to encourage you to complain to the DOT and to pressure them to enforce these rules. Lack of access to fare rules is perhaps the largest impediment to consumers' ability to use the Internet to find the best fares. All U.S. airlines already maintain their tariffs (fares and rules) electronically. They have to have access to them from their ticket sales Web sites in order to determine what prices to charge for tickets. Airlines could make their complete tariffs available to their passengers on the airlines' own Web sites with minimal programming and no new databases or links. They don't do it because they don't want to make it easier for travelers to find out about cheaper possibilities. They won't do it unless they are compelled to, and the DOT already has the legal power to force them.

Second, airlines' failure to disclose their fare rules and terms may negate the restrictions on your ticket: "A passenger shall not be bound by any terms restricting refunds of the ticket price [or] imposing monetary penalties on passengers...unless the passenger receives conspicuous written notice of the salient features of those terms on or with the ticket." (14 CFR 253.7) If you buy an e-ticket from an airline Web site, your first chance to find out the full terms of your contract with the airline is when you check-in for the flight. If you ask for the terms of the fare and the airline's conditions of carriage at the check-in counter, and are unwilling to accept them, you are entitled to your money back without penalty, *even if your ticket was supposed to be nonrefundable* unless the airline provides their terms on their Web site or sends you a separate written notice in advance of the flight.

You may have a hard time getting your money back from the airline, especially if you've already paid your credit card bill for the ticket. This is, perhaps, an appropriate place to remind you that I am not a lawyer and that nothing in this book should be relied on as a substitute for professional legal advice. But the law is quite clear. If enough people use their unwillingness to agree to terms and conditions that they didn't know about when they bought their tickets as a way to obtain refunds of otherwise "nonrefundable" tickets, airlines will have to start making their complete fare rules and conditions of carriage available on their Web sites. This will make it much easier for travelers to figure out how to qualify for the lowest fares.

State Laws on Sellers of Travel

In the absence of U.S. Federal regulations, at least six states— California, Florida, Hawaii, Iowa, Ohio, and Washington—have enacted their own laws requiring the registration of sellers of travel. These laws affect customers in these states, customers buying from travel companies in these states, and even, in some respects, travel consumers anywhere in the country.

The California Seller of Travel (CST) law is the most important, because of the concentration of Internet businesses in California, because of California's share of the national travel market (10 percent or more by some estimates), because the California law offers greater protection than those of any other state, and because it is being used as a national model.

I was skeptical of the California law when it came into effect in 1996. It was badly written by people who didn't understand the industry they were trying to regulate. Its applicability is limited, as are the remedies it provides. It's unclear how it applies in many common real-world situations that its drafters didn't anticipate. It's impossible for travel agents to comply with some provisions, and unrealistic to expect them to comply with many others.

The California Seller of Travel law has, nevertheless, proven to provide travelers with a higher level of consumer protection than in any other U.S. state. The registration and disclosure requirements of the CST law, if enforced online, could be especially valuable to travel consumers everywhere in the U.S., even when dealing with non-California companies. Because no major national travel company can afford to refuse all business from California customers, all national U.S. travel Web sites are subject to at least some provisions of the California law.

The CST law (Business and Professions Code Section 17550, **www.leginfo.ca.gov**) requires any travel company in California, or with customers in California, or which advertises in California, and which sells air or sea transportation, to:

(1) register with the state;

(2) include their CST registration number in all their advertising from or to California (including Web sites anywhere);

(3) provide customers, before accepting any payment from them for travel services, with a statement of their rights under the CST law; and

(4) if the company is located in California, participate in a state fund that reimburses California customers for losses from the failure of participating travel companies to provide transportation or travel services for which they were paid.

Note that the CST law does not apply to accommodations, ground transportation, or tours, or to agencies that sell them, unless they are included in packages that also include air or sea transportation.

As with other Internet laws, the proof is in the policing. California has prosecuted travel sales Web sites that failed to register or disclose their CST number on their sites. Deputy Attorney General Michael B. Hughes, who oversees enforcement of the CST law, says he has referred as many as 200 travel Web sites a month to his staff for issuance of warning letters. "A handful of deputies go out on the Internet" checking for violations, although none of them do so full time. The CST enforcement program also gets referrals from a national network of state agencies monitoring travel scams. Hughes says a lot of cases don't come to litigation. "Almost invariably the out-of-state sellers of travel that we've contacted—even some penny-ante people operating out of their apartments—either register or decide to stop accepting business from California customers."

That's a good record, considering the limited resources available for enforcement. Yet my own research suggests that noncompliance among those who haven't gotten threatening letters from the California Department of Justice remains widespread, especially online.

CST numbers are much less common on Web sites than in printed travel ads and tour brochures.

The CST law requires travel agencies to include their CST numbers in every "advertisement," which broadly defined, would include every Web page or banner ad. The two largest online travel agencies, Travelocity.com and Expedia.com, for example, added their CST numbers to their Web sites (but not, in Expedia.com's case, their home page) only after I asked the CST enforcement office about them during my research for this book. Neither of them consistently puts their CST number in their ads. No travel site I know of puts their CST number on every Web page, which would appear to be required by the law. I've never seen a CST number in a travel banner, and rarely in the first page I get to when I click on a travel banner ad.

Does it matter if a company doesn't comply with the CST law? In order to get a CST number, a business must provide complete details of its legal name and aliases ("doing business as"), state of incorporation, places of business, owners' and officers' names and home addresses, and the location and number of the bank account in which they deposit client funds. All this is on file with the Seller of Travel Program. I wouldn't rely on it as my sole source of information about the proprietors of the Web based business. I also wouldn't do business through any Web site that doesn't prominently state the true legal name and physical address of its owner. But if they have a bona fide CST number, you have a much better chance of being able to track them down and collect from them than if they've given a bogus address, or try to hide behind an anonymous URL or e-mail address. If they do business nationally but haven't bothered to register in California, or don't have their CST number on their Web site, that's a sign that they are lax in their concern for customers' rights and the law. You shouldn't do business with them.

The CST law also mandated the establishment of a state-supervised consumer protection fund, financed by mandatory levies on CST registrants in California. The restitution fund of the Travel Consumer Restitution Corp. (TCRC) only reimburses customers in California who purchase travel services through companies in California registered under the CST law. Of 1,300 claims to the TCRC in its first three years of operation, (1996–1998), *none* involved purchases or reservations made on the Internet! In that same time, the TCRC paid out a total of $700,000—a small fraction of the amount of money lost by Californians to travel scams in that time. TCRC claims are decided entirely on the basis of whatever written documentation you can provide as to what was promised, what you paid, and what you did or did not receive. TCRC lawyers recommend strongly that you read and print (or save *and backup*) any travel Web site's complete terms and conditions, their statement of your rights under the CST, and your itinerary *before* you authorize a credit card charge or send any money. Presumably, that's the same documentation that the TCRC will expect you to produce if you have a claim.

State E-Commerce Laws

Several states have adopted e-commerce consumer protection laws that apply to travel sales. Here again, the most significant is in California, and its most important provisions require Web sites to say who is really behind them and where they really all are. Since the law applies to all businesses that advertise or accept business from customers in California, it affects all national U.S. Internet travel advertisers, except those refusing bookings from Californians, and benefits consumers everywhere.

"Before accepting any payment or processing any debit or credit charge or funds transfer, the vendor shall disclose to the buyer in writing or by...e-mail or an on-screen notice, the vendor's return and refund policy, the legal name under which the business is conducted and...the complete street address from which the business is actually conducted. If the disclosure of the vendor's legal name and address...is made by on-screen notice,...[it] shall be accompanied by an adjacent statement describing how the buyer may receive the information at the buyer's e-mail address. The vendor shall provide the disclosure information to the buyer at the buyer's e-mail address within five days of receiving the buyer's request." (California Business and Professions Code Section 17538; **www.leginfo.ca.gov**).

The existence of such a law may come as a surprise to those who are accustomed to buying things on the Internet. Compliance is spotty at best. Online businesses of all sorts, including many in California and others that sell primarily to Californians, routinely identify themselves by their URL only, not their legal name, and omit their street addresses from their Web sites. I have yet to find *any* e-commerce site with the required button or auto-responder address to request a "Who and where we are" statement by e-mail. Amazon.com, which probably does more of its sales in California than in any other state, lists only its post office box on its Web site, unaccompanied by any mechanism to request further details by e-mail. I'm not trying to pick on Amazon.com in particular. It's just the best known and a most conspicuous example.

Travel Purchases from Other Countries

One of the big advantages of the Internet is that it makes it easy and cheap to get information about, and to book directly with, accommodations providers, tour operators, and travel agents almost anywhere in the world. The attraction of lower prices overseas is gradually overcoming Americans' fears of doing business with foreigners in foreign countries.

As a rule, your rights as a consumer when you buy something from someone in another country will be governed by the law of whichever country is more favorable to the seller. That's because the seller usually is able to dictate, somewhere in the fine print, which country's laws will govern the transaction.

The good thing is that, perhaps to the surprise of most Americans, consumer protection law in the United States is extremely weak compared to that of most other First World countries. If you make your reservation with a Western European tour operator, and they don't deliver as promised, you're probably much better protected than if the same thing happened with a tour operator in the United States.

The bad thing is that some countries have no meaningful consumer protection law at all, or have legal systems hopelessly stacked in favor of local citizens against foreigners, and in favor of businesses against their customers. Unless you know the law of the specific country, you have to assume the worst.

While the United States has been slow to recognize the special regulatory, and enforcement, and jurisdictional issues of the Internet, most other countries have been even slower. Even when they have laws on the books that, in theory, apply to e-commerce, they rarely police the Internet or take action against online fraud. The United Kingdom (Great Britain and Northern Ireland), for example, has perhaps the world's best systems of consumer protection for travelers, the Air Travel Organisers License scheme. But the ATOL enforcement office had never thought about most of the questions I raised with them about Internet travel purchases. A year and a half after they invited me to submit a list of hypothetical cases for their lawyers to review, they still couldn't decide in which, if any, situations the ATOL law applies to international sales on the Internet.

Passage of this law was not accompanied by any appropriation of money to monitor compliance. State officials were unable to provide me with details of any enforcement action against any Internet-based or travel business under this law. If enough people start demanding it, maybe they'll start to provide these important, and legally required, consumer disclosures.

Protecting Yourself Against Fraud and Scams

By now, you've probably gotten the message that protection against travel rip-offs is largely a matter of self protection. Aside from your protection against unauthorized credit card charges, and your right not to pay for tickets or services you don't receive, the law is little help. Existing consumer protection laws are, at best, laxly enforced on the Internet, and the largest category of online travel sales—ticket sales by airlines—is exempt from most such laws.

Consumer self protection entails:

- careful scrutiny of travel sites before you book with or buy from them,
- care in how you pay,
- careful record keeping so that you can prove your case if you have to, and
- knowing what to do—and how to do it—if things go wrong.

WHAT TO LOOK FOR BEFORE YOU BUY

The best time to take precautions is *before* you click on the "buy" button. If your reason for using the Internet is to save time and effort, the last thing you want to do is to read and print interminable disclaimer and detail pages about Web sites' owners and policies before you even make a booking. If you're like most people, after the first few times you buy things online, and nothing goes wrong, you'll get complacent and start clicking, "I accept these terms", without bothering to read, much less print, what you are agreeing to. Eventually, something will go wrong, and you'll have no recourse. The precautions I discuss below will only protect you if you always follow them.

Who Are These Guys?

The first question to ask about any Web site is who is behind it.

The nature of the Web makes it easy for one site, or even one Web page, to contain links to products or services from many different providers. It's not always obvious with whom you are dealing when you make a reservation or purchase. Intermediaries, sometimes several layers of them, make travel products especially confusing in this regard.

You might arrange a flight on Airline A through a Web site run by Company C, and only later, if you fail to read the fine print, find out that your contract is really with Broker B, whom you have never heard of. In such a case it's quite possible that neither A nor C can be held responsible if B never sends you a ticket, or sends you a meaningless "confirmation" number or a worthless "voucher".

The question that really matters is the legal one: with whom is your contract? When you make a booking, are you entering into a contract with the airline or hotel directly? With a travel agency or reservation service, as a legal agent for the airline or hotel? With an agency, broker, consolidator, packager, or tour operator who has bought a "block" of rooms or seats for resale and is acting as a principal in their own right? Multiple resellers and wholesalers can make the situation and allocation of responsibility even more complex if something goes wrong.

Even which Web site you are dealing with—much less what company is behind it—isn't always obvious. Links from a Web page can take you not just to other pages on the same site, but to pages anywhere on the Internet. I get e-mail regularly from people who found my answers to Frequently Asked Questions (FAQ) about airfares from a link on the Yahoo site, and didn't realize that my FAQ is actually located on another site entirely, not on Yahoo. Even if you realize what's going on, framing can complicate the establishment of liability. Whether the site with the frames or the supplier of the framed information is legally liable for mistakes (or, in some cases, copyright violations) has led to some of the first and fiercest Internet liability lawsuits. (For links to some law review articles about these issues in the United States, see: **www.dpg-law.com/main/9808-enuf/ tr9808-frames.html**, and for international implications: **www.jura .uni-tuebingen.de/~s-bes1/lcp.html**).

In Microsoft Internet Explorer, the default settings don't show full URLs of pages and links. In MSIE 5, if you want to know where on the Internet you are, and where you are being taken, you need to check both "Toolbar" and "Status bar" in the "View" menu, then go into the "Options" panel, check the "Address bar" box on the "General" tab and un-check "Show friendly URLs" on the "Advanced" tab. By default, MSIE shows truncated, partial URLs. These so-called "Friendly URLs"—a term used only in Microsoft-speak—are incomplete and can be misleading. In Netscape, keep the "location toolbar" open; if it's closed, choose "Show location toolbar" from the "View" menu. Most other browsers show your full location (URL) by default.

"Frames" can further obscure who you're really interacting with. Just as one Web page can include text from one source, images or photographs from a second, and a banner advertisement from a third, a single page can include "frames" of all these types of material from multiple sources. Web designers work hard to make adjacent frames blend together seamlessly, and framing may not be detectable unless you look at the HTML "source" code for the page. On many travel sites, a frame in which you make reservations or purchases is surrounded by frames with someone else's name, logo, and advertising.

Why would a legitimate Web site want to hide the name of their real supplier of travel services? Many sites run by companies that aren't in the travel business want to add reservations and ticket sales as an additional source of revenue. Online travel services are willing to pay them hefty fees to have them steer travel business their way. When Preview Travel (which has since merged with Travelocity.com) bought the right to be AOL's exclusive travel service provider, it was the most expensive marketing deal in the history of the Internet.

Reservations and purchases made through AOL Travel, Yahoo! Travel, Netscape Netcenter Travel, Excite Travel, or Lycos Travel are all actually made with Travelocity.com. You can use AOL, Yahoo, Excite, or Lycos links that will take you to Travelocity.com's competitors, but bookings actually made on the Yahoo, Excite, or Lycos sites are really with Travelocity.com. Naturally, Web sites with arrangements like this do their best to make their own brand-name and image the one that is most conspicuous and that sticks in your mind.

Where Is the Court Of Cyberspace?

You have to read the finest of the fine print, in most cases, to find out which state's (or country's) courts a Web site recognizes as having "jurisdiction" over their business.

Regardless of any explicit designation of a jurisdiction, you can take it for granted, as a practical matter, that if you have sent your money to another country, and it is too late to contest the charge to your credit card, you will have to go through that country's courts, if you want to get your money back. In practice, that means you can kiss your money goodbye. Making reservations in advance directly with

You Can't Sue a URL

Before you do business with anyone on the Internet, you need to know their legal name and status (corporation, partnership, or proprietorship) and the physical location (street address) of their place of business (and, if it's a corporation, its place of incorporation). An e-mail address is not a name, a Web site is not a "person" or "company", and you can't sue a URL.

Ultimately, what matters is whether you know enough about them to be able to sue them to get what you paid for, or to get your money back if you didn't. It might not matter in the case of credit card chargeback. But if a chargeback isn't available, such as when you've already paid your credit card bill, it's another story. If you don't know, before you pay, what name you would put in the space for "defendant" on a complaint form in Small Claims Court, or to what address you'd send someone to deliver that complaint, you're putting your money, and your trip, at risk.

There are no courts or process servers in cyberspace. Knowing what URL you went to when you made your reservations, or the domain name or e-mail address of the people who took your money, may help you find them but is not sufficient to hold them responsible. It may seem antiquated in the age of virtual reality, but to bring a lawsuit you have to put a physical copy of the complaint into the hands of a live human defendant, or their (human) legal representative.

I hate to have to say this. Don't think me litigious: I'm an anarchist. I hate lawsuits, and regard them as appropriate, if ever, only as a last resort: usually ineffective and often counter-

foreign hotels or tour operators is one thing, but sending payments overseas in advance is much more risky. Never do so if you have a choice or if the amount is so large that you aren't prepared to lose it to tuition at the school of hard knocks, unless you know the country well enough to be confident of your ability to get redress through their local consumer protection system if you have any problems.

With large hotels, except at holidays and especially busy seasons, it's usually possible to send only a single night's deposit in advance, even if you've made reservations for a considerably longer stay. That way if the place isn't as advertised on the Internet, you're only out the charge for one night. Smaller places and bed-and-breakfasts often want

productive. I've never sued anyone, nor been sued, and I hope to preserve that record. My point is not that you're not likely to have to sue anyone. Most travel companies are completely legitimate, and most travelers have no serious complaints. But *if* you need to sue, as can sometimes happen, you need to know whom to sue.

More can be accomplished, more easily and effectively, through contesting a credit card charge than through a lawsuit. If a travel company is out of business, a lawsuit will get you only an uncollectible judgment. If the company is still in business, and you have a legitimate complaint, the threat of a credit card chargeback will usually prompt them to negotiate a financial settlement of your claim.

Unfortunately, many travel purchases are unlike most Internet purchases, where merchandise is delivered within days or weeks. Often you have to pay for travel well in advance, and have long since paid your credit card bill when you take the trip. Even if you receive tickets or vouchers as soon as you pay, there's almost no way to tell if they are legitimate until you try to use them. In such cases, you make sure that you'll be able to find the seller again if you have a complaint.

If you didn't pay by credit card, or it's too late to contest the charge, and you don't even know who has your money or where they are (in the real world, not in cyberspace), they are likely to realize that you couldn't sue them even if you wanted to. You have no leverage—other than an appeal to their business ethics, if any—to prompt them to enter into negotiations. In such a case, you can expect to get the brushoff.

a larger deposit, but you should still try to negotiate for something less than full pre-payment. If a foreign hotel insists on the full amount up front, it's safer (although usually more expensive) to book and prepay through a travel agent or reservation service in your home country.

Foreign tour operators are a bigger problem. Many require full payment well in advance, so that you'll already have paid your credit card before you arrive for the promised tour. Even 25 percent or 50 percent of the cost of a modest tour may be more than you're willing to risk. Yet one reason to use the Internet for foreign travel is to find local tour operators who aren't represented in the United States, or whose tours are twice as expensive if booked through agents in the

How Far Would You Go to Collect a Debt?

Among other things, what you don't want to see in a Web site's fine print is a line saying something like, "User agrees that all use of this site shall be governed by the laws of the Cayman Islands/Cape Verde/Chechnya (or some other offshore "haven"), and accepts the exclusive jurisdiction of the courts of the Cayman Islands over all disputes related thereto." Nothing personal against the Cayman Islands, mind you (I haven't been there yet, as it happens, nor to Cape Verde or Chechnya) but it's a lot more convenient to be able to bring suit in small claims court in my home town in the United States. Suing in a foreign country or even another state is usually expensive because of the necessity of hiring a local lawyer there. Even suing in a Western European country with better consumer protection law than the United States is likely to cost more than the value of most travel complaints. Most countries' laws—especially those of countries that compete to offer the most favorable legal climate to offshore businesses—are biased toward nominal "locals" in disputes with foreigners like you. Places that offer businesses a nominal home as a jurisdiction of convenience operate for the convenience of the businesses that support them, not the convenience of consumers like you. And if you have to go to a place as dangerous as Chechnya to collect a debt, you're probably better off writing it off.

United States. They often have to lay out much of the money for the services you will use before you arrive, so they're quite justified in asking for a sizable percentage up front. It's not fair to try to talk them out of any deposit. How do they know that they can trust you? They are taking the risk that you might cancel without remembering to tell them. Unless you're on a very rushed schedule, I think there's much more risk in pre-paying foreign tour operators than in waiting until you arrive to make tour arrangements. Use the Internet to gather information, but don't commit your money until you get there.

PAY BY CREDIT CARD

The single best way to protect yourself—on the Internet or in any other purchase—is to pay by credit card whenever possible. The strongest consumer protection provisions in the United States are those applicable to credit-card purchases.

By U.S. federal law, you are not required to pay credit-card charges for goods or services you didn't receive. If you haven't received your tickets, you can contest the charge when your bill arrives. The burden is on the merchant to prove that you authorized the charge and that you got what you paid for. They must come up with proof: a written and signed charge authorization or electronic signature, or copies of purchased tickets, or the charge will be removed from your bill without you ever having to pay.

KEEP RECORDS

You should save and print your itinerary and the complete contact details, terms and conditions of the agency, tour operator, or booking service with which you are making your reservations or from whom you are purchasing your tickets, *before* you send any money or authorize any charges to your credit card. Don't count on the seller to send you a confirmation notice after you've completed your booking. If you hadn't first saved or copied the itinerary and price you were led to expect, what would you do if you got a confirmation notice showing a higher price than the one you agreed to? If you don't read and save their terms and conditions, what can you do if they change them after the fact to exclude the cause of your complaint?

I keep a folder of printouts of specifications, itineraries, prices, terms and conditions, and charge authorizations for all my online purchases. You may prefer to keep an electronic file of these on your computer, but if so, make sure you always keep it backed up. If you think my preference for hard copies anachronistic, consider that the credit card companies that stand to gain the most from online credit card use recommend that you keep *paper* records of all online credit card authorizations. For travel purchases, I recommend that you check your file against each credit card statement, and save the documentation (what

---

IF I MAY REITERATE: PAY BY CREDIT CARD

If you pay by cash or check, they have your money. If they don't deliver, you may have to sue, and the burden is on you to prove that you didn't get your tickets or whatever you paid for. If the company that took your money goes out of business before you can get a legal judgment, and collect on it, you're out of luck. It's typical that when a travel company goes bankrupt, those who paid by credit card get their money back from their card issuers, while those who paid by cash or check lose out.

you expected to receive, how much you expected to be charged for it, and the terms and conditions) for each reservation or purchase until after you have completed your travel and settled all the bills from the trip. Most of the time you'll never need it, and you'll be tempted to give it up as a waste of time, disk space, and paper. The one time that something goes wrong, it will be essential.

LIMIT YOUR CONSENT TO "ELECTRONIC SIGNATURES"

Under a Federal law that came into effect October 2000, an "electronic signature" can have the same legal validity as your written signature, and electronic documents can satisfy all legal requirements for written notice. If you "agree to use or accept electronic records or electronic signatures", they can be used to do anything that previously required a physical signature or documentation on paper.

"Agree" implies a process of mutual negotiation. In reality, of course, your only real choice is to accept the terms offered by an online business, or to take your business elsewhere. That doesn't mean you should accept a Web site's terms unthinkingly, however. E-commerce companies know that on the Internet, "the competition is always just one click away". If enough people go elsewhere, sites will be forced to change their policies.

Why shouldn't you agree to give your electronic signatures the legal status of a written signature? Requirements that documents be signed in person, and that notice be given in writing, are important consumer protections designed to limit the danger of fraud and false impersonation.

Acceptance of electronic signatures shifts the burden of proving that someone else has used your password without your permission from the merchant to you. That means consumers instead of e-commerce companies will bear the cost of online fraud.

The worst case will be if a single electronic signature becomes recognized for all purposes, instead of your having separate passwords for each site. This would be very convenient, but very dangerous. Only one password for you to remember, and

— VOTE WITH YOUR MOUSE —

One of the most significant consumer victories over intrusive online "profiling" of Web site visitors has been in travel: the removal of registration requirements by online travel agencies. People voted with their mice, and simply went elsewhere when asked to provide detailed personal and market-research information before being allowed to check prices.

only one password a bad guy knows to be able to steal everything but the clothes on your back. Right now, someone who gets your password to one site can only use it on that one site.

I expect that travel reservation and sales sites will start using electronic signatures as soon as they can figure out how to do so, and will add "consent" to this to the fine print in their terms and conditions. To limit your risk, and the amount of damage an identity thief can do:

■ If possible, avoid sites that require you to agree to use of electronic signatures in place of written signatures.

■ If you have to agree to make an electronic signature equivalent to your written signature, make sure the agreement is limited to use with that one company for specific purposes. Under no circumstances should you agree to give an electronic signature unlimited validity for all purposes.

ELECTRONIC SIGNATURES AND IDENTITY THEFT

Once you give your consent to use of an electronic signature, there is no limit to what an identity thief can do with it: open and close bank or brokerage accounts in your name, change the beneficiary of your life insurance, sell your house, obtain complete copies of your medical or financial records. A forged electronic signature will be, by definition, a perfect forgery, and the burden of proof will be on you to prove it was forged. No current electronic signature system provides any means by which victims of identity theft would be able to prove forgery.

What to Do When Things Go Wrong

TO WHOM SHOULD YOU COMPLAIN?

Complain to the people who caused the problem. If it's a complaint about service by an airline, complain to the airline. If you don't like a hotel, complain to the hotel management. Travel agencies are limited in their ability to control suppliers' behavior or obtain redress for grievances against them, especially as to the quality of service.

If you have a financial dispute, complain to whomever you gave your money to. Your money may have been passed on to someone else—it's not uncommon for there to be a chain of three or four intermediaries between a retail agency and the airline or supplier of travel services, especially if the supplier is in a different country—but it should be possible to forward your complaint and claim down the same chain.

Good businesses *want* to hear from dissatisfied customers, and would rather have a chance to make things right, than have you denounce them for something that might not have been their fault, or for which they would have been willing to compensate you. Be realistic and fair, and specify exactly what you want done, or how much you want to be paid.

A mediator can often help both sides see each other's points of view and settle their differences without the expense and acrimony of a lawsuit. A mediator might be simply an uninvolved acquaintance who can help you keep your cool, a trained volunteer from a mediation service, or a full-time professional mediator for hire.

For an incomplete index of some mediators and mediation services by state, zip code, and specialization, see the Mediation Information and Resource Center Web site at **www.mediate.com**. If you can't find a community mediation service in your locality, and you're interested in helping set one up, contact the Community Board Program, **www.mediate.com/cbp**.

APPEALING TO AIRLINES AND OTHER SUPPLIERS

Notwithstanding what I've just said about complaining to the party you believe to be responsible for the problem, appealing to an airline, cruise line, or tour operator can be an effective way to put pressure on a recalcitrant travel agent. Travel agents are "appointed" by the airlines, etc., to represent them and sell their travel products. Agents are at their suppliers' mercy: if an airline revokes the appointment of an agency, that agency can no longer sell tickets on that airline (or can only do so awkwardly and at additional cost through intermediaries).

On the other side of the fence, airlines and other big suppliers of travel services don't like having their reputations damaged by unscrupulous-seeming agents. If a supplier gets a complaint about an agent who's taking payment without delivering tickets or vouchers, or is refusing to provide a refund, and the complaint sounds legitimate, their next call will be to the agent to ask them what's going on. Their big stick is the threat to revoke the agent's appointment. The more the agent's profits depend on selling that particular supplier's products, the more likely the agent is to give in, and do what the supplier demands.

If the amount of money in question is large, and/or the supplier is a small one with whom the agent can afford to stop doing business, the agent may say no and burn their bridges with the supplier. But if it's an important supplier—an airline, a cruise line, a big name-brand tour operator, or a supplier with whom the agent has preferred relationship or special prices—the agent will do what the supplier says.

Appeals to suppliers are especially effective in disputes with discounters of airline tickets and other travel products. Almost by definition, discounters depend on their preferred relationships with the airlines or other suppliers that give them special prices. Justified complaints from customers that make it back to the supplier are a major black mark against them when it comes time to renegotiate their special prices. Nothing scares an agent more than a call from one of their key suppliers questioning their treatment of a customer.

If you have a problem with a discounter, ask them for the name of their sales representative with the supplier, or at least for which sales office of the supplier they deal with. They probably won't tell you but your asking will put them on notice and may spur them to reconsider a refund or settlement. Even if they won't tell you exactly to whom to go, you can contact the supplier's main office and ask to be referred to the sales office or representative who handles the agent's account. Tell them your story, and if they think you're in the right they'll see that you are taken care of, or that the agent is reprimanded and perhaps loses their appointment, preferred status, or special prices with that supplier.

INDUSTRY SELF-REGULATION ORGANIZATIONS

The Better Business Bureau (BBB)
Many U.S. and Canadian businesses belong to local Better Business Bureaus. In theory, a Better Business Bureau (BBB) provides assistance in resolving complaints against members, and a way to check members' complaint histories. BBB's are locally organized; see: **www.bbb .org/bureaus/index** for a directory of BBB's by geographic location.

Kinds of Disputes With Travel Agencies and Travel Service Providers

Disputes between travelers and travel companies break down into four quite distinct categories, with quite different patterns of liability and chances of success.

1. Scams

Most Internet travel complaints involve out-and-out scams. In general, these are the same scams that have been around for years as telemarketing, mail-order, or face-to-face cons. All that's changed is that they've migrated to the Internet.

A search on the keywords "travel" and "scams" will locate a plethora of Web pages of victims' stories and scam advisories from government agencies, nonprofit consumer organizations, and industry associations of legitimate travel businesses.

Travel scams typically involve "free" trips, "gifts", or "prizes" that cost more to redeem—in service charges, shipping and handling, or other mysterious fees—than they are worth, or are only available in conjunction with a package that's overpriced by more than the "free" component is worth. Or they involve travel products or services that are grossly overpriced even at prices that seem (in light of the glowing hype) too good to be true. The "resort" turns out to be a flophouse, the "cruise" a short ferry ride, and so forth.

When you've been had in a scam like these, there is usually no doubt about it. The problem is finding anyone from whom to collect, since con artists who specialize in this field are experts at sending out a wave of solicitations, collecting as much money as they can in a hurry, and moving on.

Notwithstanding the poor chances of recovering your losses, you should report this sort of fraud to the local police or prosecutor's fraud squad or the Attorney General of the state where the scam was based. At least the police might get them shut down, or limit the number of people who continue to get fleeced.

2. Bankruptcies And Business Closings

When a travel business closes its doors, the failure is usually precipitated by a cash-flow crisis. Typically, some travelers are left holding the bag: they paid their money, but they had not yet received their tickets, or they are left holding worthless vouchers. (Airline tickets, it should be noted, almost invariably remain valid even if the issuing agency goes out of business immediately after they are issued.)

Since there is often no crime in such a case, merely a bankruptcy, finding the principals of the failed business may do you no good. If it was a corporation, and is bankrupt, the principals aren't usually personally liable (that's a major reason businesses incorporate). You're probably out of luck unless you can prove that they took your money in bad faith, or never intended to deliver what they promised. Your best chances of recourse are through a credit card chargeback, or trip cancellation and interruption insurance).

3. Quality-Of-Service Complaints

Quality-of-service complaints involve things that weren't the way you thought they should be: the promised 4-star hotel turns out to be what you'd call a 2-star hotel; the tour skips one of the stops on the itinerary in the brochure; you find the "gourmet" meals unappetizing; the flight is hours late; the staff are rude; etc.

Some people regard a trip as a commodity like a sewing machine or a case of canned tomatoes. You buy a "travel product", take it out of the box, and compare it with the specifications list. If it doesn't measure up, you feel cheated, and you go back to the store to ask for your money back.

Other people (myself included) regard travel as an experience, like anything else you do in life. You buy a ticket, and you pay people to provide certain services, but you can't buy a trip. The trip is what happens, and what you do. No one can guarantee what it will be like, or if you will like it. You can't judge a provider of travel services solely by whether you have a good time.

In most Western European countries, the descriptions in travel brochures are treated as legally binding promises about exactly what will happen. In the United States, travel brochures and descriptions on Web sites are allowed more leeway for "puffery" and hype as long it's not a flat-out lie. It's still essential, however, to be able to prove how the trip was described. If you made the booking based on a description on a Web site, that means you'll need to be able to produce printouts of all the Web pages describing what you bought, as they appeared at the time you made the purchase.

The most important factor in how such a complaint will be resolved is where the person making the decision is on the continuum from "travel as commodity" to "travel as life experience". It's impossible to predict whether you're more likely to have better luck on this score with an arbitrator, a bank chargeback officer, or a judge in Small Claims Court.

Continues on next page

Part of the problem is that the travel "industry" is in the business of selling fantasy fulfillment. Given the way they advertise, it's understandable that some people will feel that they haven't gotten what they paid for if their fantasies aren't fulfilled. But all anyone can promise is to provide certain services. No one can guarantee that you'll have a good time.

It's hard when a trip has been a letdown, but try to step back for a minute and ask yourself if it's their promises, or your hopes and expectations, that weren't fulfilled.

Whether you are trying to negotiate with the provider of travel services, getting an intermediary like a travel agent to negotiate on your behalf, referring the dispute to a bank chargeback officer by disputing a credit card charge, or bringing suit in Small Claims Court, it's important first to figure out what you want. Do you want money back? Are you primarily concerned with insuring that other travelers won't have a similar bad experience in the future? Or do you want an apology? If you don't start by stating explicit, realistic goals, you can scarcely complain if you don't like what you are offered in settlement.

Notice that I said "settlement," not "victory". Quality is inherently subjective. Is a hotel "charming"? Is the pace of a tour "relaxed"? If they aren't, how much money is that worth? How do you determine what fraction of the value of a travel package should be attributed to any particular component? Reasonable people will disagree, and there are differences of opinion about what's a fair settlement of almost any complaint. A fair settlement almost certainly won't make either party entirely happy.

4. Refunds For Trips Not Taken

Refunds of payments and deposits for trips that aren't taken, or services that aren't used, are a common cause of disputes with travel companies. "I had to cancel my trip because of a death in my family. I got seasick, so I didn't eat the meals on my cruise. I only used half of my round-trip ticket. I want my deposit back. Where's my refund?"

First, has the travel company agreed that you are entitled to a refund? Did you get it in writing? If so, it's just like collecting on any other debt. You can contest the credit card charge, or go to Small Claims Court if you've already paid your credit card bill.

The only possible area of dispute will be how long it's reasonable for you to have to wait for your refund. Refunds are slower than most people expect. After you return the unused tickets or vouchers to the original seller of travel, it can take six to nine months for some airlines to process your refund claim.

I can't overstate the importance of finding out whether you will get a refund before you decide to change your plans, and of getting the answer in writing. Oral assurances that unused tickets, vouchers, or services will be refundable are frequently false, always unprov able, and never to be relied on.

Only the travel agency or airline from whom you purchased a ticket can tell you whether you are entitled to a refund. An airline can waive its own rules, and refund any ticket it feels like. So if the travel agency says you aren't entitled to a refund, you can ask the airline for a refund. But that's a matter of discretion, not rights.

Always try to exchange your old tickets before you think about buying new ones. It's particularly common for airlines to tell you that you can get a refund on your original tickets from your travel agent, in order to sell you new tickets when your plans change. What do they care? You can't prove what they said, you can't get a refund, and they've sold two tickets while only having to fly one person. If they won't accept the old tickets for refund on the spot, giving you a written receipt showing the amount of the refund due, assume the tickets won't be refundable through your travel agency either.

If you don't have a written promise of a refund, it's a different situation altogether. Everything depends on the exact terms and conditions of the original purchase. If there is no explicit provision for refund, your payment is nonrefundable.

If you read none of the other fine print, read the cancellation and refund rules. If you print out none of the other terms and conditions applicable to your itinerary, print out the cancellation and refund rules. Before you pay.

Don't say, "I'm sure of my plans, and I don't expect to change them." Most trips are canceled for reasons that couldn't have been anticipated. Don't assume that deposits or purchases will be refund able in case of family emergencies or other unexpected exigencies. Don't assume that tickets can be exchanged for other tickets unless you see it in writing. No law requires a travel company to give you a refund just because you don't use the services you paid for. If you buy a ticket to a movie or a concert, and can't go, does the law require them to give you your money back? No. It's the same with tickets and travel vouchers. Unless it's in the written rules, it doesn't matter that you didn't take the trip because your mother died yesterday, or you were in the hospital. That's not the travel company's fault, nor their financial responsibility.

Complaining to the BBB is often a waste of time. The BBB is not a consumer organization but a business organization. Like most self-regulation schemes, its main purpose is to enable businesses to claim that the government doesn't need to protect consumers because merchants are policing themselves. It is designed by businesses to protect their images, not to be an advocate against them.

The BBB has no enforcement power whatsoever. It can cancel a merchant's membership if it doesn't answer your complaint at all, but as long as the business sends any response a complaint is simply logged and forgotten as unresolved. Neither the "participant profiles" on the BBB Online site, **www.bbbonline.org/reliability/index .html**, nor the ratings available by calling or writing local BBB chapters give consumers access to actual records of complaints or how they have been "resolved". The BBB will tell you only that the member's complaint resolution record is "satisfactory" or "unsatisfactory". The BBB is, in my opinion, a sham; many businesses know it is, and refuse to waste their money on membership. Membership or non-membership in a BBB is no measure of legitimacy.

The national Council of Better Business Bureaus runs a central "BBB Online" site for Internet businesses at **www.bbbonline.org**. Aside from requiring participating businesses to provide the name, Internet and postal address, and telephone number of a customer service contact, it's not of much use. Because the Council of BBB's charges substantial additional fees for participants in the BBB Online program, in addition to membership fees in a local BBB chapter, most BBB members aren't listed on the BBB Online site. The only way to tell if a business is really a BBB member is first to find out their physical location, and then check with the local BBB chapter in that place.

The American Society Of Travel Agents (ASTA)

Although it is also an industry self-policing organization, the American Society of Travel Agents (ASTA) **www.astanet.com/** has a much better track record than the BBB's of pursuing consumer complaints. ASTA requires its members to adhere to certain standards of ethics and business practices, including responding to complaints, and can expel members who don't. In the U.S., I would hesitate to do business with an agency that is not a member of ASTA, and would not do business with one whose membership has been revoked.

ASTA's Consumer Affairs Department provides an informal mediation service to assist in resolving disputes with members and a complaint reference service that will give you a profile of past complaints to ASTA, if any, about travel companies. You can check with the department for an agency's complaint record and membership status, or for information on how to pursue a complaint against a member. Information is available online at **www.astanet.com /www/asta/pub/info/consprotection.htmlx**, but note that as of this willing all requests for information or assistance with complaints must be made by phone or postal mail, not by e-mail or through the Web site. You can contact ASTA at:

American Society of Travel Agents
Consumer Affairs Department
1101 King St., Ste. 200
Alexandria, VA 22314
telephone 703-739-8739

Remember that all agencies are likely to have had at least some complaints. The red flags are: numerous complaints, recent complaints, a high proportion of unresolved complaints, revocation of ASTA membership, or use of the ASTA logo despite not being an ASTA member.

You may be able to turn to ASTA for help with travel companies other than travel agencies, or outside the United States. Because of the importance of the American market and ASTA's global role as an industry networking group, many other sorts of travel companies are ASTA "associates", and many non-U.S. tour operators and travel agencies with clients from the U.S., or going to the U.S., are ASTA members. There's a fair chance that any major travel firm in any country may be a member. ASTA will get involved in mediating disputes with any member, even ones involving local transactions with local customers by members in countries outside the U.S.

The Association of British Travel Agencies (ABTA), **www .abtanet.com**, offers similar services for consumers in disputes with its member agencies in the U.K. See the ABTA Web site and the "How to complain" FAQ in the alt.travel.air.uk, newsgroup for details of what to do if you have a problem with an ABTA member.

Arbitration

A disturbing recent anti-consumer trend in the travel industry is the introduction of "arbitration" requirements into the terms and conditions of tour operators and some other travel businesses. You should look closely for, and reject, these terms.

Businesses tout private arbitration as simpler and cheaper than government courts. For large cases, it sometimes is. But it's unusual for consumer disputes with travel companies to involve so much money, at least $1,500 in every state, as not to be eligible for Small Claims Court, especially in the majority of states with limits of $5,000 or more.

The whole point of Small Claims Court has been to address exactly the problems which arbitration is supposed to solve. It's not perfect, but it serves consumers pretty well. Small Claims Court already provides a relatively simple, fast, accessible, no-lawyer-required dispute resolution forum. The biggest problem with Small Claims Court, in fact, is that few states have raised their dollar limits for "small" claims enough to keep pace with inflation.

Businesses don't like Small Claims Court because they perceive it as being biased toward consumers. That's why they've lobbied against raising the claim limits. Businesses prefer private arbitration, and are trying to impose it on consumers, because they think arbitrators are more likely to decide in their favor than are judges.

— BUSINESSES PREFER ARBITRATION TO SMALL CLAIMS COURT

Arbitration is more expensive, more complicated, and, for the consumer, less likely to produce a favorable result than Small Claims Court.

If they are right in preferring arbitration that's reason enough for you to insist on retaining your right, if you're not satisfied, to submit your case to an elected or government-appointed judge rather than an arbitration firm hand-picked in advance by the other party to the dispute. It's because the arbitration service is chosen entirely by the company that requires arbitration as part of their terms that I'm discussing arbitration here as a form of "self-regulation", rather than as a neutral judicial or impartial dispute resolution system.

In some cases, courts have held mandatory arbitration clauses in contracts to be unenforceable. But you can't count on it. Your only defense against being forced to submit your complaint to an arbitration firm handpicked by the merchant as being the one most likely to decide in their favor, rather than at least nominally impartial Small Claims Court judge, is not to agree to those terms in the first place, and not to do business with companies that insist on them.

I recommend strongly against giving your business to a travel company (or any merchant) that requires you to submit disputes to binding arbitration. Arbitration makes sense only if both sides mutually agree to it, and on the choice of an arbitrator, after the dispute arises, and if either the amount of money in question is too large for Small Claims Court or the case raises technical issue more likely to be understood by a specially chosen arbitrator than by the average judge.

CREDIT CARD CHARGEBACKS

Credit card chargebacks are the power tools of Internet consumer protection. Chargebacks are really pretty simple—simple for consumers, that is; they're a nightmare for businesses and banks—but understanding them is essential to protecting your rights.

E-commerce companies, naturally, don't like a system that favors consumers over merchants. They want to replace credit cards with electronic transfers directly from your bank account to theirs, and replace banks' requirements for written signatures with electronic signatures, in order to shift the burden of proof and the burden of liability for fraud. These anti-consumer changes should be vigorously resisted.

Your rights in credit card chargebacks and other disputes with online merchants could be significantly altered by the Electronic Signatures Act which went into effect in October 2000. How bank chargeback departments will interpret and apply this new law's provisions is hard to predict.

Why Travel Businesses Fear Chargebacks

All merchants, but especially travel agents and travel companies, are terrified of chargebacks. Most travel companies are more intimidated by the threat of a large chargeback than by the threat to bring a Small Claims Court suit for a similar amount. It's harder for them to contest a chargeback than a lawsuit as they have to meet a higher burden of proof, and it's easier—virtually certain and instantaneous—that you'll get the money if your chargeback is successful.

Chargebacks damage businesses in ways that lawsuits don't. Lawsuits are a matter of public record, but how many people really check them before deciding to do business with someone? Chargebacks are known only to a business and its bank. But bankers judge businesses by their chargeback percentages in deciding how creditworthy they are. Even unsuccessful chargeback attempts are expensive for the bank to administer, and leaves a black mark on the business's credit record. If a business fails, the bank with which they had their credit card merchant account may end up liable through chargebacks, for consumers' losses. So giving a business a credit card processing

> ## CREDIT CARD CHARGEBACKS — POLICE THE NET
>
> It's been said that there is no cybercash, and that there are no courts in cyberspace. That's not true. Credit cards are the de facto universal currency of the Internet. Credit card chargebacks are the de facto courts of cyberspace, with bank chargeback officers as their de facto judges, juries, and enforcers. They work, and work well, for consumers.

account is a substantial statement of a bank's faith in their solvency and legitimacy, and involves a considerable assumption of risk by the bank on the business' behalf.

Banks regard travel companies as more prone to disputes and chargebacks than businesses selling tangible merchandise. In some countries and some U.S. states it's almost impossible for a travel agency to get a credit-card merchant account. As smaller businesses, travel agencies have to pay much higher percentage fees for processing of charges than do the airlines, even when they can get their own merchant accounts. If a travel agency charges $100 to your card, it only gets $95–98; the bank with which it has its merchant account keeps the other 2–5 percent as what it calls its discount. Too many chargebacks, and the bank will raise the "discount" it charges the merchant, or shut the business down by canceling its merchant account. They'll either lose their ability to accept payment by credit card, or will have to look elsewhere, at higher cost, for merchant account services. Either could be devastating.

How To Dispute a Credit Card Charge

Making a chargeback is easy. All you have to do is send a letter to your credit card issuer at the postal address in your credit card statement. It doesn't have to be a legal document; it just has to be in writing. Unless your credit card agreement specifically provides for them, an e-mail message doesn't count as proper notice of a dispute.

There are actually three separate provisions of U.S. Federal law for unauthorized charges (15 U.S.C. section 1643), billing errors (15 U.S.C. section 1666), and disputed charges (15 U.S.C. section 1666i). Your rights under each of these provisions are slightly different, and more than one provision may be applicable in the same case. For the details, enter the title and section numbers in the U.S.C. search page at **law.house.gov/uscsrch.htm**.

In general, it's best to challenge a charge first as "erroneous" or "unauthorized", or simply notify your card issuer that you need further information to verify whether the charge is correct, rather than trying immediately to charge it back. An immediate chargeback only makes sense if the company is out of business, and/or has refused to talk to you and has no intention whatsoever of providing any part of what you paid for.

You can only charge back a disputed charge *after* you have "made a good faith attempt to obtain satisfactory resolution of a disagreement or problem...from the person honoring the credit card," but *before* you have paid your credit card bill for that charge. An unscrupulous business will typically try to stall you for long enough that you've paid your bill in full, and thus forfeited your chargeback rights.

The best way to avoid this pitfall is by questioning a charge as unauthorized or erroneous as this will delay your having to pay the bill and thus preserve your right to charge-back the as-yet unpaid amount.

The merchant is compelled, through your bank and theirs, to produce written documentation justifying the charge. The law specifically defines an "error" as including any item for which the customer "requests additional clarification including documentary evidence" for any reason. It's not necessary to make any accusation of wrongdoing on anyone's part. On receipt of your written request, your bank is required to investigate and send you a written report. If you further request, they are required to send you the documents on which their report was based. They must remove the disputed amount from your bill until their investigation is complete and they've sent you their report and documentation. Once again, e-mail is unacceptable for any of this correspondence unless specifically provided for in your credit card agreement.

Your request for documentation makes the merchant work, think about your claim, and assemble a file of documentation on your claim to send to their bank. It puts the merchant on notice that you are seriously considering a chargeback. That's usually enough to get them to negotiate an acceptable settlement of your complaint. If they don't offer a satisfactory settlement, follow up with a second letter to your credit card issuer identifying the charge as disputed; documenting your purchase, what went wrong, and your unsuccessful attempt to resolve it with the company that made the charge; and requesting a chargeback.

How Chargebacks Are Handled

Once you dispute a charge, the matter is referred to the chargeback departments of the bank that issued your card and the bank with which the agency has its merchant account, both of which function as arbiters. Together they decide whether the merchant has proved that you authorized the charge and got what you paid for. Your bank takes over as your advocate with the merchant's bank: you don't have to do the work of making demands on the merchant or trying to collect.

A credit card chargeback will get you your money back even if the company that charged your card has skipped town or gone out of business. It's the bank that advances money to the merchant, and the bank that is required to absorb any uncollectible losses from disputed charges.

— GO FOR THE GOLD

There are usually separate customer service and chargeback departments for holders of higher-fee premium (gold or platinum) credit and charge cards. In disputes with merchants, banks are more likely to give the benefit of the doubt to premium cardholders than to holders of standard cards. This is the best reason I know of to pay the extra fee for a gold or platinum card.

How aggressively the charge-back department will pursue your dispute with a merchant, and how willing it will be to remove a disputed charge from your bill, depends to a significant degree on the status of your account and how much the card-issuing bank wants your business. In my experience, American Express is significantly more likely to side with the customer than are Visa or Master-Card issuing banks. A bank where you also have other accounts will go further to keep your business than one with which you only have a credit card.

A successful chargeback is not a final or legal judgment. The merchant can still sue you to try to collect what they think you owe. For that matter, you can still sue the merchant if your chargeback attempt fails. But since the merchant has the burden of proof in a chargeback, and you have the burden of proof in court, you have next to no chance of winning a lawsuit if you lost a chargeback. For all practical purposes, though, a chargeback is the end of the matter.

Documenting a Chargeback

Chargebacks don't involve trials, hearings, or witnesses. You'll never meet, and probably never talk to, the people in the chargeback department at your bank who decide on your claim. Their decision will be based solely on your letter, the travel company's written reply, and whatever copies of documents you each send with your letters. Remember what I said about printing out confirmations, terms and conditions, and orders. Never send originals, save those in case you need to go to court.

Since the travel company has the burden of proof, you don't necessarily have to provide any documentation at all. You only get one chance at a chargeback, however, so it's best to supply copies of whatever paperwork you have in support of your claim. There's no appeal unless you go to Small Claims Court, and if the company is bankrupt even that will get you nowhere.

Exactly what sort of proof the travel company has to supply to defeat your chargeback is governed by who they are and their agreement with their bank. The highest standard of proof is that required of travel agencies selling airline tickets at official fares. You may have noticed that when you buy airline tickets from most travel agents, whether on- or offline, the charge appears on your credit card statement in the name of the airline, not the agency. That's part of the basis of the agency's claim to be "acting only as agent for" the airline.

The nuances of agencies' relationships with the airlines are far too complicated to go into here, and, for what it's worth, involve an additional intermediary called the Airline Reporting Corporation (ARC) that serves as a collective financial clearinghouse between airlines and their U.S. agents. The key point here is that, as a condition of their appointment to represent the airlines, and the airlines' agreement to process credit card charges for them, travel agents have been required to accept absolute and unconditional liability to the airlines for all chargebacks. This is true even in cases where they do not have a physical imprint of the credit card and an in-person (not even a fax will do) signature of the customer on a credit card authorization form. On the Internet, of course, this is never the case. Since it's the airline (in whose name the charge was made) that has to answer your chargeback, but they are not the ones who will have to pay if they lose—their agreement permits them to take the money directly out of the agent's bank account—airlines make only a perfunctory attempt, if any, to contest chargebacks concerning tickets issued by agents.

This system gives travel agencies that sell tickets online virtually no chance of contesting chargebacks. Let me make myself perfectly clear: if you dispute a charge for an airline ticket purchased online from an agency at a published fare, and your claim is even vaguely plausible, your chargeback will be successful and you won't have to pay. This is as true with the largest online agencies as with the smallest. Frankly, as a travel agent, I'm tempted not to tell you this. Many travel agents will be mad at me for revealing this, and many of you will abuse this knowledge. But it's the truth, and I would be remiss not to tell you so.

When I asked the president of Travelocity.com, Terry Jones, about his company's chargeback record, he said their number and percentage of chargebacks was "probably no worse than" other comparable businesses. They can't contest chargebacks in the absence of signatures or credit card imprints. He declined to comment on just how much Travelocity.com loses in uncontestable chargebacks, but made clear that they have no choice but to write them off as a cost of doing business. That's also why online travel companies were among the leading proponents of making electronic signatures a legally acceptable alternative to pen and ink autographs.

All this could change significantly as a result of passage of the Electronic Signatures Act of 2000. Any changes are almost certain to be in travel agencies' favor, and at consumers' expense. Conceivably, they could shift the effective burden of proof in many chargebacks. But exactly how the airlines, the ARC, travel agencies, and bank chargeback departments will revise their agreements, policies and procedures in light of this law remains unknown at press time.

Limits On Chargebacks

Some of your chargeback rights—especially if you did authorize the charge, but didn't get what you paid for—are limited to your dealings with businesses within 100 miles of, or in the same state as, the address to which your credit card bill is sent. It's a backward rule. Consumers need more protection when dealing with distant, out-of-state merchants than when buying from local vendors they can more easily sue in local Small Claims Court. But that's the law.

In practice, though, disputes with merchants anywhere are referred to the same bank chargeback departments regardless of location. Banks will usually honor a chargeback even when they aren't legally obligated to do so, in the interest of keeping your account and to avoid being accused of being complicit in any fraud or illegal activity by the merchant. Unless the vendor is out of business, the bank that makes the decision generally has nothing to lose. The merchant agreements typically permit the bank to pass the cost of the chargeback on to the merchant even if they are in a distant state from you, or in another country.

You can only charge-back the amount that you haven't yet paid. As I've noted above, you can postpone payment, typically for two or three months, by requesting documentation of the charge. If they come up with the documentation while you're still trying to negotiate a settlement with the company that made the charge, or are unsure if you're going to get what you paid for, it may be worth the finance charges not to pay the amount in dispute, or to make only the minimum required payment. I use my charge cards for convenience not credit—almost any other source of credit except a loan shark is cheaper—and pay my bills in full each month. The only times I've deliberately carried a credit balance were when I had made large purchases that remained in dispute.

Playing Fair With Chargebacks

Don't go overboard with chargebacks. They are appropriate mainly in cases where a merchant doesn't deliver at all, or is out of business;

Tradeoffs of Out-of-State Purchasing

Some Internet (and mail or phone order) shoppers make a point of buying from out-of-state vendors to avoid having sales tax collected by the vendor. However, by doing so, unless the vendor is across a state line but still within 100 miles of their home, they are forfeiting their chargeback rights. That's a mistake. Sales tax is a small price to pay for the benefits of chargebacks.

You're still legally obligated to pay tax on out-of-state Internet purchases. You are supposed to report those purchases yourself to your state's tax authorities. Of course, no one does. Conceivably you could get in trouble in a state tax audit if it came to light that you had failed to report large out-of-state Internet purchases. But I've never heard of it happening, and you could probably get away with pleading ignorance—at least if you don't tell them you've read this book!

When the price difference was large, I've occasionally bought merchandise like computer parts or software (not travel or services) over the Internet from companies I'd never heard of. But I'll only do that if the amount of money is small enough that I'm prepared to risk losing it completely, or if the vendor clearly identifies itself as operating from a location within my state or within 100 miles of my home.

Avoidance of state sales tax shouldn't be a factor in online travel purchasing anyway. Travel purchases are not subject to any state sales taxes that I know of. There are many federal, local, and foreign travel taxes, some collected in advance and payable locally on arrival or departure, but all the same taxes will be collected by any online travel company regardless of what state they are located in.

they are not an appropriate way to deal with disputes over terms and conditions. Don't charge-back an entire amount if only part of it is in dispute. Treat a chargeback as only half a step short of a lawsuit: a next-to-last resort before turning to the courts. Merchants justifiably don't like people who initiate legal action without first trying to resolve their disputes informally, and the law requires that you make a good-faith effort to resolve the dispute with the company that charged

Translation, Please

It's particularly easy to (ab)use a chargeback to get out of a penalty by claiming that you weren't advised of it, even if you were. This is fraud. Sad to say, it happens every day. Often, it's engaged in by people who are ashamed to admit that they didn't read the fine print or think carefully enough before they made their reservations or purchase. Like shoplifting, pilferage, or other forms of "shrinkage", this forces prices to be raised for everyone to cover the losses from fraud by consumers against travel companies.

Otherwise-honest travelers who discover that they have committed themselves without sufficient thought to expensive penalties or nonrefundable deposits can and do routinely defraud travel agencies with illegitimate chargebacks. The ease and the frequency with which they do this is the major reason for the reluctance of travel agents to trust their customers.

your card before you initiate a chargeback. Once you start a chargeback, you have defined the relationship with the merchant as adversarial, and can expect few concessions. If a dispute is a matter of judgment, interpretation, or misunderstanding, rather than of simple nondelivery, your best bet is to try to negotiate a settlement directly with the merchant before initiating a chargeback.

Unjustified chargebacks against travel agents usually involve people who change their minds after authorizing a charge for tickets or other travel arrangements, but before receiving their tickets or vouchers or leaving on their trips. They think that because they hadn't received their tickets yet, or never used them, they shouldn't have to pay. It doesn't work like that. From the moment you authorize a charge for tickets or travel arrangements, you are morally and legally bound to pay the bill. The agent relies on your authorization to start sending payments to airlines or other suppliers as soon as your charge is approved, and a tour operator may start spending money and making commitments to set up the tour. If you dispute the charge, you are stiffing them unfairly. If you change your plans, you must pay the bill, send any tickets or vouchers you have received back to the agent or supplier, and wait—perhaps several months—for any refund, less any cancellation penalties.

TRIP CANCELLATION AND INTERRUPTION INSURANCE

Trip cancellation and interruption insurance is the best way of protecting yourself if you have to put down money far in advance of your trip, or if you are dealing directly with a travel company in another country where it wouldn't be practical for you to sue them if they took your money and ran.

Trip cancellation and interruption insurance is available either separately or as part of a package that also includes travel health insurance, baggage insurance, etc. The cost is a fixed percentage of the cost of your air tickets (if that's all you buy in advance) or total trip costs (if you pre-book a full package), typically 5–8 percent, regardless of the length of your trip. This covers any cancellation or refund penalties and the cost of getting home on an alternate route if you have to cancel or cut short your

--- **No Condition to Travel** ---

Road accidents—which can leave you in no condition to continue your trip, in need of lengthy rehabilitation, and follow-up treatment that you would prefer to undergo at home—are the other common reason for trip cancellation and interruption insurance. I even once had a client get in a car accident on his way home from picking up his tickets at my office, although his tickets were such that he could postpone his trip without penalty and didn't end up needing the trip insurance.

trip for a variety of reasons, typically including your own serious illness or injury; death, serious illness, or injury of a traveling companion or a member of your immediate family; bankruptcy or default of a travel agent, airline, tour operator, or other provider of travel services; and, under some plans, wars or terrorist acts or threats in a country you are in or to which you had planned to go.

Although most airline tickets will allow you to make changes for a fee, these change fees have increased sharply in recent years, and are often substantially higher than travelers expect. Standard fees for most U.S. airlines for changing domestic U.S. tickets *start* at $75; change fees on many international tickets range from $150–250 up to 100 percent, i.e. completely nonchangeable. U.S. air travelers have also gotten used to being able to exchange "nonrefundable" tickets for travel on different dates or even different routes. But more and more tickets, and in particular more and more of the airlines' Internet special fares, are now genuinely nonrefundable and nonchangeable: you have to use them on the ticketed flights or throw them away.

The alternative, of course, is to pay the much higher prices for full-fare, fully refundable, freely changeable tickets. But the cost of trip cancellation and interruption insurance is a tiny fraction of the difference in cost between fully refundable, freely changeable tickets and discounted nonrefundable, nonchangeable tickets. It's much cheaper to get tickets with penalties and get trip cancellation and interruption insurance than to get full-fare tickets.

Trip cancellation and interruption insurance won't cover you if you simply change your mind, or if the reasons for a business trip change. Some plans cover you if you are denied a visa or denied entry to a foreign country. Most won't cover you for pre-existing medical conditions.

Family emergencies are an especially common reason to need trip cancellation and interruption insurance. Most people are uncomfortable with acknowledging that a parent or other immediate family member is in sufficiently poor health that cutting short a trip in case of hospitalization or death might be necessary. But this is actually a common reason to come home early, and if you bought insurance at least your choice of whether to come home if someone gets sick or dies won't have to be influenced by concerns of cost.

If you think about it, the longer your trip will be, and the farther in advance you buy your tickets, the more likely you are to need to change your plans. The insurance costs the same whether you are leaving tomorrow or in a year, so it's a bargain for both long trips and trips you plan well in advance.

Some travel agents and tour companies provide information on travel insurance, but you should never buy travel insurance directly from a travel agent or tour company. Your payment should be made directly to the insurance company. If you pay travel agents or tour companies for insurance, and they go bankrupt, you are apt to find that they had failed to pass on your insurance premium to the insurance company and that you are not insured. This has happened in several recent major travel company bankruptcies.

If you're making payments directly to travel companies in other countries, trip cancellation and interruption insurance is the only way to obtain meaningful or comprehensive protection. Read the fine print closely, however, as most travel insurance policies will not cover purchases made directly from suppliers or agents in other countries. There are some travel insurance policies that will cover you when dealing directly with tour operators, resorts, hotels, etc. abroad, but it can take some effort to find them.

I get more questions from my readers about travel insurance than anything else except airline tickets. Clearly, there's a demand—greatly enhanced by the ease with which the Internet makes it possible to deal with foreign tour companies—for travel insurance with truly global coverage. I'd offer references or recommendations to specific insurance companies or policies if I could, but the limited offerings of this sort in the U.S. change too often for that to be possible.

Worldwide travel insurance coverage is widely available in many other countries, especially the United Kingdom and Australia. But the U.S. insurance business is incredibly provincial, and protectionist U.S. regulations make it hard for the foreign firms to sell insurance in the U.S.(So much for "free trade" and "globalization".) Check both with travel companies and with your regular insurance agent for possible sources of appropriate coverage. And, I repeat, read *all* the fine print to make sure that your sort of travel purchase isn't excluded, in which case the insurance policy would be a complete waste of money.

Some tour companies allow you to pay an additional fee, up front, in exchange for a waiver of their usual penalties if you have to cancel your trip. In effect, this means that you are paying a higher price for a less-restricted ticket or package. This is not really insurance, but has its own legitimate reasons and uses. It may or may not be a good deal, depending on the relative sizes of the waiver fee and cancellation penalties, but you should at least look at the numbers and consider it.

COMPLAINTS TO GOVERNMENT ENFORCEMENT ORGANIZATIONS

Police and government regulators won't, for the most part, help resolve your individual complaint. Their function is to get businesses to comply with government rules, or to shut them down if they don't. They are more concerned with systematic and ongoing illegality. If you have an individual or isolated complaint, and a credit card chargeback isn't possible, you can bring your own individual lawsuit, probably in Small Claims Court. With that caveat, following are some of the agencies responsible for different aspects of Internet travel policing and enforcement.

U.S. Federal Complaint and Enforcement Organizations
1) The Department of Transportation (DOT): The Department of Transportation, which is supposed to enforce federal laws affecting airlines, gives out one address for consumer complaints and another for enforcement requests.

DOT's Aviation Consumer Protection Division operates a "complaint handling system for consumers who experience air travel serv-

http://www.ftc.gov
The Federal Trade Commission accepts privacy complaints through this Web site. But most online privacy invasion is currently legal, so the FTC isn't likely to act on your complaints unless and until U.S. federal privacy law is improved.

ice problems." Your letter to this office "will be reviewed and, in most cases, will be forwarded to an airline official for further consideration." Sounds like a big help, doesn't it? To be fair, I should note that they at least count the letters before they forward them, and publish monthly reports as to the numbers and general nature of complaints against each airline. It's mostly a system for monitoring quality-of-service issues rather than real enforcement, although in theory the complaint records can be used as a basis for rule making. I don't know anyone who's gotten a satisfactory response to a letter to this office, but if you want to try it, their address is:

Aviation Consumer Protection Division
U.S. Department of Transportation
Room 4107, C-75
400 Seventh St., SW
Washington, DC 20590
telephone 202-366-2220
www.dot.gov/airconsumer/

Requests for enforcement action by the Department of Transportation, as opposed to requests for resolution of individual disputes with the airlines, should be directed to the Office of Aviation Enforcement and Proceedings. This is the office, for example, to which to send complaints of such fraudulent and deceptive airline practices as code sharing and labeling of "change of equipment" flights as "direct", or reports of violations by the airlines of federal truth-in-advertising laws. Be sure to make clear that you are making a legal request that the DOT initiate an investigation and consider whether enforcement proceedings against the airline are warranted for the violation or practice in question—not merely asking for your letter to be passed on to the offending airline for a formulaic reply from their customer-relations department. Enough sacks of mail, dear readers, and maybe DOT will get the message:

Office of Aviation Enforcement and Proceedings (C-70)
Office of the General Counsel
U.S. Department of Transportation
400 Seventh Street, SW
Washington, DC 20590
telephone 202-366-9342
www.dot.gov/ost/ogc/org/aviation/

2) The Federal Trade Commission (FTC): The Federal Trade Commission enforces most consumer protection rules related to businesses other than airlines, cruise lines, railroads, interstate bus companies, and other interstate "common carriers". The FTC also enforces the laws against breach of privacy promises on the Internet. "While we do not resolve individual consumer disputes," says the FTC, "your complaint, comment, or inquiry may help us spot a pattern of law violations requiring law enforcement action." Complaints to the FTC can be made online using the form at **www.ftc.gov/ftc/complaint.htm**. The FTC also has regional offices around the United States, at addresses listed in **www.ftc.gov/ro/romap2.htm.**

Spam ("Unsolicited Commercial e-mail") can be forwarded directly to the FTC at uce@ftc.gov for logging and possible enforcement action. This e-mail address is provided solely for forwarding of spam. No explanation or further messages are necessary. Just forward any unwanted spam you receive, including all headers if possible.

3) The Secret Service: Technically, the Secret Service has jurisdiction over violations of federal credit card laws. Why the Secret Service? Although it's better known for protecting the President, the Secret

Service is actually a division of the Department of the Treasury. Its responsibilities include enforcing federal banking and financial laws, including those governing credit card transactions, computer fraud, electronic funds transfers, and counterfeiting. For details of the S.S. Financial Crimes Division, see **www.treas.gov/usss/financial _crimes.htm**.

Secret Service investigators really do go to travel agencies to investigate complaints of interstate credit card fraud on rare occasions. The Secret Service generally takes an interest only in large cases ($100,000 is small to the Secret Service). Most customer disputes with travel companies are smaller and can be resolved more easily through chargebacks. The Secret Service would only be likely to get involved in the case of a large-scale so-called "bust-out" scam where a company takes many people's money, delivers nothing (or worthless stolen, or counterfeit tickets or vouchers), and absconds. The victim in such a case is more likely be the company's bank.

You'd only be likely to need to contact the Secret Service if you didn't discover you'd been ripped off until it was too late for a chargeback. By that time, any competent con artist has probably long since skipped town, and you can't hope for too much even if the Secret Service takes an interest in your situation. Should you wish to give it a try, though, addresses and phone numbers (no e-mail addresses) of Secret Service field offices are listed on the contact page on their Web site at **www.treas.gov/usss/**.

State and Local Law Enforcement

The wide variation in state and local legal rules and procedures makes it impossible to give a universal or comprehensive guide to consumer protection resources. You'll need to check with the relevant authorities or applicable regulatory agencies in both your state and locality (city, town, county, etc.) and that (or those) in which the company with which you have a problem operates, is incorporated, or recognizes jurisdiction.

1) **Local police and prosecutors:** Most local police and prosecutor's offices have some sort of "fraud squad" or consumer protection unit, and more and more such agencies have some sort of computer crimes department. They don't usually act on isolated complaints or against businesses that only occasionally break the law. Their main interest is in shutting down swindlers who are defrauding many people. They tend to be familiar with the standard travel swindles, but other than that they know little about the travel industry. I have seen

local prosecutors put dishonest travel agents in jail for fraud, but I've also seen them completely misunderstand, and misjudge, complex and (to outsiders) strange-seeming but legitimate industry practices.

Criminals can be ordered to pay restitution as a condition of a sentence or settlement, so there's some chance that the police or district attorney's office could help you get your money back. The ratio of cash flow to profits in the travel business is so high, however, than even if someone is found and held legally responsible, they aren't likely to have enough assets to make restitution to all their victims at more than pennies on the dollar.

2) State "seller of travel" offices: State regulation of sellers of travel seems to be spreading, albeit slowly. Check with your state government to see if some such system has been put in effect in your state.

As of this writing the most important state regulatory scheme was that of the California Seller of Travel (CST) law.

Complaints about travel companies doing business in, or with customers from California, and that have failed either to register under the CST law, to include their CST number in all advertisements (including on the Internet), or to provide customers with the required statement of their rights under the CST law, can be made through the form on the Web at **caag.state.ca.us/piu/mailform.htm**. There's also a version of the same form at **caag.state.ca.us/piu/form.htm** that you can print out, complete and mail.

For more information, you can call the Public Inquiry Unit of the California Department of Justice at 800-952-5225 (toll free from California only) or 916-322-3360.

California travel consumers who don't get what they paid for from travel companies registered under the CST can apply for restitution from the Travel Consumer Restitution Corporation. The TCRC has no Web page or e-mail address. For information, or to request a claim form, you can contact the TCRC at:

TCRC
P.O. Box 6001
Larkspur, CA 94977-6001
telephone 415-924-1881
fax 415-927-7698 or 415-924-2033

Foreign Government Law Enforcement Organizations
1) The U.K. Air Travel Organisers License (ATOL): Sellers of air tickets, or packages including flights, in the United Kingdom are required to be approved by ATOL and to include their ATOL number

in all their ads, booking forms, and receipts. The applicability of the Air Travel Organisers License regulations to Internet purchases from other countries are, at best, ambiguous. But even though you aren't protected under ATOL, you shouldn't deal with a U.K. air ticket seller who doesn't display an ATOL number.

Travel consumers' rights under the ATOL scheme are described at **www.caaerg2.org.uk/atol/leaflet.htm** (general information) and **www.caaerg2.org.uk/atol/gdnot16.htm** (purchases involving customers, suppliers, or flight origination outside the U.K.). Contact information for complaints, claims, and enforcement requests is at **www.caaerg2.org.uk/atol/consumer.htm**.

You'll have to call, fax, or write (by snail mail) to the U.K. The ATOL enforcement office does not (yet) provide services or accept inquiries or complaints by e-mail, nor do they have a Web-based ATOL number or licensee verification system.

To verify that an ATOL number in an ad or on a Web page is valid, contact the ATOL Consumer Advice section of the U.K. CAA at telephone +44-207-832-5990 or fax +44-207-832-5298. (From the United States, dial 011 first; from within the United Kingdom, start with 0207- instead of 44-207-.) Complaints related to the ATOL scheme should be directed to ATOL Enforcement at telephone +44-207-832-6600, fax +44-207-832-5802. Remember, when it's 9 a.m. in San Francisco and noon in New York, it's 5 p.m. in London.

Government Organizations In Other Countries

Every country has its own rules and procedures for consumer protection and regulation of travel industry. Enforcement procedures and their availability to foreign citizens and residents vary as well. If you think you've been ripped off by a foreign travel company, and it's too late for a chargeback or you didn't pay by credit card, check with that country's embassy or nearest consulate for guidance on what rights, if any, you have under that country's laws, and how to proceed. At a minimum, they should be able to tell you to what agency or officer of their government you can direct a letter of complaint or request for enforcement action. Don't get your hopes too high, but many countries have better consumer protection laws and closer government supervision of the travel industry than the laissez-faire United States. Be patient, you might be pleasantly surprised by the response to and eventual result of your complaint.

See the U.S. Department of State Web pages at **www.state.gov /www/about_state/contacts/diplist/** for street addresses and, where available, telephone and fax numbers of all accredited foreign

embassies in the United States (mostly in Washington, DC), and **www
.state.gov/www/travel/consular_offices/fco_index.html** for similar information on foreign consulates elsewhere in the United States.

GOING TO COURT

As I've mentioned already, lawsuits are a last resort. Credit card
chargebacks are easier, cheaper, quicker, and have a better chance of
success. Consider a lawsuit only if you didn't pay by credit card, or if
you've paid your credit card bill before you found out that there was
a problem.

Principals, Agents, and Liability

Before you can file a lawsuit, you have to figure out whom to sue. In
legal terms, who is "liable"? This isn't as simple a question as you
might think when you are dealing with a travel agency.

The terms "agency" and "agent" are not just names. They are
terms of art describing a legal relationship. Without getting into a
treatise on the law of agency, the important thing for you to know is
that, in general, it's the "principal", *not the agent,* who is responsible
for whatever their agent does.

If a travel agency, including an online travel agency, mis-advises
you about the penalties on a ticket, or misrepresents the facilities at a
hotel, you probably have no legal claim against the agency. If you
want to sue, you usually have to sue the principal: the airline, hotel, or
whatever. If your suit against the principal is successful, the principal
may—depending on the terms of their agreement appointing the agent
to represent them—be entitled to recover the principal's costs from the
agent. But that has no affect on your rights, and doesn't usually entitle
you to collect directly from the agent.

This can be good or bad, depending on the circumstances. Suppliers of travel services generally have deeper pockets and are less
apt to go out of business or abscond than are agents. But they are
usually less accessible, less likely to be located in the same jurisdiction and so you may have to go to a distant state or country to sue
them. They also have the resources to put up more of a fight than a
typical local travel agency.

Travel agencies' terms and conditions invariably include a statement that they "act only as agent for airlines and other suppliers" of
travel services. If true, this means that they have little or no liability
for anything they do within the scope of their agency. It also means
that, as the exclusive agent of the supplier, they are legally obligated

to do their best to advance the interests of the supplier. They have no comparable obligation to serve the customer nor to inform the customer of things that might advance the customer's interest, such as the potential availability of lower fares.

Travel agents are, most justifiably, tired of being blamed for mistakes and mis-treatment of travelers by airlines and other travel companies over which agencies have no control. But from the traveler's point of view, it would be best to be able to hold both the agency and the supplier accountable, and to get the agency to commit to serve the traveler's interests.

The best way to do this is to pay the agency a service charge or consulting fee. Insist on paying a separate service fee, even it's only $1, or of having your payment clearly labeled as including a fee for the agency's services. Make sure you get a receipt specifically acknowledging your payment of a fee to the agency. Fortunately for you, the agency will probably be happy to be paid even a nominal fee. Few travel agents realize the legal significance of service fees.

By accepting a service fee, a travel agent becomes your agent, with a legal duty to advance your interests, as well as the suppliers' agent. As your agent, even if they are also the supplier's agent, they have a much greater legal duty of disclosure of facts or choices (if known to them) that might affect your interests.

The theory of "dual agency" as established by service charges has already been used in some legal cases to hold travel agencies liable for actions against customers' interests that, in the absence of service fees, would have been permitted or even required by their obligations to their suppliers, or for which only the suppliers could have been held responsible. Travel agencies will gradually come to understand that accepting service fees changes their legal relationship to their customers, and gives them additional responsibilities. In the meantime, it's likely to help you only if your dispute gets to court

Small Claims Court

Every state and the District of Columbia has some sort of Small Claims Court. The idea is to make the courts more accessible and to simplify the resolution of minor disputes. In Small Claims Court, you don't need a lawyer, the filing fees are lower, the procedures are simpler, and cases are usually heard sooner than regular courts. You'll probably only have to spend one day in court. There's no jury, just a judge. A Small Claims Court lawsuit can be worth the time and trouble for a dispute over as little as a few hundred dollars.

There's a limit to how much you can be awarded if you win your

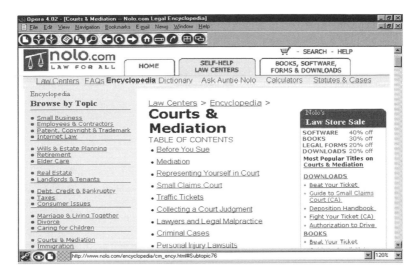

http://www.nolo.com

Legal self-help publisher Nolo Press has a useful online guide to courts and mediation, including how and why to avoid resorting to a lawsuit and a table of small-claims court limits by state.

case in Small Claims Court. Current limits are at least $1,500 in all states, $3,000–5,000 in most, and up to $25,000 in one. Nolo Press, the best-known publisher of legal self-help books and software for non-lawyers, has an unofficial index of Small Claims Court limits by state at **www.nolo.com/ChunkCM/CM19.html**. The same site also has useful excerpts from Nolo's how-to books on Small Claims Court at **www.nolo.com/ChunkCM/CM.index.html#2**.

General nationwide advice has limited value in preparing for Small Claims Court because each state has slightly different rules and procedures. Government and private consumer organizations provide online guides to Small Claims Court for most individual states. Use a search engine to look for pages mentioning both "small claims court" and the name of the appropriate state in which the travel company you want to sue is located or incorporated (for example, search for + "small claims court" + "new york" to retrieve only pages including both phrases).

Winning a case in Small Claims Court isn't the end of the matter and doesn't necessarily get you your money back. Once you win, it's up to you to find a bank account or other property owned by the loser which you can have seized to pay the judgment. Often the bank account in which they deposited your check is an "escrow account" for client funds which is immune from seizure. If you don't know where to find them, or they've already absconded with all their assets, or gone bankrupt, it may not be worth your trouble to get an uncollectible judgment against them.

Proving What Happened In Cyberspace

E-commerce disputes raise novel issues about "evidence" and "proof" that the courts haven't yet decided how to handle. I've been unable to find any published legal decisions concerning what evidence would be admissible, or decisive, in proving what happened in cyberspace. It's already clear, however, that these won't be easy questions to answer. You may be right, but how will you prove it to the judge?

If you, the consumer, request a credit card chargeback, the burden of proof is on the merchant. If you sue someone, the burden of proof is on you, the plaintiff. It's possible to prevail in Small Claims Court if it's "your word against theirs". Your chances will be much better, and it will be much harder for the defendant to get away with lying or manufacturing evidence if you have written records of what you paid for or authorized, what you were supposed to receive, and on what terms and conditions. You'll only have these, of course, if you always print them out and save them before you book, pay, or authorize a charge. If you think I'm beginning to sound like a broken record about this, that's because it really is as important as I make it out to be.

The e-commerce industry's response to the hard time they have contesting consumer claims against them is the Electronic Signatures Act. Courts are now required to give the same weight to "electronic signatures" as to written signatures. But this law doesn't specify what constitutes an electronic signature, or establish any technical standards for how they will be used. It's vague, in some respects self-contradictory, and it hasn't yet been tested in court. So how much this law will shift the burden of proof, or reduce consumers' rights, probably won't be sorted out for years.

Federal Court

Airlines are largely exempt from the jurisdiction of state and local courts as a result of the same "preemption" by the federal government that removes them from the purview of state consumer protection law and local police. If a credit card chargeback is unavailable or unsuccessful, the only forum in which you can pursue a dispute with an airline may be federal court.

For legal details on federal preemption of airline regulation, and its limits, see 49 U.S.C. Section 41713, as interpreted in *American Airlines vs. Wolens* (1995) and *Morales vs. TWA* (1992).

There is no federal Small Claims Court. Making a federal case out of something is slow, expensive, and very rarely worthwhile. If you want to try it anyway, consult a lawyer.

Using The Internet While Traveling:

Advice For Road Warriors and Road Warrior Wannabes

Some of you may be happy—determined, even—to log off the Internet once your travel plans are finalized, leave the computer behind when you depart, and ignore the Internet while traveling. If so, you can skip this chapter and count yourself lucky. Others, however, want or need to get online on the road: perhaps you need to check your e-mail once a week, or perhaps you need a constant wireless Internet connection wherever you are. Whatever your needs, there are many choices.

The first time I saw a portable device for connecting to a computer was when my father brought one home in the early 1970s, around the time I started writing programs in the BASIC computer language in junior high school. It consisted of a sort of teletype that used rolls of thermal paper like a fax machine, and connected to an acoustic coupler (sort of like a pair of inverted foam-lined earmuffs into which you stuck the telephone handset). I don't remember if it was 110 baud or 300 baud (today's standard modems are 56,000 baud). By a miracle of miniaturization, all this was squeezed into a slightly oversized attaché case that weighed only about 35 pounds! Of course, it used far too much power to run on batteries, and it was strictly a "dumb terminal:" it couldn't do anything at all when not connected to a mainframe computer.

Times changed. By the late 1980s, the totem of the connected traveler, the newly christened "road warrior," had become the genuinely portable laptop computer—even though everyone cursed its weight. By the mid 1990s, it seemed that almost every business traveler had a laptop computer.

Today, times have changed again. As the Internet becomes omnipresent, it becomes ever more possible to stay connected without having to schlep around your own computer. Many business travelers are finding it unnecessary to carry a laptop to stay connected—even if they still bring one for video gaming in waiting rooms and on airplanes. A wider variety of smaller Internet connection devices are becoming available. At the same time, there are more and more public Internet access points for those without their own computers. That means more possibilities, and more choices, for staying connected while on the road.

LET YOUR COMFORT LEVEL BE YOUR GUIDE

Don't try something just because I recommend it in this section. I mention a wide range of connectivity approaches and devices, including some that are quite unusual. Let your own comfort and confidence level be your guide. If, like most people, you rely heavily on a particular friend or colleague for computer assistance, give great weight to what they are familiar with. Ask them point blank, "If I try X, Y, or Z, and have a problem, will you be able to help me?" If you're prepared to solve problems on your own with the assistance you can get over the Internet, you can consider trying something more exotic.

There's more to mobile computing, though, than throwing a laptop in your luggage, or knowing that cybercafes exist. How do you find a cybercafe, or get on the Internet without one? What can and can't you do over the Internet while on the road? What preparations do you need to make before you leave to stay connected? And what do you need to watch out for?

In this chapter, we'll address the sometimes difficult choice of whether to bring a computer with you, and how to decide. We'll look at some of the alternate ways to get access to the Internet while traveling, with or without your own computer, and their pros and cons.

Ways of connecting to and using the Internet while traveling vary greatly in how much computer expertise they require. Internet-using travelers have a wide range of computer skills. Different suggestions in this chapter will be appropriate for different people depending on your needs, your situations, and your technical levels. Use what you can, ask a more computer-savvy friend about things that seem interesting or that you aren't sure how to do on your own, and feel free to disregard whatever is over your head.

However you plan to connect, the keys to making successful use of the Internet while traveling are preparation and practice. Try doing

>> KEY ADVICE
About Using the Internet While Traveling

- Don't bring a computer with you unless it's essential. Computers are expensive, fragile, heavy, and theft-prone. Connecting your own computer to the Internet while traveling can be unexpectedly complex and problematic. You can find cybercafes or other public Internet access points anywhere in the world.

- Whatever you're going to want to do while traveling, try it before your trip from a friend's house or a public Internet terminal in your home town. Problems or complications you don't discover until you are on the road can be much harder to deal with.

- Plan carefully how to deal with your e-mail while you are traveling. If you can't empty your mailbox, and it fills up, you may not be able to get any more messages—even short ones.

- Don't count on finding any particular hardware or software on a public computer. The more types of computers and standard Internet programs you're familiar with, the better your chances of getting your work done wherever you find yourself.

- Don't count on a fast connection to the Internet while traveling. Familiarize yourself in advance with how to get your work done over a slow connection.

whatever it is you'll want to do on the road from a cybercafe or public Internet terminal in your hometown. Try to check your e-mail or transfer a file from a friend's computer you haven't used before, with a different ISP. Take your laptop computer to a friend's house or pay phone, and try to connect.

Maybe everything will work right the first time. If so, you're lucky. More likely, you'll find that there's some missing piece of hardware or, more likely still, some software compatibility or configuration glitch that limits what you can do. In that case, you're even luckier that you found the problem before leaving home, while you still have a chance to solve it before your trip. If you discover a software or connection problem after you're already on the road, you often can't solve the problem until you come home.

- For convenience, consider bringing a couple of floppy disks with your e-mail address list and Web bookmarks or favorites for use at public internet terminals.

- Make sure you have at least two backup copies of *all* your important electronic data, including the information on your laptop, your e-mail address list, your electronic organizer or PDA, your cell phone speed-dial list, and any computer disks you're bringing with you. Carry your backups separately, if possible, in different pieces of luggage.

- Test your backups. Make sure you have them in a form that will be accessible and usable when you need them. Think about exactly what you will do when (not if) your hard disk crashes or your computer is stolen and you have to continue your trip without it.

- If you're bringing a computer, check local dial-up numbers and charges for using them before you go, to avoid long distance calls or unexpected charges.

- International travel can pose *much* more complex Internet connection problems. Consider using cybercafes or public terminals abroad, even if you take your own laptop computer on domestic trips. If you're taking your computer abroad, prepare carefully. See if a global roaming service would cut your connection costs.

Cybercafes and Public-Access Internet Terminals

Staying connected on the road no longer has to mean carrying a heavy, fragile, and expensive laptop computer. The Internet is truly everywhere, as there are Internet-connected computers available to you almost anywhere you might think of going.

There are still reasons to carry a laptop—if you want to spend many hours working on it. But just wanting to connect to the Internet is no longer reason enough.

You might think that the more remote the location, the more

Where to Look for Internet Connections

- Cybercafes (**www.cybercafe.com**)
- Hostels (**www.iyhf.org; www.hostels.com**)
- Libraries
- Computer stores
- Photocopy shops
- Airports
- Truck stops
- Hotel business centers
- Convention centers
- Colleges and universities
- Your friends and hosts

In addition to their uses for travelers, all of these places provide Internet access for people who don't (yet) have computers of their own, or who only have Internet access at workplaces where Internet use is monitored or restricted to business purposes.

necessary it would be to have your own computer. But that would be wrong. The more remote the location, especially in the Third World, the greater the advantages to paying a small fee to someone else to find an Internet service provider, a reliable power supply and to get a phone and network connection to work. The places where cybercafes are easiest to find and make the most sense are places where it takes a cybercafe professional to get a reliable connection and keep it working. I get e-mail every day, for example, from clients at cybercafes in Kathmandu and on Kuta Beach in Bali. I wouldn't want to have to make a dial-up connection from my own computer in either of those places.

— TRAVEL LIGHT

These days when people ask me, "What's the best type of computer to carry with me on a long trip?", my first answer is usually, "None!"

Drop me in a city of half a million people or more, anywhere in the world, and within a day I'll find a way to send you e-mail. How do you find a public Internet connection? Here are some places to look:

CYBERCAFES

In much of the world, cybercafes are the standard mode of Internet access and most people's introduction to Internet use. Why not? Where local phone calls are metered, Internet access from a cybercafe can be little or no more expensive than from home. Either you pay by the fraction of an hour to use an Internet terminal, or Internet use is included in the de facto "cover charge" of the price of refreshments. In recent years it's become relatively easy to find a cybercafe in any major tourist or business center around the world.

In the United States, however, cybercafes are fewer and farther between than in most other countries. In the United States, more people than anywhere else have computers of their own, local phone calls to Internet service providers (ISPs) are free and unmetered, and most ISPs provide unlimited access time for a flat monthly rate. So relatively few people choose to pay by the hour to access the Internet from a cybercafe.

Since most business travelers bring their own laptop computers, cybercafes in the United States are mainly used by leisure travelers. That means cybercafes in the United States are still largely confined

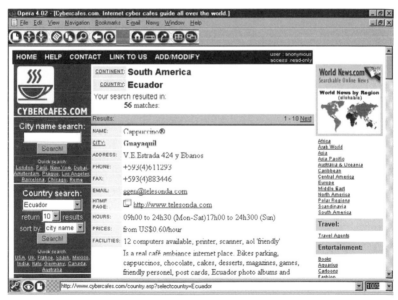

http://www.cybercafes.com
With so many cybercafes in even small, third-world countries, do you need to bring your own computer? The 56 cybercafes listed in this online directory are actually only a few of the hundreds in Ecuador.

Should You Bring a Laptop Computer With You or Rely on Public-Access Computers?

When to bring a computer with you:

- You need to spend a lot of time using a computer, especially if much of your time on the computer will be offline.

- You want to be able to work on airplanes, trains, taxis, or in hotel rooms.

- You need to use your computer in a specific location (e.g. at a specific work site) where a computer isn't available.

- You need to use specific or unusual software, or a specific system configuration. You can't count on finding any operating system other than Windows and any applications other than Microsoft Office—sometimes not even that—and a browser and Telnet client on a public-access computer. You can't count on finding any specific software version; in particular, you can never count on which Web browser or which, if any, e-mail program you'll find.

- You need to have special peripheral hardware with you that might not work with just any computer.

- You need to use remote access, remote control, or file synchronization software on your laptop to connect to, or exchange data with, your home or office computer.

- You need to send sensitive or private information. You can install software on your own computer to enable you to send information over the Internet with reasonably high security, although most people don't bother. When you use a public terminal, there's always a risk that some subsequent user might be able to see some or all of whatever you did, such as the e-mail you sent or received or which Web pages you looked at, or that your online activities might be monitored or logged.

- You only know how to use one Web browser or one e-mail program, or you aren't comfortable using a computer that isn't configured just the way you like it and are accustomed to.

You still, of course, need to be prepared to deal with whatever goes wrong on the road. It's much better to be literate in all the major programs you might encounter on the road.

■ Your computer is configured with accessibility tools like speech recognition, a screen reading program, or special input and/or output devices.

■ You are skilled, experienced, and confident about being able to deal with connectivity issues on your own. Bringing a laptop with you if you aren't confident about debugging problems you encounter is a recipe for frustration.

When not to bring a computer with you:

■ You only need to access the Internet intermittently (e.g. to check your e-mail or the Web).

■ You won't need a computer much, if at all, except when you are actually online (e.g. if you only need a computer to access the Web). Because so many computers can access the Web, getting Web access is easier than finding a computer that will run any specific application.

■ You need to transfer files, or need access to your files while traveling, but you know that any application(s) needed to open or use your files will be available where you're going (or you can bring the programs with you and you will be able and permitted to install them).

■ Your connectivity needs are limited and standard.

■ You lack skill, experience, or confidence in your ability to diagnose and solve connectivity problems by yourself. (At a cybercafe, the connection is supplied for you. If you have a problem, there is always someone—if only another patron—to offer assistance.)

Don't Mix Cybercafes and Money Management

Never access a money management site from a cybercafe, library, public terminal, any computer you did not personally configure, or any computer belonging to anyone you wouldn't trust to hold all your money in cash. All cybercafes and public terminals are inherently insecure, even when you're accessing a highly secure website.

Everything you type, every mouse click, and everything you see on the screen can be, and often is, monitored and logged by the cybercafe proprietor or network administrator. Ignore anything the Web service or the cybercafe says about their security procedures. Because the data can be captured before it is encrypted for sending to the public Internet, local logging or remote monitoring over a LAN renders any website or browser security irrelevant, and can be completely undetectable even to a computer security expert. Network administrators or hackers can install software to monitor other users on the LAN without the knowledge of the cybercafe.

Cybercafes, libraries, and the like install monitoring and logging software for a variety of reasons: to keep track of time online for billing; to log sites visited for market research or "data mining;" to assist in providing technical support to people who are having trouble using the computers; to prevent children from accessing adult sites; or to prevent hackers from using cybercafes as anonymous bases for attacking other computers. Or because they're bored and curious about what people are doing, and want to snoop on their e-mail. Or because they are crooks. Even if your password can only be used to pay a prearranged list of bills, a thief can charge things to your credit card, then use your password to pay your credit card bill before you have a chance to contest the unauthorized charges.

to tourist centers, especially those that attract foreign visitors who are more accustomed to cybercafes and for whom phone calls home are more expensive.

The biggest difficulty in finding cybercafes is that people who live in a place are most likely to have their own computers, and thus least likely to use a cybercafe. In a typical American city, most locals wouldn't know that a cybercafe existed, much less where it was located. You'll do better asking other out-of-towners or foreign visitors!

It also doesn't help that the best way to locate a cybercafe is on the Internet. Presumably, when you're looking for a cybercafe, it's because you're *not* on the Internet at that moment. So remember to take the time before you leave on a trip to log on and look up whether there's a cybercafe where you're going, and how to find it.

The "alt.cybercafes" FAQ, currently at **cybercaptive.com/faq .shtml**, includes links to some online directories of cybercafes. Large cybercafe directories with good search engines for finding cybercafes by city or country include those at **www.cybercafe.com** and **cybercaptive.com**. You can also try posting a query in the "alt.cybercafes" newsgroups to the effect of, "Does anyone know if there is a cybercafe in Podunk, New York, United States," or wherever. Be sure to specify the country and state or province to avoid any confusion between similarly named cities or towns. If there's a cybercafe in Podunk, there's a good chance the proprietor reads that newsgroup, wants your business, and will reply.

HOSTELS

Can't find a cybercafe? Look for a youth hostel or backpacker guesthouse, even if that's not where you want to stay. Hostellers and backpackers are the core market for cybercafes everywhere. More and more hostels have added in-house cybercafes, or Internet terminals in their lounges, to serve their guests and make a little extra money. Even if a hostel doesn't have its own cybercafe or public Internet terminal, the hostel proprietor *will* know where one is.

Hostelling International (formerly known in the United States as "American Youth Hostels") has its own network of Internet terminals in selected hostels around the world. Many of these terminals can be used to access both the Internet and Hostelling International's internal "International Booking Network" (IBN) for advance hostel reservations, guaranteed by credit card. (As of this writing, the IBN isn't accessible

INTERNET ACCESS IN HOSTELS

Internet terminals in hostels generally cost about as much as those in cybercafes, although hostellers are less likely to be pressured to buy overpriced refreshments while they surf than patrons at cybercafes. Occasionally hostel Internet terminals are inside the "guests only" area of the hostel. But I've never heard of anyone being refused admission if they ask politely and say they've come to spend money on Internet access.

from the Internet, but that may well change by the time you read this.) See **www.iyhf.org** for the complete directory of worldwide hostels accredited by the International Youth Hostel Federation and its affiliates.

For-profit private hostels have been even quicker to recognize the potential incremental revenue in installing Internet terminals, and most now have them. The most comprehensive online directory of private hostels is at **www.hostels.com**.

Although hostel managers have recognized the importance of Internet access for their guests, hostel organizations and guidebooks have been slower to catch on. The Hostelling International directories have elaborate coded listings of hostel features and services, but don't mention Internet access. Most publishers of guidebooks for hostellers and backpackers don't yet include whether hostels have Internet terminals in their standard accommodations listings.

Even more surprisingly, neither the Hostelling International (**www.iyhf.org/**) nor Hostels.com offline hostel directories indicate which hostels have Internet access available. So for now, the only way to find out which hostels have Internet access is the old-fashioned way of calling them on the phone, or asking when you arrive.

LIBRARIES

Libraries are among the most under-appreciated resources for travelers. I'll restrain myself from singing the general praises of libraries (the way I sing, that's doing you a favor). But I wouldn't want you to forget the local library when you need to get online while away from home.

Virtually all public libraries in the United States either already provide Internet access for patrons, or are making concerted efforts to do so as soon as they can afford it. There are tens or hundreds of times as many public Internet terminals in U.S. public libraries as in U.S. cybercafes. If there's a public Internet terminal in a small American town that's not a tourist center, it's almost certainly in the library. Better still, there's a good chance that it's free or at minimal cost.

The free public library is a grand American institution dedicated to making information available to all. Even when there is a charge for Internet access at a library, it's usually less than at a cybercafe. The dilemma for American librarians is that—while libraries have done a better job than any other institution in bridging the digital divide between computer haves and have-nots—the importance of that role hasn't been recognized with adequate funding. Libraries simply haven't got the money they would need to give all comers all the access they want to the Internet.

As a result, libraries are forced to ration Internet access. Rationing means setting and enforcing priorities. Unfortunately for travelers, their needs generally and justifiably rank lower on libraries' priorities than those of local residents and library patrons. So as a visitor using the Internet for purposes unrelated to library research, you may have to wait for a terminal, be allotted only a limited amount of time, or be kicked off if library patrons want to use the Internet.

If all the obvious Internet terminals are in use, see if you can access the Internet from a library catalog terminal. In larger libraries with older mainframe-type catalog terminals, you may find text-only Internet access buried in one of the menus of the catalog system. If you don't see anything labeled "Internet," look for a listing for the text browser "Lynx." Because most people don't realize that a text-only terminal could possibly provide Internet access, and/or don't know how to use Lynx, these terminals are often available without a wait.

Librarians are generally staunch defenders of library patrons' privacy. They are much more attentive to the risks that users of public or shared Internet terminals take in terms of inadvertently revealing private information. Cookies can sometimes enable the next user of a public terminal to log into your account on a Web-based service. But if cookies are disabled completely, you can't log on to sites that require them. Librarians are stuck in the middle. As I've noted in the chapter on privacy and security, browser software designers haven't made it easy for them. For a window into librarians' debates on balancing privacy protection, functionality, and security, see the "Web4Lib" mailing list at **sunsite.berkeley.edu/Web4Lib**.

The key to maximizing your ability to use the Internet from libraries is thus to check in advance that any sites you rely on are accessible from text terminals, without cookies, Java, or ActiveX. The easiest way to find out is simply to try them out with Lynx, and with cookies disabled, before you leave home. If you can't or don't want to get Lynx installed and working on your own computer, try connecting by Telnet to some of the public Lynx sites listed at **www.trill-home.com/lynx/public_lynx.html**. Try doing some of the things you might want to do on the Web when you're on the road.

You will get a good sense of what your favorite sites will look like on a library catalog terminal.

The most likely problem is that your Web-based e-mail provider relies on cookies, which are blocked by many libraries and corporate firewalls. Microsoft Hotmail and Netscape Mail, among other Web-based e-mail services, require cookies. Yahoo Mail uses cookies in ways that are contrary to the standard cookie specifications, and thus are blocked by most versions of Lynx even if cookies are enabled. You'll need to find some other e-mail service if you don't want to limit your access options. It's not impossible to find one, and it's worth the effort.

If you can't find a service that does what you want without cookies, at least try to find one that doesn't rely on images, frames, Java, or, worst of all, ActiveX. Any or all of these are likely to be disabled, for good reason, by libraries and others concerned about privacy and security.

COMPUTER STORES

Computer stores might seem an unlikely source of Internet access. After all, you don't want to buy a computer, you just want to use one for a little while. But many computer stores have demo models connected to the Internet. As long as you don't hog a computer for too long or get in the way of customers more eager to buy, they usually don't care whether you are checking your e-mail or just playing with the machine to try it out. In a big warehouse-type store with few salespeople walking the floor, it's easy to spend half an hour on the Internet—on the fastest and fanciest new machine—before anyone bothers to ask, "Can I help you?"

— BROWSERS WELCOME

Some computer stores explicitly invite browsers to use their demo computers as a free cybercafe. The downtown CompUSA nearest my office has half a dozen iMacs set up as demo Web browser stations, in the hope that people who try them will decide that they want their own iMac at home. There's no sign on the door of the store that says, "Free public Internet access inside," but they've begun to attract an increasing stream of guests from the hostels down the street.

COPY SHOPS

After libraries, copy shops are the most numerous and widespread providers of public Internet access in the United States. Places that used to describe themselves as "photocopy shops" have morphed into one-stop providers of a wide range of services for small and home-based businesses—often including Internet access. They can be especially useful if you need to do something elaborate, since they often cater to people who have a low-end computer but need to rent time occasionally on a high end machine with an oversize display, a high-resolution or large-format printer, or expensive image manipulation software.

One reason people go to a service bureau is to deal with files in formats that their own computers can't handle. The larger copy shops cum computer service bureaus have the widest possible range of hardware and software. Many also have on-site computer consultants to help show you how to get your work done, often for no extra charge if they aren't too busy or you only need a limited amount of assistance. Some even offer classes or private tutoring in the applications of your choice. If you just want to check your e-mail, having to pay for time on a high-end graphics workstation is expensive overkill.

HOTELS

Hotels that cater to business travelers often have "business centers:" miniature all-purpose service bureaus that provide faxing, photocopying, printing, Internet access, and sometimes other services such as rush business card production, secretarial services, and/or foreign language translation.

Hotel business centers are mainly oriented to serving business travelers who have their own laptop computers but who need access to a desktop machine, a printer, software that doesn't fit or won't run on their laptop, or an Internet connection. Their greatest use is by people who just need to print a file.

The biggest drawback to business centers in hotels is that their prices per minute for Internet access tend to be higher than any alternative. For that reason, I generally look elsewhere whenever possible. On the other hand, in a poorly-connected country, the hotel where the international businesspeople and journalists stay may be the only place with a reliable Internet connection, even if it relies on a satellite dish on the roof (to bypass the dysfunctional local phone system) and costs $5 a minute.

CONVENTION CENTERS

Convention centers and exhibit venues provide Internet access in two ways: at "business centers" or service bureaus like those in hotels, and

Not Intended for the General Public, But...

Occasionally and unpredictably, hotels have free (semi-) public Internet workstations. More than once I've wandered into a high-end business hotel to find a free Internet terminal somewhere in the lobby or the coffee shop. These terminals aren't necessarily intended for the general public. They are more of a convenience for the businessperson who happens to be without their laptop, like the complementary toothpaste for guests who didn't bring their own. But I've never been kicked out for using a hotel's free Internet station, either. The most it's cost me has been the price of a cup of coffee in the hotel lounge. The more expensive and business-oriented the hotel, the more likely it is to provide services like this to guests (and clever budget travelers).

at cybercafes or "Internet zones" set up on trade show, convention, and exhibit hall floors as part of the events themselves. These days, most large trade shows include a bank of Internet terminals, available free to anybody with access to the show floor. It's paid for by a sponsor who gets to put their advertising in the Internet area (a popular area of any show since so many attendees will go there to check their Web based e-mail) and on the start page of the Internet terminals.

AIRPORTS

Many airports—especially hub airports where lots of people have to wait while changing planes—have some provision for Internet access. Look for airport Internet terminals either in freestanding Internet kiosks in waiting areas, or in cubicles in a phone booth or "business center" area.

Typically, though, airport access is inconvenient (such as kiosk workstations with no place to sit) and/or expensive. Prices are set for the business traveler who urgently needs to send or receive an e-mail message no matter what it costs. If you really need the Internet right away, you'll be grateful. If you don't, or need to be online for a significant amount of time, you're probably better off to wait and look elsewhere.

— LAST RESORT

A $20 minimum is not uncommon for even a few minutes' use of an airport Internet terminal.

TRUCK STOPS

It may come as a surprise to white-collar readers, but the best place to find public Internet access on American highways is at truck stops. People in cars are generally only on short trips, and can check their e-mail before they leave or after they arrive. But there are literally millions of long-haul truckers in the United States who are often on the road for days at a time. E-mail is a vital tool for truck drivers wanting to stay in touch with family, fellow drivers around the country, and friends.

Many truckers now have laptop computers in their cabs for satellite tracking and dispatching. Others use Internet kiosks in truck stops. People who live in mobile RVs are in the same situation, and usually either have laptop computers or use Internet kiosks and

> ## TRUCKSTOP RULE OF THUMB:—
>
> The place with the most big rigs in the parking area is the one most likely to have the comprehensive array of services for truckers that would include an Internet kiosk.

cybercafes. However, highway rest stops for cars rarely have Internet terminals.

Truck-stop Internet kiosks are typically like the worst of those in airports. The computer is sealed in the kiosk housing, all the ports and disk drive slots are inaccessible, and there's no printer. So you can't copy anything to or from a disk or print anything out. They're only good for surfing the Web and using Web-based services. You'll need to write down by hand anything you want to save. But they're often the only public Internet terminals for miles, and among the few open 24 hours a day. You can find them through truckers' portal Web sites, the trucker newsgroup misc.transport.trucking, or directories of kiosk providers like DriverNet (**www.drivernet.com/locate.asp**).

COLLEGES AND UNIVERSITIES

College students, faculty, and staff generally have Internet access through campus networks and terminals. As a rule, these aren't open to the public. And since all legitimate members of the campus community can get accounts on the campus network, there's little or no need for a cybercafe on most campuses.

So why am I talking about colleges and universities? Sure, it's on the gray side, and most campus network administrators would be annoyed with me for suggesting it. But... few students are overly concerned with official rules on authorized access. In a pinch, it never hurts to ask around on a campus: "Hi! I'm visiting from out of town and haven't been able to find a cybercafe anywhere around here. Do you perhaps know of somewhere I might get on the Internet to check my e-mail?" If you come across as a nice person, there's a good chance that someone will take pity on you and let you use their account on an unguarded terminal, or in their dorm room or office. As in libraries, many older campus terminals have only text Internet access, not a graphical browser. So you stand the best chance if you know how to do what you want in Lynx or a Telnet session, as well as in Netscape and MSIE.

YOUR FRIENDS AND HOSTS

About half of all U.S. households now have Internet access from home. If you're visiting friends or relatives, they're as likely as you are to have their own computer and Internet connection. Be considerate—don't take over the computer or the phone line when your hosts need them— but don't be afraid to ask, politely, if you can use their computer to check your e-mail or look up something you need to find on the Web.

Bringing a Computer With You

TYPES OF INTERNET ACCESS DEVICES

It's possible to access the Internet with a variety of devices from full-sized, full-featured laptop computers to Palm Pilots and cellular phones. Here are some of the pros, cons, and peculiarities of these different types of devices for travel.

Repetitive Stress Injury

Repetitive stress injury (RSI) is the leading cause of occupational disability in the USA, and computer use is one of the leading causes of RSI. My mother needed surgery on both her wrists for carpal tunnel syndrome, some of my friends have been injured so badly they can no longer work, and I am dictating this book using voice recognition software because of the damage done by computer use.

Mobile computing can exacerbate the risks of RSI. At home, you can—if you make it a priority, as you should—set up your computer workstation carefully and comfortably. On the road, you are less likely to have a custom-fitted or ergonomic workstation.

Laptop computers aren't necessarily less ergonomic than desktop ones. The touchpad on a laptop, for example, puts much less stress on your hand and wrist then does a mouse. But it's just as important to consider ergonomics when choosing a laptop as when choosing a desktop computer.

Using a computer in an airplane seat or some hotel rooms is inevitably awkward. Limit your computer use as much as possible in settings like these where it stresses your body. Wheverer you are, try to set the computer up as carefully and comfortably as possible. Take the time to adjust it, and pay attention to your posture.

By the time you feel pain from RSI, the damage to your body is often permanent. Ignore RSI risks from computer use at your own peril. If you notice any physical discomfort associated with computer use, see an RSI specialist immediately.

If you are buying an Internet-access device with travel in mind, get the smallest, lightest device that will serve your purposes. Before you buy a full-size laptop computer, find a rigid object of similar size and weight, then carry it around all day, treating it as though it were worth several thousand dollars and could never be left unattended. Which features do you actually need? How will you actually use it? How much time will you spend carrying it around? As technology evolves, you can do more and more with a notebook or even a palmtop with a touch-typing keyboard, modem, Web browser, and e-mail program. Before each trip, especially a lengthy trip other than for business, or overseas, think, "Do I really need to bring my computer?"

Avoid carrying a laptop computer in a fancy case or one with a computer company name or logo that says, "Steal me." Use a nondescript case, preferably one that doesn't look like a computer case at all. One of the overlooked advantages of computers smaller than standard laptops is that they are less conspicuous and less likely to be recognized as computers. Most people think that the case for a subnotebook, even with its power supply, accessories, and spare batteries, is a slightly odd-shaped purse too small to be a computer.

There are no hard and fast lines between laptop, notebook, subnotebook, and palmtop computers. Some of the devices I like best are the ones that critics find hardest to fit in these pigeonholes. There's much more of a continuum from the largest to the smallest computers than is often acknowledged. What matters is how well a device serves your needs, not what anyone calls it. If you look long and hard enough, you'll find there's a mobile Internet access device for almost every need.

Laptop Computers

Full-sized laptop computers can do anything and everything that full-sized desktop computers can. But you pay for all that flexibility, in both dollars and pounds. If you really need to run the same operating system and all the same programs while traveling (even oversized and inefficient applications like Microsoft Office), with all the same peripherals (CD-ROM drive, speakers, microphone, large display, high-resolution color graphics, etc.), you can do it on a laptop computer.

The price you pay is high, in both money and weight. Flat-screen displays are still much more expensive than television-type CRT tubes, and miniaturization costs money. A laptop typically costs at least twice the price of a desktop computer with comparable features. Including the "power brick" or batteries and other essential cables and accessories, a full-sized laptop can weigh as much as 10 pounds. The bigger and heavier it is, the bigger, heavier, and more awkward and conspicuous the case you need to carry it around and protect it from breakage.

On the road, a full-sized laptop makes sense only if you need to spend a lot of time doing work on your computer, rather than the Internet. As an Internet access device, a full-size laptop is overkill. The more your work on the road relies on the Internet, the more you can limit your traveling computer gear to whatever is needed for a portable Internet access terminal.

Used and Older Laptop Computers

If you don't need the highest possible performance you might consider a second-hand laptop computer. Most laptops are owned by business people who trade them in more frequently than their desktop computers. Used laptops tend to be even more of a bargain than used desktops. Any Windows laptop with a modem is an adequate Internet terminal. Prices for new current-model Windows laptops start at $1,200–1,500. You can get refurbished rental laptops (with warranties), or discontinued ones that were state-of-the-art last year, for $400–800. Check with online surplus, closeout, and clearance vendors.

For those who are prepared to try it, Linux may be the best way to get more performance out of an "obsolete" laptop. Once it's installed and configured, Linux is an excellent operating system for an Internet terminal. Linux is so much more efficient that a computer that plods in Windows will race in Linux. Since Linux is the most widely used operating system for Web servers, all new Internet programs are available for Linux. Many a first-generation 486 laptop that would otherwise have been scrapped or given away has found a second life as a portable Linux box.

The need for Microsoft compatibility doesn't rule out Linux. Sun's free Star Office suite for Linux **www.sun/com/staroffice** provides a complete graphical desktop; Internet and office tools; and the ability to open, edit, and save files and documents in all Microsoft Office formats. Star Office is also available, free, for Windows, if you need to deal with other people's documents in proprietary Microsoft formats. If, like me, you prefer WordPerfect's word processor, Word-Perfect Suite for Linux is also free from Corel at **linux.corel.com /products/linuxproducts_wp8.htm**.

Linux is not for everyone—not yet. But its inherent suitability for portable Internet use makes Linux a likely candidate for the laptop operating system of the future. In 1999, Dell and Compaq started selling desktops with Linux pre-installed. By the end of 2000, IBM was shipping laptops with Linux installed at the factory. You can also get "dual-boot" systems with both Linux and Windows 2000, so you can use Windows-only programs when you really have to.

Even someone who's perfectly happy using Windows on their desktop computer might prefer Linux on their older laptop when all they're doing with their computer on their vacation is surfing the Web or reading e-mail. If you're interested in trying it out with your existing laptop, check out the "Linux on Laptops" page at **www.cs .utexas.edu/users/kharker/linux-laptop** for resources and links

Software to be Familiar With

You never know what sort of computer you'll find available. The more types of hardware and software you're familiar with, the better your chances of being able to do what you need to do on the road. It's better to spend a little time familiarizing yourself with these before you go—at a friend's home, say—than when you are paying by the hour at a cybercafe.

Here's some of the software with which it's most useful to have at least a little practice:

- **Windows:** Even if you have a Macintosh (or a Linux or Be Box) at home, you can't count on finding one on the road. Learn at least the basics of Windows. Windows 2000, NT 4.0, 98, and 95 are all similar enough that familiarity with any one of these flavors of Windows is adequate to accomplish basic tasks on any of the others.

- **Mac OS:** PowerBooks have always been the prima donnas of laptop computing. And ever since the introduction of the iMac, Apple has been on the rebound. In a service bureau cum cybercafe that caters mainly to graphic artists, or in a friend's house, you'll sometimes find only Mac's. Prepare yourself. Mac devotees will tell you that Mac's are intuitive and that no training or practice is needed to use them. There's some truth to that, but it's equally true that to think like Apple you have to "think different" from Mr. Bill. If you can, spend an hour before you start traveling getting the lay of the land in Mac-world with a Mac-using friend for a guide.

- **Netscape Communicator (includes Navigator and Messenger) and Microsoft Internet Explorer and Outlook:** Virtually any graphical Internet workstation will have one or the other of these browsers and e-mail clients, but many don't have both. You have to be prepared to use whichever is available. It's actually a good idea to have both Netscape and MSIE on your computer. Some badly designed sites only work with one and some only with the other.

- **Lynx (lynx.browser.org):** Never heard of Lynx? You may have used it without realizing it, as the interface to a library catalog or other database. Lynx has near total domination of the market for text-only Web browsers, with many millions of users. Lynx is available on many text-only terminals in libraries, on campuses, and elsewhere. Lynx is the only browser you can run within a Telnet session, if no browser is installed on the machine to which you have access. If you are at an old computer or dumb terminal with a modem but without TCP/IP (Internet) networking capability, or something is wrong with the TCP/IP services or settings, you can use a simple terminal program to dial in to a "shell" account and run Lynx on the host. (Many libraries and freenets provide limited free shell accounts.) If you can't figure out how to run Lynx, but you can get to some sort of command prompt or shell, just try typing "lynx" and pressing return. Learn a little Lynx, and many more potential points of Web access will be available to you.

■ **Pine:** What Lynx is to Web browsing, Pine is to e-mail. Virtually all text-only Internet terminals use Pine for e-mail. (Try typing "pine" or "mail" from a shell or command prompt.) Because it runs on more types of computers and terminals than any other e-mail program, it's standard in many academic and other large organizations with diverse hardware—so it's what you'll have to work with if someone in such a place offers to let you use their account to send an e-mail message. And it's the only common e-mail program you can run in a Telnet window (see below). It may seem more complicated than Web-based e-mail. But once you get the hang of it, checking mail on your own ISP or mail host with Pine in a Telnet window is actually far faster, easier, and more powerful than Web-based e-mail. When hackers want to check their e-mail remotely, they run Pine in a Telnet window.

You can download a free version of Pine for the PC from **www.washington.edu/pine/pc-pine**. But don't let its limitations discourage you: the host-based version you can get to with Telnet is much easier to use and more powerful than PC-Pine.

■ **Telnet:** Telnet is a protocol that lets you open a text-only, command-line interface (like a DOS window) to another machine across the Internet. Why should you care? Some sort of Telnet program is included in almost any Internet-capable operating system. Even if there's no browser installed, Telnet is almost certainly available. (Search for a file or directory with "Telnet" in its name, or just try typing "Telnet" at a command prompt.) Maybe the terminal isn't capable of displaying graphics, or is too old and slow to run a graphical browser. Telnet to your ISP (if your Internet account includes "shell" access) or to a public-access Lynx server (bring a copy of the list at **www.trillhome.com/lynx/public _lynx.html**), and you're on the Web. You can also use Telnet to get to your e-mail.

including an index of configuration tips and advice for Linux on specific and mostly "obsolete" laptop models.

Notebook Computers

If what you want is a portable Internet terminal, a stripped-down "notebook" computer may be a better choice than a full-sized laptop.

The CD-ROM and floppy disk drives are not only large and heavy but the most power-hungry components, requiring more than their own weight in additional batteries. Without them, without built-in speakers, and with a slightly smaller display, the total weight in your luggage of a typical notebook computer is half that of a full-sized laptop.

The limiting factor in getting things done on the Internet is typically connection speed, not processor speed. Notebooks, laptops, and home computers are all limited to the same 56K bps over dial-up connections. For anything on the Internet except bleeding-edge multimedia, a notebook computer is just as useful as a bigger laptop. And unlike palmtops, notebook computers generally run the same versions of Windows as larger laptops and desktop computers. There hasn't been a Macintosh notebook—yet.

The ideal machine of this type would be the smallest one capable of running the latest version of your preferred desktop operating system and applications, with the smallest keyboard on which you can comfortably type, and the smallest screen you can comfortably read.

Unfortunately, there's been relatively little effort put into development of good Internet-terminal notebooks. Most laptop computers have been used primarily as stand-alone portable PCs, not Internet devices. That's starting to change, but don't be discouraged if most laptop salespeople start out by showing you things that are way too big to lug around all the time. The models and makers keep changing, but for at least five years there have been a couple of models at a time available in this "notebook" niche from one or another manufacturer.

Subnotebook Computers

What disappears next as you go down the scale of portable computer size? The hard disk drive and the ability to run normal Windows applications. Subnotebook and palmtop computers use smaller, simpler operating systems and programs, and store their data in memory chips or "flash" memory cards. They have built-in or PCMCIA PC-card modems, and can exchange data with other computers by cable linkage or over the Internet. They come with software for synchronizing files with those on a desktop computer.

What do you get in exchange for giving up the familiar operating system, applications, and storage methods? Hugely increased battery life, greater durability, and another halving of size and weight.

Even notebooks rarely get more than a couple of hours out of a battery charge. Windows CE or Psion subnotebooks can run for 8–20 hours on a set of batteries. Some even use standard AA batteries instead of the typical $100 + special-purpose laptop or notebook batteries. You can bang a palmtop around quite a bit without the risk of crashing the hard disk. Oh, and they turn on and off instantly.

At the top end, a variety of Windows CE and Psion subnotebooks now have touch-type keyboards and high-resolution color graphic displays as large as those in many notebooks and some laptops.

In the United States, Windows CE machines are more visible. In Europe and the world as a whole, Psion (**www.psion.com**) dominates this category. Microsoft has come to this category from above, trying to strip down its bloatware to fit on small machines. Psion has come to it from below, gradually adding modems, the ability to download programs, larger keyboards and displays, and finally a color graphical display and Web browser to its industry-leading line of electronic organizers.

Both Windows CE and Psion subnotebooks include all the programs you need for Internet access and basic office tasks: Web browser, e-mail, calendar and address book, word processing, and spreadsheets. For other, specialized applications, there's more software available for download for the EPOC operating system on Psions than for Windows CE, and more of it is free.

Psion subnoteboooks and even palmtops can run downloaded Java programs, giving them access to a much wider range of software. Microsoft has promised to add Java support to Windows CE, but hasn't yet.

I'll be frank: I was fascinated by the first notebook and subnotebook computers I saw. I got one as soon as I could afford it, and I've used one ever since. For several years a notebook was my only computer, and I wrote most of my first book on one. For me, notebooks and subnotebooks are the optimum compromise between size, performance, and price. (Did I mention that top-of-the-line subnotebooks cost only about $1,000, compared to at least twice that for low-end new laptops?)

If I were buying a new device solely to use for Internet access while traveling, my choice would probably be a Psion palmtop (Revo or 5MX) or subnotebook (Series 7 or NetBook). Compared to Windows CE, Psion's greater software and hardware reliability, superior and more compact design, and availability of downloaded software more than make up for the need to install a small link program or use e-mail to exchange files with other Windows computers. Compared to a laptop, the limited functionality, which still includes all the essential Internet and office tasks, is more than made up for by the savings in size, weight, and battery life.

Palmtop Computers

"Palmtop" computers are pocket-sizes devices that, like subnotebooks, mostly run Windows CE or the EPOC operating system used by Psion (and a few others), and have about the same processor capabilities. The main difference between a subnotebook and a palmtop is the size of the keyboard and display. Palmtops typically have black-and-white displays that show only a few half-lines of text, and keyboards you can only type on with a stylus. That's just too small for most people to find really useful for extended work. Think of a palmtop as an electronic organizer (calendar and address book) with a modem that you can use to check your e-mail or send a fax in a pinch, or as a Palm Pilot with a sub-miniature keyboard.

If you find the display screen and keyboard size adequate for your purposes, however, there may be no need to carry anything bigger than a pocket-sized half-pound (including batteries and built-in modem) Psion or HP palmtop. I've been tempted to get one as an emergency backup Internet access device for trips on which I don't bring my notebook computer.

How useful one of these will be to you probably depends on whether your needs are more for e-mail or for Web access. Many people find palmtops acceptable for reading and writing brief, text e-mail messages. But almost no one would want to have to do any real research or other work on the Web on a palmtop. Your personal taste for the size and feel of the keyboard and display is crucial for devices in this size range, so don't buy one without a chance to play with it first.

Palm Pilots, PDAs and Cell Phones

You've heard the hype: soon everything from your toaster to your flashlight will be connected to the Internet, the songs you're listening to on your Walkman will be interrupted by a robotic voice reading your e-mail and instant messages, and we'll all be browsing the Web from our two-way wrist TVs. As we enter the third millennium, is any of this yet real?

You can send and receive e-mail on a palmtop (with a modem

or a wireless transceiver) or on a cellular phone. You can even browse specially-adapted "lite" versions of some Web sites on a Palm Pilot or similar "personal digital assistant" (PDA). Currently, a Palm Pilot or cell phone is no real substitute for a device with a full keyboard and larger screen for general Internet access. Given the limitations of small displays and of text entry without a keyboard, the text messaging capability doesn't amount to much more than enhanced paging. And only being able to browse selected content from a few Web sites eliminates most of the versatility and value of access to the Web. But this is one area where technology is changing especially quickly, with the emergence of pocket-sized gadgets that combine cell phone, PDA, and wireless e-mail, and Web access in one device.

COMPATIBILITY AND CONNECTIVITY

Power

If you travel internationally, the problems can start as soon as you try to plug your computer into the outlet ("mains" in British and much international usage). It's more complicated than you might think.

There are two standard voltages (110 volts and 220 volts), two standard AC frequencies (50 and 60 Hz), and about 10 different types of wall outlets and corresponding plugs in use in different parts of the world. The United States uses 110–120 volts, 60 Hz AC, and three types of partially compatible plugs and outlets

> **CHECK THAT OUTLET**
>
> If you just plug it in without first checking whether the outlet has the right power for your computer, you could completely destroy your computer.

(two-prong, two-prong polarized, and three-prong). Not all countries have a single national standard; you may find three different kinds of plugs or two different voltages or frequencies in different parts of the same country. In rare instances you may even encounter DC or other voltages.

There is no easy, simple, or cheap device that will enable you to use electronic devices with power systems other than those for which they were designed. General-purpose voltage and frequency converters are too big, heavy, and expensive for travel use. Smaller, cheaper voltage-reduction devices are often sold for travel but are useless for computers, as they can be used only with lights or heaters and not with most electronic devices.

Plug adapters are deceptively cheap and simple. Most electrical and electronic equipment will not work on the wrong voltage. Using an adapter to plug something into the wrong voltage can ruin the equipment or cause it to overheat, catch fire, or explode. The danger is greatest if you inadvertently plug 110-volt devices (used in the United States) into 220-volt power supplies (used throughout most of Europe).

Some—but *not* all—laptop computers come with multiple-voltage power supplies capable of operating from all standard power types with only plug adapters and no need for external voltage or frequency converters. These aren't standard yet, and the specifications don't always distinguish whether the power supply is available in two alternative models, one for 110–120 volts and one for 220–240 volts, or whether there is a single model capable of operating on either voltage. You may have to go pretty deeply into the manuals or call the manufacturers' technical support line to get a definite answer.

— PULL THE PLUG

Don't buy a laptop computer for travel without a demonstration that it won't be damaged by a power failure. One approach is to have the salesperson yank the plug out of the wall when the machine is running. Computer still okay? Then take it on the road with confidence.

The key words to look for or ask about are an "auto-switching" or "universal" power supply, at least 110–240 volts, 50–60 Hz. The one on my computer is rated 90–264 volts, giving it a decent tolerance for brownouts and surges. I still use a surge suppressor for protection against lightning and voltage spikes. Avoid power supplies with a manual 110/220 voltage switch: unless you also carry a voltmeter, you don't always know the voltage before you plug in your computer. The wrong setting on a manually-switched dual-voltage power supply could ruin your computer.

Third World power supplies pose additional problems, even if you have the proper plug adapters and equipment with a universal power supply. Power supplies in much of the world are intermittent. That a country or city has a central electrical power supply does not imply that power is available 24 hours a day, every day. Power may be supplied only for certain hours each day, or at unpredictable hours if the generators or their fuel supply are unreliable. Power lines may go down or short out, and distribution problems may make power outages common even where there's no problem with generation. In some places there is no city power, and hotels or other buildings have electricity only while they run their own generators, which they don't usually do around the clock.

If generating capacity is inadequate to meet city or countrywide demand, the most common load-management strategy is that of "rolling blackouts," when power is deliberately shut off to some areas to keep the overloaded system from shutting down entirely. Depending on the extent of the capacity shortfall, your hotel's neighborhood may have power for 20 hours a day or only two. Sometimes there is a predictable daily or weekly schedule or rotation, sometimes not. This is a problem if you are using a computer that can be damaged by a power failure while it is plugged in and in use.

If the batteries are in the computer charging and the power goes out, some equipment can be damaged or lose stored settings or data. Try to find a computer designed so the batteries can be removed while charging. If you have a second set of batteries, this also enables you to leave one set in your hotel room charging while you are out on the town with the other, so you can come back to a freshly-charged set.

Telehones and Modems

"What's the big deal with telephones? You just plug your modem into the jack, right?" Wrong. Even within the United States and Canada, first-time laptop-toters tend to underestimate the potential problems of digital and hardwired phones and operator-assisted modem calls from hotels. Internationally, things can get really weird, from a wild variety of phone jacks (see illustration) to periodic modem-destroying high-voltage pulses on phone lines used for billing in some European countries.

Telephones are even less standard internationally than are power supplies. A "universal" (110–240 volts, 50–60 Hz, AC) rechargeable power supply and 10 plug adapters will enable you to power up almost anywhere for minimal cost. A complete set of 39 adapters to connect your modem to all the types of telephone jacks in the world will set you back $450; adding equipment to con-

---

UNMETERED LOCAL CALLS A RARITY

When connecting your computer to the Internet, don't forget to consider the price of the phone call. In the United States and Canada, it's a simple matter of asking a hotel whether local calls are free. In the rest of the world, you don't have to ask: take it for granted that the answer is, "No". Almost no other country in the world offers unmetered local calling, even for residential phone users. "Free" Internet access in most countries means that you pay the same per-minute charge for calls to an ISP as for any other local calls. It may be "only" the equivalent of a few cents a minute, but it can still add up if you're on the Internet for hours.

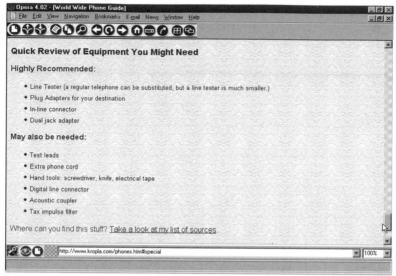

Quick Review of Equipment You Might Need

Highly Recommended:

- Line Tester (a regular telephone can be substituted, but a line tester is much smaller.)
- Plug Adapters for your destination
- In-line connector
- Dual jack adapter

May also be needed:

- Test leads
- Extra phone cord
- Hand tools: screwdriver, knife, electrical tape
- Digital line connector
- Acoustic coupler
- Tax impulse filter

Where can you find this stuff? Take a look at my list of sources.

http://www.kropla.com

Road warrior Steve Kropla's international telephone guide is an Internet classic of voluntary mutual aid and information sharing, with a worldwide network of contributors.

nect to non-modular phones (hardwired, PBX, digital, and pay phones) almost doubles that price. The whole kit-and-caboodle for worldwide connectivity is larger and heavier than many computers.

Power plug adapters are widely available; only a few specialty companies like Teleadapt (**www.teleadapt.com**) sell telephone and modem adapters, and even fewer know which types are required for which countries. Most travel stores and mail-order suppliers get their telephone adapters from Teleadapt. You might as well buy from Teleadapt directly; as you get a lot of extra advice and support if you buy direct.

To figure out what type(s) of telephone plug(s) and other connectivity peculiarities to expect in any given country, check Steve Kropla's excellent noncommercial Web site at kropla.com (maintained with the assistance of volunteers around the world) or the Teleadapt database at **www.teleadapt.com/Web/destinations/destination** (very authoritative, but lists plug types only by Teleadapt model number). Both these sites have online primers going into more detail.

Outside the First World, modular phone connections and international direct dialing are rare. You have to be prepared to open up

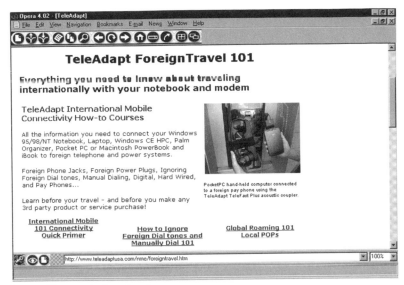

http://www.teleadapt.com

Whether or not you buy anything from them, you can find a wealth of practical advice about mobile connectivity on the Teleadapt Web site.

strange phones and connect your modem to the right terminals (the wrong connections can ruin your modem, if not your computer) and place modem calls through an operator, or carry and know how to use an acoustic coupler in places where international calls can only be made from phone booths where you aren't allowed to dismantle or wire into the phones. Your equipment should tolerate noisy lines and be able to fall back to slower speeds than you are used to. I've encountered phone lines that were unreliable for data communications at more than 300 bps. Connecting to the Internet through a cell phone avoids many of these pitfalls, but the cost is usually prohibitive.

The weight and expense of all the adapters and tools is, for some people, the deciding factor against trying to maintain e-mail access, or even bringing a computer at all, on long or multi-country trips. I don't bring a computer except on business trips within the First World, and I buy telephone adapters one at a time as I need them for those particular countries I visit on business.

In high-tech countries, most hotel rooms have direct-dial phones. In low-tech countries, and in low-budget hotels in the United States, you may have to go through an operator to get an outside line. Different countries use different sounds for "dial tone," "ring," and "busy". Your modem may not recognize these correctly. Learn how to tell your modem software to dial even if it doesn't think it hears a dial tone, and to connect without dialing when you've placed a call manually. Teleadapt (**www.teleadapt.com**) produces a series of concise instructional "cheat sheets" on how to do this with many common programs.

Whatever equipment you plan to bring, try it out before your first trip. Take your new laptop to a friend's house and try to get on the Internet. Familiarize yourself with how to indicate whether or not your modem should dial the area code, how to get your modem to dial whatever string of numbers a hotel requires to get an outside line, and how to get your modem to connect after placing a call through an operator.

Local Dial-Up Numbers

Most Internet users connect by having their modem dial the phone number of their Internet service provider's (ISP's) nearest "point of presence." At home, you set this up once and forget about it. On the road, how do you find a local dial-up access number?

First, check with your present Internet service provider (ISP). Some ISPs include a list of their dial-up access numbers with their setup software, or with their printed user information. With most others, or if you want the most up-to-date list, you'll need to check your ISP's Web site or contact them by e-mail or phone. Remember to copy down the access number(s) in the place(s) you're going *before* you leave, since when you need them you won't have access to the Web.

The easiest way to do this is usually to find your ISP's Web page listing all their dial-up numbers in different places, and save it on your laptop (and your backup floppies) in a place and with a filename that you'll remember. (Note to ISPs: to make life easier for travelers, don't just have a search tool that shows the access number(s) for one location at a time. Provide a way to get a page or text file that can be saved as an index of *all* your access numbers in all locations.)

Check the fine print in the list of dial-up numbers to see if there are per-minute surcharges for using some or all of them. If your ISP operates in only one region, they may have arrangements with a larger company to offer access outside their territory—but at an extra charge of anywhere from 5–50 cents a minute. Access through a toll-free 800, 888, or 877 number (the default choice for AOL users in places where AOL doesn't have a local access number, for example) is almost always surcharged. It's often cheaper to make a long distance call to your ISP than to use a surcharged local or 800 number.

If you're traveling internationally, check with your ISP to see if you need to make special provisions in advance. To cut down on fraudulent use of their international access numbers, some ISPs block access from outside the United States and Canada by anyone who hasn't specifically requested it. This may be appropriate, since most people in the United States never leave the country. But you need to make sure you get your international access turned on before you leave the country.

Roaming Numbers

Some ISPs have "roaming" programs for subscribers traveling outside their service area. If you're traveling to a place where your ISP doesn't have a local point of presence, check if they belong to either "iPass" (**ipass.com**) or "GRIC" (**www.gric.com/zone**), or offer some other roaming service.

iPass and GRIC are each a consortium of ISPs who have joined together to offer each others' subscribers reciprocal access through their local dial-up numbers. Per-minute charges vary depending on both your ISP and the one whose access number they use, so you need to check the rates with your ISP for access through specific numbers. Some ISPs also charge a one-time setup fee for a roaming account, and/or a fee for each month you use roaming services or have them activated.

GRIC and iPass each include member ISPs with thousands of dial-up numbers in more than 150 countries each—far more than any single ISP. The complete list of iPass locations is at **ipass.com/accesspoints** and GRIC members are listed at **www.gric.com/zone/isplocator**.

There's a good chance your ISP belongs to iPass, GRIC, or a similar alliance. If your ISP doesn't, suggest it to them. It's beneficial both for them and their subscribers.

AOL and Compuserve provide global roaming access through GRIC, but only allow AOL and Compuserve subscribers to use some, not all, GRIC access numbers.

To use either of these services, you have to set up a roaming account and get the list of access numbers from your ISP in advance. Your roaming user ID and password are different from those you use for your own ISP's dial-up numbers, so you'll need to make a few small changes to your dialer settings. You can do this manually, or through software downloaded from iPass or GRIC.

Access through GRIC or iPass isn't cheap, but it's usually cheaper than making a direct international call to your ISP's access number in the United States. Since you only need to make a local

Airlines at Forefront of Global Networking

The roaming Internet access network with the most thorough worldwide coverage is a spinoff of the airlines' own communication network. (Remember when I said that it was the airlines, not the Internet, who were the real pioneers in global networking?) Equant **www.equant.net** was originally the network infrastructure built by the airline cooperative SITA **www.sita.int**. Most international businesses concentrate on a few major financial hubs. Airlines were the first businesses to need real-time electronic communications for their operations in even the more "peripheral" parts of the world. So SITA ended up with the world's most comprehensive dial-up data network. They also had more bandwidth than they needed: airlines need reliable communications anywhere they fly, but in places with few flights they don't use their data lines that much. So in 1995 SITA formed a division, which eventually became Equant, to market its excess capacity to businesses and the public. Equant services aren't cheap, but there are countries where they have just about the only reliable access lines. Among their users are Non-governmental organizations (NGOs) and war and disaster relief organizations that do work in the Third and Fourth Worlds.

call, it's also simpler, more reliable, and likely to get you a faster connection than an international call.

Advertiser-Supported Dial-Up Numbers

"Free" internet access means you agree to a barrage of ads, and to letting the service provider monitor your online behavior and perhaps sell that information to the highest bidder. That's a dreadful bargain at home or anywhere you can find a local access number. But it sometimes makes sense if you need to spend hours online in a remote place where your ISP doesn't have a local access number and calls are expensive.

Advertiser-supported Internet access is a good deal if you're using it for something that doesn't require you to look at the screen, so you're not distracted by the ads. Why would you want Internet access when you're not looking at the screen? When you're transferring large files, that's when. Dial in to the local access number of an advertising-supported Internet service, start a transfer, close the computer, and leave the transfer running while you do something else. Go out to eat, and all your e-mail will have been downloaded when you get back. Go to sleep, and you can back up all your work over the Internet overnight with no connection charges, and without having to watch the ads. "Free" access services have been trying to find ways to force users to look at the ads, but thus far without success.

In their attempt to keep you from turning off the ads while you surf, all the advertiser-supported Internet services I've reviewed rely on proprietary Microsoft technology. They run only on Windows, and only with MSIE version 4 or above. No other operating system or browser allows commands from the Internet to take over your computer the way advertisers want. Obviously, this involves some security risk. I've seen little discussion of exactly how dangerous it is to use these services. All these services are in the business of selling information about your Web surfing to their advertisers, and all are inherently privacy-invasive. How do you say, "Buyer beware!," when you are referring to something "free"?

Wireless Internet Access

In a few years devices smaller than a cell phone, attached to or built into our computers, will give them seamless roving high-speed wireless network connectivity. We're not quite there yet, but it's coming.

Wireless home networking is becoming popular with people who don't want to have to run wires through the walls between rooms, or who want to use their laptop from their lawn chair. But no standard has yet emerged for portability between local wireless networks. New Apple computers have built-in wireless networking transceivers, but you can't count on finding a compatible Apple wireless network base station on the road.

YOU GET WHAT YOU PAY FOR

So-called "free" Internet access isn't. You pay for it by allowing the service to take over part of your screen and use it to flash advertising at you for the entire time you're connected, and by allowing them to monitor and collect information about where you go and what you do online.

Connecting a laptop to a regular cell phone, while possible, is still too slow, expensive, and cumbersome. GSM cell phones can connect directly to the Internet without a modem, but on most wireless service plans the per-minute charges make this option unattractive.

The largest wireless Internet access service is the Ricochet network **www.ricochet.net**. It works like this: you buy a special Ricochet modem ($300) about the size of a cellular phone. You connect it to your computer just like any other external modem. Once your account is activated, you can connect to the Internet from anywhere in the Ricochet coverage area.

At about the price of DSL or a cable modem for unlimited connection time, it seems like a good deal to me. Friends who have Ricochet service love it. You can connect anywhere as long as you're within the coverage area. You never have to find a phone or plug-in to check your e-mail or browse the Web, and you never have to change any settings to connect on-the-fly. If your sole or primary computer is a laptop, and you don't have higher-speed access through DSL or a cable modem, I'd seriously consider Ricochet as your ISP. As with voice calls on cell phones, there are "dead spots" within Ricochet coverage areas where connections aren't possible. Try to borrow a Ricochet modem and test the coverage before you buy.

Richochet covers a growing number of major U.S. cities, and the speed of Richochet connections is being upgraded to 128k bps (the same speed as an ISDN line). Check the Richochet Web site for current coverage.

Internet Access Through a LAN

Local area networks (LANs) are becoming as ubiquitous as the Internet. Within a few years, dial-up modems will be considered obsolete, and a standard method of mobile connectivity will be to plug your laptop directly into the network, not to plug your modem into the phone line.

It's already common, if you're visiting a company on business, to be offered a chance to plug your laptop into their LAN. If not, it's most likely due to concerns about network security rather than about technical feasibility. Cybercafes often prefer to have you use your own laptop over their LAN, since that way you aren't tying up one of their workstations. Indeed, most home "broadband" connections to DSL or cable modems are via a small-scale home Ethernet LAN.

Why bother, when it's less common and, with most currently-available computers, takes more effort to figure out? Why not just dial-in with your own modem, especially if your ISP contract allows unlimited nationwide dial-up Internet use?

In a word, speed. Some cybercafes, especially in less well-connected parts of the world, and home networks are connected to the Internet only by a shared dial-up modem. But most of the time when you have a chance to connect via a LAN, it will have a fast (ISDN,

Checklist for Connecting Your Laptop Computer to the Internet Over a LAN

Questions For You About Your Computer:

■ Does your laptop computer have a built-in Ethernet interface, or do you have an Ethernet PC card?

■ What kind of connector does it have? (Look for an RJ45 jack like an oversized modular phone jack.)

Questions for your host about their hardware:

■ Do you have an Ethernet LAN connected to the Internet?

■ What kind of cable connectors does it use? (RJ45?)

■ Do I need to bring my own cable or do you have a spare?

Questions for your host about their software:

You or your network-savvy friend will need the answers to configure your TCP/IP software. Once again, if the terms below are all Greek to you, you probably aren't ready to try this by yourself.

■ Should I Use DHCP or a fixed IP Address?

■ If I should use a fixed IP address, what is it? (It will look like "192.168.1.64", or some other string of 4 numbers separated by periods. The most likely first 2 numbers are "192.168", for reasons you probably don't want know.)

■ Do I need to specify a default gateway? If so, what is it? (This will also be a four-part numeric IP address.)

■ What are the primary and secondary DNS's? (These will be more IP addresses; there might not be a secondary DNS.)

This might sound nightmarish if you've never done it before, but with experience it's not really so bad. Just don't try it unless you are sure you know what you are doing: if these questions don't make any sense to you, you probably aren't ready for this.

DSL, cable modem, T1, or better) connection to the Internet. That means much faster file transfers, and makes possible many things that would take a prohibitively long time over a dial-up connection. Downloading a 10 MB PowerPoint presentation might take 45 minutes over a modem connection but only 45 seconds over a LAN with a broadband connection.

Suggested Travel Connectivity Packing List

Essentials for modem connectivity within the USA and Canada

- ■ Computer (laptop, notebook, or palmtop)
- ■ Modem (built-in, PC card, USB, infrared, or other)
- ■ Computer power supply and cord
- ■ Phone cord (RJ11)
- ■ Power and modem surge suppressors
-    Line tester(s) for reversed polarity and digital lines
-    List of ISP's or roving partner's dial-up access numbers
- ■ Any needed user names and passwords (ideally, memorized; if there are too many to memorize, carry them in a safe and secure place like on waterproof paper in a money belt)
-    Printout of ISP's server and TCP/IP settings (Even if you don't understand them yourself, a technician will need them for troubleshooting, or to configure a replacement if your computer is broken or stolen.)
- ■ ISP's phone number in case of connection problems
- ■ Two tested emergency bootable floppy disks with basic diagnostic software, one carried separately from the computer
- ■ Two backup copies of any crucial data, carried in different places (floppy disks, Zip disks, or CD's)

Recommended Additions If You Have Room

- ■ 3-prong adapter for older 2-prong power outlets
-    Power and telephone extension cords (The only accessible power outlet in a hotel room may be in the bathroom, and the phone jack may be at the far side of the room.)
-    2-to-1 RJ11 telephone line doubler (so you can plug in both the phone and your modem if you have to go through an operator to place or receive calls)
-    RJ11 telephone cable gender changer (you never know if the available phone connection will be male or female)
-    2-line to single-line RJ11 adapter (so you can plug a single-line modem into the jack for a 2-line phone)
- ■ Spare batteries for computer and accessories
-    A few spare floppy disks

Useful If You Have Them and Have Room

- ■ Portable Zip drive with power cord and/or battery pack, cable, and a couple of Zip disks
- ■ CD-R or CD-RW with data backups (2 copies)

- Tiny flashlight (sometimes you have to work on a telephone connection in a dark corner of a hotel room)

Essential Additions for Lan Connectivity

- Built-in, PC card, or other external network adapter and any needed cables, connectors, and/or "dongles"
- Printout of your network settings (so you can reset them if they are changed to connect through a LAN)

Essential Additions For International Travel

- Modem plug adapter(s)
- Power plug adapter(s)
- "Universal" or auto-switching power supply (check with the manufacturer if you aren't sure if the power supply works with multiple frequencies and voltages without a converter)
- Line tester or filter for detecting or blocking high-voltage pulses used for billing in some countries
- Screwdrivers for connecting to hard-wired phones
- Alligator-clip and spade-lug to RJ11 adapters
- Non-toll free (not 800, 888, or 877) U.S. telephone support numbers, or local numbers in the countries where you will be
- Before departing, learn how to get from the Windows and Mac desktop to MSIE and Netcape, and navigate in either major browser, without reading anything. If you are going someplace where the predominant language is not English, you'll find this trick invaluable if all the on-screen menus, prompts, and labels are in another language. Turning off the labels on the toolbars will help you practice

Not Recommended Except In Rare Cases

- Acoustic coupler (in places where you would need an acoustic coupler, connection problems are often so severe that you're better off using a public connection in a business center or cybercafe)
- Satellite phone (unless you use it all the time, it's cheaper to pay a hotel for satellite phone time when you need it)

If this list seems daunting, you may want to reconsider your assumption that it would be easier to bring your own computer than to rely on cybercafes or other public terminals. And if you think it seems excessive, think again. There's been a time when each of the items listed as "essential" has been just that for me.

Warning: despite its advantages, this is about the most technically difficult thing I will discuss in this book. I think it's worthwhile to learn how to do this, but if you're afraid to tinker with your computer and don't have a more knowledgeable friend around to hold your hand or bail you out if you screw up, please skip the rest of this section. Don't try this at home unless you're sure you know what you're doing.

The point of this section is not to provide a technical lesson or comprehensive manual, but to point out some of the problems you are likely to encounter, and to give you a checklist of the hardware and software you'll need. If your eyes glaze over as you read this section, you probably don't want to try this.

When people talk about a LAN, they usually mean an Ethernet LAN. Connecting your laptop to the Internet through an Ethernet LAN in someone's office or home, or in a cybercafe, requires either built-in Ethernet capability or an Ethernet PC card for your laptop's PCMCIA slot.

Most new laptops have built-in Ethernet interfaces. Most older Windows laptops need an Ethernet PC card. Apple Powerbooks, like all Apple computers, have built-in Ethernet and AppleTalk network interfaces, although some older Powerbooks require a special cable adapter to connect their AppleTalk port to an Ethernet. Windows 98 or later Windows computers with USB ports can be connected to an Ethernet LAN through a special USB-to-Ethernet cable adapter.

Most Ethernet LANs use six-wire cable that looks like slightly oversized telephone extension cable and connects through an RJ45 modular connector very similar to, but slightly larger than, the standard four-wire RJ11 modular telephone connector. If there's a connector on your laptop slightly too large for a telephone plug, it's probably for a built-in Ethernet interface. A few older Ethernet LANs use thicker coaxial cable with threaded BNC connectors. This is less and less common, but for maximum compatibility, all else being equal, get a PC card with both types of connectors. Most people who have a LAN will have a spare network cable, although it doesn't hurt to carry your own just in case.

Unfortunately, computer and operating system manufacturers are behind the times when it comes to supporting mobile Ethernet connectivity. You'll probably have to do some manual reconfiguration of your computer each time you switch between connecting to the Internet over a phone line and over a LAN.

If you travel often, though, it's well worth the effort to learn how to put your laptop on a LAN, and switch back and forth

What Happens if Your Laptop is Stolen?

If the thief is stupid, your computer will be fenced to someone who wants a cheap computer. If the thief is more knowledge-able, your computer will be fenced to someone who will try to use the data on it for "identity theft".

Imagine everything that's stored on your laptop computer or in your electronic organizer—in the hands of someone smart, greedy, and unscrupulous. Even if it doesn't include any passwords or PIN numbers, it's probably enough to enable them to impersonate you and get credit cards in your name sent to their address. Even if the banks absorb the thief's charges, it could destroy your credit rating for years.

A password-protected screen saver will barely slow them down in getting the data from your laptop. You need stronger measures if you want to protect the data on your laptop, such as software that encrypts the files on your laptop. It slows down access to those files, and you may not feel it's worth it on a computer that never leaves your home. But on a computer as vulnerable to theft or snooping (if you leave your laptop in your hotel room, do you want the cleaners to be able to browse through your electronic briefcase?) as a laptop, it's worth considering.

between modem and LAN network settings. Just don't try it for the first time on the road, or on your own if you're not sure of yourself. Practice first at home, with your most network-savvy friend available to help you.

LAPTOP THEFT, BREAKAGE, AND INSURANCE

Laptop computers are extremely vulnerable to both theft and breakage. Insure your laptop. Safeware, Inc. (**www.safeware.com**), the leading personal computer insurance company, estimates from its claims and other data that over 300,000 laptop computers, worth over $800 million, were stolen in the United States in 1999. Another 770,000 laptop computers suffered $950 million in accidental damage. That means the average accident (most often simply dropping the laptop) did $1,200 in damage, typically by crashing the hard disk, breaking the screen, or both. And that doesn't count the cost—usually much greater—of lost data or the time it takes to recreate it. At $50–100 a year for a typical laptop, insurance is a bargain.

Safeware has been in the computer insurance business since 1982, and dominates the category. I've insured some of my computers with them, but luckily haven't yet had a claim to file. Homeowners' or renters' insurance doesn't always cover laptop computers when they aren't in your home or apartment, and usually has significantly more exclusions than separate policies designed specifically for laptop computers. As with all insurance, read the fine print carefully before you buy.

Some of the most common ways laptops are stolen or damaged:

- Theft from unattended vehicles. This is so common that it's the one major cause of loss that Safeware won't cover.
- Power surges and lightning. Carry surge suppressors for both your laptop's power supply and its modem connection, and always use them. A top-quality portable combined power and modem surge suppressor costs only $30 and adds only a few ounces to your luggage.
- Loss or theft in transit. One common scheme is for someone to cut in front of you at a security checkpoint, after you've put your laptop on the x-ray conveyor belt but before you've gone through the metal detector. While they delay you, usually by deliberately setting off the metal detector, a confederate who's already gone through the security checkpoint picks your laptop up off the other end of the conveyor and walks away with it. To prevent this, and if you're traveling with another person, have one of you go through the metal detector and station themselves by the far end before you put any your luggage on the x-ray conveyor. If you're traveling alone, don't let anyone get between you and the metal detector after you've put your laptop and any other carry-on baggage on the belt.
- Water damage. No matter how careful you are, drinks can still get spilled on your laptop. It might survive a spill, but it might not. Insurance and regular backups are your only protection.

Ultimately, most other laptop computer thefts are due to carelessness. Never forget that your laptop computer is expensive, conspicuous, portable, and easy to fence.

Accessing, Exchanging, and Backing Up Your Data

The hard drive of a typical laptop computer holds as much as thousands of floppy disks or tens of Zip disks. That makes it tempting to use a laptop as a way to carry around a lot of data.

Don't do it. There are reasons to bring a laptop with you, but carrying a lot of data is generally not one of them. A laptop hard drive is about the least reliable means available for transferring or transporting large databases or other files. Hard drives on laptops crash far, far, more frequently than those on desktop computers. They are smaller and more fragile, and laptop computers simply aren't designed to withstand many of the bumps and shocks they get in routine use. A fall of six inches or a foot will often crash a laptop's hard drive or break the screen. A laptop dropped from waist height is likely to be a total loss. And then there's the possibility that your entire laptop could be stolen, as several hundred thousand are each year.

It's axiomatic that no matter how tedious backups are, they take less time and effort than re-creating all your data from scratch. When your hard drive crashes, you won't regret the time you spent making backup copies of all your data—unless you find that you can't use your backups! This is surprisingly common. The only way to be sure your backup procedure works is to test your ability to restore the data from a trial backup set.

> ## BACK UP THOSE FILES
>
> Someday, your hard drive *will* crash. The only question is when. Murphy's law says it will crash just before a crucial presentation, just after you have done a lot of work on the computer, and just before you get around to the backup that you've been putting off because it would take too long.

If you don't have a laptop with you, or can't rely on it, how can you carry your files, data, electronic documents, bookmarks or favorites, and get access to them on the road, or back them up so they won't get lost? Use the Internet, of course. Let me count the ways:

PERSONAL WEB PAGES

Obviously, one way to avoid carrying your data around with you is to store it in a way that's accessible over the Internet. One of the simplest ways, for information you don't need to keep private, is simply to post it on your personal home page. When you get where you're going, open any Web browser anywhere, go to your URL, and you are at your personal start page. Some browsers, including Netscape, store their bookmark files in HTML format. If you know anything about HTML editing, this makes it easy to copy your bookmarks into the HTML code of your home page.

If you don't already have a personal home page or Web site, don't let that deter you. Most ISPs include a certain amount of space for your own Web pages in the price of their standard dial-up access account. Some ISPs also provide tools or "wizards" to help you create a basic page if you don't know how.

If your ISP doesn't give you any Web space, many sites on the Web will be happy to give you space for your Web pages as long as you let them include ads on your pages. Some of the most widely-used of these sites are also among the most annoying. When someone goes to your page on one of these sites, they not only get ads but also pop-up advertising windows. Yuck. Most people only use these sites because they don't know that there are advertising-free alternatives. It's worth the effort to find a truly free Web space provider that doesn't inflict ads (much less pop-ups or multi-media ads) on you or your visitors.

E-MAIL

What about any personal or private information that you don't want to post on your Web page for everyone in the world to read? How about e-mail? E-mail isn't usually thought of as a way of storing data, but it's often used that way.

Just e-mail whatever file(s) you'll need to yourself, at an e-mail address that you'll be able to access from where you're going. Most often that means sending a small key file, such as a copy of your address book, to a Web-accessible e-mail address.

— A MESSAGE TO YOURSELF

E-mail any small text files you'll need on the road to an address accessible from where you're going. Or you can create a file while traveling, and e-mail it to yourself at home.

Similarly, if you create a file while traveling, and want to make sure it gets back safely to your home or office computer, just e-mail yourself a copy. Better still, since any given e-mail message might not be received, e-mail two different copies to yourself at two different addresses. It's cheap and easy insurance, although time-consuming if the file(s) are large. Do be careful. If you are unfamiliar with the e-mail software you are using, it's more likely you'll do something wrong. You may think you've sent a message, or many messages, when they really haven't gone anywhere.

E-mail isn't the most sophisticated technique for remote access or backup, and it's not good for anything large. Be especially careful not to send anything so large that it will exceed your e-mail storage quota. If you do, it will be lost. But it's simple, it works, and it makes whatever you sent accessible to you from wherever and however you can reach your e-mail and with the same level of security and privacy as your e-mail.

FTP SITES

For larger private files you might need while traveling, especially binary (non-text) data, consider putting them on an FTP ("File Transfer Protocol") server.

If you've never used it before, FTP can sound intimidating. Relax. If you've ever downloaded a file from the Internet, you've probably used FTP—your browser used it behind the scenes. Learning to use an FTP program to transfer files across the Internet (to and from an FTP server) isn't much more difficult than learning to use the Windows Explorer to move or copy files between directories on your own computer. Many FTP programs for Windows have drag-and-drop interfaces that look and work very much like the Windows Explorer. If you don't have an FTP program, you can download your choice of free ones.

Why bother with FTP? Because if you try to e-mail yourself very large files, you may accidentally fill up your mailbox. If this happens, you won't be able to receive any other e-mail, not even short messages. FTP is much more powerful and efficient than sending files by e-mail, especially if you need to transfer or synchronize many files. For files in any format other than plain text, FTP is faster. Unlike FTP transfers, e-mail is really only text. All binary files or attachments, including word processor document files, have to be encoded as ASCII text before they can be sent by Internet e-mail. That's why HTML-mail or word processor documents always take so much longer to download to your e-mail box than plain text e-mail, and why you should never send HTML-mail or attach word processor documents to your e-mail messages unless it's necessary.

As with Web space, FTP space is provided by many ISPs as part of their standard accounts, as well as from many other providers, some of them free.

INTERNET FILE STORAGE SERVICES

Several companies offer space on their servers, accessible over the Internet, for you to store backups or other files. Some of these services allow you to upload and download files through a Web browser and/or FTP client from any Internet-connected computer. Others require you to install special software on your computer to use their service. In several cases, their software makes your space on their Internet service look like an extra drive on your computer. Once it's installed—but only from the machine on which it is installed—you can save or copy files back and forth the same way you do between local drives.

Most of these services offer a limited amount of space "for free," i.e. in exchange for viewing ads on their Web site, and then charge by the megabyte for additional space. Some also require you to agree to receive promotional e-mail—spam—in exchange for using their services. Find one that doesn't. At the moment, I'm using **www .driveway.com**, but there are many others.

These services can be a useful secondary supplement to local backups on disks, tape, or writable CDs. But I wouldn't rely on them as a primary or exclusive backup method. Too many of my friends have lost vital data stored with ISPs and other Internet companies that failed. All of the current Web storage companies are startups, that can and do go out of business often and without warning. Analysts expect that only a few of the companies offering any given service like this will survive. If you guess wrong, and store your only copy of a file with a service that goes out of business, you'll be out of luck.

With the caveat that you shouldn't rely primarily on any such service, here are some things to keep on such a service, as a secondary emergency backup in case all else fails:

- Address book
- Scanned images of tickets and other vital documents to facilitate replacement if they are lost or stolen; note that you'll need copies of tickets, not just ticket numbers, to get them replaced
- Telephone numbers and addresses for follow-up letters for reporting loss or theft of each of your credit cards, telephone calling cards, and the like
- Scanned images of insurance policies and other documents from your safe deposit box in case of fire, flood, earthquake, or other disaster at your home while you are away
- Web browser bookmarks, favorites, or hot list

Virtual Address Book

A variety of companies offer services to allow you to keep your calendar, address book, or other data directly on their servers and access them over the Web. These service providers include many of the same ones that offer Internet-accessible file storage space. Internet address book and calendar services have all the same problems as Internet backup services—and then some.

Most people's address books are some of their most critical data. Backing up your address book, including making off-site backups over the Internet, is a good idea. Entrusting the primary copy of your address book to someone else who might disappear with it at any time is a dreadful idea. I've had at least two friends who kept their address books on their Internet service providers' servers, and had their ISP go out of business or shut them off unexpectedly without giving them a chance to copy their data. For each of them, it was a disaster.

You may say that you wouldn't do that. "I'll back up my address book often," you say. I don't believe you. Unless it's a completely automated process, almost no one (and I certainly include myself) backs up their data as often as they should. If you keep your primary address book or calendar on someone else's computer, elsewhere on the Internet, you'll probably let it go months between backups. If the service fails, changes its policies, or decides to drastically raise its prices, you'll lose recent updates that may be among those you most need.

As with any other mode of backup, Web-based storage is only as useful and reliable as your own discipline in remembering to back things up. If you have to restore from a backup, you lose everything you've created or changed since the last one. One of my grandmother's sayings was, "Turn your bacon often while it's cooking. You may get tired, but it won't." The same might be said for backups. When you need them, you won't regret the time it took to create them and to update them often.

REMOTE ACCESS AND REMOTE CONTROL SOFTWARE

Most remote access and remote control software works only if you have the same program installed on the computers at both ends.

Since you can't usually install programs on other people's computers, that usually precludes their use unless you have your own laptop with you. But as more and more computers have always-on connections, and the Web browser becomes the de facto standard for access to any Internet application, makers of remote control software are beginning to add browser-based remote control to their features. As of this writing, the bugs are still being worked out of these products, but they could be ready for prime time before you read this.

The leading contender at the moment for Windows is Desktop On-Call from IBM, **www.direct.ibm.com**. Desktop On-Call was developed by IBM's subsidiary in Japan, and new versions have been released in Japan much sooner than in the United States. If you can't find the U.S. version, consider getting a copy of the Japanese version. The current Japanese distribution CD includes an English-language version of the program (version 3) more recent than the ones currently packaged by IBM for the U.S. market. VNL, a similar but less user-friendly program from ATT is available free for a wide variety of operating systems at **www.uk.research.att.com.VNL**

Web-based remote control works like this: Install the program on your home or office computer, choose your user name and password, and leave the program running, with your computer on and connected to the Internet. More and more computers are connected all the time through office networks, DSL, or cable modems. You can leave your computer on the Internet using any of those connections, without having to tie up your phone line—although at the price of putting it at risk to hacking 24/7.

Then, from anywhere on the Internet, open a Web browser and enter your computer's address or that of the service that keeps track of your computer's dynamic IP address. Sign in with your user name and password, and an image of your home or office computer's screen will appear in the browser window. Then, as you type or click or move the mouse, your keystrokes and clicks and movements will be sent to the computer you are controlling, and the on-screen results will be sent back to your browser window. All this will be familiar to users of existing remote-control products, except for seeing them in a browser window.

Remote control lets you do anything you could do if you were sitting at the remote computer—but slowly. The key limitations to Web-based remote control are that:

■ Remote control over a dial-up connection to the Internet is slow; some tasks will prove too slow to be workable. Try it out before you hit the road. Set up remote control on the computer you want to use; go to a friend's house, a cybercafe, the library, or some other computer and try some sample tasks by remote control.

- Some Web-based remote control programs require specific Web browsers and downloadable ActiveX controls or plug-ins. If the computer you find at your destination doesn't have the right browser, or has ActiveX or plug-in downloading and installation disabled, you're out of luck. Desktop On-Call and VNC use a downloadable Java clients that will run in any Java-enabled browser on any operating system, which is a much more promising and universal approach. It takes about a minute to download and launch the Java client over a 28K baud dial-up connection. Any slower of a connection wouldn't be suitable for remote control.

- If the power fails, or you manage to crash your computer by remote control, or the remote control software itself hangs, you lose your access to the remotely controlled computer. You can try to set up your computer to automatically restart and reboot, but that's not totally reliable either. So you can't count on remote control for essential data or critical tasks. I use remote control regularly, but occasionally the computer I'm controlling freezes or crashes, and I can't use it until I get home and can reboot it.

- Any remote control program provides a way for unauthorized or hostile hackers to get into your computer and any others to which it is connected. Don't enable remote control of your computer unless you're sure you understand how to do so securely. Don't rely on remote control software vendors' security claims. Of course they all claim their products are secure. Your remote control password is the key to everything on your computer. Use a password that isn't a word in any dictionary and contains a mix of letters and numbers.

- Because of the risks it poses, installing a remote control program violates almost any company's computer security rules. Don't install such a program without asking first for permission from the person in charge of computers in your office. The problem isn't so much that such programs are inherently insecure as that most people don't set them up securely. So you might get permission if you ask first, and allow the network administrator to supervise the installation. If you don't ask, and get caught later, you could be fired. For now, and the foreseeable future, remote control through a

Web browser is a fairly limited option. But keep an eye on the current state of software development, as in the future this could become a much more useful tool for travelers. If it works well, especially as high-speed and always-on connections become routine at both ends of remote control sessions, it could largely eliminate the need for anyone to carry a computer with them to stay connected to their home and office data.

FLOPPY DISKS

If all you need are your bookmarks or favorites and a copy of your address book, they will probably fit on a single floppy disk. Some address book programs bloat their files too big to fit on a floppy, but most address books will fit just fine if you export them to, or save them as, a text file.

The best thing about floppies is that, except for iMacs and some public Internet terminals sealed in kiosks (especially at airports), any computer you use to access the Internet will have a floppy drive. Stick in your floppy disk, open your bookmark file (either from the browser menu or by entering a "file://" URL), and you can go directly to any of your bookmarks.

If you need to save or print a downloaded document, or transfer data from or to a computer not on the Internet, an IBM-compatible DOS or Windows-formatted 1.44MB 3 inch floppy disk is currently, and for the foreseeable future, the most universally compatible medium of data exchange. A good indication of the degree of de facto standardization on the floppy disk is the extent to which criticism of the iMac and iBook has focused on their lack of a floppy disk drive. I always carry two copies of my most essential data on floppy disks, as well as a few spare blank floppy disks.

— LOSING CONTACTS

As a travel agent, I hear regularly from travelers whose belongings have been lost, stolen, or broken. The worst thing of all to lose while traveling, because it's usually the most difficult—often impossible—to replace or to reconstruct at any price, is your contact list. That's equally true whether your address book is hand written (and subject to getting ruined if it gets wet), or stored on a computer (that can crash), a Palm Pilot or other electronic organizer (which you can lose), or the server of a Web-based service (which could shut done without warning). I've had clients lose their contact lists in all of these ways. However you maintain it, back it up often and in several copies.

ZIP DISKS

Modern commercial "bloatware" stores data in ever larger files. Even the shortest document in Microsoft Office format can be too large to fit on a floppy disk. The most standard portable storage medium for files too big to fit on floppies is the 100 MB Zip disk. There are other high-capacity disks and removable storage media, but none you can count on finding on the road.

Only the largest digital audio, video, or multimedia files are too large to fit on a Zip disk. Zip disks can go bad unexpectedly, but it's easy enough to carry two copies.

As with floppy disks, DOS/Windows PCs can read only DOS/Windows formatted Zip disks, while Macs can read either DOS/Windows or Mac formated disks. So for maximum compatibility, use DOS/Windows formatted Zip disks even if you create your files and do most of your work on a Mac.

PORTABLE ZIP DRIVES

If you need access to a large volume of data, don't necessarily need a laptop computer with you, and aren't sure that a Zip drive will be available where you are going, consider carrying a portable Zip drive instead of a whole computer.

Depending on your system, you can get a USB Zip drive for newer Windows and Mac computers, or a Zip Plus drive that can connect to DOS/Windows PCs (parallel port) or older Macs (SCSI). At less than $200, either costs less than a tenth of what a laptop computer costs. They weigh less than half as much as even the lightest full-size laptop, and they're much less fragile. Even if a drive breaks, you don't lose your data (as you do if you drop a laptop and crash the hard drive), and it's easy, quick, and relatively cheap to replace the drive. And it makes it easy to keep backups of that vital data you're carrying around, and any changes you make to it.

CDS (CD-R OR CD-RW)

If you have a CD writer, you can burn up to 650 MB of data onto your own CD to bring with you while traveling. This is by far the easiest, fastest, and most compact way to carry really large volumes of data. If you need to, you can even copy the program(s) needed to read the data onto the CD as well. The drawbacks are that you can't change or add to this data on the road (unless, of course, you get lucky and find another CD writer at your destination) and that some CDs will only work in the same drive on which they were recorded. This is basically a quality-control and alignment problem, and happens sometimes with floppy disks as well. After you've burned a disk, test that you can read it in a different drive.

In addition to their speed, CDs have a substantial advantage in being less fragile than magnetic tapes or disks. Unlike hard drives—their only rivals for capacity—they have no moving parts. And as optical media they are immune to damage from metal detectors or x-ray inspection.

While you can't count on finding a Zip drive in every home or office, you can count on finding a CD-ROM drive on every new computer. A CD writer (CD-R or CD-RW drive) is currently priced from about $150 as an add-on, less if purchased as part of a new system. It's well worth it if you need to carry extensive multimedia business presentations, collections of digital photographs to show your relatives, large databases, complex spreadsheets, or any other files too large to send over the Internet. Adding a CD writer to your home or office computer might enable you to swap your laptop computer and accessories for a pair of CDs in jewel cases on your next trip. Why two CDs? Always have two copies of any data in case one gets lost, broken, or scratched. For an extended trip, if you don't have a CD writer, you could ask a friend to burn a couple of copies of a CD with your travel data.

E-mail on the Road

E-mail is *the* critical Internet application while traveling. Research on the Web is generally done before you leave, and you can ask someone else to look something up for you on the Web in a pinch. Asking someone else to retrieve your e-mail for you can be more problematic—especially if it's a personal message when you're at someone's office, or a message from your office about confidential information or negotiations you're having with a company or client whom you are visiting. Receiving e-mail is usually the primary reason for wanting to get on the e-mail while traveling. When you need to get an e-mail message, you sometimes need it *now*.

As a travel agent specializing in trips around the world and other long-term, multi-continent journeys, I deal daily with the problems and pitfalls of e-mail communication with customers traveling in every part of the world. I've become, of necessity, an expert on how to make Internet work and on everything that can go wrong in trying to stay in touch by e-mail.

There are lots of different ways to get your e-mail while traveling. Each of them requires different sorts of advance preparations. Here are some of the alternatives for dealing with your e-mail while you're traveling.

LEAVE YOUR E-MAIL UNTIL YOU GET HOME

Even if you plan to ignore your e-mail while you're away, you need to think about a couple of things:

First, you need to make sure that people know that you aren't reading your e-mail. Otherwise they may think you haven't gotten a message, and keep sending it repeatedly. Or they may think you have gotten a message, when you haven't. Of course, in any business, it's essential to make sure that people who do business with you by e-mail aren't left in the lurch while you are gone. Just as you need to put a message on your voice-mail to say that you're gone, whether or not you will be checking messages, and who can be contacted in your absence, you need to do something with your e-mail. Either set up a vacation reply, or have your e-mail forwarded to yourself on the road, or to someone else who can handle it while you're gone.

Second, if you don't check your e-mail it can easily fill up your virtual mailbox. Most e-mail accounts have a limited storage capacity. You may never notice it when you're home and checking your e-mail every day. But once your limit is reached, new messages will either be rejected and returned to sender, confusing the sender, or worse, thrown away unread. Now the sender doesn't know that their message wasn't

THE JOY OF BEING ———
OUT OF TOUCH

If you're traveling for pleasure, and don't want or need to stay in touch with people at home, you might want to consider just saying no to e-mail on the road. Part of the joy of taking a vacation is escaping from constant e-mail and voice-mail messages, pages, faxes, and cell phone calls. To some people, having to check their e-mail every day is like being on an electronic leash. When I go on vacation, I don't check business e-mail (or voice-mail, or anything else). Otherwise it's not a vacation. If your employer is so dependent on you that you can't go away for two weeks without checking in, they've got a problem. (And you deserve both a raise and a real vacation!)

received, and you don't know that anybody tried to send you messages after your mailbox was full. I've had people send me e-mail messages every week, not realizing that their incoming mailbox was full. Each time I would try to send a reply, but only got a "mailbox full" rejection message.

E-mail tends to accumulate faster than people realize. Perhaps we don't want to think about how much spam we delete each day! And you may not be certain how many megabytes of e-mail storage space you have. If you aren't sure, try changing your settings to leave all the e-mail you've read on the server for a week or two, instead of deleting it. Note that this is not the same as leaving the e-mail in Outlook or Eudora after you've read it. I'm talking about the server it's on *before* you download it to your computer. Send yourself a test message every day. See how long it takes before your mailbox fills up, and if you get a warning message when it does.

It's always possible to get a burst of spam, or a single message with an oversized attachment, that fills up your e-mail box all at once. I recommend against ever ignoring your e-mail for more than a few days without setting up mail forwarding or a vacation message, or both.

VACATION MESSAGES

If you're not going to be reading your e-mail for while, it's customary and useful to set up a "vacation message" to be sent in reply to each e-mail message received. You may be able to set this up in the e-mail program on your own computer (on Windows, this is easiest in Pegasus Mail), but it's better to set it up with your ISP so that the vacation message is sent automatically, even if you never download the e-mail to your own computer. Different ISPs have different systems, but most allow you to set and change vacation settings through a page on their Web site. Don't forget to turn the vacation message off when you get home!

— THE DREAD MAIL LOOP —

Warning: an automatic vacation message can interact with an automated mailing list to create a "mail loop". It happens this way: You get a message from the list. The vacation program sends its "I'm on vacation" message in reply. The reply is to the list, so it is broadcast to everyone on the list—including you. So the vacation program sends its message again, and so on *ad infinitum*.

Vacation and list programs are set up to try to prevent this accumulation, but don't always succeed. And there's no need to tell everyone on a mailing list that you're on vacation. It's better to have

Things to Include in Your Vacation Message:

- When you expect to be reading and responding to e-mail to this address again.

- Whether your e-mail is being saved for your return, or whether it is being (or might be) deleted. This tells people wether they should just wait for a reply, or whether they should send their message again after you are back offline.

- If you can be contacted (and want to tell people so) at some other e-mail address or by some other means. Include the circumstances in which it is appropriate for people to use this alternate contact, whether it is yours or someone else's, and whether it's a home or an office. For example, "In case of emergency only, you can reach me by phone at the home of Jane Doe in Hilo at +1-808-555-1212 between 9 a.m. and 10 p.m. Hawaiian Time (09:00-22:00, GMT -10)".

- If there is some other person to whom questions should be directed while you are unavailable. For example, "If you need to speak with someone by phone about the Foobar Project in my absence, please call Richard Roe in our office in Malaysia at +60 3 123-4567 (08:00-17:00, GMT +8)."

- If you are referring people to a phone number, include at least the area code, time zone, and acceptable hours to call. It's best to include the country code (1 for the United States and Canada), in the "plus" format as in the examples above. An email address does not indicate your geographic location. The United States has six time zones and Canada has seven. I often get calls at odd hours, generally from people who should know better but who forget that people on the Internet might be in a different time zone.

- A URL or other source of information, if appropriate. For example, "If you want more information about me while I'm offline, see my home page at hasbrouck.org."

all your mailing list subscriptions go to a different e-mail address on which you don't use a vacation message.

A burst of activity on a mailing list can fill up your e-mail box suddenly and unexpectedly. If you don't need to read list postings while you are traveling, unsubscribe or temporarily suspend receiving messages from the list.

If you subscribe to several lists, it's easy to forget to unsubscribe from them all. Many Web site and product registrations automatically put you on mailing lists you didn't know about. And spammers have ways of getting lists of subscribers to mailing lists.

To reduce the amount of nonessential e-mail you have to deal with while traveling, I recommend using a different e-mail address for all mailing list subscriptions and registration forms. Don't forward mail from your list address to your travel address unless you really must. That way a "mail loop" on one of your lists, a flurry of postings to a list, a list message with a humongous attachment (very bad netiquette, but it happens), or a burst of spam to list members won't exceed your e-mail storage quota and block you from receiving more important e-mail messages.

WEB-BASED E-MAIL SERVICES

As you probably know, you can send and receive e-mail from a Web browser by getting a "free" account with Microsoft Hotmail or any of hundreds of similar services. Most people equate all Web browser access to e-mail with these services. That's a mistake, and a potentially costly one.

As I'll discuss below, you can easily access most standard e-mail accounts from the Web—as well as by POP (when you're on your own computer), Telnet, and often IMAP. A multi-protocol account gives you the flexibility to use whichever access method works best for you wherever you are.

— CHECK YOUR E-MAIL ON THE WEB

You don't have to get a Web-based account to get e-mail over the Web. You probably have Web access to your existing e-mail account without even realizing it.

Web-mail accounts are typically accessible *only* from the Web. As the price of being "free," they put ads in all your messages. In order to make sure that you can't get your e-mail without seeing the ads on their Web page, most of them won't forward your e-mail. You can forward e-mail from other addresses to Hotmail, but not from Hotmail to another address. There's no reason to accept those limitations or pay that price when advertising-free Web/POP/IMAP e-mail accounts are available as part of standard-rate e-mail access packages, or for free from other providers such as Altern.org (altern.org).

The major claimed advantage to purely Web-based e-mail systems is that they are set up to allow you to store your address books and message archives on their server. That also means that you are dependent on them for your e-mail archives and address book. If they decide to discontinue their "free" service, or start charging for it, you're stuck. I know of too many people who lost their e-mail archives and address books when e-mail providers went out of business or changed their services to entrust such important data to someone else's Web server.

E-MAIL SERIVICES ESPECIALLY FOR TRAVELERS

Some travel agencies provide travelers with e-mail accounts as an added-value service. Since they aren't trying to provide e-mail for everyone in the world, just for their customers, they can offer more and better services than typical Web-only e-mail accounts, without the "free" advertising.

Frank disclaimer: I work for, and have an interest in, one such company, AirTreks.com (**www.airtreks.com**). Each AirTreks.com customer gets a "TripMail" account accessible by POP, IMAP, Telnet, or from the AirTreks.com Web site. The AirTreks.com Web interface for clients' TripMail is accessible with text-only browsers and doesn't require cookies, Java, or ActiveX. Any or all of these are disabled on some terminals, which precludes access to Web-mail sites that require them. No advertising is added to TripMail messages sent or received. Whether or not you get your tickets from AirTreks.com, that's the sort of e-mail service you should expect from a travel agency committed to serving wired travelers.

ACCESSING YOUR HOME MAILBOX

E-mail Forwarding

If you can't access your primary mailbox directly while you are traveling, you can arrange to have all your messages forwarded to another address. Typically, people forward their e-mail to a Microsoft Hotmail or Web-based e-mail account, although it's better to forward your e-mail to an address accessible by other means than just the Web.

Configuring an e-mail program on your PC to forward your e-mail (on Windows, this is another e-mail task that's easiest in Pegasus

A Few Words About AOL

AOL is the world's largest ISP (some people say it's technically not an ISP, but I'm not going to get into that debate here). But AOL may be a poor ISP of choice for travelers.

AOL only lets you read your e-mail from a computer with an AOL account and AOL software installed, or from the AOL Web page **www.aol.com**. You can't use any e-mail program to read e-mail addressed to you at AOL except AOL's customized version of Microsoft Outlook. You can't have your e-mail forwarded to any address outside AOL. You can't connect to your AOL e-mailbox by any of the industry-standard POP, IMAP, or Telnet protocols described in the following sections. You can't use any new software or services that are developed for these standard protocols.

If you go to a public Internet terminal that doesn't have AOL software installed (a few cybercafes do, but not many), or you're at a friend's home or an office where they don't have AOL, your only option is to read your AOL e-mail in AOL's Web interface. If you've got AOL-mail, it's AOL or nothing else. If you want maximum access to your email while traveling, get a different ISP.

Mail) will have no effect unless your PC is set up automatically to connect to your e-mail server and retrieve your e-mail for forwarding. That may sound obvious, but it's a common mistake. If you have a typical dial-up POP e-mail account, your e-mail will only be forwarded if you set up your PC to autodial and run your e-mail program at regular intervals. Even then, PCs just aren't reliable. Too many things can go wrong, a power failure, for example, that will cause your PC to go down and your e-mail can't be retrieved or forwarded.

Much better to have your e-mail forwarded by your ISP, whose servers are much less likely to go down. Most ISP's allow you to have all your e-mail messages forwarded to any other address of your choice at no additional charge. The exceptions are "proprietary" systems like AOL, Compuserve, Prodigy Classic, and Web TV, as discussed in the sidebar above. Most ISPs have a section of their Web site to specify a forwarding address for your e-mail and to start and stop the forwarding service.

If you use an e-mail program that runs on your ISP's host in a "shell" account, or on an office computer that's always connected to the Internet and kept running even when you're traveling, you may be able to set it up to sort and filter your e-mail before it is forwarded. That way only e-mail from certain people, or that meets certain criteria, will be forwarded.

If you use a typical dial-up account, however, e-mail forwarding by your ISP is an all-or-nothing proposition. Every piece of spam will be forwarded along with the messages you really need right away, the chain letters and jokes sent to lists of acquaintances, and the messages that could wait for you to read them when you get home.

Nobody ever likes spam, of course. But spam is most costly when you're paying for connection time to download it at a cyber-cafe or over a long distance or surcharged hotel phone line.

Never make your travel e-mail address public, never use it in your e-mail signature or return address, never use it for posting to newsgroups or mailing lists, and never allow it to appear on any Web page. Give it out only to a few people who really need to reach you while you're traveling:

Fight Spam

Want to do something about spam? Join and support the Coalition Against Unsolicited Commercial e-mail, CAUCE, **www.cauce.org.** In the meantime, you can limit the amount of spam you have to deal with while traveling by using a separate travel e-mail address.

your family and one key contact at your office, for example.

ISPs typically provide anywhere from 2 to 10 e-mail addresses or "aliases" for the price of a single account. You can get as many advertising-supported e-mail addresses as you want from any of dozens of providers. Some organizations provide genuinely free e-mail without adding advertisements to your messages. They come and go, and are more of a challenge to find, but IMHO ("in my humble opinion"), it's worth the effort not to inflict someone else's advertising on all your correspondents.

At last count, I had 10 e-mail addresses. If you want to reach me, please send your message to edward@hasbrouck.org, or see my Web site at **hasbrouck.org**. The addresses I actually check when I'm traveling don't appear anywhere in this book, in print, on the Internet, or in my outgoing e-mail. None of these travel addresses has ever received a single piece of spam except what made it through the filters and was forwarded from one of my other addresses.

Retrieving POP Mail

Standard e-mail accounts are so-called "POP" (Post Office Protocol)

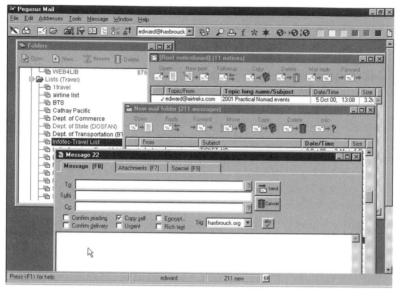

Pegasus Mail is free and more powerful than any other Windows e-mail program. It's especially good at filtering mail, and at dealing with multiple e-mail accounts from the same computer, or the same account from multiple computers—as travelers often must.

accounts. When someone sends you an e-mail message, it's routed across the Internet to your ISP. Your ISP's "mail server" receives it and stores it for you until you log in to retrieve it. When you call in, your e-mail program uses "POP" commands to tell the e-mail server your mailbox name and password and request your e-mail.

Once the server has sent all your messages to your PC, your e-mail program usually tells the server to delete it. It's possible, however—and sometimes desirable when traveling—to leave your e-mail on the server, so you see it again the next time you retrieve your e-mail.

Because the POP protocol is a standard, you can retrieve your e-mail from a POP mailbox with any POP mail program: Microsoft Outlook, Netscape Messenger, Pegasus Mail, Eudora, and many others. There are POP mail programs for Windows, DOS, Macintosh, Unix, Linux, EPOC (the operating system used by Psions and smart mobile phones), Palm OS, and so on.

If you don't already have a preferred e-mail program, or aren't satisfied with the one you are using, I recommend Pegasus Mail (**www.pmail.gen.nz** or **www.pegasus.usa.com**). Pegasus Mail is free

Settings You Need to Know to Get Your E-mail from a POP Mailbox

Before you change any of those settings on someone else's computer, (1) ask permission and (2) write down the original settings so you can change them all back when you are done. If you can, set up a separate "user profile" or "identity" for yourself in the e-mail program, and delete it when you are done.

- What is your POP server? If you have an account with "isp.com", your POP server might be "pop.isp.com", "pop3 .isp.com", "pop2.isp.com", "mail.isp.com", "postoffice .isp.com", or just "isp.com"—or something else entirely. Occasionally, it might be specified as a numeric IP address like "207.82.250.251", rather than as a name.

- What is your POP user name? If your e-mail address is foobar@isp.com, your POP user name is almost always "foobar". Global roaming systems may require you to use a different dial-up login name when you connect through other services. But your POP user name is the same wherever you've connected from.

- What is your POP password? Usually your POP password is the same as the password you use to connect to your ISP's dial-up access number. Like your user name, your dial-up password may change with global roaming, but your POP password won't.

Your computer uses different servers to send and to receive e-mail, even from within the same program. To *send* e-mail, you need the name of an "SMTP" server. "SMTP" stands for Simple Mail Transport Protocol, which is anything but simple. Fortunately, it's unnecessary to reconfigure the SMTP settings on a computer you're using to send e-mail. You can generally use the existing settings to send e-mail. It may appear to come from some different address, but that's OK if you make sure to identify yourself and include a return address in the text of each message.

and more powerful than any of the competing programs, even expensive ones like Eudora Pro. What more could you want? Pegasus Mail is especially good at handling multiple e-mail addresses and accounts, and at automatically sorting and filtering e-mail—features that are key for travelers. Like Linux, Pegasus Mail is supported by a global following of (some would say cult-like) devotees, as well as by its author. It's not the easiest program to configure, but once you get it set up and learn how it works, I don't think you'll want to go back to Eudora, Microsoft Outlook, or Netscape. As of this writing, the latest version of Pegasus Mail is available only for Windows. A Linux version may be available by the time you read this, as may an update of the older Macintosh version.

If you have your own laptop, getting your e-mail is the same on the road as it is at home. Once you're connected to the Internet, you can use the same e-mail program, with the same settings, regardless of where or how you are connected. On other people's computers, it's another story.

If you've never tried to check your e-mail from another computer, you may be surprised to find that you can't just open "Mail" on someone else's computer. Before you can retrieve e-mail from your POP mailbox, you have to configure the e-mail program, as discussed in the sidebar. When you're done, you'll have to change all the settings back *exactly* the way they were before. It's easiest to do this if you create a separate "user profile" or "identity."

Be extremely careful about downloading your e-mail in someone else's copy of an e-mail program. Ask permission before you change the e-mail configuration or download e-mail into someone else's mailbox. Unless you know how to set up a separate e-mail directory, all the e-mail you download will get mixed in with all the e-mail that has previously been downloaded on that computer.

If the person whose computer you are using has set up their e-mail program to sort or filter incoming e-mail, messages newly retrieved from your POP mailbox could be deleted automatically before you see them, forwarded to lists of people you've never heard of, or filed in places you'll never find them.

If the e-mail program permits it (in Windows, this is easiest in Netscape), set up a separate "user profile" or "identity" whenever you use a terminal other than your own to get your POP mail. Delete it when you are done. It only takes a few seconds; it keeps your e-mail folders separate from anyone else's, and it keeps any changes you make to settings from messing things up for anyone else.

Newly-arrived e-mail is stored on your ISP's or e-mail service's server, and can be downloaded from anywhere as long as you have the right configuration. Keep in mind, however, that address books, copies of outgoing messages, and messages you've previously received are generally stored only on the computer on which you created or retrieved them, and will *not* be available when you open the same e-mail program on another computer on the road. Bring copies of your address lists and any e-mail messages that you will need to refer to on floppy disks, or store copies of them somewhere that you can access over the Internet.

Because of the potential problems of different users' e-mail getting mixed together or misfiled, most cybercafes and operators of public Internet-access terminals forbid you to reconfigure their POP e-mail programs. In such places, you have to use IMAP, Telnet or the Web to retrieve your messages, as discussed below.

Web-To-POP Gateways

Many ISPs provide a way to check your e-mail from their Web site. If yours doesn't, there are several sites on the Web that will check any POP account for you. You enter your POP server, user name, and password on a form on their Web page, and they retrieve your e-mail and let you read it, delete it, or answer it. You don't have to reconfigure anything or forward your e-mail. Unless you choose to delete your e-mail, it's still on the server for you to download and save when you get home.

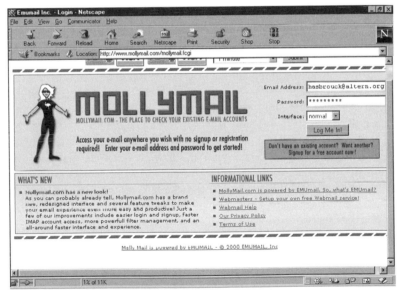

http://www.mollymail.com
Web sites like "Mollymail" let you check your existing e-mail account from any Web browser, without having to get a new e-mail account or transfer your mail to a different system.

Among useful sites of this type are MollyMail (**www.mollymail .com**), ThatWeb (**www.thatWeb.com**), and mail2Web (**www.mail2Web /.com**), and MailStart (**www.mailstart.com**). Before you get a Web-only e-mail account, try out some of these services with your existing POP account. I like MollyMail because it's quick and easy, it doesn't require you to register before you can use it, it's accessible with a text browser, it has only minimal advertising, and it doesn't use Java or ActiveX. My only criticism of MollyMail is that it needlessly requires cookies, which rules out its use in some places. ThatWeb and Mail2Web are more cluttered and heavier with graphics and ads, but neither requires cookies.

IMAP

IMAP (Internet Mail Access Protocol) is a more recent and sophisticated system than POP for accessing a e-mail server from a remote computer. IMAP is designed for roving e-mail users, and offers them many advantages. Universities and larger companies have been the first to switch to IMAP, but more and more ISPs now offer IMAP e-mail access in addition to POP.

The majority of people who still use POP or Web-mail haven't noticed, but all the major e-mail programs (Netscape Messenger, Microsoft Outlook, Eudora, Pegasus Mail, and others) have added support for IMAP as well as POP. If a current version of any of these programs is on the computer you're using, you can access your mailbox by IMAP from anywhere on the Internet. If you're at a computer without an IMAP program, you can access your IMAP mailbox over the Web, from your browser, through MollyMail (**www.mollymail.com**). Choose "Options" to switch to IMAP from the default POP mode.

Configuring IMAP on someone else's computer is much simpler than configuring POP. Every e-mail program I've seen that supports IMAP supports multiple IMAP accounts and mailboxes. You can add a temporary IMAP mailbox without changing any of the existing settings for other users, and you can easily delete it when you're done. There's almost no risk of getting your e-mail mixed up with that of someone else who uses the same computer.

Your mailbox stays on the server, so you can view it without having to download any more than you actually need. If the header says, "Spam," you can delete the message from the server before you waste your time downloading it. You can sort and file your messages either on the server or on your own computer, and you can copy whichever messages or folders you want back and forth. If you want to be able to refer to a file of messages while you are traveling, copy it to the server. If you only need it at home, delete it from the server.

Your address books, as such, stay on the computer on which they are created. But it's easy to copy your address books into an e-mail folder and store them in your mailbox on the server. Then you can access them from anywhere, along with your saved e-mail.

IMAP isn't a replacement for POP. IMAP is more complicated and slightly less reliable. You can't always count on finding an IMAP program on any computer you use. And you can't easily Telnet to an IMAP server. All this means that you should look for an account accessible at any time either by IMAP or POP, not an IMAP-only account. There's no incompatibility between IMAP and POP as I've connected to the same mailbox using both IMAP and POP at the same time.

Free IMAP accounts are relatively hard to find, though some exist. Try to find an ISP that includes IMAP access along with POP in their standard services, or a travel agency that includes them with their services. If your ISP doesn't offer IMAP yet, tell them they're falling behind the times and urge them to upgrade their e-mail server

Remote Control or Remote Access
Some business travelers receive all their e-mail on their office PC, and use a remote control program or remote access service to get their e-mail from wherever they are. I mention this strategy because it can work. But it is dependent on someone making sure that the computer you are accessing is always working, even when you are on the road. If it goes down, you're cut off from your e-mail until someone fixes the problem and starts it up again. You shouldn't try a setup like this unless your company has a professional IT support staff to install and administer it—in which case you shouldn't need my help or advice.

Telnet To a Shell Account
If you have a "shell" account, you can Telnet to your host and read and send e-mail with Pine or whatever other mailer your host provides, although it's probably Pine. You never have to download anything except what you actually read or send, so it's usually the fastest way to check your e-mail.

What's a shell account? Basically, it's an account that let's you run programs (like an e-mail program or text-based Web browser) on your ISP's "host" system, rather than on your local PC. All you need on your local PC is any terminal with a Telnet program, and all that has to be transmitted is the text you type and that appears on the screen. It's limited to text, but it's amazingly fast compared to a graphical interface. One picture can be worth a thousand pages of text download time. The more technically skilled and experienced the traveler, and the more remote the places they travel to, the more likely they are to rely on a Telnet connection to a shell account.

How do you get a shell account? First, ask your ISP. You may have a shell account without knowing it, or be able to get one for the asking. Some ISPs include shell access. Small, local ISPs often throw it in for no extra charge. Many Web-hosting accounts include shell access, since it's sometimes needed to administer a Web site. If your ISP doesn't provide shell access and most of the big national name brands don't, you can get a shell account from another ISP for $5 a month or so.

Free shell access is provided by a mix of small, low-budget "freenets" and other volunteer organizations, and newfangled advertising-supported startups like **www.freeshells.com**. One list of free shell providers is at **members.spree.com/messer/site/geo/shell.html**. Almost all shell accounts include an e-mail address to which you can send or forward e-mail and read it in the shell. I have a shell account with Grex, **www.grex.org**, which is a busy site and you often wait to log on, but provides a way-cool, free, ad-free e-mail address. It's accessible only from their shell at "cyberspace.org". Some systems provide a choice of command-line or menu-based shells. If you have a choice, and don't know Unix, choose a menu-based shell to start with. You can always change it later.

To get to your shell account at, let's say, "isp.com," just type "telnet isp.com" from a DOS, Windows, or Unix command line, or type "telnet://isp.com" into the URL entry field of a Web browser. Once you've logged in, you might get a menu with an obvious choice for "mail". If not, try entering "m," "M," "pine," "mail," or, of course, "help," "h," "H," or "?". In Pine, you can read, send, sort, file, and delete messages; maintain an address book; and so forth. Since all your e-mail, address books, etc. stay on the host (as with Web-based e-mail), you don't have to carry anything with you—but you are vulnerable to losing it all if the host goes out of business.

Further instruction in how to use Unix or a shell account is beyond the scope of this book, but that's all you need to know to read and send e-mail.

Telnet To Your POP Server

Even if you don't have a "shell" account, or are using a computer without a browser or e-mail program, you can use Telnet to connect directly to your POP mail server to read your e-mail from anywhere on the Internet. See **help.mindspring.com/modules/00100/00129.htm** or **help.netscape.com/kb/corporate/19990415-8.html** for instructions and a list of POP commands for dealing with your e-mail. POP is a method of receiving e-mail, not sending it; you'll have to find another way, such as getting someone else to let you send a message from their account, if you need to send e-mail.

For example, if "www.myisp.com" gets you a message that cookies are required, but you're at a library Web terminal where cookies are disabled, you may still be able to get your e-mail by Telnet. Try typing "telnet pop.myisp.com 110" from a DOS, Windows, or Unix shell command line. If you're at a kiosk or dedicated Web terminal where you can't get out of the Web browser, type the telnet command into the browser window in URL format: "telnet://pop .myisp.com:110". (The "110" is the standard port number for POP mail, in case you're curious.) Telnet will get through many firewalls that block cookies, Java, ActiveX, specific free e-mail Web sites, or all Web browsing.

One nice thing about connecting to a POP server by Telnet is that mistakes are unlikely to be disastrous. You can't mess up any one's e-mail program configuration, and it's quite hard to delete messages inadvertently. Messages aren't deleted automatically when you read them; you have to give a specific delete command. If you delete a message by mistake, you can "Undo" the deletion at any time until you log out of the POP server. And if you are disconnected without logging out properly, any deletions are undone and all messages are saved.

Using a Telnet connection to a POP server is a little awkward, but extremely useful in a pinch. Try this from a computer at your home, office, or a library before you go, to get a feel for it.

VOICE ACCESS TO E-MAIL

E-mail by voice? Why not? I'm writing this, as I've written most of this book, by dictating to a speech recognition program. There's nothing natural about a keyboard. Repetitive stress injury from keyboard use is the leading cause of occupational disability in the United States. The next generation of user interfaces and operating systems will have integrated voice recognition and speech synthesis. Mac OS version 9 already does, to a limited degree, but enough to read you your e-mail.

Several services already allow you to access e-mail by voice. Most

— Robot Readers

If you'd like to call from any phone in the world and have a robot read you your messages, then voice access to e-mail is for you.

of them work like this. First, you get an e-mail address and PIN number on their system. If you want to access some other e-mail address, you have to forward it to their address. Then they give you either a toll-free number or a set of local numbers in different cities to call for your e-mail. When you call in, you enter your username and PIN number and a robot reads you your e-mail.

Obviously such a service isn't cheap to provide and one way or another, you have to pay for it. You can subscribe to a so-called "free" advertising-supported service. This means that every time you call, you have to listen to ads before you hear if you have any e-mail, as well as between individual messages. There's also a service that charges by the minute for time you spend listening to your messages.

Some services allow you a limited number of free messages or time each month, as a come-on to get you to pay for more messages or time. Be careful as it would be easy to get a burst of e-mail messages, and end up having to pay a lot to find out whether there was a pearl in the mountain of spam oyster shells.

Getting your e-mail by voice is tedious at best. People often don't get to the point at the start of their message. Sending e-mail in reply by voice with current technology is difficult or impossible. I'd reserve voice access for the rare times and places when I can't get my e-mail by any other means.

Internet References Mentioned in This Book

About This Book and the Practicalnomad.com Website

This book is published in conjunction with the *Practical Nomad* Web site at **www.practicalnomad.com**. Some information is repeated in both places, but not everything in this book is on the Web site, and not everything on the Web site is in this book. I've tried to put each type of information in the place where it will be most useful.

It's easier to read explanations and descriptions in a book. It's easier to use lists of Internet resources on a Web site, where they can be linked directly and updated more often, and you don't have to type in Internet addresses.

This is a short, partial list of key Internet resources for travelers, including those mentioned in this book. But there are many more, as well as more detailed reviews of specific Web sites (and their links) on the *Practical Nomad* Web site. That's also the place to look if something mentioned in the book has moved, or if you want to find out about new Web sites or other changes since this book went to press.

Undoubtedly many things will have changed by the time you are reading this. If you don't find what you are looking for here, check the PracticalNomad.com Web site. If an update or correction isn't on the Web site, please let me know.

Internet Research Tools and Sources

SEARCH ENGINES AND DIRECTORIES
Web Directories
About.com (formerly The Mining Co., miningco.com) •
   www.about.com
Ask Jeeves • **www.ask.com**
GO Network • **www.go.com**
LookSmart • **www.looksmart.com**
Open Directory • **dmoz.org**
Snap • **www.snap.com**
Yahoo! • **www.yahoo.com**
Search Engine Watch • **www.searchenginewatch.com**
Web directory sizes (from Search Engine Watch) •
   www.searchenginewatch.com/reports/directories.html

Keyword Search Engines
AltaVista • **www.altavista.com**
AltaVista (text only) • **www.altavista.com/cgi-bin/query?text**
Excite • **www.excite.com**
FAST Search • **www.alltheweb.com**
GO Network • **www.go.com**
Google • **www.google.com**
Hotbot • **www.hotbot.com**
Inktomi • **www.iwon.com** (and other sites)
Lycos • **www.lycos.com**
NorthernLight • **www.northernlight.com**
Alexa (division of Amazon.com) • **www.alexa.com**
search engine tips and reviews (from Search Engine Watch) •
   www.searchenginewatch.com/facts
Copyright infringement issues with Web archives (National Writers
   Union) • **www.nwu.org** • **www.nwu.org/tvt/tvthome.htm**

USENET NEWSGROUPS
English-language Usenet travel newsgroups
(see also listings of international newsgroups below)
alt.travel
alt.travel.road-trip
alt.travel.rides

alt.travel.marketplace
bit.listserv.travel-l
rec.travel
rec.travel.air_
rec.travel.bed 1 breakfast
rec.travel.budget
rec.travel.budget.backpack
rec.travel.caribbean_
rec.travel.cruises_
rec.travel.marketplace_
rec.travel.misc_
rec.travel.resorts
rec.travel.resorts.all-inclusive
rec.travel.usa-canada
Deja.com author posting history
   www.deja.com/profile.xp?author=president@whitehouse.gov
   (substitute any e-mail address for "president@whitehouse.gov")
Answers to Frequently Asked Questions (FAQs)
   from Usenet newsgroups • **www.faqs.org** • **ftp://rtfm.mit.edu**

MAILING LISTS
Infotec-Travel ("information technology in travel and tourism")
   www.infotec-travel.com
Green-Travel ("sustainable travel and tourism including
   ecotourism and adventure travel") • **www.green-travel.com**
Liszt (searchable directory of mailing lists compiled by Topica.com,
   but not limited to lists hosted by Topica.com) • **www.liszt.com**

E-MAIL NEWSLETTERS
Smarter Living (weekly compilation of airline specials) •
   www.smarterliving.com
(see also the Web sites of most major online travel agencies
   for their weekly e-mail newsletters of airline specials)

AUTO-REPLY ROBOTS
Frequently-Asked Questions about international airfare discounts •
   faq@hasbrouck.org
Web access by e-mail • **mail-server@rtfm.mit.edu** • e-mail message
   text (on one line, without the quotation marks): "send
   usenet/news.answers/internet-services/access-via-e-mail"

GOPHER

All the Gophers in the world • **gopher://gopher.tc.umn.edu**

EVALUATION OF INTERNET INFORMATION AND SOURCES

Online! A Reference Guide to Using Internet Sources •
www.bedfordstmartins.com/online
Evaluation of Information Sources (The WWW Virtual Library) •
www.vuw.ac.nz/~agsmith/evaln/evaln.htm
Evaluating Information Found on the Internet •
miltonsweb.mse.jhu.edu:8001/research/education/net.html

Domain Names

Top-level domains and their registrars (Internet Assigned Numbers
Authority) • **www.iana.org/domain-names.htm**
2-letter country codes used in domain names
ISO (International Standards Organization) 3166-1
www.din.de/gremien/nas/nabd/iso3166ma
Web-based WHOIS queries (.com, .net, .org, and .edu only) •
www.crsnic.net/whois

WHOIS Programs

Sam Spade (Windows) • **www.samspade.org/ssw**
WsFinger (Windows) • **www.tidesys.com/wsfinger.htm**
VisualRoute (Java; for multiple platforms) • **www.visualroute.com**

Internet Travel Planning and Research

TOURIST BOARDS AND TRAVEL INFORMATION CENTERS

Tourism Offices Worldwide Directory • **www.towd.com**

CLIMATE, WEATHER, AND WHEN TO VISIT

World Weather and Climate Guide•
www.onlineweather.com/world.html
World Travel Guide Online • **www.wtgonline.com** (pick a country,
then choose "Climate" from the menu)
The Worldwide Holiday and Festival Site • **www.holidayfestival.com**

SPECIALIZED AND SPECIAL-INTEREST TRAVEL

(see also Usenet newsgroups and specialty Web sites for particular
communities, interests, and activities)
eGulliver.com • **www.egulliver.com**
Specialty Travel Index • **www.specialtytravel.com**

Active, Outdoor, and "Adventure" Travel

Adventureseek (partially owned by REI) • **www.adventureseek.com**
Adventurocity • **www.adventurocity.com**
Away.com (formerly greentravel.com and adventurequest.com) •
away.com
GORP (Great Outdoor Recreation Pages) • **www.gorp.com**
iExplore (partially owned by National Geographic Ventures, the for-
profit division of the National Geographic Society) •
www.iexplore.com

Ecotourism and Responsible Travel

Green-Travel (now Away.com) • **www.green-travel.com**
Tourism Concern • **www.tourismconcern.org.uk**
The International Ecotourism Society (trade association of self-
described ecotourism companies) • **www.ecotourism.org**

Older Travelers

International Travel News • **www.intltravelnews.com**
Marco Polo ("The Magazine for Adventurous Travelers Over 50") •
www.travelroads.com

Women Travelers

Journeywoman • **www.journeywoman.com**
Maiden Voyages ("Travel and Transformation for Women") •
www.maiden-voyages.com
Passionfruit ("A Women's Travel Journal") • **www.passionfruit.com**

Gay and Lesbian Travelers

Our World ("International Gay and Lesbian Travel Magazine") •
www.ourworldmag.com
Out and About • **www.outandabout.com**

Student Travelers

Abroad View • **www.abroadviewmagazine.com**
• **www.abroadview.com**
Student World Traveler • **www.studenttravels.com**

Travelers Of Color
Pathfinders Travel ("The Travel Magazine for People of Color")
- www.pathfinderstravel.com

Travelers With Disabilities or Special Needs
We Magazine • www.wemagazine.com

SPECIALTY MAP, GUIDEBOOK, AND TRAVEL STORES
The Bookwire Index: Travel Booksellers (USA) •
  www.bookwire.com/index/Travel-Booksellers.html
Independent Travel Stores Association (ITSA) •
  www.travelstores.org
International Map Trade Association (directory of specialty
  map and travel book stores) • **www.maptrade.org**
ITMB Publishing (International Travel Maps and Books)
  • **www.itmb.com**
Map Link • www.maplink.com
Recreational Equipment, Inc. (nonprofit membership cooperative)
  • **www.rei.com**
U.S. Geological Survey (includes links to other U.S. government
  mapping agencies) • **mapping.usgs.gov**

GUIDEBOOK PUBLISHERS AND ONLINE GUIDEBOOKS
(all these publishers have at least some of their content,
including updates to guidebooks, on their Web sites)

Avalon Travel Publishing
www.travelmatters.com
Moon Travel Handbooks (United States, North America and
  worldwide) • **www.moon.com**
The Practical Nomad • **www.practicalnomad.com**
Rick Steves' Guides (Europe) • **www.ricksteves.com**
Road Trip USA • **www.roadtripusa.com**

Other Guidebook Publishers
Footprint Handbooks • **www.footprintbooks.com**
Let's Go Publications, Inc. • **www.letsgo.com**
Lonely Planet Publications • **www.lonelyplanet.com**
Rough Guides • **travel.roughguides.com**

PERSONAL CONSULTING WITH GUIDEBOOK WRITERS

Guidebookwriters.com • **www.guidebookwriters.com**
Twelve Degrees Corp./Korobra Corp. • **www.12degrees.com**
  • **www.korobra.com**

SHARING INFORMATION WITH FELLOW TRAVELERS

(searchable archives of travel journals and stories)
BootsnAll.com • **www.bootsnall.com**
Rec.Travel Library • **www.travel-library.com**
Trip Journal (AirTreks.com) • **www.tripjournal.com**

Online International Travel Information

INTERNATIONAL PORTAL SITES AND DIRECTORIES

International Affairs Resources (The WWW Virtual Library) •
  www.vlib.org/InternationalAffairs.html • **www.etown.edu/vl**
Orientation.com • **www.orientation.com**
WorldSkip • **www.worldskip.com**

U.S. GOVERNMENT SURVEYS AND REFERENCES

Background Notes (U.S. Department of State)
  • **www.state.gov/www/background_notes**
CIA World Factbook • **www.odci.gov/cia/publications/factbook**
Country Studies and Area Handbooks (U.S. Library of Congress)
  • **lcweb2.loc.gov/frd/cs**

ONLINE MAGAZINES FOR INTERNATIONAL TRAVELERS

Big World • **www.bigworld.com**
Escape ("The Global Guide for the Adventurous Traveler") •
  www.escapemag.com
Third World Resurgence • www.twnside.org.sg •
  www.southside.org.sg

Transitions Abroad ("The Magazine of Work, Study, and Travel Overseas") • **www.transitionsabroad.com**

World Press Review • **www.worldpress.org**

EXPATRIATE AND INTERNATIONAL COMMUNITY WEB SITES

expatexchange.com • **www.expatexchange.com**

GoAbroad.com • **www.goabroad.com**

iAgora.com ("The Place for People Abroad") • **www.iagora.com**

INTERNATIONAL USENET NEWSGROUPS

alt.travel.eurail.youth-hostels

rec.travel.africa_

rec.travel.asia_

rec.travel.australia + nz_

rec.travel.caribbean_

rec.travel.europe_

rec.travel.latin-america

rec.travel.usa-canada_ _

soc.culture.afghanistan

soc.culture.african

soc.culture.african.american

soc.culture.african.ashanti

soc.culture.african.ewe

soc.culture.african.hausa

soc.culture.african.ibo

soc.culture.african.mandingo

soc.culture.african.somali

soc.culture.african.swahili

soc.culture.african.tuareg

soc.culture.african.xhosa

soc.culture.african.yoruba

soc.culture.african.zulu

soc.culture.albanian

soc.culture.algeria

soc.culture.antarctica

soc.culture.arabic

soc.culture.argentina

soc.culture.armenian

soc.culture.asian

soc.culture.asian.american

soc.culture.assyrian

soc.culture.asturies

soc.culture.australian

soc.culture.austria

soc.culture.azeri

soc.culture.baltics

soc.culture.bangladesh

soc.culture.bashkir

soc.culture.basque

soc.culture.bavarian

soc.culture.belarus

soc.culture.belgium

soc.culture.bengali

soc.culture.berber

soc.culture.bolivia

soc.culture.bosnia-herzgovena

soc.culture.brazil

soc.culture.breton

soc.culture.british

soc.culture.bulgaria

soc.culture.burma

soc.culture.cambodia

soc.culture.canada

soc.culture.caribbean

soc.culture.catalan

soc.culture.celtic

soc.culture.chaldean

soc.culture.charnego

soc.culture.chile

soc.culture.china

soc.culture.chuvash

soc.culture.cis

soc.culture.colombia
soc.culture.cornish
soc.culture.corsican
soc.culture.costa-rica
soc.culture.croatia
soc.culture.cuba
soc.culture.czech
soc.culture.czecho-slovak
soc.culture.dominican-rep
soc.culture.druse
soc.culture.ecuador
soc.culture.egyptian
soc.culture.el-salvador
soc.culture.eritrean
soc.culture.esperanto
soc.culture.estonia
soc.culture.ethiopia
soc.culture.europe
soc.culture.filipino
soc.culture.french
soc.culture.galician
soc.culture.galiza
soc.culture.german
soc.culture.greek
soc.culture.guinea-conakry
soc.culture.haiti
soc.culture.hawaii
soc.culture.hmong
soc.culture.honduras
soc.culture.hongkong
soc.culture.icelandic
soc.culture.indian
soc.culture.indian.american
soc.culture.indian.assam
soc.culture.indian.bihar
soc.culture.indian.delhi
soc.culture.indian.gujarati
soc.culture.indian.info
soc.culture.indian
   .jammu-kashmir
soc.culture.indian.karnataka
soc.culture.indian.kerala

soc.culture.indian.marathi
soc.culture.indian.muslims
soc.culture.indian.orissa
soc.culture.indian.rajasthan
soc.culture.indian.telugu
soc.culture.indian.uttar-pradesh
soc.culture.indonesia
soc.culture.intercultural
soc.culture.iranian
soc.culture.iraq
soc.culture.irish
soc.culture.israel
soc.culture.italian
soc.culture.jamaican
soc.culture.japan
soc.culture.jewish
soc.culture.jordan
soc.culture.kashmir
soc.culture.kazakh
soc.culture.kenya
soc.culture.korean
soc.culture.kurdish
soc.culture.kuwait
soc.culture.kyrgyz
soc.culture.laos
soc.culture.latin-america
soc.culture.latin-america.aztec
soc.culture.latin-america.gaucho
soc.culture.latin-america.guarani
soc.culture.latin-america.quechua
soc.culture.latvian
soc.culture.lebanon
soc.culture.liberia
soc.culture.lithuanian
soc.culture.macedonia
soc.culture.maghreb
soc.culture.magyar
soc.culture.malagasy
soc.culture.malaysia
soc.culture.mexican
soc.culture.mexican.american
soc.culture.misc

soc.culture.mongolian
soc.culture.multicultural
soc.culture.native
soc.culture.nepal
soc.culture.netherlands
soc.culture.new-zealand
soc.culture.nicaragua
soc.culture.nigeria
soc.culture.nordic
soc.culture.occitan
soc.culture.pacific-island
soc.culture.padania
soc.culture.pakistan
soc.culture.pakistan.education
soc.culture.pakistan.history
soc.culture.pakistan.politics
soc.culture.pakistan.religion
soc.culture.pakistan.sports
soc.culture.palestine
soc.culture.peru
soc.culture.polish
soc.culture.portuguese
soc.culture.provence
soc.culture.prussian
soc.culture.puerto-rico
soc.culture.punjab
soc.culture.quebec
soc.culture.rep-of-georgia
soc.culture.romanian
soc.culture.romany
soc.culture.russian
soc.culture.ruthenian
soc.culture.sardinian

soc.culture.scottish
soc.culture.siberia
soc.culture.sicilian
soc.culture.sierra-leone
soc.culture.sindhi
soc.culture.singapore
soc.culture.slovak
soc.culture.slovenia
soc.culture.somalia
soc.culture.south-africa
soc.culture.south-africa.afrikaans
soc.culture.soviet
soc.culture.spain
soc.culture.sri-lanka
soc.culture.swiss
soc.culture.syria
soc.culture.taiwan
soc.culture.tajik
soc.culture.tamil
soc.culture.tatar
soc.culture.thai
soc.culture.tibet
soc.culture.turkish
soc.culture.uighur
soc.culture.ukrainian
soc.culture.uruguay
soc.culture.usa
soc.culture.uzbek
soc.culture.venezuela
soc.culture.vietnamese
soc.culture.welsh
soc.culture.yugoslavia
soc.culture.zimbabwe

LANGUAGE RESOURCES

Babelfish (online Web-based translations) • **babelfish.altavista.com**
Systran Software, Inc. (Web-based translations and Windows
   translation software) • **www.systransoft.com**
Transparent Language, Inc. • **www.freetranslations.com**
   (Web-based translations) • **www.transparent.com**
Travelers' language tools (vocabulary and pronunciation)
   • **www.travlang.com/languages** (Windows translation software)

PASSPORT, VISA, AND IMMIGRATION INFORMATION

Passports

U.S. Passports • travel.state.gov/passport_services.html
Canadian passports • www.dfait-maeci.gc.ca/passport/passport.htm
U.K. passports • www.ukpa.gov.uk
Irish passports • www.irlgov.ie/iveagh/services/passports
Australian passports • www.dfat.gov.au/passports
New Zealand passports • www.passports.govt.nz

Visas and Other Entry Requirements

Travel Information Manual (through Travel.com.au gateway)
- www.travel.com.au/tools/visa.html
- www3.travel.com.au/everest/index.cgi?E=bevisreq

Foreign embassies in Washington, DC
- www.state.gov/www/about_state/contacts/diplist

Foreign consular offices elsewhere in the United States
- www.state.gov/www/travel/consular_offices/fco_index.html

Foreign Entry Requirements for U.S. citizens (informational, not authoritative) • travel.state.gov/foreignentryreqs.html

HIV Testing Requirements for Entry into Foreign Countries
- travel.state.gov/HIVtestingreqs.html

U.S. trade sanctions and travel restrictions • www.treas.gov/ofac

Visa requirements for foreign visitors to the United States
- travel.state.gov/visa_services.html

POLITICAL AND SAFETY ADVICE AND INFORMATION

Consular Information Sheets and Travel Warnings (U.S. Department of State) • travel.state.gov/travel_warnings.html

Tips for Travelers (by country and region) (U.S. Department of State) • travel.state.gov/travel_pubs.html

Travel Information and Advisory Reports (Canadian Department of Foreign Affairs)
- www.dfait-maeci.gc.ca/travelreport/menu_e.htm

Travel Advice (U.K. Foreign & Commonwealth Office)
- www.fco.gov.uk/travel

Consular Travel Advice (Australian Department of Foreign Affairs and Trade) •
www.dfat.gov.au/consular/advice/advices_mnu.html

TRAVEL HEALTH
Health and Medical Advice/Information
Centers for Disease Control and Prevention (U.S. Department of
Health and Human Services) • **www.cdc.gov/travel**
Staying Healthy in Asia, Africa, and Latin America
• **www.moon.com/staying_healthy**

Travel Medicine and Immunization Clinics
American Society of Tropical Medicine and Hygiene (ASTMH)
• **www.astmh.org**
International Association for Medical Assistance
to Travelers (IAMAT) • **www.sentex.net/~iamat**
• **www.cybermall.co.nz/NZ/IAMAT**
International Society of Travel Medicine (ISTM) • **www.istm.org**

Travel Insurance and Emergency Medical Services
Medical Information for Americans Traveling Abroad
(U.S. Department of State; includes informational directories
of medical evacuation and travel insurance companies) •
travel.state.gov/medical.html
MEDjet International, Inc. • **www.medjet.com**
Specialty Risk International, Inc. • **www.specialtyrisk.com**
Travel Insurance Services • **www.travelinsure.com**
Worldtravelcenter.com • **www.worldtravelcenter.com**
Worldwide Assistance Services, Inc. • **www.worldwideassistance.com**

Internet Travel Shopping

BUYING AIRLINE TICKETS ON THE INTERNET
Automated Published-Fare Internet Travel Agencies
Travelocity.com • **www.travelocity.com**
Expedia.com • **www.expedia.com** • **expedia.microsoft.com**
Trip.com (Galileo) • **www.trip.com**
American Express (GetThere.com/ITN) • **travel.americanexpress.com**
• **www.itn.net/cgi/get?itn/pl/amex_personal/index**
Biztravel.com (Rosenbluth International) • **www.biztravel.com**
Amadeus.net • **www.amadeus.net**
GENESIS • **www.ustar.com**

Automated Online Consolidator Ticket Agencies
1travel.com / onetravel.com • www.1travel.com
- www.onetravel.com
- www.farebeater.com (direct link to airfare search)

Hotwire • www.hotwire.com
Cheaptickets.com • www.cheaptickets.com
Lowestfare.com • www.lowestfare.com
Priceline.com • www.priceline.com

Student and Youth Fare Specialists
Council on International Education and Exchange • www.ciee.org
Council Travel • www.counciltravel.com
STA Travel • www.sta.com (USA) • www.statravelgroup.com
    (worldwide)

Online Ticket Purchases Directly From Airlines
International Air Transport Association (IATA) (links to all IATA
    member airlines' official Web sites) • www.iata.org/membership
Orbitz • www.orbitz.com

Flights From the United Kingdom
Farebase • www.farebase.co.uk
Teletext • www.teletext.co.uk/holidays (follow
    the "TV text ads" link)

Flights From Europe (United Kingdom and Elsewhere)
Flights.com (formerly TISS.com) • www.flights.com •
    ebookers.com • www.ebookers.com

Flights From Australia
Travel.com.au • www.travel.com.au • www.travel.com.nz
Cyber Air Broker (Phil Travel) • www.airdiscounter.com

Flights From Other Countries
Association of Special Fares Agents (ASFA) • www.asfa.net
Association of International Travel Agents (AITA) • www.aita.org

Multi-Stop International Tickets
AirTreks.com • www.airtreks.com
Air Brokers International • www.airbrokers.com
Around The World Travel • www.netfare.net
Avia Travel • www.avia.com • www.igc.org/avia

BUYING TRAIN TICKETS AND PASSES ONLINE
Amtrak • **www.amtrak.com**
National Association of Railway Passengers (NARP)
   • **www.narprail.org** •
Amtrak Travel Tips (NARP) • **www.narprail.org/tips.htm**
VIA Rail Canada • **www.viarail.ca**
Eurail • **www.eurail.com**
Rail Europe • **www.raileurope.com**
Eurotunnel • **www.eurostar.com**
Rail Australia • **www.railaustralia.com.au**
worldwide passenger rail links (Trainweb) • **www.passengerail.com**
worldwide railfan links (Trainweb) • **www.trainweb.com**

AVIATION PORTAL SITES—INCLUDING DIRECTORIES OF AIRPORT WEB SITES
Aerolink.com • **www.aerolink.com**
Landings.com • **www.landings.com**

RESERVING ACCOMMODATIONS ONLINE
Hotel Brokers
Hotel Reservations Network (HRN) • **www.180096hotel.com**
   • **www.hoteldiscount.com** • **www.hotelreservationsnetwork.com**
Priceline.com Hotels • **www.priceline.com/hotels**
Expedia.com "Hotel Price Matcher" • **www.expedia.com**
   • **expedia.microsoft.com**

Hostels
Hostelling International • **www.iyhf.org**
HI-AYH (formerly American Youth Hostels) • **www.hiayh.org**
Hostels.com • **www.hostels.com**
The Hostel Handbook for the United States and Canada •
   www.hostelhandbook.com

Campgrounds and RV Parks
U.S. Federal government campgrounds • **www.recreation.gov**
   • **www.reserveusa.com**
U.S. National Park Service • **www.nps.gov**
U.S. state park campgrounds • **www.reserveamerica.com**
Parks Canada • **parkscanada.pch.gc.ca**

Home Exchanges
Homelink • **www.homelink.org**

HomeExchange.com • **www.homeexchange.com**
Intervac • **www.intervac.com**

Hospitality Exchanges
Free Stay • **www.free-stay.com**
Hospitality Exchange • **www.goldray.com/hospitality**
Servas • **www.servas.org**
Stay4Free • **www.stay4free.com**
Travelhoo International Hospitality Exchange • **www.travelhoo.com**
Wildflower Travel Community • **www.escape.ca/~livana**

BOOKING OTHER TRAVEL SERVICES ONLINE
Vacation.com • **www.vacation.com**

Consumer Protection, Privacy, and Security

PRIVACY AND SECURITY
European Union Privacy Protection Law
European Union data privacy directive (full text)
- **europa.eu.int/eur-lex/en/lif/dat/1995/en_395L0046.html**

General information on the EU data privacy directive
- **europa.eu.int/comm/internal_market/en/media/dataprot**

Privacy Invasion Techniques Used By Websites
Gibson Research Co. (Steve Gibson) • **www.grc.com**
Internet privacy issues (Richard M. Smith)
- **www.tiac.net/users/smiths/privacy**
- **www.tiac.net/users/smiths/privacy/banads.htm**

MSIE cookie security and privacy problems (Peacefire)
- **www.peacefire.org/security/iecookies**

Privacy on the Internet (John Navas, The Navas Group)
- **cable-dsl.home.att.net/#Privacy**

Privacy Invasion on the E-Commerce Web (Matt Curtin)
- **www.interhack.net/people/cmcurtin**

"What's Related? Everything but Your Privacy"
- **www.interhack.net/pubs/whatsrelated**

Privacy Advocates and Organizations
Center for Democracy and Technology • **www.cdt.org**
Electronic Privacy Information Center (EPIC) • **www.epic.org**
Junkbusters Inc. • **www.junkbuster.com**

Web Browser Privacy Testing Sites
(demonstrates what your browser reveals to each
Web site you visit)
Junkbusters, Inc.
- **www.junkbuster.com/cgi-bin/show_http_headers**
- **www.junkbusters.com/cgi-bin/privacy**

Privacy.net (Russell Smith) • **www.privacy.net/analyze**

Internet Security Testing Sites
(tests how easily your computer can be spied
on from the Internet)
HackerWhacker • **hackerwhacker.com**
Shields Up! (Steve Gibson) • **grc.com**
- **https://grc.com/x/ne.dll?bhObkyd2**

WebTrends ("The Portal Site for Internet and Intranet Professionals")
- **www.webtrends.net/tools/security/scan.asp**

"Spyware" Detection and Removal Software
Ad-aware (Windows) • **www.lavasoft.de/free.html**
Opt Out (Windows) • **grc.com/optout.htm**

Privacy Protection and Security Software
(proxy servers, cookie blockers, and personal firewalls)
Internet Junkbuster Proxy (Windows, Unix, Linux)
- **www.junkbuster.com**

Junkbuster for Windows
- **ourworld.compuserve.com/homepages/gtschech/ijb95_en.htm**

Proxomitron (Windows) • **proxomitron.tripod.com**
Web Washer (Windows) • **www.webwasher.com**
AdSubtract (formerly InterMute; Java for multiple platforms)
- **www.adsubtract.com**

Zone Alarm (Windows) • **www.zonelabs.com**
Net barrier (Mac OS) • **www.intego.com/netbarrier**
Macintosh security links • **www.macintosh.com/security.html**

CONSUMER PROTECTION
Credit Card Chargebacks
Unauthorized charges (15 U.S.C. section 1643),
    Billing errors (15 U.S.C. section 1666),
    Disputed charges (15 U.S.C. section 1666i)
- **law.house.gov/uscsrch.htm**

Consumer Protection Laws
United States Code (U.S. federal laws) • **law.house.gov/uscsrch.htm**
Code of Federal Regulations
- **www.access.gpo.gov/nara/cfr/cfr-retrieve.html**

California Seller of Travel (CST) law (Business and Professions
    Code Section 17550) • **www.leginfo.ca.gov**
California e-commerce disclosure law (Business and Professions
    Code Section 17538) • **www.leginfo.ca.gov**

Law Enforcement Agencies
Aviation Consumer Protection Division (U.S. Department of
    Transportation) • **www.dot.gov/airconsumer**
Office of Aviation Enforcement and Proceedings
    (U.S. Department of Transportation) •
    www.dot.gov/ost/ogc/org/aviation
Federal Trade Commission (FTC)
- **www.ftc.gov/privacy** (privacy policy and enforcement)
- **https://www.ftc.gov/ftc/complaint.htm** (online complaint form)
- **www.ftc.gov/ro/romap2.htm** (regional offices)
- **uce@ftc.gov** (reports of "unsolicited commercial e-mail",
    or spam)

California Travel Consumer Restitution Corp.
- **www.gocalif.ca.gov/agents/seller.html**

Complaints against California sellers of travel
- **caag.state.ca.us/piu/mailform.htm**
- **caag.state.ca.us/piu/form.htm**

Airlines and state law enforcement (California Attorney General's
    Office) • **caag.state.ca.us/piu/airlines.htm**
Air Travel Organiser's License (ATOL) Section (U.K. Civil Aviation
    Authority) • **www.atol.org.uk**
- **www.caaerg2.org.uk/atol/leaflet.htm** (general information)
- **www.caaerg2.org.uk/atol/gdnot16.htm** (purchases involving
    customers, suppliers, or flights originating outside the U.K.)
- **www.caaerg2.org.uk/atol/consumer.htm** (complaints, claims,
    and enforcement requests)

Industry Self-Regulation Organizations
American Society of Travel Agents (ASTA) • **www.astanet.com**
ASTA Alerts for Consumers (common travel scams, etc.)
  • **www.astanet.com/www/asta/pub/info/info.htmlx**
ASTA Consumer Affairs Department (informal mediation)
  • **www.astanet.com/www/asta/pub/info/consprotection.htmlx**
Better Business Bureaus • **www.bbb.org**
BBB Online • **www.bbbonline.org** •
Association of British Travel Agencies (ABTA) • **www.abtanet.com**
ABTA complaints and arbitration
  • **www.abtanet.com/holcheck.html#PROBLEMS**

Mediation Services
Mediation Information and Resource Center • **www.mediate.com**
Community Board Program • **www.mediate.com/cbp**

Small Claims Court
Nolo Press index of Small Claims Court limits by state
  • **www.nolo.com/ChunkCM/CM19.html**
Nolo Press guide to Small Claims court
  • **www.nolo.com/encyclopedia/cm_ency.html#Subtopic76**

Using the Internet While Traveling

PUBLIC-ACCESS INTERNET TERMINALS
Cybercafes
Cybercafe directories • **www.cybercafe.com** • **cybercaptive.com**
Cybercafe newsgroup • **alt.cybercafes**

Hostels
Hostelling International • **www.iyhf.org**
Private hostels • **www.hostels.com**

Libraries
librarians "Web4Lib" mailing list • **sunsite.berkeley.edu/Web4Lib**

Truck Stops
DriverNet • **www.drivernet.com/locate.asp**

BRINGING A COMPUTER WITH YOU
Portable Computers and Internet Access Devices
PDA Street (reviews, etc., of a wide range of handheld devices)
- www.pdastreet.com

Psion • www.psion.com

Linux on Laptops • www.cs.utexas.edu/users/kharker/linux-laptop

Star Office • www.sun.com/staroffice

WordPerfect Suite for Linux • linux.corel.com/products/wp8

Compatibility and Connectivity
Teleadapt (telephone and modem adapters and advice)
- www/teleadapt.com

APCC (power and phone line protection) • www.apcc.com

Teleadapt's directory of power and phone systems by country
- www.teleadapt.com/web/destinations/destination

Teleadapt's Mobile Connectivity 101
- www.teleadaptusa.com/nme/mb101.htm

Steve Kropla's Help for World Travelers • kropla.com

Steve Kropla's Worldwide Phone Guide • kropla.com/phones.htm

Steve Kropla's Worldwide Electric Guide • kropla.com/electric.htm

Roaming Internet Access
GRIC • www.gric.com/zone

GRIC member ISP's • www.gric.com/zone/isplocator

iPass • ipass.com

iPass dial-up locations • ipass.com/accesspoints

Equant • www.equant.net

SITA • www.sita.int

Wireless Mobile Internet Access
Ricochet • www.ricochet.net

Portable Computer Insurance
Safeware, Inc. • www.safeware.com

INTERNET FILE STORAGE SERVICES
Driveway • www.driveway.com

FreeDrive • www.freedrive.com

i-drive • www.idrive.com

Xdrive • www.xdrive.com

E-MAIL ON THE ROAD

TripMail from AirTreks.com • **mail.airtreks.com**
Coalition Against Unsolicited Commercial e-mail (CAUCE)
   • **www.cauce.org**

Web Gateways To Standard E-Mail Accounts

MollyMail (POP and IMAP) • **www.mollymail.com**
Mail2Web • **www.mail2web/.com**
MailStart • **www.mailstart.com**
ThatWeb • **www.thatweb.com**

Shell Accounts

directory of free shell account providers
   • **members.spree.com/messer/site/geo/shell.html**
Grex • **www.grex.org**

POP E-mail By Telnet

instructions for accessing a POP account by Telnet:
   • **help.netscape.com/kb/corporate/19990415-8.html**
   • **help.mindspring.com/modules/00100/00129.htm**

Internet Software

INTERNET SUITES

(each of these suites includes a Web browser,
      e-mail program, and newsreader)
Microsoft Internet Explorer (MSIE) and Microsoft Outlook Express
      (Windows and Mac OS) • **www.microsoft.com/windows/ie**
Netscape Navigator/Netscape Communicator (many platforms)
   • **www.netscape.com/download**
Opera (many platforms) • **www.opera.com**
Star Office (Windows, Unix, Linux) • **www.sun.com/staroffice**

WEB BROWSERS

Lynx (many platforms) • **lynx.browser.org**
public Lynx servers accessible by Telnet
   • **www.trill-home.com/lynx/public_lynx.html**
iCab (Mac OS) • **www.icab.de**

E-MAIL PROGRAMS

Pegasus Mail (Windows) • www.pmail.com • www.pmail.gen.nz
Eudora (Mac OS, Windows) • www.eudora.com
Pine (Unix, Linux) • www.washington.edu/pine
PC-Pine (Windows) • www.washington.edu/pine/pc-pine

NEWSREADERS

Xnews (Windows) • xnews.3dnews.net
SLRN (Unix, Linux, Windows) • space.mit.edu/~davis/slrn.html
SLRN for Windows • www.vex.net/~cthuang/slrn
SLRN under Windows (tips for installation, configuration, and use)
    • thingy.apana.org.au/~fun/slrn
Free Agent (Windows) • www.forteinc.com/getfa/getfa.htm

INTERNET REMOTE ACCESS AND REMOTE CONTROL SOFTWARE

IBM Desktop On-Call (Windows, Mac OS, Linux)
    • www.ibm.co.jp/pspjinfo/javadesk • www.direct.ibm.com
    • ftp://ftp.ibm.co.jp/pub/pspj/dtoc40/trial
LapLink (Windows) • www.laplink.com

OTHER SOFTWARE FOR TRAVELERS

The Postal Business Companion, Global Edition (Windows)
    free from the U.S. Postal Service •
    800-THE-USPS, ext. 2113 (800-843-8777, ext. 2113)
World Watch • www.cxptech.com

OPEN ACCESS TO THE INTERNET

"Best viewed with any browser" • www.anybrowser.org/campaign/
"Lynx friendly" •
    www.cs.umanitoba.ca/~djc/personal/lynxfriend.html
Web Accessibility Initiative (World Wide Web Consortium) •
    www.w3c.org/wai
"Bobby" (accessibility and browser compatibility testing tool) •
    www.cast.org/bobby

The Practical Nomad

The Practical Nomad • www.practicalnomad.com
Edward Hasbrouck • hasbrouck.org

Glossary

This isn't a comprehensive glossary of travel industry, computer and Internet, or consumer protection and legal terminology. Nor do I expect that anyone will want to read it straight through! It's intended as something to refer to if you encounter unfamiliar terms in the book, or want a bit more background about some of the more technical issues. I've tried to define terms in a way that will be comprehensible to non-specialists, but also to suggest some of the deeper issues.

Travel agents, computer and Internet professionals, and lawyers will each find some of the definitions in their respective fields unnecessary, oversimplified, or technically imprecise. But few readers, I suspect, will be familiar with the jargon of all these fields, and I hope that these definitions will be useful to some of you.

404—Web server error code for "I can't find the Web page you asked for. Either the URL is wrong, the Web page has moved, or the page no longer exists."

ActiveX—software included in MSIE that allows a Web page to send programs and make them run on your computer. If you allow an ActiveX program from a Web page to run on your computer, it can do *anything* you could do from the keyboard, including sending all your files anywhere on the Internet or deleting them and reformatting your hard drive. There's no intermediate control: it's all or nothing. Web sites that depend on ActiveX may not work with any browser except MSIE. Disable ActiveX, and avoid sites that require it if you have a choice.

address—In Internet usage, an address can mean either a URL, an e-mail address, or some other sort of Internet address.

agency—a business that acts as an "agent" or representative for a "principal." *see* "agent" and "principal"

agent—a person or company that acts as a representative of someone else, rather than providing goods or services itself. In general, it's the principal, not the agent, who is responsible to the customer if there are problems—even if the problems are the agent's fault. Standard travel agency terms and conditions say that the agency "acts only as an agent for suppliers of travel services," and is not responsible for their actions. *see* "principal"

airfare—*see* "fare"

AIRIMP—*see* "Air Interline Message Procedure"

Air Interline Message Procedure (AIRIMP)—the protocol used for messages between airline computer systems and CRS's. *see* "protocol"

Airlines Reporting Corp. (ARC) www.arccorp.com —the central financial clearinghouse established by the airlines to process all payments for airline tickets issued by travel agencies in the United States

air tariff—the schedule of published airfares and associated rules, generally distributed electronically through IATA, ATPCO, and the CRS's. The air tariff doesn't actually put price tags on tickets. It says, in effect, "*If* there is a reservation on such-and-such an airline, in such-and-such a class, on such-and-such a route and schedule, then a ticket can be issued for this price."

Air Tariff Publishing Co. (ATPCO) www.atpco.net —The principle compiler and distributor of published airfares. ATPCO gets fares from the airlines, IATA, and the government (which has to approve some international fares), and distributes them to travel agencies and the CRS's.

Air Travel Organiser's License (ATOL) www.atol.org.uk —the licensing and consumer protection system for airline ticket and package holiday purchases in the United Kingdom (Great Britain and Northern Ireland). Don't buy tickets, or a package holiday including flights, from an agency in the United Kingdom unless they have an ATOL number in all their literature.

America Online (AOL) www.aol.com —AOL gives subscribers access to most things on the Internet, as well as its own proprietary content available only to AOL members. AOL is thus both more and less than an ISP. Little of the AOL proprietary content really adds to what you can find on the Internet, and the fact that AOL isn't a standard ISP makes connecting on the road more difficult in some places. If you ask a question of the entire Internet, you're more likely to get an answer than if you only ask other AOL users. If you use AOL, be aware of when you are in areas open only to AOL subscribers, and when you are in Internet areas.

American Society of Travel Agents (ASTA) www.astanet.com — the principal trade association of travel agents in the United States. ASTA operates a mediation service for consumers with disputes with members.

AOL—*see* "America Online"

application, application program—software that you use to accomplish something (as opposed to the operating system that just keeps other programs running). Applications are usually the purpose of having a computer; the hardware and OS exist to enable them to do their work. Web browsers, e-mail programs, word processors, and spreadsheet programs are all applications.

ARC—*see* "Airlines Reporting Corp."

ASTA—*see* "American Society of Travel Agents"

ATOL—*see* "Air Travel Organiser's License"

ATPCO—*see* "Air Tariff Publishing Co."

availability—whether seats are available in a specific booking class on a specific set of airline flights, whether cars are available in a certain category from a certain company in a specific place on specific dates, whether cabins are available in a specific category on a specific sailing of a specific ship, etc. Fares, rules, and availability together determine the price.

BBB—*see* "Better Business Bureau"

Better Business Bureau (BBB) www.bbb.org, www.bbbonline.com —a "self-regulation" organization funded by businesses and designed to make members seem more legitimate. It's not a bad organization, but it has little real power and is generally ineffectual.

booking (n.), to book (v.)—To make a booking means, "to make a reservation." Buying a ticket is a separate step, even if the ticket is an e-ticket. There is no such thing as "booking a ticket."

booking class—a category of availability. There are many booking classes on each flight, and each fare has rules requiring that reservations be made in a specific booking class. Seats may be available in one class on a flight, and not in other classes. Airlines use booking classes as a tool to help them get each person to pay as much as possible, and maximize their profits. *see also* "availability," "fare basis"

bookmarks—stored links to URLs of Web pages you want to be able to go back to quickly, without retyping the URLs. Most browsers, except MSIE, call them bookmarks; Microsoft uses the nonstandard term "favorites." Netscape and most other browsers store all your bookmarks as one file, which you can copy to use on another computer. MSIE stores each favorite as a separate file, so to copy or move your favorites you need to copy or move the whole directory.

browser—*see* "Web browser"

BTW—"By The Way" (commonly used in newsgroup postings)

California Seller of Travel (CST) Law—A California state law requiring travel agencies to register with the state, include their registration number in all their advertisements, and participate in a state fund to reimburse customers of failed or fraudulent travel companies. Any travel agency anywhere that accepts business from customers in California is subject to the law.

case—Capital letters are "UPPER CASE," small letters are "lower case." *see* "case sensitive

case sensitive—If something is "case sensitive," that means it matters whether you type it in capital letters or small letters. Domain names aren't case sensitive, but parts of URLs and e-mail addresses sometimes are. If an Internet address doesn't work in all lower case, try reproducing the combination of upper case and lower case letters exactly, no matter how weird it looks.

chargeback—A disputed credit card charge. Chargebacks are decided by the banks where you and the merchant have your credit card accounts. If a chargeback is successful, you get your money back from the bank, even if the merchant is out of business.

CFR—*see* "Code of Federal Regulations"

CLI—command-line interface

client—a program that interacts with a server. When you browse the Web, your Web browser is the client of the Web server. *see* "client/server computing," "server"

client/server computing—a computer operation that involves two programs, a client and a server, interacting with each other. Browsing the Web is the most common use of client/server computing: the browser (client) on your computer sends a request to the Web server; the server sends back some data (text, images, etc.); and then your browser renders that data as a Web page on your screen.

Code of Federal Regulations (CFR)—the compilation of all regulations issued by federal agencies in the United States, including those that regulate the airlines.

codeshare—a flight that is labeled with the flight number of one airline, even though it is actually operated by a different airline. Sometimes the same flight will have four or five flight numbers designating it as a flight of different airlines. Codesharing serves no legitimate purpose, and has no benefits for travelers. Airlines do it solely to deceive you. I (and many others) think it's fraud, but DOT allows it.

command-line interface—a text-based user interface. Operating systems with command-line interfaces include DOS, UNIX, Linux, and (optionally) Windows NT. You can get to a command-line interface on a remote computer over the Internet by using Telnet or connecting to a shell account. You can browse the Web from a command line interface using the text browser Lynx. Most travel agents use command-line CRS interfaces, but since the demise of Easy Sabre there is no publicly-available command-line interface to any CRS or airline computer system.

computerized reservation system (CRS)—a computer system used by online and offline travel agencies, airlines, hotels, car rental companies, etc. Through the CRS's, travel agencies and other travel companies can get information about fares and availability, make reservations, and issue tickets. Almost all airline reservations that aren't made directly with the airlines are made through CRS's. Most online travel agencies rely exclusively on a single CRS for all price and availability information.

confirmed seat—a confirmed seat guarantees that you will get on the plane (or the airline has to compensate you). A confirmed seat doesn't guarantee any particular seat on the plane. If you ask, "Do I have a confirmed seat," all you are asking is whether you are confirmed. If you want to know if you have seat assignments, ask, "Do I have a pre-reserved seat?" *see* "pre-reserved seat"

connecting flights—a set of flights that involves a change of planes at an intermediate airport. *see* "direct flight," "nonstop flight"

consolidator—a travel agency that has a contract with an airline that enables the agency to sell tickets for less than published fares. Some consolidators are wholesalers who only sell through other retail travel agencies; others sell directly to the public.

consolidator agency—a travel agency that sells consolidator tickets, either issued itself under its contract with an airline, or purchased from wholesale consolidators.

consolidator price—a selling price for a ticket that is less than the official published fare. Consolidator prices are set by individual travel agencies, *not* by the airlines. Consolidator tickets have the published fare (or no fare at all) printed on them as their face value, not the actual price you paid.

cookie manager—a program that allows you to control what happens to cookies that Web sites send to your computer: which Web sites (if any) are allowed to store cookies on your computer, or receive cookies from your computer, whether cookies are saved or deleted when you close your Web browser, etc.

cookies—small pieces of information that Web sites send back and forth to and from your computer. If you allow Web sites to "set" cookies (store them on your computer) and retrieve them, they can use them to correlate what you do on one Web site with what you do on another, compiling a log of all your Web browsing and a profile of you and your interests and activities.

country code—The same set of two-letter country codes is used in geographic Internet domain names, in international airline ticketing, and as the first two letters of the three-letter currency codes seen on airline tickets and at many currency exchanges. These codes are defined in ISO standard 3166-1, **www.din.de/gremien/nas/nabd /iso3166ma**

credit card chargeback—*see* "chargeback"

CRS—*see* "computerized reservation system"

currency code—The most universally understood and unambiguous way to specify monetary units is the set of three-letter currency codes defined in ISO standard 4217 **www.bsi.org.uk/bsi/products/standards /products/cur rency.xhtml.** (The first two letters of the ISO 4217 currency code are the same as the ISO 3166-1 two-letter country code.) Prices on almost all Web sites are in the local currency of the place where the site is located, and/or in currencies designated by the ISO 4217 codes. These codes are also used at banks and currency exchanges around the world. Get familiar with the more common of these codes if you ever travel abroad or look at Web sites with prices in any currency other than your own.

Department of Transportation (DOT) www.dot.gov —the federal agency in the United States responsible for approving international airfares and enforcing anti-trust and consumer protection laws involving airlines, cruise lines, railroads, and interstate bus lines.

DHCP—*see* "domain host control protocol"

directory—folder. What some operating systems and programs call directories and sub-directories, others call folders and sub-folders. Generally, command-line OS's like DOS, UNIX, and Linux use the term directory; graphical OS's like Windows and MacOS refer to them as folders. Occasionally, "directory" is used in a completely different sense as shorthand for "Web directory".

direct flight—a "flight" that has the same flight number from where you get on to where you get off. A direct "flight" might actually consist of connecting flights, with one or more changes of plane at intermediate points, as long as they have the same flight number. I think this is fraud, but DOT allows it. *see* "connecting flight," "nonstop flight"

discount fare—To the airlines, anything less than the highest, unrestricted fare. A discount fare isn't necessarily cheap. *see* "discounted ticket"

discounted ticket—can mean either (1) a ticket at a discount fare, or (2) a ticket sold at a discount from the published fare, i.e. a consolidator ticket. These are very different. *see* "discount fare," "consolidator price"

domain host control protocol (DHCP)—a system used to make it easier to move a computer from one network to another, with less manual reconfiguration. It's much easier to put your laptop on the LAN at a cybercafe, for example, if they use DHCP.

domain name—the domain name is the part of a URL that identifies who owns the Web site. If the URL is www.foobar.com/gobbledegook/example.html, the domain name is "foobar.com". You can use a WHOIS program, or a WHOIS lookup Web site, to get the name and contact information of the owner of the domain from the domain registrar for the top-level domain (in this example ".com"). The system of domain names is administered by IANA and ICANN.

domain registrar—one of the organizations and companies that registers domain names. Whoever registers a domain effectively owns it. Each top-level domain has one or more domain registrars who maintain records of who has registered each name in their domain. Registrars and WHOIS servers for all top-level domains are listed at **www.iana.org/cctld/cctld-whois.htm**

DOT—*see* "Department of Transportation"

electronic signature—under the Electronic Signatures Act, an electronic signature can be legally equivalent to a written signature. The law doesn't define an electronic signature—apparently it can be anything you agree to—so it's best not to consent to allow a password or anything else to be used as an electronic signature unless you're very certain that it can't be intercepted or forged. If someone gets your electronic signature, there's no legal limit to what they can use it for.

electronic travel authorization (ETA)—the electronic equivalent of a visa. ETA's are not yet available through the Internet, only from travel agencies and airlines that obtain them for you through CRS's and airline computers. Always carry printouts of any ETA's in case the computers are down when you arrive in the country.

electronic ticket—*see* "e-ticket"

endorsements—notations printed or written on the ticket as to the rules, refundability, change fees, etc. Endorsements are coded, cryptic, and easy to misunderstand. If in doubt, ask the airline what the endorsements on your ticket mean. Endorsements override the rules of the fare shown on the ticket.

ETA—*see* "electronic travel authorization"

Ethernet, Ethernet network—the most common system for local-area networking. If someone mentions a LAN without mentioning what type of LAN it is, it's probably an Ethernet LAN. If your computer has a network port, network card, or network adapter, it's probably for an Ethernet connection.

e-ticket—a ticket that isn't printed, but is kept electronically in the airline's or CRS's computer database. Many tickets purchased on the Internet can only be issued as e-tickets. E-tickets have significant disadvantages; it's worth a few dollars more for paper tickets.

FAQ—*see* "frequently asked questions"

fare—a price for an airline ticket and an associated set of rules (route, schedule, booking class, etc.) that a reservation has to satisfy to qualify for that price. Existence of a fare does not imply that there are any flights, or available seats, that satisfy the rules of the fare. In general, "fare" is used to mean "published fare." Technically speaking, there are no consolidator fares, only consolidator prices. Fares advertised on Web sites may include none, some, or all of the required taxes. *see* "price"

fare basis—a string of letters and numbers designating the fare (and thus the official price and the rules) applicable to a ticket. There are some general customs about how the letters and numbers for a fare basis are chosen, but you can't necessarily infer anything from the code itself. In a CRS (but not with most online travel agencies or airline Web sites) you can use the fare basis code to look up the rules of the fare.

fare rules—fare rules include what airline(s), booking class(es), route(s), and schedules qualify for the fare; minimum and maximum stay; refund and change fees; etc. You can buy two tickets for the same flights, at different fares, with completely different rules. If you later have to make changes, the cheaper ticket with change fees could end up much more expensive. You should be allowed to read the complete rules before you buy a ticket, but in practice that's rarely possible.

favorites—Microsoft-speak for what most other Web browsers call bookmarks.

firewall—software and/or hardware for protecting your computer against Internet hacking, vandalism, data theft, viruses, etc. The simplest and easiest form of firewall for a home PC is a "personal firewall" program that monitors and controls your Internet connection to stop unauthorized activity. That provides less protection than a physically separate firewall between your computer and the Internet—but much more than no firewall at all. Most people have no protection for their Internet connection, and vandals generally go for the easiest targets.

folder—directory. "Folder" and "directory" are different names for the same thing, used interchangeably. *see* "directory"

frame—a rectangular section of a Web page that has its own URL, and can be used to show all or part of another Web page, even one from a completely different Web site. Frames are often used to make it looked like the "framed" page comes from the site that puts its border around it, and to hide or confuse you about its true source. Learn how to recognize frames and display their individual URLs in your browser, so you can tell where the information in them really comes from.

freeware—software that you don't have to pay to download, install, and use. *see* "shareware"

FYI—"For Your Information" (commonly used in newsgroup postings)

Federal Trade Commission (FTC) www.ftc.gov—the federal agency in the United States responsible for enforcing consumer protection laws (except for airlines, cruise lines, railroads, and interstate bus lines) and privacy regulations (which for the most part don't exist).

file transfer protocol (FTP)—the system used by your browser or a separate FTP program to download and upload files to and from other computers on the Internet. If you've ever downloaded and installed a program, you've probably used FTP.

flight number—a single flight number may designate a set of connecting flights that requires a change of planes and may even be operated by different airlines. *see* "direct flight."

FWIW—"For What It's Worth" (commonly used in newsgroup postings)

Frequently Asked Questions (FAQ)—"FAQ" is used to refer both to frequently asked questions and to answers to frequently asked questions. Most Web sites and almost all newsgroups have FAQ's. (My FAQ on discounted international air tickets **hasbrouck.org/faq** has been posted monthly in the rec.travel.air newsgroup since 1991.) Before you ask a question in a newsgroup or by e-mail, check if it's answered in the FAQ.

FTC—*see* "Federal Trade Commission"

FTP—*see* "file transfer protocol"

gopher—a system for organizing and retrieving information on the Internet, widely used before the creation of the World Wide Web. Occasionally you'll still find useful information on a gopher site. Any major browser can retrieve and display gopher pages the same way it retrieves Web pages; just type in the URL. Gopher URLs look like gopher://gopher.foobar.edu/menu/submenu/subsubmenu/filename.ext

graphical user interface (GUI)—a system that lets you interact with a computer through icons and other graphic and pictorial elements on a screen, rather than text. Operating systems with GUI's include MacOS and Windows. Most Internet applications for Windows or MacOS have GUI's, but it's possible to browse the Web, send and receive e-mail, participate in newsgroups, etc. from a command-line interface, especially in UNIX or Linux. It's useful to learn how to do this in case the only available public Internet terminal is a text terminal.

GUI—*see* "graphical user interface"

home exchange—an arrangement for you to stay in someone else's home, while they stay in yours, usually with no money changing hands.

hospitality exchange—a mutual agreement among members of a hospitality club or other affinity group to put each other up in each others homes when they are traveling. A guest needs to ask permission well in advance, and a host can always decline. But membership in such a group gives you access to a network of potential hosts, in exchange for putting up guests yourself.

hotel broker—hotel brokers or hotel consolidators are travel agencies that negotiate contracts with hotels allowing them to offer rooms for less than the "rack" rate. Typically, you have to pay a hotel broker in full, in advance.

hotel consolidator—*see* "hotel broker"

HTML—*see* "hypertext markup language"

http—*see* "hypertext transfer protocol"

https—"secure HTTP." If you see that you are at a URL that begins with "https://", you'll probably also see the security icon in your browser that indicates that the messages between your browser and the Web site are being encrypted (sent in code). Note that this only protects against data theft on the Internet. Information can still be intercepted on the computer (especially if it's a public terminal), before it is encrypted for sending across the Internet.

hypertext markup language (HTML)—the code used on a Web page to indicate which parts of the page are the headings, which is the body text, which things are a numbered list, where to find the images for the page, etc. HTML is actually text. Most browsers will let you look at the HTML for the current page by choosing "view source." HTML can be used to try to control exactly how the Web page looks on your computer screen, but it wasn't designed to be used that way, and it tends to cause problems when it is.

hypertext transfer protocol (http)—the system by which your Web browser gets information from a Web site. In a URL, it tells the Web browser to use that method to get the Web page.

IANA—*see* "Internet Assigned Numbers Authority"

IATA—*see* "International Air Transport Association"

ICANN—*see* "Internet Corporation for Assigned Names and Numbers"

identity theft—using personal information about someone to impersonate them for fraudulent purposes, such as getting purchases billed to them, obtaining credit cards in their name, or transferring money out of their bank account

IMAP—*see* "Internet mail access protocol"

IMHO—"In My Humble Opinion" (commonly used in newsgroup postings)

International Air Transport Association (IATA) www.iata.org — the international cartel and trade association to which almost all major airlines worldwide belong (including all major U.S. airlines except Southwest Airlines)

International Organization for Standardization (ISO) www.iso.ch —sets international standards including those for country and currency codes used in Internet domain names, airline ticketing, and by banks and currency exchanges.

Internet—the global network of networks of computers connected using the Internet protocol and reachable from each other by IP address.

Internet address—Internet addresses include URLs (for Web pages), e-mail addresses, etc. Microsoft uses "Internet address" in a nonstandard way to mean "URL," which confuses the Internet with the Web and overlooks the other kinds of Internet addresses.

Internet Assigned Numbers Authority (IANA)—one of the administrators of the system of top-level domain names.

Internet Corporation for Assigned Names and Numbers (ICANN)—one of the administrators of the system of top-level domain names.

Internet mail access protocol (IMAP)—a system for accessing e-mail that allows you to leave your e-mail on the server, download what you want, but still work with e-mail folders on the server as though they were on your computer. It's a substantial improvement over POP mail, especially for travelers.

Internet protocol (IP)—the system by which all computers on the Internet talk to each other by breaking up large messages and files into many small "packets." *see* also "IP address"

Internet service provider (ISP)—the company that provides you with a connection to the Internet. There is only one Internet. Once you are connected to the Internet you have access to all the same information regardless of which ISP you use, *unless* your ISP is a proprietary service like AOL or Compuserve that gives less than complete Internet access.

IP—*see* "Internet protocol"

IP address—a number like "207.46.130.14" that distinguishes your computer from all the others on the Internet. Your browser sends your IP address with each request for a Web page, to tell the Web server where to send that page in reply. When you dial into the Internet with a modem, your IP address is usually assigned automatically. If you're connecting your computer to the Internet through a LAN, you may need to set its IP address manually.

ISO—*see* "International Organization for Standardization"

ISP—*see* "Internet service provider"

itinerary—written details of a set of travel reservations. An itinerary can serve as a schedule of flights, a reference for where and when you have reservations, a specifications list for a tour, and an invoice for tickets and/or travel services. Proofread your itinerary carefully before you click "buy."

Java, Java applet—Java is a programming language used, among other things, for programs that can be downloaded from a Web page by your browser and run on your computer. Java applets are supposed to be limited in what they can do, so they are somewhat safer than ActiveX. But you still shouldn't let them run on your computer, or say "yes" to any requests they make for privileges, unless you are sure the site that sent them is trustworthy and competent.

LAN—*see* "local-area network"

local-area network (LAN)—despite the name "local," a LAN is usually not just a way to connect local computers, but also a way to link them all to the Internet. Usually a LAN is an Ethernet network, although it might be a different type of network if you have a Mac. An Internet connection through a LAN can be much faster than a dial-up modem connection, so if you have a choice it's usually preferable to connect through a LAN.

location—"location on the Internet." Netscape uses "location" to mean URL. This suggests that a URL corresponds in some way to a physical location, which it doesn't. There's almost no way to tell where a Web server is physically located, and anyone anywhere in the world can register a domain name in any "geographic" domain. Domain names, in URLs or elsewhere, say nothing about the physical location of the company or Web site.

Linux—an operating system similar to UNIX that runs on the same computers that can run Windows. Linux isn't (exactly) UNIX, but most UNIX programs run under Linux.

Lynx lynx.browser.org—the most widely-used text Web browser. Lynx is available on many library catalog terminals and other text-only terminals that don't have MSIE, Netscape, or another graphical browser. If you know how to use Lynx, there are many more places where you can get access to the Internet than if you don't.

machine name—the part of the URL before the domain name, which indicates the specific computer to which you are trying to connect. For example, Foobar.com might use two machine names, "mail.foobar.com" as its e-mail server and "www.foobar.com" as its Web server. Both might actually be the same physical machine.

Microsoft Internet Explorer (MSIE) www.microsoft.com/ie—the most widely used Web browser for Windows and the Macintosh. So many Web sites work only with MSIE that you need it on your computer to make full use of the Internet, even if it's not your default browser. The AOL Web browser is still, as of this writing, a customized version of MSIE, even though AOL owns Netscape. Some people refer to MSIE simply as "Explorer."

mirror, mirror site—one of several copies of the same Web site on different servers at different URLs. For example, there are at least a dozen mirrors of my FAQ (and of most newsgroup FAQ's) on different sites around the world. If there are mirrors of a site in several countries, try to find the closest. Browsing a nearby mirror of a Web site is usually much faster than browsing a site on the other side of the world. Mirror sites aren't always kept up to date, however, so if you really need the most recent information you should check when the mirror was last updated, or try to find the primary site.

MSIE—*see* "Microsoft Internet Explorer"

munge—to "munge" an e-mail address is to change it, usually by inserting extra characters into the middle, in a way that will defeat spam robots, but that a human being will be able to correct. For example "edwardnospam@hasbrouck.org" instead of "edward@hasbrouck.org". Many people munge their e-mail address in newsgroup and bulletin board postings. Unfortunately, spammers are getting sneakier, and this is getting less useful. Using an alternate, expendable e-mail address is more effective in limiting spam. But munging your address is better than nothing.

Netscape—(1) a division of AOL (2) Netscape's Web browser **www.netscape.com/download**, which in different versions is called "Navigator," "Communicator," or simply "Netscape." As with MSIE, enough Web sites work only with Netscape that it's worth having on your computer even if you don't want to make it your default browser.

news—messages in Usenet newsgroups

newsgroup—a collection of electronic messages on a common topic. Newsgroups include both "private newsgroups" which are available only from one server, like a bulletin board, and Usenet newsgroups which are mirrored on many thousands of news servers around the world. *see also* "Usenet"

newsreader—a program for reading newsgroups. Both Netscape and Microsoft Outlook can be used as newsreaders, but if you spend a lot of time reading or participating in newsgroups you may be better off downloading and installing a program that's designed specifically as a newsreader like Xnews or slrn.

nonstop flight—a flight that isn't scheduled to land anywhere between where you get on and where you get off. "Nonstop flight" means what it says—unlike "direct flight." *see* "connecting flight," "direct flight"

offline—that which is not the Internet. Also known as "the real world." Try to remember that even if you plan and arrange your trip online, real travel takes place offline.

online—technically, online information and activities include both things on the Internet and those on proprietary online systems such as AOL. Since this is a book about the Internet and travel, and because I think proprietary online sources have very little to add to what's available on the Internet (and reach a smaller and less diverse audience), I use "online" in this book in its looser sense of "on the Internet."

Opera www.opera.com—currently the third most popular Web browser after MSIE and Netscape. Opera is much faster than MSIE or Netscape, and is especially popular with people who need to use the Web to get their work done, such as journalists and researchers. Particularly advantageous for travelers because of its speed (often you're in a hurry and paying more for connection time while traveling) and usability on low bandwidth and small-screen portable devices.

operating system (OS)—the software that handles the most basic functions on a computer and serves as an intermediary between application programs and the hardware. Windows, MacOS, and Linux are the most common PC operating systems. Some badly-designed Internet sites can only be used from computers with a certain operating system (usually Windows), but with competently designed Web sites it shouldn't matter which operating system your computer uses.

OS—*see* "operating system"

PC—*see* "personal computer"

Pegasus Mail www.pmail.gen.nz—the most powerful standalone Windows e-mail program. Freeware. Includes e-mail filtering, forwarding, and automatic processing features that are especially useful for travelers.

personal computer (PC)—a single-user desktop microcomputer. Some people use "PC" or "personal computer" in a narrower sense of "DOS/Windows PC," but I think it's more appropriate and useful to consider Windows computers, Mac's, and Linux and Be boxes as all being varieties of PC's.

Pine www.washington.edu/pine— "Program for Internet News and e-mail." Pine is the most common e-mail program usable on text only terminals, in a Telnet window, and/or on a shell account. There's a version for Windows, but it doesn't work nearly as well as the host-based UNIX version.

platform—the combination of hardware and operating system required for a particular software application. The Intel processor chip and associated hardware, and the Microsoft Windows operating system, make up the "Wintel" platform.

plug-in—a sort of "helper" program that enables your Web browser to do things, or deal with files of a type, that the browser can't handle by itself. Plug-ins are mostly used for multimedia and special effects, and generally only work in specific browsers. Avoid Wseb sites that rely on plug-ins, especially if you might need to use them while traveling, since the plug-in might not be installed and might not even be available for that platform.

POP—*see* "post office protocol"

portal—a Web site that wants you to use it as your gateway to everything else on the Internet. Most portals include a travel section, although you can generally find better travel information on more specialized sites.

post, posting—a public message in a newsgroup or on an electronic bulletin board, available to anyone who reads the newsgroup or browses the bulletin board

post office protocol (POP)—the most common system for retrieving your e-mail from your ISP or other mailbox. You can retrieve mail from a POP server with an e-mail program on your computer, or with a browser through a POP-mail Web site.

prereserved seats (PRS)—specific seat assignments on an airline flight, made in advance. Pre-reserved seats are never guaranteed; they are subject to reassignment by the airline at any time and for any reason. *see* "confirmed seat"

price—What you pay. Make sure you see and print out a bottom-line price including all taxes, shipping, surcharges, etc. before you agree to authorize a charge. *see* "fare"

principal—the person or company who is actually getting your money, and who is responsible for providing products or services. When you buy an airline ticket from a travel agency, the airline is the "principal." That's why the charge shows up on your credit card statement in the name of the airline, not the agency. Relationships like this are governed by the law of agency. If the agency accepts a service fee, they become your agent, as well as the airline's agent, with much greater legal responsibilities to you. *see* "agent"

private-label Web site—A Web site that is actually run by one company, but is made to look like part of another company's site. The travel reservations sections of many portal and other Web sites are actually private-label versions of the Web sites of major online travel agencies.

protocol—a set of standards, e.g. for how messages are formatted and sent between two computers. All computers on the Internet communicate using the Internet protocol (IP), so even computers with different hardware and operating systems can talk to each other on the Internet. CRS's and airline computers have a different network message protocol called AIRIMP ("Air Interline Message Procedure"). That's one of the reasons you can't access them directly from the Internet: you need a gateway that interprets between the Internet and airline/CRS protocols.

proxy server—a program that serves as a buffer between your Web browser or other application programs and the Internet. The program you are using talks to the proxy server, and the proxy server talks to other computers on the Internet, instead of the program connecting directly to the Internet. By controlling what messages it passes on, in both directions, a proxy server can help protect against a variety of security and privacy risks. A proxy server can also be used to enable several computers to share one Internet connection. A proxy server is often combined with, or included in, a firewall.

published fare—an official fare (price and rules) set by an airline, filed with the government, listed in CRS's, and available from the airline or any travel agency. Most online travel agencies only sell tickets at published fares, and only published fares are listed in CRS's.

query syntax—how you formulate your questions or requests, e.g. for information from a search engine, or for airfare and flight possibilities from an airline or travel agency Web site. One of the most important things you can do to improve your ability to find things on the Internet is to learn how to use the query or search syntax of the sites you use often. *see* also "syntax," "search engine"

rack, rack rate—the highest rate a hotel ever charges. All "discounts" on hotel rates are calculated form the rack rate. Sometimes shortened to just "rack": "I've never paid rack."

referer header—a message your Web browser attaches to each request for a Web page, telling the Web server what link from what site you followed to get there. Unless you suppress these headers, they allow sites to track you from site to site, click by click. You can set some browsers like Opera or Lynx not to send referer headers, but with MSIE or Netscape you can only remove them with a separate proxy server or firewall.

registrar —*see* "domain registrar"

RTFM—"Read The F__ing Manual." Frequently said in response to questions asked in a newsgroup that are answered in the FAQ for the group. *see* "FAQ."

scripts, scripting languages—programs that are downloaded through your browser, as part of a Web page, and then run on your computer. Scripts can compromise your privacy and/or security, and you shouldn't allow them to run unless you are sure that you trust the site that's sending them to you.

search engine—a Web site with a searchable index of key words on Web pages. Search engine indexes are created by robots, not people. They don't try to categorize pages; they just index the words they find. *see* Web directory

shareware—software that you can download and try before you decide whether to buy it. Some shareware is freeware, but some requires you to pay if you want to use it for longer than a trial period. Don't steal software just because the author is generous enough to give you a free trial. Good software that you use regularly is usually worth much more in the time that it saves than what it costs. Efficient software is most valuable for travel, to optimize what you can do with an expensive or slow connection to the Internet.

shell, shell account—an account that lets you log on to a host computer, usually by Telnet, and run programs on the host computer from the command line or a text menu. Sometimes referred to as a "UNIX shell" or "UNIX shell account," even if it's really on Linux or some other OS. Many Web hosting plans include a shell account; there are also some non-commercial systems that provide free shell accounts. The advantage to a shell account is that it lets you run programs on the host instead of your local computer, which can be faster and solve software compatibility or availability problems on the road. A menu-based shell, if available, lets you run basic programs like a newsreader, e-mail program, or text Web browser without really having to know anything about UNIX or Linux.

shill (n.), to shill (v.)—in carnival and gambling con-game lingo, a "shill" is someone who's part of the con, or working with the house, who conceals their real role and pretends to be a satisfied customer or winner in order to lure suckers to put up their money. Common forms of Internet shilling include using friends or phony names to make bids on things you are selling at auction to drive up the price; posting favorable "testimonials" about hotels or resorts in newsgroups or on bulletin boards without saying that the proprietor is a friend or relative; and making paid advertisements from sponsors of travel sites look like impartial "reviews" or "recommendations."

shovelware—a Web site or other collection of information assembled as though with a shovel, i.e. by throwing together a lot of stuff without much selectivity or organization. You can find useful things on shovelware sites, but it takes work to find them in the clutter, and sort them out from the worthless junk.

snail mail—non-electronic mail, such as from the U.S. Postal Service.

surcharges—"fuel surcharges," airport fees for flights or car rentals, shipping, rush charges, etc. To avoid having to pay surcharges that weren't disclosed in advance, keep a printout of your complete itinerary, showing the total that was supposed to be charged, until well after the trip is complete.

syntax—in computing, the "grammar" of how you specify commands or requests. Computer syntax is often non-intuitive, and it's worth looking at the "help" or "how-to" screens to see how best to formulate your request to get the answers you want.

tariff—a schedule of fares or prices. *see* "air tariff"

taxes—may or may not be included in fares or prices in advertisements, Web sites, itineraries, etc. Always check before you authorize a charge to make sure that all taxes are disclosed.

Telnet—a program that enables you to connect to a remote computer, on a LAN or on the Internet, and work as though you were logged in directly to a command-line (text) interface on the remote computer. Telnet enables you to run programs on the remote computer that aren't installed, or wouldn't run, on the computer or terminal you are actually using. The combination of Telnet, a shell account, and a command-line e-mail program like Pine is the way most hackers deal with their e-mail on the road, rather than through Web-mail. I use Telnet to a shell account for reading newsgroups and sometimes for e-mail. Telnet itself is a very simple program installed on virtually every Internet-connected computer as part of the operating system.

ticketless travel—a misleading term for travel with an e-ticket, which isn't really ticketless. E-tickets are stored electronically rather than printed out, but they are still tickets with all the other attributes of paper tickets.

TLD—*see* "top-level domain"

top-level domain (TLD)—the last element of the domain name, such as ".com" (commercial), ".au" (Australia), or ".int" (international organizations). Anyone can register a name in any geographic domain, so a ".au" site could actually be owned by an American company. Only a few TLD's tell you something meaningful about who owns the site.

United States Code (USC)—the compilation of all U.S. federal laws in effect

uniform resource locator (URL)—the address of a particular Web page, downloadable file, or other "resource" on the Internet. The same Web page or file may be retrievable at many different URLs, but each URL specifies a unique page or file. URLs cannot contain spaces; they are sometimes case sensitive. Generally speaking, a URL consists of (1) the protocol ("http" for a Web page) to be used to retrieve the data, (2) the server or computer ("www.example.com"), and (3) the path to the file from the root directory of that server or machine ("/directory/subdirectory/webpage.html").

UNIX—the dominant operating system for Internet server computers. *see also* Linux

UNIX shell, UNIX shell account—*see* "shell," "shell account"

URL—*see* "uniform resource locator"

USC—*see* "United States Code"

Usenet, Usenet news, Usenet newsgroup—the Usenet is the network of computers that mirror the Usenet newsgroups. Whenever anyone posts a message in a Usenet newsgroup, it is copied to all the other Usenet news servers around the world. So anyone can participate in a collective worldwide discussion, without having to be connected to the same server or at the same time. Most Usenet news is distributed via the Internet, but it also reaches some computers beyond the Internet. Because of their wide reach and open participation, Usenet newsgroups are one of the most valuable feature of the Internet for travelers. If you want to "ask the Internet" for its collective wisdom on some issue or topic, the place to do so is a Usenet newsgroup.

user interface (UI)—what you see (displays, menus, etc.), the way you control a program or operating system (typing commands, clicking on icons, etc.), and what choices and tools the software gives you. User interfaces are largely divided into command-line interfaces and graphical user interfaces. For an essay on the difference between them, and its significance, see **www.cryptonomicon.com/beginning .html**. Web user interfaces are emerging as a third type of UI. Data does you no good if the user interface doesn't let you get to it, or use it the way you want. This is the problem with Web-based user interfaces to CRS's and airline computer systems.

Web—*see* "World Wide Web"

Web browser—a program that retrieves Web pages from servers on the Internet, and displays them for you. The best-known Web browsers, MSIE and Netscape, are actually Internet suites that come with e-mail programs, newsreaders, etc. Other browsers worth considering include Opera, Lynx, and iCab.

Web directory—an index of links to Web pages by topic, usually organized like an outline or encyclopedia. Web directories are sometimes referred to as search engines, although they aren't. The best-known general-purpose Web directories are Yahoo.com and About.com; there are also many specialized Web directories on specific topics. *see also* "search engine"

Web-mail—an e-mail service that lets you send and receive e-mail from a Web browser rather than an e-mail program. Most Web-mail accounts are accessible *only* over the Web, but there are other Web sites you can use to check and send e-mail to and from most regular e-mail accounts.

Web page—a collection of information retrieved from a single URL, and generally displayed as one "page" in a browser window. Can contain any number of files (text, images, multimedia, etc.) and frames from different Web sites, domains, or servers.

Web server—a computer that stores the contents of Web pages and sends them to your browser when your browser asks for them. *see also* "client-server computing"

Web site—a group of related Web pages on the same server, in the same domain or sub-domain.

WHOIS—a request for the name, contact information, and other public records of the owner ("registrant") of a domain name. You can get WHOIS information over the Web from your browser, or through a separate WHOIS program.

World Wide Web (WWW)—collectively, all the public Web pages and other data available from all the Web servers connected to the Internet, and the set of links that can lead you from one place in that network to another.

WWW—*see* "World Wide Web"

Index

A

About.com, 14, 93, 203, 374
academic Web sites, 57-58
access
  Internet devices, 322-331, 391
  remote, 351-354
  to e-mail (voice), 371-372
  to fares, 150-152
  to files, 347-356
  to online tools, 154-155
accommodations
  reservations, 188-210, 386
  trains, 182
accuracy, of online
  information, 9, 11, 47-52,
  96, 376
ActiveX, 227, 318, 353, 371
adapters, 331-336, 341-343
address
  alternate e-mail, 36, 215,
  237-238, 360
  books, online, 351, 354, 360-
  361, 368
  e-mail, 363, 405
AdSubtract, 236, 388
advance, purchase, 162-164
advantages
  to online purchasing, 170-171
  of working with travel
  agents, 101-102
Adventuocity.com, 42-43, 377
adventure travel, 62, 377
advertisements
  for accommodations, 191
  and dial-up numbers, 338-
  339
  and search engines, 23-25
  deceptive, 8, 50, 111-113, 278
  laws, 259-260, 264-265
  on Teletext, 144-145

on Web sites, 233, 237,
  264-265
advice
  do-it-yourself travel agent,
  99-103
  from fellow travelers, 81-84
  how to word questions,
  86-87
  for online consumers,
  214-215
  purchasing airline tickets
  online, 97-99, 103-113
  researching travel online, 8
  trains, 186
  using the Internet while
  traveling, 306-309
Aerolink.com, 88, 188, 386
Agent (browser), 32
agents, legal, 301-302, 394
agreements, Web sites, 248-249
air passes, 117-118
Air Travel Organizers License,
  266, 389, 395
airfares
  discounts, 106-108, 109
  domestic, 168-169
  international, 168-169,
  173-176
  pricing, 150-180
Airline Reporting Corporation,
  289, 395
Airline Tariff Publishing Co.
  (APTCO), 174, 395
airline tickets, purchasing
  online, 103-113, 384-385
airlines
  and consumer complaints,
  276-277
  commissions to travel agents,
  104-105, 108, 114-115
  ownership
  of CRSs, 126
  of online travel agencies,
  126, 133, 139-142

"Best Fare," 154, 158-162
BestFares.com, 38
Better Business Bureau, 223,
    277, 282, 390, 396
biometric passwords, 243
Biztravel.com (Rosenbluth
    International), 118, 119, 123,
    124-125, 384
"bloatware," 355
booking
    class, 158-162, 166-168, 396
    reservations, 177, 180, 395
bookmarks, 348, 396
books, travel, 88, 90
boolean operators, 21, 23
bootleg, articles online, 21, 28
borders, crossing international,
    75-77
boutique hotels, 196-198
Britrail, 182-185
brochures, online, 88
brokers (consolidators), hotel,
    193-196, 386, 404
browsers, 18-19, 32, 326-327,
    392-393, 397, 414
    display full URLs, 17
    graphical, 34
    privacy, 226-227, 230-238,
        388
    secure, 240-241, 244
bulletin boards, 30, 237-238
bumped, from flights, 167
buses, local/regional, 85, 185,
    187-188
business centers, Internet
    access at, 319
business travelers, 123-125

C

cache sites, 21, 28
California Seller of Travel (CST)
    law, 91, 262-265, 298-299,
    389, 397

campgrounds and
    RV parks, 202-203, 386
Canada
    airfares, 106-108, 113-116
    Via Rail, 182-185, 386
cancellations
    airline tickets, 157, 280
    insurance, 293-295
    train tickets, 184-185
"cannot connect to server"
    (error message), 28-29
capitalization, in URLs, 26, 397
cars, renting, 180-181
case sensitive, URLs, 26, 397
CDs, 355-356
cell phones, 330-331
Centers for Disease Control
    (CDC), 79-80, 384
certificates, 52
    see also scams
changes
    e-tickets, 179
    fees, 293
    train tickets, 184-185
chargebacks
    credit cards, 214, 270-271,
        285-292, 389, 397
    illegitimate, 290-292
chat rooms, 237-238
Cheaptickets.com, 115, 119,
    129, 385
clients, e-mail, 18-19, 397
climate, 59-61, 376
clinics (travel), medical, 81,
    384
clothing, shopping online, 88-
    90
Coalition Against Unsolicited
    Commercial E-mail (Cause),
    363, 392
codes, error, 25-29
colleges, Internet access at,
    321-322
color, travelers of, 378

principals, lawsuits, 301-302, 410
privacy
and Usenet newsgroups, 34-36
browsers, 226-227, 230-238
consumer rights, 216-219, 222-223
invasion of, 212-239, 387-390
laws, complaints and enforcement, 238-239
protecting, 229-238
public Internet terminals, 238, 306-322
Web site policies, 213, 215, 218, 222-223, 230
"private label," 111, 120, 410
Prodigy Classic, 362
products online, specialized, 171
profiles
author, 35, 45-46
personal, 213, 222-223, 228-229, 247, 274
preference, 155, 160-161
programs, newsreader, 31-36, 83, 393, 408
proof
legal, 304
of onward passage, 179
propaganda, 75, 88
protecting, your privacy, 229-238
protection, against fraud and scams, 270-275
Proxomitron, 236, 388
proxy servers, 215, 231, 233, 236-237, 388, 410
Psion, 329-330, 364, 391
public, transportation, 185, 187-188
public Internet terminals, 224, 225, 238, 310-311, 314-322, 390

published fares, 168-169, 173-176, 410-411
international, 141, 151-153
online travel agencies, 118-126, 384-385
on Web sites, 111, 116-126
publishers, guidebook, 378

Q

query
fees, 154, 160-162, 172
syntax, 12, 19-23, 411
WHOIS, 42-43, 94-96
questions, how to phrase, 65-68, 86-87

R

"rack" rate, 189, 193-194, 411
Rail Australia, 182-185, 386
RailFans, 186
rebates, 105, 173 176
recommendations, 81-84, 86-87
"recommendations" (by shills), 8, 16, 46, 50, 191
records
legal, 304
of online purchases, 214, 273
Web browsing, 219-229
Recreational Equipment, Inc (REI), 89
reference information, 7-9
references, U.S. Government, 379
"referral logging," disable, 231-232
refunds, 125, 157, 280-281, 293
registrar, domain names, 94-96, 400, 411
registrations, Web sites, 160-162, 228-229, 237, 247-250, 274
regulation
of international airfares, 107
of the Internet, 254-267

Acknowledgments

First and foremost, now and always, I acknowledge my profound gratitude to Ruth Radetsky, my Best Beloved (who must *not* be forgotten), for her support, close reading, advice, and sustaining love. Steve Homer, the best friend a writer could hope for, provided extraordinarily prompt, thorough, and constructive criticism of the manuscript at exactly the right moment, and spared me from what would otherwise have been some grievous errors. Marguerite Helen, Jim Pilaar, and John Taylor also took time out of their busy schedules to offer comments on portions of my drafts at various stages. I apologize for those of their suggestions that I've been unable to incorporate in this edition, and take full blame for the mistakes I'm sure remain.

This book draws on technical knowledge in at least three fields: airline ticketing and the travel industry, consumer protection and privacy law, and computing and the Internet. For contributing to my understanding in these and other areas, I thank especially J.P. Whitecloud, Brook Schoenfield, Caryn Navy, David Holladay, W. Alexander Hagen, George Gleason, Will Doherty, Hermine Craven, and Ron Boyer. In their own ways, my father and grandfather, L.P. (Phil) Hasbrouck, Jr. and Louis P. Hasbrouck, both introduced me to the mindset of the engineer, and gave me confidence in my own technical abilities. My mother, Marguerite Helen, passed on to me her love of well-chosen words, and gave me respect for women like her in technology and law.

Thanks to Dragon Systems, Inc., without whose voice-recognition software this book could not have been written, and to Opera Software and Wordperfect, without which it would have been much slower and more difficult. For their software gifts to the Internet community, thanks to David Harris for Pegasus Mail, to the Lynx and SLRN development volunteers, and to Jason Catlett for the Internet Junkbuster Proxy.

All Internet travelers are indebted to Marcus Endicott, Brian Lucas, and John Levine for their early and continued volunteer contributions to online travel information sharing.

Thanks to Philip C. Wolf of PhoCusWright, Inc., for giving me access to some of the key people in the online travel industry at PhoCusWright events. For making me feel part of the travel writing community, thanks to Tom Brosnahan, Paul Grimes, Carl Parkes, Chris Baker, and the Bay Area Travel Writers.

Participants in newsgroups and mailing lists, attendees at my seminars, readers of my other writings, and e-mail corrspondents too numerous to mention have been a helpful sounding board and source of ideas and issues needing to be addressed. Many thanks to all of you who've taken the time to send me your comments, questions, feedback, and corrections.

It would have been impossible to write a book while working for a dot-com without a great deal of support, tolerance, and flexibility from both Avalon Travel Publishing and AirTreks.com. Both those teams have my heartfelt gratitude for allowing me the lattitude I needed to see this through. Everyone at AirTreks.com has contributed to this book in one way or another. Thanks to each of you. Special bows to Jim Pilaar, Tom Michelson, Jesse WalkerShaw, Lorin Kalisky, Aimée Barile, Paul Ethier, John Taylor, Cat Leppo, Ben Scarola, and David Derrick. At Avalon Travel Publishing, I especially appreciate the editing and encouragement of Erin Van Rheenen and Angelique Clarke, the patient confidence of Pauli Galin and Bill Newlin, the enthusiasm of Amanda Bleakley and Mary Beth Pugh, and the contributions of those whose work on getting this book into print and into your hands has yet to come.

About the Author

Edward Hasbrouck (edward@hasbrouck.org, **hasbrouck.org**) is the world's best-known authority on around-the-world travel and an expert in international airfares, with a global reputation founded on his writing on the Internet and in the *Practical Nomad* series of travel how-to and advice books, including the acclaimed *The Practical Nomad: How to Travel Around the World* (1st edition 1997, 2nd edition 2000). His definitive set of answers to Frequently Asked Questons about airfares (**hasbrouck.org/faq**) has been posted monthly on the "rec.travel.air" Usenet newsgroup since 1991.

(Continues next page)

In addition to his writing, speaking, and seminars, Edward is a full-time Internet travel agent specializing exclusively in around-the-world travel and airline tickets. Currently, he is a travel consultant, industry analyst, and the "Travel Guru" for AirTreks.com. He also answers travel questions for travelmatters.com, Guidebookwriters .com, AllExperts.com, and on Usenet travel newsgroups, and gives travel planning seminars throughout North America and overseas.

Edward Hasbrouck grew up on Massachusetts' Route 128 ("America's Technology Highway"), in a community and a family dominated by the computer industry. His father started his 30- plus year career as a computer programmer in the late 1950's, shortly before Edward was born, and his mother's jobs including editing a computer-industry trade journal and technical writing for a high-tech startup. Edward went from walking around inside the giant computers in his father's workplace as a small child in the 60's, to programming minicomputers himself in junior high school and high school in the 70's, to first encounters with the Arpanet and Usenet newsgroups through BBN and DEC in the early 1980's, to getting an Internet account in his own name in 1991. He's been an active "netizen", Internet travel agent, and Internet travel writer ever since.

Edward has traveled around the world twice, visited 48 U.S. states and 22 countries, and worked with thousands of independent travelers to help them plan and organize their trips. His clients have included educational groups, environmental organizations, development NGO's, aid volunteers, and human rights workers—as well as, of course, vacationers and business travelers. Edward is an evangelist for travel as a positive force for global understanding and change as well as personal growth and empowerment.

Edward is a member of numerous professional associations and peace and human rights groups, including the International Airlines Travel Agent Network, the Association of Special Fares Agents (Vice-President, the Americas, 1998–2001), Partners in Responsible Tourism, Tourism Concern, Guidebookwriters.com, Bay Area Travel Writers, the National Writers Union, the National Lawyers Guild, the War Resisters League, the National Association of Railroad Passengers, the Train Riders Association of California, and the San Francisco Bicycle Coalition. When he has time, Edward is an avid traveler, bicyclist, internationalist, and activist for peace and freedom. When he's not traveling, he lives in San Francisco with his partner of 19 years, Ruth Radetsky.